Power and City Governance

Globalization and Community

Dennis R. Judd, Series Editor

Power and City Governance

Comparative Perspectives on Urban Development

Alan DiGaetano and John S. Klemanski

Globalization and Community / Volume 4
University of Minnesota Press
Minneapolis • London

MINNESOTA

Published by the University of Minnesota Press
111 Third Avenue South, Suite 290
Minneapolis, MN 55401-2520
http://www.upress.umn.edu

Library of Congress Cataloging-in-Publication Data

DiGaetano, Alan.
    Power and city governance : comparative perspectives on urban
development / Alan DiGaetano and John S. Klemanski.
        p.   cm. — (Globalization and community ; v. 4)
    Includes bibliographical references and index.
    ISBN 0-8166-3218-9 (alk. paper). — ISBN 0-8166-3219-7 (pbk. :
alk. paper)
        1. City planning—Cross-cultural studies.   2. Urban policy—Cross-
cultural studies.   I. Klemanski, John S.   II. Title.   III. Series.
HT165.5.D54   1999
307.1'216—dc21   99-31736

Contents

Preface

Early in this century, the comparative analysis of cities focused on the structures and functions of local government (see Fairlie 1901; Dawson 1916; Munro 1927). Its descriptions of local government offices, legal powers, and formal responsibilities, although quite detailed in certain respects, failed to paint a complete picture of how cities were governed. The struggles over burning issues, the give and take of delicate negotiations, and the triumphs and defeats of campaigns and elections were largely missing. Simply put, these careful and precise comparisons of urban *government* omitted essential analysis of urban *governance*. In their expurgated version of events, politics was left out.

Recent comparative urban political analysis, although a major step forward (see Savitch 1988; Barnekov, Boyle, and Rich 1989; Judd and Parkinson 1990; Logan and Swanstrom 1990; Keating 1991; Stoker and Mossberger 1994; Judge, Stoker, and Wolman 1995), suffers somewhat from similar deficiencies. One of the chief problems arises from a strength of comparative urban scholarship — the recognition that countries differ, often dramatically, in the institutional structures of their governing systems, such as organization and legal competencies. That is, much of the recent comparative literature on urban politics has tended to exaggerate the influence of different national contexts on urban governance (see Kantor, Savitch, and Haddock 1997; Wolman and Goldsmith 1992; Fainstein 1994). This failure to consider important similarities in the way cities of different nations are governed has impeded the development of cross-national urban political theory beyond the study of comparative differences (DiGaetano 1997).

This book attempts to avoid these pitfalls in cross-national comparison by recognizing that, although different histories and institutional structures breed differences in political processes, common traits lie at the core of liberal democratic governance. To distinguish these commonalities as well as the differences in urban politics, we have developed an analytical framework for making cross-national comparisons, referred to here as *modes of governance*. Modes of governance are the structures and processes that shape local political decision making (DiGaetano 1997). Using this framework, we hope to add to the research and thinking in both comparative urban politics and regime theory. This investigation also develops a systematic account of how cities have begun to take control of their own destinies by defining their own policy agendas. Our detailed investigation of four cities illustrates varying degrees of success in asserting local control, but these local attempts also are reminiscent of Richard Knight's (1989: 225–26) notion of the "intentional city."

The focus of this study is urban development politics. Four cities are compared, two British (Birmingham and Bristol) and two American (Boston and Detroit). The comparative analysis of urban development politics is based on research conducted in each of the cities from 1991 to 1998. In addition to newspapers, documents, and reports, our primary sources include more than 200 interviews with local government officials, business leaders, community activists, and academics over a seven-year period.

Chapter 1 establishes the comparative framework for analyzing urban politics in the United Kingdom and the United States. First, we explain the pivotal element of the modes of governance theory: the urban governing alignments such as governing coalitions and power structures. Modes of governance operate in a larger regional, national, and international environment. To provide a comparative frame of reference for our case studies of Birmingham, Boston, Bristol, and Detroit, chapter 1 situates the analysis of the modes of governance in a comparative political economy framework.

In chapter 2 we seek to explain the mutual influences of the economic and demographic environments on a city's governing arrangements, and the strategic decisions made that create a locality's development agenda. We term this context *urban structuring and restructuring*. Included in the economic environment are the long-term forces of economic restructuring as well as the shorter-term force of the business cycle. Social trends, including population movement patterns, the racial and ethnic mix of a city, and the relative wealth and educational level of local residents, also are important in influencing the alignments of political power in a locality.

In chapter 3 we investigate what we call *state structuring and restructuring*, which is an additional contextual dimension that influences a locality's governing alignment and agenda. This environment includes a variety of influences on a locality, especially the political, legal, fiscal, and administrative parameters, as well as partisan or political influences. This context may constrain or provide greater capacity for localities to pursue their governing agendas, as well as order and reorder local governing alignments.

In chapter 4 we specify the relationship between the political-economic context of our four cities and the rise and development of local modes of governance between 1970 and 1997. We argue that differences between cities in the same countries demonstrate that urban politics are not simply products of particular national contexts. Furthermore, the chapter reveals how governing alignments and realignments in each city are both products of, and mediating institutions between, economic and state structuring or restructuring and the local responses to a shifting urban political economy.

We begin chapter 5 with a discussion of specific examples that build on the theoretical and contextual chapters by comparing the politics involved in constructing and implementing regional capital strategies in Birmingham, Boston, Bristol, and Detroit. To varying degrees, each city pursued a strategy that promoted a mix of business, commercial, and cultural or tourism developments in its downtown or city center. In the postindustrial urban hierarchy, each city adopted a regional capital emphasis that achieved different levels of success in the period after 1970.

Chapter 6 analyzes the politics of industrial development in the "Motor Cities" of Birmingham and Detroit. Both cities faced the challenge of deindustrialization after 1970, and have pursued various courses in attempts to regain their former status as world automobile manufacturing centers. Our comparison of these two cities illustrates the similarities and differences in industrial development politics among cities. Despite each city's attempt to focus on a regional capital strategy noted in chapter 5, each also remained fundamentally committed to the automobile industry.

In chapter 7 we compare the politics of urban social reform—that is, the politics of redistributive justice—in Boston and Bristol. Social reform failed to emerge as a governing agenda in Birmingham and Detroit in the post-1970 period. But our analysis, focusing on the relationship between community movement mobilization and the formation of local social reform governing coalitions, finds Boston and Bristol to be an interesting study in contrasts. Despite their social and economic similarities, Boston saw the rise and development of a powerful social reform governing alliance while Bristol did not, even though Bristol's context might have suggested such an alliance.

Chapter 8 is a comparison of growth management politics in Boston and Bristol. Growth management politics entails the use of regulatory planning systems and development controls to protect the urban environment from the externalities of rapid economic growth. Growth management politics emerged in the 1970s in Bristol, enduring the recession of the early 1980s. In contrast, Boston's growth management governing coalition formed much later, in the mid-1980s, and survived only until the collapse of the city's development boom in 1990. As with social reform, a growth management movement failed to materialize in the nongrowth cities of Birmingham and Detroit.

In chapter 9 we draw together the strings of comparative analysis that run throughout the book: urban political economy, governing alignments, and governing agendas. Indeed, based on the case studies, this chapter both broadens and refines the modes of governance approach by explaining the respective roles of urban and state structuring and restructuring, governing alignments, and leadership in progrowth, social reform, and growth management politics. The chapter also revisits the question of urban power structures, elaborating upon the typology developed in chapter 1.

Acknowledgments

This book grew out of a mutual interest in urban development politics shared by the authors, and a growing interest in local governance in the United Kingdom. The project started after Professor Klemanski spent the 1989–1990 academic year, funded by a Leverhulme USA-Commonwealth Fellowship, living in London while attached to the School of Policy Studies, Cranfield Institute of Technology (now Cranfield University), located in Bedfordshire, England. In the summer of 1991, Professors DiGaetano and Klemanski began conducting interviews and collecting primary research information in England. Professor DiGaetano has been able to return each summer since 1993 to conduct follow-up interviews and locate the most current budget reports and primary data for our two British cities. During the summer of 1992, and between 1993 and 1998, interviews were conducted and information gathered in Boston and Detroit.

One benefit of our visits to the United Kingdom has been the formation of a number of professional associations and friendships, especially with people based in Birmingham and Bristol. Many gave tremendous amounts of time over the past seven years. We would especially like to thank Chris Collinge, Murray Stewart, Gerry Stoker, and John Stewart for their assistance, collegiality, and friendship. In the United States, Tom Halper in particular read drafts of the manuscript, offered insights, and made constructive comments as we developed our work. Robin Boyle and Michael Keating also offered suggestions. Moreover, having conducted over 200 interviews during the course of this project, we owe a tremendous debt of gratitude to the many government officials, business leaders, community activists, and scholars who took time from their busy schedules to meet with us.

Dennis Judd, the editor of the Globalization and Community series for the University of Minnesota Press, has been a strong supporter of this work from the beginning. Dennis is also a top-flight editor, who helped us revise the manuscript in several crucial ways. Barbara Ferman read early draft chapters and provided useful recommendations for improvement. Alan Harding reviewed the entire manuscript, offering a number of constructive suggestions. The staff at the University of Minnesota Press was consistently competent and encouraging, and we would especially thank Carrie Mullen and Robin A. Moir for their contributions to the completion of this book.

Partial funding for research in all four cities was provided by the Research Foundation of the City University of New York, and, through Oakland University, a Faculty Research Fellowship (1991), a Small Grants Award (1994), and the Political Science Development Fund (1991, 1992).

A project that takes seven years to complete and requires large amounts of time away from home inevitably takes a toll on the quantity and quality of one's home life. A huge acknowledgment of appreciation for their understanding, support, and patience goes to our wives, Denise Nickel and Sheryl Clark Klemanski. That is why this book is lovingly dedicated to them.

Introduction

In the past, British and American cities functioned as centers of production and distribution, of learning and entertainment, and of regional, national, and international public affairs. After World War II, however, many larger cities in Britain and the United States (and elsewhere in the industrialized world) appeared to be in danger of losing their centrality to economic, cultural, and political life. The main feature of postindustrial spatial development in Britain and the United States has been population deconcentration, brought about by dramatic processes of suburbanization. Moreover, as the middle classes moved to the urban periphery, they left behind an increasingly impoverished big city population. Economic functions also dispersed, with many retail and service firms abandoning central cities for suburban malls or other settings. Manufacturing also departed from central city locations, finding new homes in suburban industrial parks or moving to other regions or offshore to countries with lower pay scales and weaker traditions of unionization (Bluestone and Harrison 1982; Jacobs 1992).

These forces of deconcentration produced uneven patterns of urban development in Britain and the United States. Some cities tumbled into social and economic decline, while others prospered by developing social and economic functions central to the workings of the changing urban system. For example, former industrial giants such as Detroit, Michigan, and Birmingham, England, experienced substantial deindustrialization, with resultant economic contraction, rising unemployment, and mounting social deprivation. In contrast, cities like Boston, Massachusetts, and Bristol, England, converted from maritime and industrial centers into regional financial and business service centers, and thus avoided the most devastating aspects of postwar urban transformation.

In the face of social and economic spatial decentralization and un-even development during the 1960s and 1970s, urban policy became a preoccupation for national governments in the United Kingdom and the United States. National urban policy in the United Kingdom in the 1970s, for example, focused on concerns of social deprivation (Barnekov, Boyle, and Rich 1989; Atkinson and Moon 1994). The Urban Programme in particular provided antipoverty aid to local authorities deemed the most needy, such as London and cities in Northern England and in Wales. In the 1980s and 1990s, however, the Conservative governments of Margaret Thatcher and John Major revamped the national urban policy agenda, emphasizing economic revitalization over community development. The Conservative governments also centralized control over urban policy implementation by imposing more restrictive guidelines on urban aid and creating govern-ment agencies that operated independently from locally elected city and county councils.

In the United States, national urban policy moved in a somewhat different direction. By cutting federal aid to cities in the 1980s and early 1990s, the Republican administrations of Ronald Reagan and George Bush retreated from the expansive urban policy agenda that had been devel-oped through the 1960s and 1970s. Also, beginning as early as 1972 with Richard Nixon's presidency, Republican administrations sought to devolve responsibility for administration of urban aid programs to state and local governments through revenue sharing and block grant programs (Judd and Swanstrom 1998).

To meet the challenges of a rapidly changing political economy, big city policy makers in the United Kingdom and the United States embraced different sorts of policy agendas that were dependent on the position oc-cupied by their city in the evolving urban system. In some declining cities, such as Glasgow, Scotland, and Atlanta, Georgia, policy makers promoted growth agendas based on local strategies of economic revitalization (Stone 1989; Boyle 1990). Other declining cities, such as Sheffield and Liverpool, England, embarked on radical regimes of local social and economic redis-tribution (Lawless 1990; Parkinson 1990). In contrast, prospering cities en-countered different problems associated with uneven development. In some, such as Cambridge, England, or San Francisco, California, local pol-icy makers became preoccupied with strong planning regimes to manage or control rapid development (Brindley, Rydin, and Stoker 1989; DeLeon 1992). In others, such as Chicago, concerns about redistributing the bene-fits of economic growth to poor and working-class neighborhoods often dominated local politics and policy agendas (Bennett 1989).

In short, the relationship between the larger urban political economy and the formation and implementation of city policy agendas is neither simple nor direct. Indeed, as responses to changes in the political-economic environment, city policy agendas have been fashioned by coalitions of city government officials, business leaders, and community activists in Great Britain and the United States in ways that reflect *local* political alignments. These ruling coalitions exercise considerable power over the shape and content of local policy agendas, leaving a distinctive imprint on the final product.

A Tale of Two Cities

Birmingham, England, and Boston, Massachusetts, have occupied very different positions in their respective urban systems, and in a number of respects local policy agendas have reflected these differences. Development policies devised by local governing alliances in Birmingham and Boston, however, were not merely knee-jerk reactions to national and global restructuring. As this tale of two cities reveals, who governed and how they governed mattered greatly in the politics of policy agenda setting and implementation in Birmingham and Boston.

Deindustrialization and deep recession gripped Birmingham's economy in the late 1970s and early 1980s. To address the city's economic woes, city council Labour leaders and the Birmingham Chamber of Industry and Commerce forged an alliance around a policy agenda to promote economic growth. This progrowth agenda featured the dual economic development strategies of city center revitalization and industrial retention. The centerpiece of the downtown renewal strategy was the development of an international convention center, financed primarily by the city council and completed in 1991. To attract and retain manufacturing, the city council, chamber of commerce, and five development companies entered into a formal partnership, known as Birmingham Heartlands, that worked to regenerate a declining industrial area in East Birmingham. In both cases, these renewal strategies were initiated by the local growth coalition, not as part of a central government program or policy. This "localized" policy agenda was highly unusual in British urban politics, in that the city's growth coalition steered clear of Conservative government intervention to the extent that it could, yet emphasized market-based economic development in ways that resonated with Thatcherite urban policies.

In the early 1990s, new bases of power emerged in Birmingham's development politics. First, leading executives from the city's financial and professional service sector organized Birmingham City 2000, which became an active participant in city center redevelopment politics. At about the same time, the Conservative government established a Training and Enterprise Council (TEC) in Birmingham, which was charged with the responsibility of overseeing government grant programs related to training and business development. This multiplication of power centers in development politics could have generated explosive conflict by pitting one agency against another. In Birmingham, however, City 2000 and the TEC integrated smoothly into existing governing alignments, engendering a broader and more powerful growth alliance. Moreover, these new entities brought to bear valuable financial and political resources in the effort to revitalize Birmingham's economy.

By the middle 1990s, governing arrangements in Birmingham underwent a partial realignment. In 1993, a power struggle within the ruling Labour group on the city council resulted in a new Labour leadership taking the helm. The new Labour leadership (led by Teresa Stewart) opened up the city council decision-making process, which had been controlled by a closed circle of Labour leaders and officers. The new leadership advocated a "back-to-basics" policy agenda, emphasizing education, housing, and social services. The growth agenda was not abandoned entirely under the new Labour leadership, as the coalition of city officials and business elites remained a powerful force in city politics. Instead, it lost its preeminent position in setting the governing agenda, which was now carried out in tandem with the emergent Back to Basics agenda.

In sharp contrast to Birmingham, Boston experienced a downtown development boom in the late 1970s and 1980s that engendered a period of relative prosperity for the city. Since at least the middle 1970s, a growth coalition composed of Kevin White's mayoral administration and real estate developers advanced a policy agenda of downtown revitalization. The election of an urban populist, Raymond Flynn, as mayor in 1984 dislodged this ruling coalition ushering in a new era of Boston politics.

Flynn owed his electoral and later policy successes in large part to the growing strength of Boston's community movement. First, community activists enlisted as footsoldiers in Flynn's election campaigns and provided him with a ready-made grassroots organization. Many community organizers, in turn, were appointed to prominent policy-making positions in his mayoral administration, giving the new ruling coalition a decidedly populist cast. Once in place, the Flynn administration united neighborhood activists and environmentalists around a dual policy agenda of affordable housing development and growth management.

A union of tenants' groups, neighborhood development organizations, citywide community associations, and the Flynn administration promulgated policies and implemented programs that both protected and produced affordable housing. For instance, limits were imposed on condominium conversions that were perceived as a threat to the existing affordable housing stock. Production of affordable housing was facilitated by a number of neighborhood development programs, which were in part financed by linkage fees exacted from downtown commercial development projects.

The Flynn administration also joined forces with environmentalists to enact growth management policies that balanced positive action to enhance the city's green spaces with more restrictive land-use policies to protect the urban environment from overdevelopment. For example, environmental groups and the Flynn administration launched a large-scale refurbishment of the city's park system. At the same time the Flynn administration introduced more restrictive zoning policies that sought to curtail large-scale development.

Governing alignments in Boston, as in Birmingham, were reshuffled in the 1990s. The collapse of the city's property market during the recession of the early 1990s affected both branches of the city's governing coalition. Coupled with federal cutbacks in urban aid, the abrupt halt of downtown development in Boston dried up the pool of financial resources necessary to implement the affordable housing agenda. Similarly, the absence of rapid development made redundant the growth management coalition's policies on limiting development. Under these less favorable political and economic conditions, the Flynn administration dropped the policy agendas of affordable development and growth management, and adopted an aggressive growth strategy. The powerful coalition of neighborhood activists and the Flynn administration weathered this shift to a growth agenda. That is, given his strong populist predilections, Flynn simply incorporated neighborhood economic development into the overall growth strategy. The alliance with environmentalists, however, collapsed, as the Flynn administration turned its attention to encouraging, rather than containing, economic development.

In 1993, after Flynn accepted a post in the Clinton administration, Thomas Menino became mayor. The change in the mayor's office brought about little change in the city's dual policy agenda of economic and neighborhood development. As a result, community activists remained key players in the city's governing coalition, although overtures to business leaders became more frequent as the Menino administration pressed ahead with the city's economic renewal strategy. The centerpiece of this agenda was the development of a new convention center, which was seen by the city's incipient growth coalition of business leaders and the Menino administration as the engine that would power downtown revival.

Toward a Theory of Urban Governance

Implicit in our tale of Birmingham and Boston is an explanation of the complex relationship between the urban social, economic, and political environment, on the one hand, and local political decision-making structures and processes, on the other. We call this explanatory frame of reference *modes of governance*; it incorporates three analytical components.

The first of these is *urban political economy,* which refers to the social, economic, and intergovernmental context in which urban governance occurs. As our story of Birmingham and Boston suggests, changes in a city's political economy set in motion a reordering of local political processes and policies. In Birmingham, the double whammy of deindustrialization and deep economic recession precipitated the rise of the city's growth coalition and agenda. The mounting strength of the city's community movement, in combination with a context of rapid economic development, ushered in an era of populist politics in Boston.

The second component of the modes of governance model, *urban governing agendas,* is a product of the governing process and embodies the strategies and policies formulated by governing coalitions. Table I.1 sets out our typology of governing agendas for urban development politics in Great Britain and the United States.

Progrowth agendas focus on the importance of encouraging business development for a city's economic well being. Progrowth agendas may contain a variety of governing strategies that seek to stimulate economic development. Regional capital strategies attempt to maintain or strengthen a city's position as a region's business, cultural, or retail center. Industrial development strategies are designed to retain or diversify a city's industrial base. Regional capital and industrial strategies generally use the public sector (both central and local government), often in partnership with elements in the private sector, to promote and subsidize private investment by supplying grants, loans, land sites, and other inducements. They may also emphasize the reduction or elimination of local governmental planning power and business regulation, thus facilitating market forces in shaping the pattern of urban development (Brindley, Rydin, and Stoker 1989:23–25; Turner 1992). Finally, human capital strategies such as the de-

Table I.1

Governing Agendas in Urban Development Politics

Governing Agenda	Governing Strategies	Programmatic Tools
Progrowth	Regional capital Industrial development	Reduce government regulation of businesses, reduce taxes, provide public subsidies, and provide necessary services and infrastructure.
	Human capital	Provide educational and/or employment programs to upgrade the skills of the work force.
Growth management	Growth control	Use planning and land-use powers to regulate the kind and rate of growth.
	Environmental improvement	Develop programs and policies that facilitate improvements in the built environment and or green space.
Social reform	Community development	Use a mixture of public and private resources for affordable housing and job opportunities for disadvantaged neighborhoods.
	Human investment	Target disadvantaged groups and individuals with educational, training, and employment programs.
Caretaker	Routine service provision	Limit or reduce role of government in development and other strategic decision-making processes.

velopment and implementation of education reform or training and employment programs may be employed as a component of a progrowth agenda.

Social reform agendas concentrate on community development rather than business development, and center on perceived issues of social or redistributive justice. Community development strategies target disadvantaged groups and neighborhoods as the locus of development efforts. The expansion of affordable housing, support of cooperatives, and improvement of neighborhoods figure prominently in social reform agendas. Depending on the nature of the programs involved, human development may also be a component of social reform agendas (see Clavel 1986; Brindley, Rydin, and Stoker 1989; Blakely 1994).

Growth management agendas are developed to protect or improve the urban physical environment. Growth control strategies are defensive in nature and seek to moderate or restrict the rate and kind of development in a locality by using local governmental land-use powers. The goals of this strategy may be preservation of certain land uses, such as open space or historical districts, or even selective screening of the sorts of economic activities that are permitted to flourish, such as high-tech industry over commercial or more traditional industrial development (see Brindley, Rydin, and Stoker 1989; Caves 1992; Stein 1993; Blakely 1994). Environmental improvement strategies attempt to upgrade the urban physical environment through historical preservation, enlarging or upgrading a city's green space, or even implementing better air and water quality programs.

Caretaker agendas are fiscally conservative and, therefore, limit tasks of governance to the performance of the routine chores of service provision. Caretaker coalitions avoid or leave to others the problem of formulating development strategies.

Finally, the key question posed by the modes of governance perspective is how and why civic and political elites enter into coalitions around particular governing agendas. Consequently, the explanatory linchpin of the modes of governance approach is the concept of *urban governing alignment.* Urban governing alignments comprise the coalitions and power structures that set and carry out governing agendas. In this sense, governing alignments and agendas are inseparable, forming integrated bundles of policy makers and policy. In table I.2, we identify the expected relationships between who governs (coalition composition) and what they seek to accomplish (governing agenda) in the politics of urban development.

Powerful leaders whose political calculus derives from an economic logic (including elected officials who see political gain in promoting growth), business elites, trade union leaders, and economic development professionals, may converge around progrowth agendas. In Birmingham, for example, pragmatic city council Labour leaders aligned with business interests around a progrowth governing agenda in the 1980s and early 1990s that included both regional capital and industrial retention strategies. Elected officials whose political interests lie in quality of life issues, city planners,

Table I.2

Governing Coalitions and Governing Agendas

Coalition Composition	Governing Agenda
Elected officials, development professionals, and powerful economic leaders (business and trade union)	Progrowth
Elected officials, planners, middle-class preservationists, or environmentalists	Growth management
Elected officials, progressive development and planning professionals, and lower-class community activists	Social reform
Fiscally conservative elected and professional officials and small property owners	Caretaker

and middle class preservationists and environmentalists may unite around a growth management agenda. In Boston, as noted, environmentalists and the Flynn administration found common ground in the areas of environmental protection and enhancement policies. Progressive elected officials and city professionals, in turn, may ally with community activists from poorer neighborhoods around a social reform agenda. For example, in the 1980s, the populist mayor, Flynn, and neighborhood activists constructed a social reform agenda based on the development and preservation of affordable housing. Finally, coalitions of fiscally conservative government officials and small property owners (such as small businesses and homeowners) center on caretaker agendas. Caretaker modes of governance failed to appear in either of the two cities.

Of course, table I.2 simplifies the independent variable (coalition composition) for the purpose of illustrating how coalition composition relates to the dependent variable (governing agenda). The array of political perspectives involved in urban politics is quite extensive and complex. We hope that the case studies presented in subsequent chapters will demonstrate the complex interrelationships among these elements of urban governance, but also how differences in patterns of governance among cities are shaped by the confluences and conflicts generated by changes in the larger urban political economy.

Part I
Comparing Urban Governance in the United Kingdom and the United States

1

Modes of Governance in Comparative Perspective

What is taken for granted in comparing cities within a single country—their intergovernmental relations or role of their courts, for example—may emerge as daunting obstacles to cross-national comparisons. The danger here is that one might be tempted to take the path of least resistance and focus simply on principal differences (see Gurr and King 1987; Kantor, Savitch, and Haddock 1997). Such a course might, however, miss what is more subtle but perhaps equally important: common traits in urban politics of liberal democratic countries, such as the informal processes of coalition building and the use of power implicated in governance. Structural, institutional, and cultural differences among countries greatly complicate the study of comparative urban governance. What is needed to overcome these difficulties is an approach that recognizes the often stark differences between countries, but strives to search out the essential commonalities in the politics of big cities.

This chapter places the modes of governance approach in comparative perspective. The first part of the chapter discusses the nature of urban governing alignments. The second broadens the conceptual compass of modes of governance by situating it in an urban political economy paradigm. The final part of the chapter unites the urban governing alignments and political economy elements into a single comparative framework. This is applied in subsequent chapters to our analysis of urban development politics in two cities in the United Kingdom (Birmingham and Bristol) and two in the United States (Boston and Detroit).

Urban Governing Alignments

Urban governing alignments actually embody two separate but related arrangements of urban governance. *Urban governing coalitions* constitute the informal political networks of city leaders that form around particular policy agendas. In other words, they are the "Who's Who" in urban governing processes. But knowing the composition of governing coalitions reveals only half the story. Another distinct and crucial element of urban governing alignments is how cities are governed. *Urban power structures* influence how cities are governed by affecting allocation of political resources among urban leaders. In short, how ruling elites govern depends in many ways on the distribution of political power in a city.

Urban Governing Coalitions

Coalition building is a practice common to liberal democratic politics. Its function, at least in the political sphere of life, is to find common ground among differing interests as a means to work out collective solutions, if possible. In this sense, governing coalitions unite civic and political leaders with different interests and outlooks around a common policy agenda. How, and even if, different interests form alliances is a matter of some debate.

Urban Regime Theory

The chief architect of urban regime theory is Clarence Stone (1988, 1993), who defines the concept of regime as "the informal arrangements by which public bodies and private interests function together in order to be able to make and carry out governing decisions" (Stone 1989:6). Regime governance, in turn, hinges on the ability to coordinate actions and deploy resources through the building and maintenance of political alliances. As Stone (1989:5) states, "*[T]hese informal modes of coordinating efforts across institutional boundaries are what I call 'civic cooperation'*" (emphasis in original). He adds, however, that a "regime involves not just any informal group that comes together to make a decision but an informal yet relatively stable group *with access to institutional resources* that enables it to have a sustained role in making governing decisions" (Stone 1989:4; emphasis in original).

This understanding of regimes is based primarily on organizational theory (see Wilson 1973; Barnard 1968). Stone (1989:4) reasons that urban regimes form around "a purposive coordination of efforts [that] often depend heavily on tacit understandings" between public and private interests about what should be done and how to carry out decisions once they have been made. Selective incentives and what Stone (1989:232) calls "small opportunities" serve as the binding agents of governing coalitions. That is, regimes are formed and maintained because members receive material and symbolic benefits in exchange for their contributions to governing coalition activities. Moreover, the resulting civic cooperation revolves around efforts to accomplish relatively manageable tasks (small opportunities) rather than around a shared ideological perspective or a "grand vision of how the world might be reformed" (Stone 1989:193).

Stone also warns that governing and electoral coalitions should not be confused (see also Ferman 1985). As he (Stone 1993:7) emphasizes, "government authority is inadequate for governing, hence the cooperation and participation of nongovernmental actors becomes essential." The central purpose of regime theory, then, is to explain how governmental and nongovernmental elites, those with access to institutional resources, form alliances around governing tasks, not how politicians mobilize electoral power to build winning electoral coalitions.

Regimes form when city elites come together in an alliance, in order to assume the task of governance. The makeup of the governing coalition and the nature of the informal arrangements that unite the governing partners determine the sorts of governing tasks undertaken. To carry out the task of governing a city, these ruling alliances work out mutual understandings of the problems of governance and tap their various institutional bases of power for the resources necessary to undertake the tasks of governance. Further, because they have access to substantial institutional resources, business leaders are most often sought out as governing coalition partners, thus creating a systematic bias in urban regime formation (Stone 1989:235–42).

Urban Governing Coalitions Reconsidered

Regime theory has gained great currency as an explanation for coalition building in urban politics (see Elkin 1987; Stone 1989; Horan 1991; Lauria 1997; Ferman 1996). It has even drawn the attention of those engaged in the study of comparative urban politics (see Keating 1991; DiGaetano and Klemanski 1993; Harding 1994; John and Cole 1998). Even though Stone's regime theory has contributed greatly to our understanding of American urban governance, a number of problems arise when applied to comparative analysis.

First, Stone presents a model of governing coalitions in which formation and maintenance are portrayed as a matter of distributing small opportunities and selective incentives to members or potential members (see Olson 1965). But building and sustaining governing coalitions entails complex calculations and adjustments. Game theory, for example, reveals that decisions to join and maintain participation in a coalition are affected by the calculated return on one's contribution to a coalition (the "power index"), the size of the pie to be cut up among participants (nonzero-sum versus zero-sum games), and the size of the coalition (for example, "grand" coalitions are more unstable than smaller ones) (see Riker and Ordeshook 1973). It is not necessary, however, to adopt game theory, which is rooted in the assumptions of rationality and individualism (see Riker and Ordeshook 1973:chapter 2), to recognize that coalitional behavior is based on more than the simple choices of selective benefits and small opportunities.

Indeed, urban governing coalitions are in some ways relatively unique political creatures. Unlike electoral coalitions or national governing coalitions, the advantages of minimum majorities, in which fewer players mean more benefits per player, do not necessarily obtain. As Stone (1989) notes, the purpose of forming urban governing coalitions is to coordinate activities around particular goals. Therefore, coalition building and maintenance is a matter of pooling resources, not winning elections or legislative votes, which is the underlying assumption for game theory (Riker and Ordeshook 1973). More members of an urban governing coalition might mean a larger institutional base of resource generation, which in turn increases the chances of accomplishing the designated task. The opposite also is true; having fewer members means fewer resources.

Nonetheless, urban leaders do make calculations about the costs and derived benefits of participation in governing alliances. Politicians are governed by a "political logic," which is based on addressing the concerns of their constituencies; business and union leaders are informed by an "economic logic," which means the effects of participation on business firms or union memberships are taken into consideration; and community activists subscribe to a "community logic" that weighs the costs and benefits of participation in a governing coalition in relation to their neighborhood or organization (see Judd and Swanstrom 1998:chapter 1). Taking these considerations into account, we think at least two sets of factors complicate the task of urban governing coalition formation and maintenance.

The first relates to strategic calculations made by urban leaders in deciding whether or not to join or remain in a governing coalition. Leaders must attempt to foretell whether cooperation will reap sufficient benefits (that outweigh costs) for the constituencies they seek to represent. If not, leaders may opt to pursue other avenues to achieve intended goals. That is, because participation in a governing coalition requires partners to compromise on desired ends, urban leaders must determine whether it is worthwhile contributing resources to a governing task that does not fully meet their perceived interests. The point at which cooperation is perceived to provide net benefits we might term the "convergence threshold." By the same token, there exists a putative "defection threshold" for coalition partners. If crossed, leaders may make the decision that it is no longer in the interests of their constituencies to remain in the governing alliance.

Another problem with Stone's formulation of regime theory pertains to the role of culture and ideology in coalitional politics. For Stone (1989, 1993), ideology or political orientation plays little or no role in urban governance because partners in a ruling alliance sacrifice political preferences on the altar of pragmatism. This instrumental conception of coalition building, which is also the basis of game theory, fails to denote key differences among different countries and perhaps cities as well. For example, Stoker and Mossberger (1994) point out that urban governing coalitions form around different senses of common purpose, which may be tradition and social cohesion (an organic coalition), selective incentives (an instrumental alliance), and strategic use of symbols (a symbolic coalition) (see also Edelman 1964).

Put simply, culture and ideology, as well as instrumentality, may constitute important bases of coalition building (see Elazar 1970; Ferman 1996; Ramsay 1996; Painter 1997). For instance, British political parties divide more sharply along ideological lines than in the United States, and the parties remain important bases of power in British cities. What is more, the rise of a New Left in a number of U.K. cities during the 1980s (see Boddy and Fudge 1984; Gyford 1985) indicates that ideology has figured more prominently in the British context. In other words, ideological polarization has been greater in British urban politics than in the United States, so that the political consensus and cooperative arrangements Stone stresses may have been a product of U.S. political culture's greater emphasis on privatism and pragmatism (see Warner 1968; Barnekov et al. 1989; Judd and Swanstrom 1998).

In sum, the predisposing logic or ideological outlook that participants carry into the political arena informs their calculations as to what is in their own interest, and therefore how much they are willing to compromise in order to accomplish some governing task, or, indeed, whether they should oppose a policy entirely (see Painter 1997). The stress laid by Stone on the pragmatic elements of alliance formation and maintenance, in the form of small opportunities and selective incentives, may underestimate the importance of political perspectives in building trust and cooperation among coalition partners, or, obversely, the obstruction to cooperation that widely divergent political orientations may pose.

Urban Power Structures

The notion of power is central to political analysis, and the study of community power structures is a well-trod path in the field of urban politics in the United States (see Hunter 1953; Dahl 1961; Gordon 1973; Hawley and Wirt 1974; Polsby 1980). If commensurate identifiable structures of urban power can be found to exist across nations, this could prove to be an important basis for comparative urban research. To this end, we endeavor to recalibrate conceptions of urban power structures for the purpose of comparative research. That is, taking as a point of embarkation basic notions of power and governance, our modes of governance approach seeks to extend the analytical reach of urban power structure theorizing.

The Community Power Paradigm

The genesis of urban power structure theory lies in the scholarly discourse of the 1950s and 1960s about who ruled U.S. cities. The community power debate pitted political pluralists (see Dahl 1961), who conceived of power as dispersed among interest groups, against elite theorists, who claimed that urban political power was concentrated and highly stratified (see Hunter 1953). Power in the community power paradigm meant the ability to get people to do something that they would not otherwise do. Although pluralists and elite theorists differed in several respects, they agreed in that they conceived of power as a phenomenon that could be "observed" by monitoring the actions taken by participants in the political process.

Peter Bachrach and Morton Baratz (1962) detected a second face of power. Drawing on Schattschneider's (1960) notion of a "mobilization of bias," they claimed that a hidden process of politics, which they called *nondecision making,* can preempt the public airing of particular issues. When this occurs, governing elites "limit decision-making to relatively non-controversial matters, by influencing community values and political procedures and rituals, notwithstanding that there are in the community serious but latent power conflicts" (Bachrach and Baratz 1963:947). This veiled use of power by community notables, according to Bachrach and Baratz, prevents controversial or damaging issues from ever reaching the public agenda, so that no observable decisions are made and the exercise of nondecision-making power goes unnoticed.

For pluralist, elite, and nondecisional theorists, power structures are a function of the distribution of resources among governing elites (see Bachrach and Baratz 1963; Dahl 1961; Hunter 1953; Judge 1995; Polsby 1980; Waste 1986). According to pluralists, resources are dispersed among organized political groupings, producing multiple centers of power within the urban polity. Elite theorists, in turn, conceive of a highly stratified system of political power, with resources concentrated in the hands of social, economic, and political elites (Hunter 1952; Domhoff 1978). Nondecisional theorists also view the configuration of political power as stratified, with the most powerful elites exercising preclusionary power (nondecision making) over the public agenda, leaving minor elites able to mobilize resources only on those issues that pose little or no serious threat to the ruling elite.

Interestingly, all three community power perspectives agree that the objective in exercising political power is the Weberian predilection to control or gain dominion over others (see Dahl 1986; Hunter 1953). Differences among these community power theorists relate to the *form* in which power is exercised, not in what power is or why it is deployed.

Urban Regimes and Social Production

Although scholarly discourse over the nature of urban power structures ebbed considerably by the end of the 1970s, interest was revived in the late 1980s by the development of urban regime theory. Clarence Stone's (1976, 1989) decades-long research into politics in Atlanta led him to understand that governance was not simply or even mostly a matter of social control, in which rival factions or coalitions seek to dominate government decision making. As Stone (1989:5–6) explained:

> "Governing," as used in governing coalition, I must stress, does not mean rule in command-and-control fashion. Governance through informal arrangements is about how some forms of coordination of effort prevail over others. It is about mobilizing efforts to cope and to adapt; it is not about absolute control. Informal arrangements are a way of bolstering (and guiding) the formal capacity to act, but even this enhanced capacity remains quite limited.

These limitations redound from the constitutionally limited scope and authority of the local state. Because localities have only weak formal means through which coordination can be achieved, informal arrangements to promote cooperation are especially useful.

In place of a social control model, Stone proposed a *social production model* of political power based on a "Tillian" view of society. According to Stone, Charles Tilly (1984), who has written extensively in the area of comparative historical sociology, comprehends society as composed of a "loose network of institutional arrangements" that is "fraught with tension and conflict" (Stone 1989:227). The power to command or dominate over others under these conditions of social complexity is, at best, difficult to achieve. Hence, "the power struggle concerns, not control and resistance, but gaining and fusing a capacity to act—*power to*, not *power over*" (Stone 1989:227; emphasis in original). That is, power is structured and exercised in an effort to produce certain kinds of outcomes or results through cooperative efforts, not to gain dominion or control over the actions of others. Stone applies the social production model to urban politics through the concept of regimes.

Reconceptualizing Urban Power Structures

The various renditions of urban power structure theory hold in common the assumption that city governance can be explained by showing how the configuration of informal relations among significant actors shapes the process of political decision making. Moreover, differences in urban power structures—pluralist polyarchy, a stratified power elite, or an urban regime—derive from the different forms of power employed. At least four distinct forms of political power can be identified.

Dominating power is used to secure compliance, and is at the crux of the community power paradigm idea of political power (Dahl 1986). Dominating power is implicated in relationships marked by conflict, where actors utilize resources to overcome or to prevent actions of others (see Stone 1986, 1988). Formal authority and informal influence can be the basis for the use of dominating power. A simple illustration of dominating power is the mayoral use of veto power to stop city council legislation that the mayor opposes.

Bargaining power is employed in building coalitions (Stone 1986:82–83), and is a "relationship between actors bargaining from autonomous bases of strength" (Stone 1988:88), where each has "complementary resources, perhaps complementary domains in which each has command power" (Stone 1986:82–83). When competing actors perceive that their conflict would be too costly to settle by use of dominating power, they move toward a more cooperative relationship of negotiation in order to compromise. This is the familiar give and take of American urban politics, in which, for instance, a police union, after rejecting a mayor's proposed contract because of one or two controversial items, enters into negotiation to work out the differences between the two sides.

Systemic power (Stone 1980) enables certain interests, particularly business interests, to influence decision making simply through their position in society. This is often done without intention or recognition on the part of systemic power holders. This formulation echoes both the elite theorists' notion of positional power (see Hunter 1953) and Charles Lindblom's (1977) argument that markets exercise disciplinary power over government. That is, because business interests control crucial resources necessary for political success, governing decisions are made in ways that seek accommodation with privileged power holders. For example, to retain or attract the business investment that generates local taxes and jobs, city officials normally take care to provide the infrastructure or services necessary for the operations of large corporations, whether corporations overtly demand them or not.

Preemptive power is the most complex form of political power. Akin to Bachrach and Baratz's (1962, 1963) nondecision making, preemptive power is the "capacity to occupy, hold, and make use of a strategic position" (Stone 1988:83). In terms of urban governance, it is the capacity of fusing dominating and systemic power, which, in turn, enables a coalition to control policy setting through the ability to hold and occupy a strategic location in the governing process (Stone 1988:90–91). As a result, those who acquire and use preemptive power can direct policy setting and discourage would-be opposition to their policy agenda by making challenges far too costly to attempt. Well-oiled urban political machines, through their control of party nomination processes and patronage distribution and often in alliance with significant business interests that sought government contracts or other largess, clearly preempted opposing or alternative policy agendas in cities like Chicago and Jersey City for decades.

Stone's conception of regime is predicated on the preemptive form of political power. That is, urban regimes are governing coalitions that exercise preemptive power in setting policy agendas and are difficult to dislodge because they blend dominating, bargaining, and systemic power in ways that discourage or subdue opposition (see Stoker 1995). Further, the ability to resist (dominating power) or coopt (bargaining power) challenges enables regimes to persist for relatively long periods of time (see Stoker 1995). The governing coalition between white business elites and city politicians in Atlanta that endured from the 1940s to the 1980s, as depicted by Stone (1989), exemplifies regime politics. But is Atlanta a typical case? That is, can the concept of regime be applied profitably to governance where power other than the preemptive kind prevails? If conflict rather than cooperation dominates the interaction among ruling elites, can this also be labeled regime politics? Suppose, in other words, that a city exists without a Stonean regime. Suppose that regimes are less the rule than the exception.

To investigate these issues we must reexamine the putative dichotomous relationship between social control and social production. Stone's social production model of political power rests on the following premise: Although dominating power exists, its use is limited; more often, bargaining or preemptive power governs the policy-making process in urban politics. Conceiving of preemptive power as the basis for regimes, however, attenuates Stone's social production model. That is, regime preemption is not only the "power to" achieve specific purposes, but also the exercise of "power over" others in setting the policy agenda. What is more, "power to" and "power over" are inseparable partners in the political process. Whether using dominating, bargaining, or preemptive power in pursuit of some governing task, it is necessary to exercise some power over others either by defeating them (dominating power), persuading them (bargaining power), or precluding them from the decision-making process (preemptive power). For example, when a mayor tries to push a budget through a city council, the mayor is clearly trying to exercise the "power to" set the municipal agenda. Simultaneously, through command or bargaining power, the mayor will also seek to gain "power over" the city council to accept the proposed budget by defeating or persuading opponents. Simply put, social control and social production are not mutually exclusive models of the political process, but instead elucidate different dimensions of the use of political power.[1]

Any model of urban governance ought to inquire into the specific nature of interaction among city leaders. Regime theory generally assumes that cooperation will eventually win out, although this may not always be the case. For example, Frederick Wirt's (1974) study of San Francisco suggests that "hyperpluralism" produced a condition of endemic conflict in city politics (see also Yates 1977). To enlarge the theoretical compass of power structure research, it is imperative that analyses of urban politics recognize the relationship between the nature of governing coalition formation and patterns of urban political decision making. The duality of political power then becomes clear, as the exercise and structuring of power is aimed at setting and carrying out one policy agenda to the exclusion of another. The difference is that in applying this broader conception of urban power structures, it is *not* presumed that governance moves inexorably toward cooperation.

A conception of urban governance based on a dual social control and social production model, then, requires a broader conception of power structure. Table 1.1 correlates the different forms of political power, types of power structures, and modes of decision making that are possible in urban politics. In decision making embroiled in conflict, power is not only fragmented but used to overcome *rival factions* by employing dominating

Table 1.1

Urban Power Structures

Type of Power	Urban Power Structure	Mode of Decision Making
Dominating	Rival factions	Conflict
Bargaining	Coalitions	Contingent cooperation
Preemptive	Regimes	Enduring cooperation

power. In contrast, cooperative decision making fosters relations among governing elites so that coalition building can take place. That is, bargaining power is used to bind *coalitions* that are marriages of convenience (i.e., contingent cooperation) around particular governing agendas. Cooperation based on preemptive power, in turn, is enduring and forms the basis of creating *regimes* that both dominate agenda setting and exclude challengers from that process. In short, using our reconstituted theory of urban power structures permits consideration of urban power structures that are not regimes.

The Political Economy of Urban Governance

Urban coalition-building and power structure theories were born and reared in the family of American political science. As a result, these urban theories have greatly benefited from the sophistication of American political science methods and discourse. They have also inherited some of its cultural biases.

Urban power structure theory is based on the assumption of a weak state where it has been necessary to construct informal structures of power to compensate for the limited authority of government. Stone (1989), for example, claims that the need for civic cooperation stems from the division of labor between state and market (see also Elkin 1985; Lindblom 1977). Governance in the United States is "constrained by the accommodation of two basic institutional principles of American political economy: (1) popular control of the formal machinery of government and (2) private ownership of business enterprise" (Stone 1989:6). That is, in democratic-capitalist societies, political power is fractured into separate spheres of influence, in which business elites control crucial capital investment resources in the economic realm and governmental officials operate the levers of public authority. As a result, government alone lacks the power to command or even coordinate market forces (Lindblom 1977). Put simply, the "inadequacies of formal government authority are the foundation for urban regimes and account for the necessity of developing informal arrangements" (Stone 1989:231).

This weak state bias means that urban power structure theory can be applied to British or other European urban governance only with great care and caution (see Keating 1991; John and Cole 1998). In Britain, for example, the institutional or sectoral bases upon which power structures might be erected differ substantially from those of U.S. cities. Because the scope of the public domain in Britain is much larger, local governments there have possessed greater resources and authority, and have required fewer private resources to undertake governing tasks. Big business interests, for example, have often been absent or excluded from city governing processes (see Keating 1991; Harding 1994), so it has not been as necessary for local government leaders to form partnerships or alliances with business sector elites, at least not until the late 1980s and 1990s. As a result, the modes of governance in Britain have not historically resembled the pragmatic American-style governing coalitions discussed by Stone (1989) and others (see Stone and Sanders 1987; Elkin 1985; Mollenkopf 1983; Logan and Molotch 1987).

American urban political studies have also tended to focus primarily on the internal mechanics of coalition formation and maintenance, concentrating on how urban power structures affect the process of politics, rather than examining the ways in which a given political-economic context delimits the scope of city governance (see Horan 1991). This "localist bias" (Harding 1994) probably inheres in the use of case studies of individual cities to confirm the propositions of community power and coalitional theories (see Dahl 1961; Hunter 1953; DeLeon 1992; DiGaetano 1989; Stone 1989; Mollenkopf 1992; Turner 1992). That is, American urban political analyses generally omit careful assessments of how a specific national political-economic context shapes or conditions urban governance.

Confining our analysis to the internal workings of urban politics, therefore, would render ineffectual a comparative study of urban governance. As Stoker (1995:66) explains, there is a focus "on the internal dynamics of the governing coalition to the detriment of contextual forces. A dilemma facing all studies of community power is how to place the analysis within the context of wider processes of change.... The crucial challenge is to connect local and non-local sources of policy change." Furthermore, because the scope and institutional resources of the local state vary historically and from nation to nation, the degree to which informal public-private sector arrangements are necessary for urban governance also varies. For this reason, a study of comparative urban governance must avoid the "localist trap" inherent in close analysis of urban governing alignments (see Stoker 1995:66–67), and instead must pay greater attention to the political-economic environment of urban governance.

The political-economic environment of a city establishes certain parameters for local governing systems and the choices that urban leaders make (see Judd and Swanstrom 1998). To avoid the pitfalls of focusing too narrowly on internal urban political processes, we propose to integrate coalitional and political economic perspectives in explaining urban governance in our comparative study of four cities. Our analysis incorporates two features of urban political economy: (1) urban structuring and restructuring; and (2) state structuring and restructuring (see DiGaetano and Klemanski 1993).

First, *urban structuring and restructuring* refers to the economic and demographic patterns that unfold in the process of urbanization. A city's relationship to the regional, national, or even international economy clearly influences local political participation and decision making. For example, recent trends in economic restructuring, including globalization, deindustrialization, and the concomitant shift to service sector employment, have altered in significant ways who participates in urban political decision making and the nature of strategic problems addressed by the governing process (see Cox and Mair 1988; Fainstein 1994). Moreover, differences in local economic performance in terms of buoyant, stagnant, or depressed local economies affect the choices that a city's ruling elites make in the politics of urban development.

Social structuring and restructuring also leave an imprint on local politics. That is, a city's demographic composition, in the form of class, racial, and ethnic groupings, may also define local political interests and affect the distribution of political resources (such as votes and control of elective office) within a locality. Migrations that entail the exodus of some social classes and racial or ethnic groups and the influx of others could alter the balance of political power within a city and disrupt a governing coalition's operation, even threatening its survival. Ethnicity and race have traditionally played important roles in urban politics in the United States, as the extensive literature on machine politics and the politics of civil rights and poverty have shown (see Piven and Cloward 1971; Reed 1988; Erie 1989; DiGaetano 1991). Alternatively, social class divisions have historically figured more prominently in British urban politics (see Katznelson 1985; Duncan and Goodwin 1988). Interestingly, ethnic power and politics have also emerged as increasingly crucial dimensions of urban governance in Britain as the proportion of ethnic minorities, particularly Asians from former Commonwealth countries, has grown in the country's larger cities. As a result, ethnic minority politicians have risen mostly through local Labour parties to key positions within many city councils, with traditional Labour politicians losing ground in local power realignments. In this way, social restructuring has effected changes in the composition of local governing coalitions directly.

Second, we seek to explain how *state structuring and restructuring* defines and redefines the functions and nature of the local state. In terms of the current study, the British unitary state and American federal system generate obvious differences in the functions and structure of local governing systems. In Britain, state transformations in the 1980s and 1990s have substantially redefined the scope and capacity of local governing systems. This new intergovernmental context occasioned new sorts of local governing coalitions and patterns of decision making. The weak state system of American federalism, in contrast, has allowed municipal governments greater latitude in local decision making, but fewer resources. In addition, state restructuring may reconfigure the boundaries of the public domain, and thus alter the relationship between the local state and the economy. For example, strengthening or weakening the planning powers of the local state affects its ability to regulate economic development and thus bargain with local developers about appropriate land use. Changes in the boundaries and structure of the local state, in short, have profound implications for urban coalition building and power structures.

Comparing Urban Governance in Britain and the United States

A comparative study of urban development politics must consider the relative contributions of different political-economic contexts and local forces in shaping patterns of city governance, something that single-case studies can never do adequately. Using the modes of governance frame of reference, we compare the politics of urban development in Birmingham, Boston, Bristol, and Detroit as a means to explain how the interplay of urban political economy and internal politics of governing alignments produce variations in the form and content of local governance. To do this, we examine how local governing coalitions respond to the constraints imposed and opportunities afforded by a city's economic conditions, state policies and modes of intervention, and demographic trends. This includes the policy responses adopted by governing coalitions that comprise a city's governing agenda.

As John Walton (1990) insightfully points out, however, comparative analysis of urban politics should be guided by an explicit analytical strategy. Walton recommends adoption of Tilly's (1984:82–83) comparative analytical strategies, which consist of the following: (1) individualizing comparisons, which "contrast specific instances of a given phenomenon as a means of grasping the peculiarities of each case"; (2) universalizing comparisons, which attempt "to establish that every instance of a phenomenon follows essentially the same rule"; (3) variation-finding comparisons, which seek to find the "principle of variation in the character or intensity of a phenomenon by examining systematic differences among instances"; and (4) encompassing comparisons, which focus on "different instances at various locations within the same system, on the way to explaining their characteristics as a function of their varying relationship to the system as a whole" (Tilly 1984:82–83).

Our comparative study of urban politics employs the method of variation-finding comparisons, in that we endeavor to explain why modes of governance vary both within and across nations. The cities under scrutiny were chosen to highlight differences within nations and similarities across them. That is, we have opted to research urban development politics in Detroit and Boston in the United States and Birmingham and Bristol in Great Britain because of the striking differences in social and economic characteristics displayed by each national pair. In addition, Detroit and Birmingham form a couplet of car manufacturing cities in economic decline, while Boston and Bristol form a pair of maritime cities turned regional financial centers, both located in regions endowed with heavy concentrations of high technology and defense-related industry.

Also, to the extent possible, state policies were held constant by the time period selected for the study. Central governments in the United States and the United Kingdom turned to the political right in the 1980s and 1990s, particularly in urban policy. However, the modes of intervention in urban policy employed by the two national leaders have contrasted markedly, with the Thatcher and Major governments opting for more direct control over local governing systems, while the Reagan and Bush administrations largely withdrew from urban affairs.

A comparison of urban development politics in our four cities based on a variation-finding research strategy also enables us to detect distinctive patterns of governance for each city that cannot be accounted for wholly by external factors such as the national and international economy or policies of national political regimes. To assess the "local" contribution to patterns of urban governance, we examine the governing alignments and

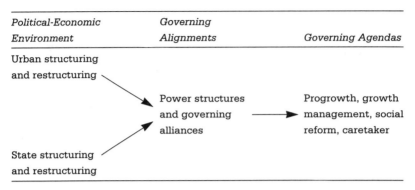

Figure 1.1. Modes of urban governance.

realignments that structure development politics in the four cities. To strengthen this analysis, however, a dynamic element needs to be injected into the modes of governance approach. As Stoker (1995) suggests, coalition building undergoes a process of coming together (formation), institutionalizing relations among the different interests involved (development), and eventually the deterioration of those relations (demise). Using this three-stage model, we can investigate the respective roles of the urban political-economic environment and local political alignments in shaping patterns of governance in the four cities.

Figure 1.1 depicts a simplified theoretical construct we use to explain urban development politics in Britain and the United States. The political-economic environment, which is the confluence of urban and state structuring and restructuring, establishes parameters for local political interaction and decision making. Conditions created by a particular political-economic environment produce opportunities for developing certain urban governing alignments (alliances and power structures) while imposing constraints on others. What is more, changes in the political-economic environment may alter the organizational bases of urban leaders, helping some, hurting others, and creating new ones. In this way, urban and state restructuring rearranges the character of and relations among interests involved in urban governance.

Urban political economy, however, does not wholly or even mostly determine the form or content of local political decision making, as structuralist urban theory would have us believe (see Gottdiener 1987; Gottdiener and Feagin 1988; O'Connor 1973; Peterson 1981). Problems generated by urban and state structuring are mediated by the form and character of the constellation of political interests that comprise the local polity, so that the governing alignments and agendas vary in relation to both the larger context and the configuration of the urban political power. In this sense, governing agendas are responses to the larger urban political-economic environment that are refracted through the prism of the local governing alignments. Furthermore, the particular sets of interaction between environment and local polity produce particular modes of governance.

Urban Structuring and Restructuring

2

Urban structuring and restructuring refers to the set of global, national, regional, and local forces that configure the socioeconomic spatial arrangements of cities. Within urban structuring and restructuring, two distinct but related patterns of development can be discerned. The first includes the spatial dimensions of work, production, and distribution of goods and services. Relevant here are the postindustrial trends of globalization of the economy, deindustrialization, and an increasing emphasis on a service economy. The second type of urban structuring and restructuring refers to the spatial implications of population shifts in a city's racial and ethnic make-up and in the relative wealth and education levels of its residents.

In this chapter, we examine the patterns of postindustrial urban structuring and restructuring for Birmingham, Boston, Bristol, and Detroit. We first discuss how postindustrial economic transformations have affected the four cities since 1970. Then we describe concomitant changes in the social structures of the cities. Finally, we develop a typology of the four cities based on economic and social characteristics that place them in a larger urban hierarchy.

Urban Economic Structuring and Restructuring

To better understand how the different economic contexts have affected governing arrangements in our cities, we can examine the effects of economic restructuring and the business cycle on Birmingham, Boston, Bristol, and Detroit. Cities in the United Kingdom and United States (as in most industrialized nations) encountered new sorts of global economic restructuring pressures beginning in the 1970s. In the United Kingdom, the decades of the 1970s and 1980s have been identified by some scholars as one of four major periods of structural change in the economy since the early 1800s (Allen and Massey 1988). Among the indicators of major structural change in the United Kingdom are a decline in manufacturing industries and employment, new production methods in leading industries including spatial decentralization of production facilities, a partial dismantling of state ownership and state provision of services, and growth in information technology, finance, and consumer services industries (Allen and Massey 1988:12). These major changes in economic structure also affected many U.S. cities in the post-energy crisis period beginning about 1973, as documented elsewhere (Logan and Swanstrom 1990; Beauregard 1989).

In addition to economic restructuring, recurring trends in the business cycle (prosperity, recession, recovery) may also have an impact on the strategies used by local leaders to define and solve problems. For example, prosperity may encourage an emphasis on amenities and quality of life issues in a city, while a depressed or declining economy often elevates economic development issues to the highest priority on a local political agenda.

Birmingham: From Industrial Revolution to Devolution

Originally a provincial market town, Birmingham's economic fortunes became heavily reliant on the manufacture of goods in the early eighteenth century. Birmingham was superbly situated to receive raw materials from around the nation and to distribute the manufactured goods produced there across the nation and beyond. During the nineteenth century, manufacturing in Birmingham largely took place in small shops and was quite diversified. Indeed, "Brummies," as locals are known, proudly boasted that Birmingham was a town of a thousand trades (Birmingham City Council 1989). Birmingham developed specialties in metal products such as jewelry, buttons, and coins; steam engines; and brass and iron tubes, pressure gauges, valves, nuts and bolts, and screws for the rapidly expanding railway system. Birmingham artisans also engaged in gun making and in the production of explosives and ammunition. Industrial restructuring began in the early twentieth century with increasing concentration on the manufacture of motor cars, and Birmingham's economy grew robustly through most of this century.

By the 1970s, however, Birmingham faced the difficulty of all cities heavily dependent on a single industry. Employment, especially in the manufacturing sector, declined at alarming rates during the 1970s and 1980s. Birmingham lost almost half its manufacturing job base between 1971 and

1997. Though the city's employment figures experienced the most rapid drop in the 1980–1985 period, the longer-term trend of economic restructuring has affected the city's economy well beyond those years.

Almost half of Birmingham's work force (47.9 percent) was employed in manufacturing in 1971. As illustrated by table 2.1, that figure had dropped to about one quarter (24.9 percent) by 1991. In the United Kingdom, the traditional employment sectors of agriculture and manufacturing decreased during the 1970s and 1980s, while the service sectors (distribution and catering; banking and finance; and other services) witnessed relative increases.

A downturn in automobile production and the related engineering and metal-based sectors was primarily responsible for job losses during this time. In 1981, about 40 percent of the Birmingham workforce was employed in manufacturing, with about two-thirds of the jobs concentrated in motor vehicle production, metal goods, metal manufacturing, and mechanical engineering.

The 1970s and early 1980s saw high unemployment in many cities because of changes in the global economy. But even within a metropolitan area, major differences in employment existed. For example, wards in and nearest the core of cities like Birmingham experienced the highest levels of unemployment, while the surrounding suburbs were relatively much better off. Some Birmingham wards had unemployment rates of between 30 and 45 percent (West Midlands County Council, County Planning Department 1983:67). Moreover, government figures indicated that in 1985, almost half (49 percent) of all unemployment in Birmingham was considered to be structural and therefore long term—the highest proportion in England (Hasluck 1987:16).

Despite its problems, Birmingham's economy possesses some strengths. As Britain's second largest city, Birmingham holds an important status position within the United Kingdom. It also has an advantage in its location, as it sits roughly in the geographic center of the United Kingdom's motorway and rail network. It is within an easy commute to and from London, so it has been able to attract some branch offices of financial institutions to its city center. As a consequence, Birmingham has been able to respond to many of the economic challenges it faced in the period after 1970. In particular, Birmingham emerged as a regional center for financial and professional services in the 1980s. Specializing in the provision of financial and professional services for the manufacturing sector in the Midlands and the North, Birmingham was not in direct competition with London's financial district. Nonetheless, Birmingham's expertise in services for manufacturing sparked fierce competition with such provincial financial centers as Manchester and Leeds, which incidentally had gone through the same transformation as Birmingham from manufacturing to regional centers.

Restructuring in Boston: The Hub Hums

From colonial times to the early 1800s, economic life in Boston revolved around its harbor, which was the nation's third largest port. Alongside maritime industries such as international trade and fishing, Boston developed a diversified manufacturing base that included the production of woolen goods, shoes, machinery, cigars, carpets, garments, and beer (Kennedy 1992). By the mid-nineteenth century, the Industrial Revolution transformed Boston's physical landscape, as factories and mills cropped up in the manufacturing belt to the south of the city center. Boston capital also financed much of New England's sprawling textile and shoe manufacturing industry. By the middle of the twentieth century, however, the maritime and manufacturing sectors contracted and Boston's economy began to undergo another transformation, this time to a service-based economy. In the postindustrial era, Boston retained its position as New England's regional corporate and financial capital, but the city's economy had largely lost its port and manufacturing bases. As table 2.2 reveals, Boston's economy suffered substantial drops in manufacturing employment between 1970 and 1990.

Still, Boston remains the "Hub" of New England, and has well-established transportation links (air, rail, and interstate highways) that have helped make the city a vital economic center. After 1970, Boston saw dramatic growth in corporate, financial, health care, higher education, and high technology jobs. As seen in table 2.2, corporate and financial sector jobs (in finance, insurance, real estate, professional, and related services) ballooned from 35.4 percent of the local labor force in 1970 to 51.3 percent

---

Table 2.1

Occupations by Industry 1971, 1981, 1991 (Percentages)

Year	Birmingham	Bristol	United Kingdom
Agriculture, forestry, and fishery			
1971	0.5	0.4	3.0
1981	0.2	0.3	1.8
1991	0.2	0.3	1.9

Table 2.1 *(continued)*

Year	Birmingham	Bristol	United Kingdom
Mining, energy, and water			
1971	n.a.	n.a.	1.6
1981	1.4	1.7	3.1
1991	3.7	2.8	4.7
Construction			
1971	5.8	6.1	6.8
1981	6.0	6.2	5.2
1991	6.5	7.3	7.4
Manufacturing			
1971	47.9	28.1	35.0
1981	41.2	27.7	26.3
1991	24.9	15.4	17.8
Distribution and catering			
1971	5.2	4.8	n.a.
1981	18.2	19.6	19.7
1991	19.0	20.5	20.5
Transport			
1971	5.5	7.5	5.8
1981	4.7	8.3	6.5
1991	5.7	7.2	6.4
Banking and finance			
1971	n.a.	n.a.	n.a.
1981	n.a.	n.a.	10.7
1991	11.9	16.4	12.0
Other services			
1971	38.4	57.9	57.7
1981	27.5	34.9	26.3
1991	27.0	29.2	28.3
Not classified			
1971	2.1	n.a.	4.4
1981	n.a.	n.a.	n.a.
1991	1.2	0.9	8.8

Source: Office of Population Censuses and Surveys (1975, 1984, 1993). Because of data collection changes, the 1971 figures are not strictly comparable to the 1981 and 1991 figures.

Table 2.2

Occupational Structure by Industry 1970, 1980, 1990

	Year	Boston	Detroit
Agriculture, forestry, and fishery	1970	0.3	0.4
	1980	0.3	0.2
	1990	0.4	0.5
Construction	1970	4.4	3.5
	1980	3.2	2.5
	1990	4.0	3.0
Manufacturing	1970	17.5	35.9
	1980	14.3	28.6
	1990	9.9	20.5
Transportation, communication,	1970	7.6	5.7
and other utilities	1980	7.3	7.7
	1990	7.0	7.8
Wholesale and retail trade	1970	19.4	18.7
	1980	16.8	16.4
	1990	16.6	18.5
Finance, insurance, and real estate	1970	9.2	4.8
	1980	9.0	5.3
	1990	10.8	6.2
Business and repair services	1970	3.8	3.4
	1980	5.2	4.1
	1990	5.8	6.0
Professional and related services	1970	25.4	16.5
	1980	31.6	23.2
	1990	34.7	25.1
Other services	1970	12.4	11.0
	1980	12.6	11.9
	1990	10.9	12.9

Source: U.S. Bureau of the Census (1973b, 1983b, 1993b).

in 1990 (U.S. Bureau of the Census 1973b, 1993b). Growth in the city's corporate and financial services sectors produced a major downtown property boom that began in the late 1970s and peaked during the late 1980s. Commercial and residential property values skyrocketed, which put the city at a relative advantage when negotiating terms with prospective property developers. During this time, the city parleyed a number of linkage agreements with developers that enabled it to secure open spaces, public access, low-to-moderate income housing, and other public goods in exchange for downtown office and hotel building permits (see chapters 7 and 8).

High-technology industries also played a large role in Boston's relative economic health because of the concentration of academic research institutions in the metropolitan area, plus the many defense-related firms that scattered along State Route 128, which encircles the Greater Boston area (Rosegrant and Lampe 1992). In particular, Boston's health care industry burgeoned, in part due to university-affiliated research and training hospitals. Health care employment grew from 66,000 in 1982 to 88,000 in 1995 (Boston Redevelopment Authority, Policy Development and Research Services 1993b:14; City of Boston 1996:7). In sum, all of these trends in economic restructuring dovetailed to propel Boston into a relatively healthy postindustrial service-based economy.

Restructuring in Bristol: Britain's Sunbelt City?

From the fifteenth well into the nineteenth centuries, Bristol flourished as one of Britain's preeminent seaports. As a major maritime center, it also benefited from the development of industries that processed imports, such as sugar refining, cocoa processing and chocolate making, and the manufacture of tobacco products. In the eighteenth century, Bristol's involvement in the notorious trading triangle of slaves, manufactured goods, and raw materials that linked Britain, West Africa, and the Americas, greatly enriched the city's economic elite, known locally as the merchant venturers. By the early nineteenth century, Bristol's economy had also spawned thriving shipbuilding, engineering, leather working, and paper product industries. By the end of the century, this diversified base also included metalworking and packaging. The first half of the twentieth century saw Bristol's economy continue to prosper as local aircraft and automobile sectors emerged and rapidly expanded in the 1920s and 1930s. Postwar Bristol experienced a "long boom," as its diversified industrial and maritime economy modernized and expanded to keep pace with global economic changes (Boddy, Lovering, and Bassett 1986).

Bristol's economy fared relatively well in the 1970s and most of the 1980s. Though questioned by some, Bristol's growth spurt in the office and service sectors during the 1980s earned it the title of Britain's "sunbelt city" (Boddy, Lovering, and Bassett 1986). Although table 2.1 indicates a mix of occupations in Bristol, the economy became especially strong in banking and finance. The city benefited to a degree from central government policy, which sought to move financial and insurance service headquarters out of overly congested London. Bristol is well situated in the country's transportation network. The city lies along the M4 growth corridor at the junction where the M4 and M5 Motorways meet. The transportation network includes a high-speed rail system, which makes travel to and from London quite convenient. This has permitted the city to lure even more financial institution headquarters and major bank and insurance company offices from London, along with retailing businesses, professional and support services, and leisure and tourism offices. Bristol has become South West England's undisputed commercial and financial capital.

Expediting Bristol's transformation into a financial services center was a downtown property development boom that occurred during the 1980s (see chapter 8). Office construction from 1980 to 1989 added 225,220 square meters of space to the city's downtown areas (Bristol City Council 1990). Bristol also is unusual in that it attracted a number of national headquarters operations for financial industry giants, such as Lloyd's Bank.

As Bristol's service sector grew, traditional industries declined. As shown by table 2.1, Bristol's manufacturing sector employed 28.1 percent of the city's work force in 1971, but the effects of deindustrialization had whittled that down to 15.4 percent by 1991 (Office of Population Censuses and Surveys 1975, 1984, 1993a). The city had not been as reliant on manufacturing as Birmingham, so the negative impact caused by deindustrialization was not as severe. Also, Bristol attracted substantial investment in high technology, particularly in the computer industry. Moreover, in sharp contrast to Boston, Bristol remains a major port city in Britain, because the city council invested millions of pounds in the 1970s to expand and modernize its Avonmouth dock facilities. Still, Bristol began the 1990s in economic trouble, with above-average unemployment.

Detroit's Economy Runs Off the Road

Begun as a French trading post in 1701, Detroit by the mid-nineteenth century had grown into a thriving commercial center that traded in lumber, furs, and finished goods. In the second half of the nineteenth century, it made the transition from a commercial center to a medium-sized industrial city. Like Birmingham, Detroit produced a diversified array of manufactured goods, including wagons, railway cars, stoves, clothing, and pharmaceuticals. Iron and steel making, printing and publishing, and shipmaking also ranked high. The twentieth century saw Detroit's rise as an industrial giant. The myriad skills developed in the city during the latter half of the nineteenth century laid the foundation for Detroit's emerging automobile industry in the early part of the twentieth century. By mid-century Detroit was unquestionably the nation's Motor City, as car manufacturing dominated almost all aspects of its economic life (Holli 1976).

The global economic restructuring that began during the mid-1970s caused a major upheaval in traditional manufacturing enterprises in industrialized countries. Major manufacturers responded to this far more competitive economic system by reducing their work forces through automation, by decentralizing the production process and outsourcing many of the production tasks, and by relocating their manufacturing sites to areas where the costs of doing business were demonstrably cheaper. Even more than Birmingham, Detroit was vulnerable to the vicissitudes of the automobile industry.

By the 1970s and 1980s, Detroit was foremost among large U.S. cities that incurred the dislocations of deindustrialization. Suburbanization of manufacturing and Sunbelt and foreign competition conspired to undermine Detroit's position as the nation's Motor City. Detroit's local economy suffered as the major automobile manufacturers left the city or simply reduced their work forces through automation and outsourcing. Detroit lost over 200,000 jobs between 1970 and 1990, nearly four-fifths of these losses (78 percent) in manufacturing. Overall, Detroit's manufacturing segment of the work force dropped from 35.9 percent of the total in 1970 to 20.5 percent in 1990 (see table 2.2). Moreover, Detroit's unemployment rate climbed from 7.2 percent in 1970 to 19.7 percent in 1990 (U.S. Bureau of Census 1973b, 1993b), paralleling Birmingham's increases at about that same time.

In sharp contrast to the other three cities, Detroit has so far been unable to convert to a service-based economy. Table 2.2 shows that Detroit's service sector as a percentage of the city's employment base expanded between 1970 and 1990. But this proportional growth is deceptive because it took place in an ever-diminishing labor force. Detroit's service sector employment actually *fell* slightly from 172,251 in 1970 to 168,215 in 1990 (U.S. Bureau of Census 1973b, 1993b). At the same time, the city also lost over 800 service-sector businesses (U.S. GAO 1993).

By the mid-1990s, however, Detroit had recovered a bit from the recession of 1990–1992, as manufacturing led the country to recovery. A healthier national and state economy certainly has helped the city, particularly because the recovery has been driven by growth in the manufacturing sector, including auto production. Moreover, an invigorated public-private relationship has occurred under Mayor Dennis Archer, who was overwhelmingly re-elected to a second term in 1997. Major investment commitments by Chrysler Corporation and a number of investments tied to the city's federal empowerment zone have breathed some new life into the local economy.

Business Cycle

The short-term economic forces that are part of the business cycle combined with economic restructuring to send shock waves through many industrialized cities in the United Kingdom and United States during the 1970s and 1980s. The business cycle is important to our understanding of how local leaders act and make public policy because the peaks and troughs of business cycle phases are part of what frames the thinking of local leaders. For example, a period of recession, with an economic downturn that features higher unemployment rates, will likely affect how localities define problems and approach local economic development solutions (e.g., demand for welfare services will climb as tax revenues decline).

During our period of study, the United Kingdom and United States each experienced two recessions between 1970 and 1997. Each country suffered through a recession in the early 1980s and another in the early 1990s. The recession in the early 1980s hit three of our four case cities quite hard (with Boston remaining relatively insulated from this downturn). Birmingham and especially Detroit reeled from the effects of that downturn.

By 1990, another recession hit the two countries, and this time all four of the cities suffered. Bristol and Boston saw property market declines in significant ways. As the prototypical single-industry city, Detroit felt the impacts of both industrial restructuring and recession swiftly and deeply. Birmingham experienced a severe economic downturn and subsequent job loss during the 1970s and 1980s, and recovery from those hardships was affected by the 1990 recession.

Cyclical Unemployment in Birmingham

By 1981, Birmingham's unemployment rate was 16.5 percent (compared to 9.1 percent for all the United Kingdom and 8.5 percent for England). As mentioned previously, much of this was part of the longer-term restructuring, so it is not surprising that the unemployment rate for the city remained high—at 19.3 percent—in 1991 (Birmingham City Council 1983,

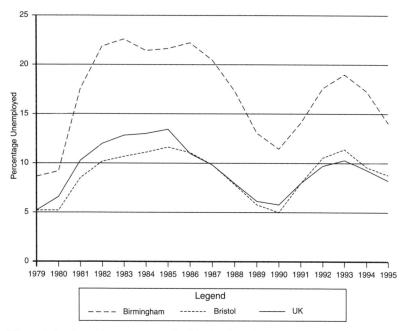

Figure 2.1. Unemployment rates for Birmingham, Bristol, and the United Kingdom, 1979–1995. *Source:* Employment Gazette 1979–1997; Central Statistical Office, *Regional Trends* (1986, 1996).

1993). Moreover, high unemployment rates were chronic problems, rather than simply the result of cyclical downturns. As the data in figures 2.1 and 2.2 demonstrate, unemployment rates in both Birmingham and Detroit consistently remained a staggering five to ten points higher than the national average during the 1970s and 1980s.

Although Birmingham's economy underwent the dislocation of automobile industry restructuring, this was confounded by hardships endured during the recessions of the early 1980s and early 1990s. Figure 2.1 illustrates the impact of the business cycle on unemployment in Birmingham, Bristol, and the United Kingdom. Birmingham's unemployment rate consistently rode 5 to 10 percent higher than Bristol's rate and the overall United Kingdom rate, peaking at 22.6 percent in 1982, and remaining at over 20 percent through 1987.

Economic recovery in the very late 1980s brought Birmingham's unemployment rates into the low double-digits for the first time since 1980. But the recession of the early 1990s visited even more hardships on Birmingham's business cycle-sensitive economy, as the city's unemployment rate again approached 20 percent (18.9 percent) by 1993. By 1997, the city saw

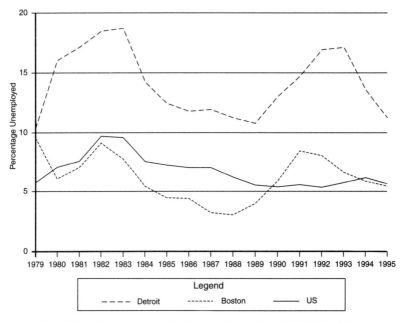

Figure 2.2. Unemployment rates for Boston, Detroit, and the United States, 1979–1995. *Source:* U.S. Bureau of the Census (1973b, 1993b); Boston Municipal Research Bureau (1990, 1995); Boston Redevelopment Authority, Policy Development and Research Department (1993); Michigan Employment Security Commission, Research and Statistics Division (1979–1995).

some recovery (along with our other cities), and its unemployment rate dipped again, to 10.0 percent in 1997, the city's lowest unemployment rate in 25 years.

Boston's Postindustrial Economy

Unlike Detroit and Birmingham, Boston has not relied on a single industry for its economic health. The city has been home to health care and higher education institutions for many years, and these two sets of institutions became two major engines of economic growth in the period after the 1970s. As New England's largest city, Boston has long served as the region's major financial center. In addition, Boston is the state's capital, and coupled with local and federal government offices, houses a large number of federal, state, and local government agencies. Because financial, higher education, government, and health care sectors have been the engines of postindustrial economic growth in the United States, the city was generally in good economic standing through the 1970s and 1980s, when many other cities suffered.

Even though Boston was subject to the business cycle, the degree of difficulties imposed on the city were mild compared to Birmingham or Detroit. From 1979 to 1997, Boston's unemployment rate at its worst reached 9.5 percent in 1979, 9.1 percent in 1982, and 8.4 percent in 1991. These rates were higher than the U.S. average in 1979 (5.8 percent) and 1991 (5.5 percent), but similar to 1982 (9.7 percent nationally). The city's official unemployment rate never reached double digits, and between 1985 and 1990, never exceeded 4.5 percent, while the U.S. national rates ranged from 5.3 percent in 1990 to 7.2 percent in 1985. Not until the 1991–1994 period did its unemployment rate exceed the national average.

Boston suffered a bit from the recession in the early 1990s, which caused unemployment rates to increase from about 3 percent in 1987–1988 to over 8 percent in 1991–1992. The recession of the early 1990s also brought downtown property development in Boston to a halt. This recession, combined with a limited supply of available properties, wilted demand for downtown real estate. This constrained the city's ability to leverage concessions from developers and required the city to alter its economic development strategy away from its downtown-centered approach of the 1970s and 1980s.

Bristol Economy Banks on Service Sector

Bristol's standing as a regional financial center generally insulated it from the problems of chronic unemployment, but it has been subject to the problems of cyclical unemployment. The recession in the early 1980s escalated Bristol's unemployment rate from 5.4 percent in 1980 to 12.6 percent by 1987 (Bristol City Council 1981, 1987). Bristol also saw economic decline by the early 1990s due to a downturn in the business cycle and the downsizing of the defense industry, but this occurred well after the dislocations felt by Birmingham and Detroit. The mid-1990s witnessed a stagnating local economy that threatened the competitive advantages that had enabled Bristol to prosper in the past.

Bristol fared somewhat better than other U.K. cities (including Birmingham) largely because of its more diversified local economy. In 1980, the city's unemployment rate was only 5.5 percent, compared with a rate for the entire United Kingdom that was almost double (9.1 percent). By the late 1980s, however, impact from long-term economic restructuring combined with a downturn in the business cycle brought about redundancies (layoffs) in important local industries such as aerospace. As a result, Bristol's unemployment rate rose above the national average, to 12.6 percent, by 1987.

During the 1980s recession, office development also slowed to a trickle, and the vacancy rate climbed (Punter 1990). The slowdown, however, was followed by an enormous office development boom that added 158,200 square meters to the city's office floor space between 1985 and 1990, with another 87,900 square meters under construction in 1990 (Avon County Council 1990).

As an illustration of Bristol's relative economic advantages compared to Birmingham, the city's highest unemployment rate was only 6.6 points higher than its lowest rate over the period from 1979 to 1997. Moreover, its highest rate (11.7 percent in 1985) was only half of Birmingham's (22.6 percent in 1983). Interestingly, Bristol—much like Boston—suffered relatively greater hardships during the 1990s recession, in that both cities had unemployment rates higher than their respective national averages.

Detroit's Economy Blows a Gasket

Detroit's extreme dependence on a single industry, automobile manufacturing, makes it acutely sensitive to fluctuations in the business cycle. Detroit already was plagued by double-digit unemployment (10.3 percent in 1979) when the recession of the early 1980s hit, forcing many permanent layoffs in the automobile industry. General Motors, Ford, and Chrysler lost a combined $3.5 billion in 1980 alone. In 1981, approximately 60 percent of all Detroit residents were receiving some form of public assistance, including unemployment compensation (U.S. GAO 1993). Detroit's unemployment rate rose quickly during the early 1980s, to 16.1 percent in 1980, then to 18.8 percent in 1983. Although some recovery occurred in the city during the mid-to-late 1980s (as unemployment dropped to 10.7 percent in 1989), the recession of the early 1990s once again raised unemployment rates, this time up to 17 percent in 1993 (a year of recovery).

By 1997, the city had entered into a recovery period, paralleling the nation's economic upturn. As the manufacturing sector in the Midwest expanded production, unemployment in Detroit fell to 8.7 percent in 1997, the lowest in 25 years. A number of commitments for industrial expansion by Chrysler, Ford, and General Motors, plans for downtown professional baseball and football stadiums, and proposals for three new voter-approved downtown gambling casinos have created considerable optimism and hope for the city's economic recovery.

Social Structuring and Restructuring

Cities must cope with forces of migration, segregation, and demographic or social change over which they have little control. Migrations into and out of large cities have been a major feature of nineteenth- and twentieth-century urbanization in the United Kingdom and the United States, and were major factors in the composition and size of each of our four cities. To better understand those forces, we investigate how social structuring and restructuring have occurred in our cities, emphasizing overall population shifts and racial and ethnic composition, as well as income, education, and poverty.

Population Migration Patterns

During the industrial era, cities acted as magnets, attracting massive in-migrations of workers for their burgeoning manufacturing and commercial sectors. In the period just after World War II, the migration patterns changed, as people began to move to the suburbs, especially in the United States. Boston and Detroit, for example, began losing population after the 1950 census (although Boston saw a slight increase between 1980 and 1990). Birmingham and Bristol both gained population through the 1961 census, but then saw declines beginning with the 1971 census (see figure 2.3). These more recent migratory movements have occasioned a spatial deconcentration of populations in the United Kingdom and the United States, resulting in a net decline in population for former industrial giants. The 1970 U.S. Census figures showed for the first time that more people lived in suburban areas than in urban or rural areas. Of course, many of those who did move were wealthier residents, which created further challenges to central city leaders. Even those cities successfully converting to a service-based economy often lost overall population in the 1970s and beyond. In virtually all cities, wealthier residents tended to be replaced by poorer ones; these poorer residents often had little or no training for jobs, if jobs were even available.

Central cities such as Birmingham and Detroit had little undeveloped land on which to build new housing. Moreover, with fewer people per household, the population of these cities has tended to decline. Improvements in transportation that enabled more affluent residents to move to suburbs have also allowed industries (and jobs) to move to the suburbs, satellite downtowns, or edge cities (Garreau 1991). This trend toward suburbanization is typical in most postindustrial nations, even where there are central cities with relatively vibrant local economies. Following na-

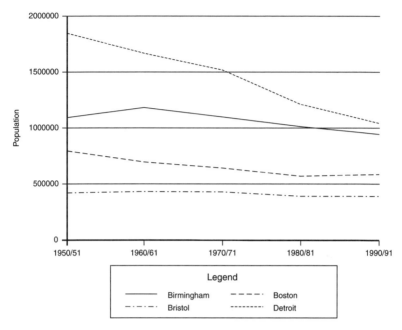

Figure 2.3. Population of Birmingham, Boston, Bristol, and Detroit, 1950–1951 to 1990–1991. *Source:* Office of Population Censuses and Surveys (1954, 1963, 1975, 1984, 1993); U.S. Bureau of the Census (1953, 1963, 1973a, 1983, 1993a).

tional trends, populations declined substantially in our four central cities after 1970. The larger metropolitan areas of Bristol and Boston grew, while the Birmingham and Detroit metropolitan areas both declined slightly.

Birmingham's population shift is similar to that of many major industrial and manufacturing centers. First, its overall population has been declining, although it continues to be Britain's second largest city. In addition, Birmingham has seen population shifts that influenced its approach to economic development policies and projects. The decade of the 1970s hit Birmingham and other industrialized cities hard, with high levels of inflation and deindustrialization, along with an outmigration of businesses and residents and an inmigration of poorer residents. Birmingham lost about 8 percent of its population between 1971 and 1981, 19.3 percent leaving the city's "old core" area. By 1991, the city's population had dropped below 1 million (937,763), marking another 6.5 percent decrease between 1981 and 1991 (Office of Population Censuses and Surveys 1975, 1984, 1993b).

Boston actually experienced a slight increase in population between 1980 and 1990, contrary to the trend in most large cities of the nation's northeast region. As illustrated by figure 2.3, Boston's population dipped slightly between 1970 and 1980 (paralleling the experience in all of our case cities, and many large cities in the industrialized world). The city lost about 70,000 people between 1970 and 1980 (12.2 percent), then gained almost 12,000 back (2.0 percent) between 1980 and 1990. At the same time, its surrounding metropolitan region grew about 2 percent, then again slightly (about 0.5 percent) between 1980 and 1990 (U.S. Census Bureau 1973a, 1983, 1993a). The city's increased population during the 1980s is indicative of the relative attractiveness and vibrancy of the local economy during that decade. Moreover, many of the city's dominant economic activities—health care, higher education, and government—generally are relatively insulated from the forces of deindustrialization or the vagaries of the business cycle.

Despite Bristol's relative prosperity, it, too, witnessed the economic and demographic trends of deindustrialization and population loss after 1970. This differs from the South West region of England as a whole, which gained population between 1971 and 1991, growing from about 3,781,000 in 1971 to approximately 4,600,000 by 1991. As a percentage of the United Kingdom's overall population, the South West region increased its share from 7.0 percent to 8.3 percent during that 20-year period. Moreover, virtually all other regions of England saw at least slight decreases in their share of overall population, including the South East (London), the North, and North West. As almost all other large cities in the United Kingdom did, Bristol lost population during this time, dropping from 427,000 in 1971 to approximately 391,000 in 1981 and another 5 percent to about 372,000 by 1991.

Detroit's population decreased dramatically between 1970 and 1990. A relatively wealthy and prominent city during the early days of the automobile industry, Detroit's population was still increasing during the early 1950s, by 1953 peaking at 1.85 million. By 1970, however, the city had declined to 1.5 million, by 1980, to 1.2 million, and by 1990 to barely one million, a 45 percent decline.

Among those who stayed behind, a disproportionate number had meager economic and educational resources. More city services are needed for these poorer residents, who at the same time are less able to pay for them. And when Detroit falls below the one million mark in population, there will be serious fiscal implications, for it will no longer qualify for federal funding that targets the nation's largest cities.

Race and Ethnicity

During the 1970s and 1980s, Birmingham and the West Midlands became a major destination for minority immigrants, especially Asians from India, Pakistan, and Bangladesh and Asians who first had emigrated to Uganda. By 1991, the West Midlands had about 424,000 ethnic minority residents out of 5.15 million people, or over 8 percent of the region's population. Ethnic minorities in all of Great Britain equaled about 5.5 percent, and only greater London had a higher percentage of ethnic minority populations than the West Midlands (Office for National Statistics 1994:25). In Birmingham itself, ethnic minority population figures reached 21.2 percent by 1991. Birmingham's relatively large ethnic population began to show greater political muscle by electing more minority city councillors (which also impacted on local public policies), but generally speaking, minorities (over time) have had higher rates of unemployment and have tended to be poorer and in need of more education and social services. Table 2.3 illustrates the recent ethnic and racial composition of selected regions in the United Kingdom as well as Birmingham and Bristol.

Beginning in the 1980s, the racial and ethnic composition of Birmingham changed dramatically. Although such information was not collected for the 1981 British Census, a local study indicated that a relatively large minority population had moved to Birmingham by 1991. By the 1991 Census, Afro-Caribbeans comprised 5.9 percent of the city's population, while the Asian population (Indian, Pakistani, Bangladeshi) constituted 13.5 percent.

Table 2.3

United Kingdom: Selected Ethnic and Racial Composition, 1991 (Percentages)

	White	Black-Afro-Caribbean	Indian, Pakistani, Bangladeshi	Other	Total Minority
England and Wales	93.8	1.9	2.9	1.4	6.2
West Midlands	85.4	3.6	7.7	1.2	12.5
Birmingham	78.5	5.9	13.5	1.8	21.2
Avon	97.2	1.2	0.8	0.7	2.7
Bristol	94.9	2.4	1.5	1.1	5.1

Source: Office of Population Censuses and Surveys (1993a, 1993b, 1993c).

Boston's racial and ethnic mix is closer to Bristol than to Birmingham and Detroit's. Though Boston's population has become more diverse since 1970, its percentage of minority residents is much smaller than Detroit's (see table 2.4). Boston's minority population increased between 1970 and 1980, and again between 1980 and 1990, and the city remains racially segregated by neighborhood. A large percentage of minority residents who live in Boston are concentrated in a few areas of the city, most notably Roxbury, Mattapan, and Dorchester.

Like Detroit, Boston faced serious social and racial tensions during the 1970s, when federal courts mandated the use of busing for public schools to achieve school desegregation. The violence and the aftermath of the busing program left an imprint on school and local politics for many years. The attempt to desegregate public schools is thought to have encouraged "white flight" to the suburbs from Boston and Detroit since the 1970s.

In contrast, Bristol and its surrounding Avon County have very small percentages of racial and ethnic minority residents. In 1991, only about 5

Table 2.4
Racial and Ethnic Populations 1970, 1980, 1990 (Percentages)

	White	Black	Hispanic	Asian, Pacific Islander	Other
United States					
1970	87.5	11.1	n.a.	n.a.	1.4
1980	83.1	11.7	6.4	n.a.	n.a.
1990	80.3	12.0	8.8	2.9	0.8
Boston					
1970	81.8	16.3	n.a.	1.4	0.4
1980	68.7	22.3	6.4	2.7	4.7
1990	59.0	23.8	10.8	5.2	1.3
Detroit					
1970	55.6	43.6	1.8	n.a.	n.a.
1980	34.4	63.1	2.5	n.a.	n.a.
1990	21.6	75.7	2.6	0.8	0.3

Source: U.S. Bureau of the Census (1973a, 1983, 1993a).

percent of Bristol's population was considered to be of any racial or ethnic minority group. In Avon County, that figure was less than 3 percent (2.8 percent). Despite these small numbers, the city has had to face a variety of social and economic challenges since the 1970s. A 1981 protest in the St. Paul's area of Bristol, which has a high percentage of Afro-Caribbean residents, illustrates the challenges that faced neighborhoods with multiple problems, including racism, very high unemployment, and high poverty rates.

Between 1970 and 1990, Detroit's racial and ethnic composition changed the most dramatically of all four cities in our study. A dual migration pattern of population movement existed in Detroit from the early 1970s on. The city lost almost a half-million people, with the percentage of white residents dropping from about 55 percent to about 22 percent. Many observers assumed that the outmigration of white residents was due to the aftermath of the 1967 riot and the busing of public school children in the early 1970s, but the city had been losing population for almost 20 years before that. Detroit's population shift is perhaps the most striking example of the social changes that have occurred as a consequence of suburbanization and deindustrialization.

Income, Education, and Poverty

In addition to overall shifts in population and racial and ethnic composition, each of our cities experienced shifts in income, educational attainment, and poverty status among its residents. An important element of a locality's vitality and potential for growth is the relative wealth and formal education levels of its residents. As previous research has demonstrated (DeLeon 1992; Herson and Bolland 1990), strong associations may exist among a population's higher levels of formal education, high per capita income, and level of political activity. Other research (Logan and Zhou 1993) has suggested that communities with high income–high education populations are more likely to have increased citizen activity around "quality of life" issues such as open spaces, landmark preservation, and growth management policies.

Income

A number of factors have contributed to a decline in income figures for large cities in industrialized countries. Higher unemployment rates, a less skilled and less educated labor force, and the postindustrial shift to lower-paying and lower-benefits service sector jobs all have combined to reduce per capita and household incomes in central cities over the past 25 years. Moreover, central cities tend to have more options that enable individuals and families with lower incomes, on fixed incomes, or on public assistance to find affordable housing. As such, income figures tend to be lower and poverty rates tend to be higher in central cities when compared with their surrounding metropolitan areas or national averages.

The comparison of average income figures for Boston and Detroit reveals a striking difference. In 1992, Massachusetts ranked third highest among all states in per capita income (with $24,059). This figure reflects in part the success of the state in converting to an economy that began to emphasize the higher levels of formal education and training required for high-technology industries. Michigan ranked nineteenth, with an average of $19,508 (Gray 1996:23). The contrasts continue when reviewing income figures for our cities specifically. By 1980, Boston's per capita income was $8,068, while Detroit's was $6,215 (U.S. Bureau of the Census 1986). Boston's 1990 census figures show a median household income of $29,180, with the city's per capita income at $15,581 (U.S. Bureau of the Census 1991). Census reports for Detroit for the same year reflect its greater economic challenges — a 1990 median household income of $18,742, and a per capita income of $9,443 (U.S. Bureau of the Census 1991). Figures on income are not kept for the United Kingdom, so comparisons of Bristol and Birmingham are not available, but educational attainment and deprivation indices may be explored.

Education

Educational achievement also becomes important as the postindustrial trend toward higher technology jobs continues, which requires higher levels of formal education and training. To accommodate changes in the labor market, the Conservative government in Britain reorganized the education system, curbing spending by local authorities, eliminating local control of polytechnics, and instituting a new evaluation system. The growth in service-sector jobs has also brought an increasing number of relatively lower-wage, part-time positions, along with lower benefits and often little or no job security. This has been true in both the United Kingdom and the United States.

Educational attainment in Birmingham and Bristol present a mixed picture. Table 2.5 shows the educational achievements in Birmingham and Bristol, along with those of their respective counties, the West Midlands and Avon County. The table indicates considerable room for improvement in all cases, but there exists variation among schools within the jurisdiction of local authorities. In the government's first national league tables reported in 1996, the top school in England and Wales was Birmingham-

Table 2.5

Educational Attainment: British Residents 18 years or older, 1991 (Percentage Qualified)

	A Level (Higher Degree)	B Level (Degree)	C Level (Diploma)	All Levels
West Midlands	0.6	4.2	4.6	9.3
Birmingham	0.9	4.9	4.4	10.2
Avon County	1.2	7.3	7.0	15.5
Bristol	1.4	8.3	5.9	15.5

Source: Office of Population Censuses and Surveys (1993b, 1993c).

based, at which students earned at least five or more grades of A-C at GCSE (General Certificate of Secondary Education), the equivalent of the previous O-Level (Birmingham City Council 1997).

A growing number of unemployed young people do not have the skills, education, or training for present and future employment, especially in the larger cities of the United Kingdom. Interestingly, younger people from minority ethnic groups in Birmingham appear to be achieving higher levels of education, which bodes well for the labor market. Many training services also have sprung up, involving a number of local business-education partnerships (including the Birmingham Education Business Partnership), and those schools that offer General National Vocational Qualifications (Birmingham City Council 1997).

Bristol's local education authority has been suffering from a common big city problem, the loss of school children to the surrounding suburban districts. Over the past few years, increasing numbers of students in Bristol (and in Birmingham) have been "staying on" in school. This is, in part, because they recognize that advanced education is required for the present and future job market. But there is also a lack of available work opportunities for younger people, as well as more stringent constraints placed by government on those claiming public assistance (Bristol City Council 1995).

Because of Boston's many higher education institutions (there are 68 colleges and universities in the metropolitan area), a relatively well-educated labor force is poised to work in a high technology-dominated economy. In fact, the New England region of the United States has the highest percentage of residents holding a bachelor's degree or higher (25.6 percent). This compares to the national average of 20.3 percent, and is far superior to the East South Central (15.1 percent), the East North Central (18.1 percent), and West South Central (18.7 percent) regions.

Boston and Massachusetts have relatively high educational achievement scores for the United States (see table 2.6). As reported by the 1990 census, 80 percent of Massachusetts residents 18 years and older had earned a high school degree or equivalency. Over half (50.3 percent) had at least some college, and over one-quarter (27.2 percent) had earned at least a bachelor's degree. For Boston, the numbers are quite impressive for a large U.S. city. When totaled, three-quarters of Boston residents (75.7 percent) had a high school degree or equivalent, almost half (45.7 percent) had at least some college, and nearly a third (30 percent) had earned at least a bachelor's degree (U.S. Bureau of the Census 1993b).

Table 2.6

Educational Attainment: United States, Boston and Detroit, 1970, 1980, 1990 (Percentages of those 25 years and older)

	United States	Boston	Detroit
High school degree			
1970	34.0	34.3	28.1
1980	33.7	35.0	31.6
1990	30.0	26.6	42.7
One to three years of college			
1970	10.2	8.8	7.5
1980	15.1	13.2	14.3
1990	24.9	19.1	9.6
Four or more years of college			
1970	11.0	10.4	6.2
1980	16.2	20.3	8.3
1990	20.3	30.0	9.8

Source: U.S. Bureau of the Census (1973a, 1975, 1983, 1993a).

As expected, a large number of Detroit residents have low levels of formal education and employment-related skills. Because the postindustrial economy demands higher levels of skill and knowledge, increasing numbers of Detroit residents, especially younger persons, are becoming marginalized in the economy. The former high paying, semi-skilled jobs that were common on the automobile production line have been drastically reduced or have relocated to the suburbs, the South, or to other countries. Many new jobs in the automobile industry now require much higher skill and training levels due to technological changes automobile production.

In 1990, over one-third of Detroit's residents (37.8 percent) who were at least 25 years old had not earned a high school degree or equivalency. The low level of educational attainment by Detroit residents remains a substantial economic and social problem. In 1990, the Detroit school district's drop-out rate was 37 percent, only one of the city's 248 schools was rated "excellent" by a recent study, and the average 11th-grade student read only at the 9.6 grade level, with mathematics skills at the 9.2 grade level (City of Detroit, Communications & Creative Services Department 1997).

Poverty

Poverty data from cities in the United Kingdom are provided as an "index of deprivation," which combines a number of economic characteristics, including unemployment rate and percentages of those living in poverty, number of single parent households, and number of income-support beneficiaries. Birmingham residents have suffered far more than Bristol's, in large part because of the changes precipitated by economic restructuring and the vagaries of the business cycle. Again, in Birmingham's case, unemployment remains a more serious problem because of the longer-term nature of the job losses. As one indication of their relative standing in terms of poverty, 1991 data show that Birmingham ranks as the fifth worst large city in England (out of 366) on the index of deprivation. Bristol fares a bit better at number 42 (Office for National Statistics 1996). When divided by region, Birmingham and the West Midlands again fare much worse than the South West and Bristol.

Poverty often is related to other problems and poses a variety of challenges to governments, including providing adequate education and job skills–development programs. This is particularly crucial to state and local economic development policies, because a work force trained especially for the demands of a high-technology economy has become central to most economic development policy decisions.

Table 2.7

U.S. Population Living in Poverty 1970, 1980, 1990 (Percentages)

	1970	1980	1990
United States	11.6	13.0	13.5
Massachusetts	8.6	9.5	10.7
Boston	6.2	9.7	18.7
Michigan	10.2	12.9	13.1
Detroit	11.3	21.9	32.4

Source: U.S. Bureau of the Census (1973a, 1983, 1993a). Figures for 1970 are for families in poverty.

The differences in poverty status between our sets of U.S. cities is illustrated by table 2.7, which shows the 1970, 1980, and 1990 U.S. Census figures in percentages for the population living below the poverty line in each city, along with comparative data for each respective state. Boston and Massachusetts have fared far better than Detroit and Michigan in the period after 1970.

In 1991, Massachusetts ranked 35th out of 50 in the percent of its population living in poverty (at 11.0 percent). Michigan's figure was worse, as the state ranked 22nd among all states, with 14.1 percent of its population living in poverty (Gray 1996:12). About one-third of Detroit's population lived below the poverty line, and with its per capita income average of $9,443, Detroit was considered the poorest large city in the United States (U.S. GAO 1993).

Conclusion

Our tale of four cities clearly tells a story of uneven urban development. Although deindustrialization and global economic restructuring have affected all four of our case cities, Boston and Bristol have been able to respond to the difficulties of restructuring by creating and sustaining postindustrial economic bases. For example, Bristol and Boston differ from Birmingham and Detroit in that each of the former cities more successfully adapted to a service-based economy in the period beginning in the 1970s. Further, Boston and Bristol generally fared well during the restructuring period after 1970, in large part because their local economies were diversified. In addition, they had already begun to emphasize postindustrial businesses and investment, such as expanding high-technology industries. Defense-related industries especially were expanded. Bristol and Boston also witnessed property development booms during the 1970s and 1980s that saw their downtown areas grow tremendously. By the late 1980s, some of that advantage was lost because the dissolution of the former Soviet Union produced a peace dividend that contributed to the 1990 recession. Yet each city also experienced a recovery in the early-to-mid 1990s, illustrating that these cities have had to face shorter-term economic downturns of the business cycle, rather than the longer-term major restructuring and deindustrialization problems of Birmingham and Detroit. Despite these differences, all four cities, with varying degrees of success, emerged as regional financial centers in the postindustrial era.

In Birmingham and Detroit, economic restructuring has eroded traditional local economic bases. These cities, once world centers for automobile production, no longer have that status (nor indeed, does *any* city). Deindustrialization and the decentralization of automobile production brought about economic dislocations in Birmingham and Detroit, beginning a trend in the 1970s that has continued into the 1990s. In their own way, each city has attempted to retain or attract prestige manufacturing facilities as part of its post-1970s development strategy. Birmingham and Detroit also suffered declines due to the business cycle, as well as the chronic unemployment patterns that came with economic restructuring. Unemployment in Detroit became a particularly troublesome matter for local policy makers because, like Birmingham, much of Detroit's unemployment was due to long-term structural change in the automobile industry that made indefinite layoffs permanent. Both Detroit and Birmingham had relied heavily on manufacturing, especially automobile production, and both did well when that industry prospered. Both confronted wrenching deindustrialization when the economy underwent significant adjustments to the more competitive global market. The result was endemically high levels of unemployment. Birmingham's unemployment rate stayed about one to two times higher than the U.K. average from 1979 to 1997, and Detroit's unemployment rate remained about twice the national average throughout the 1980s (see figures 2.1 and 2.2).

This analysis of urban structuring and restructuring provides an understanding of the socioeconomic context for local politics and policy in four cities. The economic context includes several forces at work that may influence the nature of local development politics. A profile or classification of cities might be suggested. For example, we could identify the combination of economic and social factors that provide the specific settings for each of our cities, and how these settings might contribute in part to the relative standing or position of each city in the urban hierarchy. Table 2.8 attempts to accomplish this, and offers a judgment about the relative standing of each city in the urban hierarchy.

Table 2.8

City Profiles: Birmingham, Boston, Bristol, and Detroit 1970–1997

Economic Factors	Social Factors	City Position
Birmingham		
Deindustrialization	Race and ethnic mix	Regional financial
Service sector expansion	High level of	center
Chronic and cyclical	deprivation	Manufacturing
unemployment		center
Boston		
Deindustrialization	Race and ethnic mix	Regional financial
Service sector expansion	High education levels	center
High skill labor market	Moderate level of	
Cyclical unemployment	deprivation	
Bristol		
Deindustrialization	Small ethnic and	Regional financial
Service sector expansion	minority population	center
High skill labor market	High education levels	
Cyclical unemployment	Moderate level of	
	deprivation	
Detroit		
Deindustrialization	African-American	Subregional
Service sector stagnation	majority	financial center
Chronic and cyclical	Low education levels	Manufacturing
unemployment	Very high level of	center
	deprivation	

In table 2.8, we show the position of each city in respect to its regional importance. Both Bristol and Boston, for example, are important regional financial centers in their respective countries. Each historically has been a dominant regional economic center, first as a port city, and later as a diversified city offering high technology and financial services. They faced some unemployment problems, but these were due mostly to cyclical and short-term downturns in their local economies. Moreover, their workforces have relatively high levels of education and skill that serve high-technology industry well. They each experienced a downtown development boom in the 1980s, then saw a recession in the early 1990s followed by a recovery period.

When compared to Boston and Bristol, Birmingham and Detroit have quite different histories and recently faced a different set of economic circumstances. Each had served as a leader in the industrial phase of national economic growth, but had relied to a large degree on a single industry, automobile manufacturing. As a consequence, these two cities experienced chronic unemployment problems after the restructuring of the automobile industry beginning in the 1970s. Both of these cities also have seen a large increase in minority residents, with Detroit's population in the 1990s about 75 percent African-American, and Birmingham's population about 20 percent ethnic minority group members, mostly Asian and Afro-Caribbean. In addition to the challenges imposed by deindustrialization and recession, Birmingham and Detroit shared the experience of substantial demographic changes since the 1970s. While many of the world's larger cities became centers for residents who were relatively poorer and less educated, Birmingham and Detroit encountered these problems at the extreme. Moreover, the large minority group populations in the two cities altered the political landscape. That is, the racial and ethnic mix in each of these cities has had a profound effect on local electoral politics since 1970, and has changed the composition of local political leadership in each city.

The condition and structure of a city's economy clearly affects who participates in a governing coalition, as well as the sorts of governing strategies that are produced. A major shift in the structure of the global economy (from industrial to postindustrial) occurred in the early 1970s, especially affecting cities that had single industry economies for many years. Indeed, recent trends in economic restructuring, along with the proliferation of multinational corporations, have altered in significant ways who participates in urban political decision making and the sorts of strategic problems addressed by the local governing process (see Cox and Mair 1988; Fainstein 1994; DiGaetano 1997).

Urban structuring and restructuring provides only a portion of our understanding of local development politics. As this study will demonstrate, similar economic contexts did not necessarily produce similar governing alignments, development agendas, or strategies. Among other factors, the political environment of each city also needs to be explored. Combined with the urban context, an understanding of intergovernmental relations and arrangements within each country can offer insights into both the constraints and the opportunities affecting local development politics, agenda setting, and policy making.

3

State Structuring and Restructuring

Differences in political institutions arise from differences in the histories and cultural moorings of different countries. Not surprisingly, most comparative studies of urban politics underscore these institutional differences (Gurr and King 1987; Keating 1991; Wolman and Goldsmith 1992). But in such differences lies a common ground for comparison that can be explored using the modes of governance model. That is, although different institutional structures create different political landscapes, what is common to them all is the use of power in the process of governance. Further, because institutions constitute bases of power for political actors, institutional structures greatly affect the nature of governing alignments. Therefore, understanding the institutional structures and processes of local governing systems of different countries is critical to the development of a comparative theory of urban politics based on the modes of governance model.

To that end, this chapter examines the limits *and* powers determined by the legal, political, and intergovernmental environment of localities. We begin by offering a general comparison of local governing systems in the United Kingdom and the United States. We then move to the question of the *scope* of local governing systems in the two countries, discussing how the modes of intervention used by the central government in the United Kingdom and federal and state governments in the United States demarcate the institutional parameters for local governance. The final section of the chapter explains the effects of state structuring and restructuring on local modes of governance.

Comparing Local Governing Systems

British and American local governing systems differ in fundamental ways. To highlight these institutional differences, in table 3.1 we have compared

Table 3.1

Comparison of Local Governing Systems

	United Kingdom	United States
Legal basis	Unitary system; *ultra vires*	Federal system; home rule
Structure	Mix of unitary and two-tier general purpose local authorities	Decentralized system of general purpose and single purpose local governments
Local government organization	Committee system; separate elected and administrative officials	Mayor-council; city manager; commission forms of government
Electoral systems	Party nominations; district elections	Direct primaries; partisan and nonpartisan elections

local governing systems in the United Kingdom and the United States on the basis of four sets of institutional features: legal basis, structure, local government organization, and nature of local electoral systems.

Cities in the United Kingdom and the United States are limited by law as to what they can do. The laws set down by Constitution, statute, and judicial interpretation establish a legal place for cities in the larger inter-governmental systems. The conventional starting point for understanding the legal authority of local governments in the United Kingdom has been to describe the nation's unitary form of government. Britain's strong state tradition provides for a centralized system in which subnational governments exercise only those powers granted to them by the national government (and therefore operate under *ultra vires*), with Parliament considered supreme. Subnational governments are therefore legal creatures of central authority that can be altered or abolished by majority vote of Parliament. This central-local arrangement has also meant that the national government in the United Kingdom is much more directly involved in the affairs of its local governments than is the case in the United States. Indeed, a number of changes in the authority and powers of local governments in the United Kingdom have occurred since 1979. Details of such involvement are discussed later, but direct intervention by central government in local life has consistently occurred in the United Kingdom during the period we are investigating, thus distinguishing the United Kingdom's central-local relations from those in the United States.

Originally, the U.S. Constitution formally provided for a system of divided federal-state powers called "dual federalism." This more delineated relationship effectively ended in the 1930s, as the Depression brought about a more complex set of responsibilities among the levels of government, sometimes likened to a marble cake (Grodzins 1966). In addition, the vaguely worded Tenth Amendment and Supreme Court interpretations of the Commerce Clause first granted broad powers to the federal government over states, then, since the 1970s, gradually devolved more powers back to the states. State constitutions, in turn, establish a legal status for cities as municipal corporations, and, at least initially, create a state-local relationship that itself could be considered a unitary form of government, for cities possess only those powers granted to them by their respective state governments. Cities can be created and abolished, just as in the case of the formal powers held by Britain's central government. Under Dillon's Rule (*City of Clinton* v. *Cedar Rapids and Missouri Railroad Company 1868*; Dillion 1911), in the nineteenth and early twentieth centuries, U.S. cities operated under the constraint of *ultra vires,* under which they could do nothing beyond what was specifically granted to them by their state legislature. During the early part of the twentieth century, many states granted "home rule" powers to some of their cities, especially their largest, such as Boston and Detroit. Home rule allowed cities (with varying limitations and exceptions) to create and amend their own charters without requiring specific approval by their state government.

With respect to structure, local authorities in the United Kingdom can be divided into two basic categories in terms of their range of powers. These are unitary authorities, which are empowered to conduct the full range of local government functions, and "two-tier" authorities, in which local powers are divided and shared between county (the so-called "upper tier") and district ("lower tier") councils. In the nonmetropolitan areas of England and in all of Wales and mainland Scotland, this two-tier structure of county and district multipurpose local governments has existed since implementation of the 1972 Local Government Act (Stoker 1988). Generally speaking, upper-tier county councils have statutory responsibilities in strategic planning, police and fire, transportation, education, and social services. The lower-tier district councils have statutory responsibility in housing, local planning, environmental health, and leisure services (Stoker 1988:31).

In 1986, under the auspices of the Local Government Act of 1985, Parliament abolished the upper-tier Greater London Council and six metropolitan county authorities, most of which were dominated by left-wing local Labour parties that were perceived as a threat and an annoyance to the Thatcher government's efforts at local government reform. For example, the Birmingham City Council operated as a district council within the larger jurisdiction of the West Midlands Metropolitan County Council from 1974 to 1986, at which time it became a unitary authority. In the early 1990s, Secretary of State for the Environment Michael Heseltine ordered a major review of local government by a commission initially headed by Lord Banham (Peele 1995). In general, the Banham Commission favored the adoption of unitary local authorities in the nonmetropolitan areas of England to replace the two-tier system where possible. The Bristol City Council, which had served as a district council as part of a two-tier system with the Avon County Council, became a unitary authority when the Banham reforms took effect in April 1996.

The structure of U.S. local governing systems has been characterized by a much higher degree of institutional decentralization than has been true for the United Kingdom. With a range of public authorities, such as general-purpose municipal governments, school districts, special districts, and county government, there are more than 80,000 local governments in the United States. Detroit, for instance, is situated within the larger Wayne County, although the municipal government is not an administrative branch of county government. Boston is located in Suffolk County, which it dominates. Until recently, Detroit's school district has been legally and institutionally separate, with its own elected school board and budget. In early 1999, the Michigan State Legislature proposed a plan to have the governor or mayor take over the Detroit Public Schools (Wheaton 1999). In 1992, the Massachusetts legislature granted Boston's mayor the power to appoint members of the school board.

The internal organization of local governments in the United Kingdom and United States also differ significantly. British city and county councils allow for no elected executive. Instead, decision-making authority is organized around a committee system in which each committee oversees the administration of particular functions. Councils are further divided between elected members (politicians) and officers. Appointment of city officers is based on professional criteria, such as experience and expertise, rather than political affiliation as is often the case in American city government. The result has been that decision making in British city and county councils brings to bear both the political logic of elected councilors and the professional logic of council officers.

The formal organization of a city's government in the United States is determined by a state-granted municipal charter. City government organization takes one of three forms: a mayor-council plan (which could have either a strong or weak mayor), a council-manager plan (in which a professionally trained chief administrative officer—a city manager—is hired by the council to administer city operations), or a commission plan (where members of the legislative body—the commission—also serve as executive department heads).

The strong mayor plan endows a mayor with relatively robust administrative authority, which includes appointment and budgetary powers not given to weak mayors. Strong mayors also exercise a degree of legislative authority through the use of veto power over city council legislative acts. Most of the largest cities in the United States, including our cities of Boston and Detroit, have strong mayor systems. Of course, a mayor's individual style and leadership abilities and the amount of resources available (including personnel and staff) also have an impact on a city's ability to develop a policy consensus and accomplish its strategic goals (Pressman 1972; Yates 1977; Svara 1990). Moreover, because heads of departments are political appointees, the role of professionals in administrative decision making is far more circumspect in American cities than in British city councils. This means that the political logic of elected mayors often overwhelms the professional logic of civil servants in American city politics.

Local electoral systems also differ markedly. In Britain local elections feature strong, competitive political parties. City council and county council candidates are nominated by district party organizations in multi-member districts with staggered electoral terms of office. This system favors responsible party government, in which the local party that captures the most seats on city and county councils effectively rules. On the occasions when councils are "hung," that is, when no party wins a majority, the largest party attempts to form a governing coalition with one of the smaller parties. A consequence of strong parties, as they operate within the committee system of British local government, is the development of a *collective* form of leadership. That is, although the majority party chooses a council leader (the political counterpart to the chief executive), party leadership is fairly broadly based across a group of executive and committee chairs.

In sharp contrast to the British local electoral system, U.S. direct primary elections and, in some cities including Boston and Detroit, nonpartisan ballots have diminished the formal role of party organizations in American municipal electoral politics. Candidate-centered campaign organizations, rather than parties, contest local elections. Under these conditions urban politicians have assumed a far more *personal* or individualistic, rather than collective, style of leadership than their British counterparts (see Stone 1995:110).

Restructuring U.K. and U.S. Local Governing Systems

The scope of local governing systems is defined by the degree of authority and discretion allowed by higher order, *sovereign* levels of government. Much of the comparative literature on local governing systems has focused on the question of local state autonomy (see Clark and Dear 1984; Cockburn 1977; G. Clark 1984; Gottdiener 1987; Gurr and King 1987). As Gurr and King (1987:62) put it, "[T]he local state is autonomous to the extent that it can pursue its interests without substantial interference by the national state." The problem with this formulation is the premise that local governing capacity is defined almost entirely on the basis of external *constraints*. State structuring, however, may enlarge as well as limit the scope of local governing systems. The local autonomy model suffers from another serious drawback; comparisons are far too static and consequently fail to account for changes in state structures that redefine the boundaries of the local state over time.

To capture the dynamic nature of local governing systems, our method of assessing the effects of state restructuring in the United Kingdom and United States compares the changes in the *modes of intervention* employed by a national government and, in the United States, by state government. Beginning in 1970, four modes of intervention can be identified. The first is termed *directive,* where national (and state) governments are extensively involved in determining, administering, or monitoring local policy and programs. Britain's unitary form of government allows central government to be much more involved in local matters generally, and it has exercised that authority regularly since the 1970s. In the United States, national government has taken a less directive role (in fact, it has had a weak urban policy in general), but this void has been filled in various ways by state governments using their discretion as they deal with their own cities. Many development policies undertaken in the United States are best understood by investigating state-local relations. In some cases, a state government may take a directive role vis-à-vis its cities. The second mode of intervention could be termed *permissive,* an approach that allows greater local discretion in local policy administration and financial support for programmatic initiatives. The third approach could be termed *withdrawal,* in which national (or state) governments substantially retract or eliminate support for local policies and programs. An emerging fourth mode can be termed *competitive,* in which cities compete against each other for limited national (or state) government resources. National governments still establish the rules of the game for grant competitions, however, thereby restricting local discretion in crucial ways (see Cochrane and Peck 1996).

Redefining the British Local State

Although it is true that the British state is legally based on a unitary constitution (all authority ultimately resides with Parliament), a fairly clear division of labor has characterized central-local relations for most of the twentieth century (Saunders 1981). As Pickvance (1990:7–8) explained, "[C]entral government makes policy, but leaves implementation to local government within a framework of legislation, departmental advice, and other controls." Under these arrangements, local authorities emerged as administrative arms of the British state, developing the expertise and organization necessary for direct service provision. Furthermore, local authorities acquired a certain degree of autonomy through the accumulation of administrative and political resources derived from their monopoly over service provision and other local functions. However, from the late 1970s, Conservative governments bent on narrowing the scope of local governing systems challenged this model of local government.

A Permissive Urban Policy in the 1970s

Urban policy in the 1970s acknowledged the administrative capacity and expertise of local authorities and, as a result, implementation of grant-supported programs took place with little interference or direct oversight by the central government. For example, in 1968 Harold Wilson's Labour government initiated the Urban Programme (UP), which was designed to combat inner-city problems by addressing issues in four areas: social, environmental, economic, and housing (Barnekov, Boyle, and Rich 1989: 146). According to Atkinson and Moon (1994:44, emphasis in original), the UP "involved *positive discrimination* in favor of selective groups or areas and typically took the form of small scale projects emphasizing experimentation, self help, coordination of existing services and the promotion of rapid results." The Home Office, the ministry under whose auspices the program was administered, provided very little in the way of direction to local authorities in the implementation of projects (Atkinson and Moon 1994:45). The Urban Programme, in other words, was quite permissive.

The passage of the Inner Urban Areas Act in 1978 altered the UP somewhat. Under the new legislation, economic regeneration received greater attention. Grants were allocated to local authorities for construction projects, which could include industrial units. Also, designated local authorities could exercise additional powers of economic development, such as the declaration of Industrial Improvement Areas, the preparation of industrial sites, the rehabilitation of industrial structures, and the dispensation of grants and loans to businesses (Spencer et al. 1986:133–34). Three designations were possible under the 1978 Inner Urban Areas Act: Inner City Partnership (which provided the most government support); Programme Authority Status (the intermediate amount of support); and Designated District (the least amount of government support) (Prestwich and Taylor 1990:239–40). These designations were based primarily on criteria of deprivation. For example, Birmingham's inner city, having suffered from substantial dereliction and poverty, was designated an Inner City Partnership area. At the same time, Bristol was consistently passed over because it was perceived as a relatively prosperous city and therefore less in need of Urban Programme funding. Overall, the amended UP narrowed local discretion to a degree, but remained essentially permissive in its mode of intervention.[1]

Directive Urban Policy in the 1980s

In 1979, the Conservative Party won the general election with a 43-seat majority, and party leader Margaret Thatcher was elected prime minister. During the Thatcher era, political and partisan divisions deepened between the Conservative-led central government and the Labour majorities that existed on many local councils. This rift between central and local governments was occasioned by a series of parliamentary attacks on local autonomy, with a large number of statutes passed by Parliament beginning in 1980 that restricted local-authority powers. A number of local governments reacted both symbolically and with real policies in an attempt to protect local governing capacity. These New Left-dominated local authorities championed a brand of municipal socialism that prescribed a more active and even expansive local state (see Stoker 1988; Boddy and Fudge 1984). In reaction to efforts by local administrations to flout the unitary nature of the system, the Thatcher government added another layer of restraints until, by the early 1990s, the degrees of freedom left to local authorities were next to nil.

One major thrust of the Thatcher government throughout the 1980s was to curtail local authority expenditures by bringing spending and revenue generation under stricter central control. The Local Government Finance Act of 1982, which dispensed with supplementary rates and provided for adjustments in the block grants that were payable to local authorities, was designed to force reductions in local expenditures. An Audit Commission to monitor local finances also was established under this act. The Rates Act of 1984, in turn, allowed for central government rate limitations or "rate capping" of local authorities, in which revenue and expenditure ceilings were imposed by central government on local authority budgets. Our two cities, Bristol and Birmingham, were never subjected to rate capping. Conflict between central and local governments was quite open and public by this time, and Parliament moved further to preempt local powers.

Central government continued its direct intervention into local authority finance by passing the Local Government Finance Act of 1988. This created the community charge or "poll tax" mechanism that took effect in 1990. The act replaced the domestic rates tax system with a per capita charge. The grants system was altered at the same time. The new mechanism lasted only two years because of its political unpopularity and difficulty in administering and collecting the tax (this has been documented in Bloch 1990). But before it was replaced, it became a political liability for Thatcher and contributed to her resignation in 1990.

In the mid-1980s, fiscal restraints were coupled with changes in the function of local authorities in an effort to redefine local-state boundaries. As noted, for most of the twentieth century, local authorities served as administrative mechanisms for the delivery of statutory services (e.g., housing, social services, transport, education). The Thatcher government wished to transform the function of local government to that of enabler or facilitator of service delivery by private, often nonprofit, organizations (see Goodwin 1992:118–20; Cochrane 1993:120). To that end, the Local Government Act of 1987 created the competitive tendering system, which required local governments to allow competitive bidding in six service areas: street cleaning, building cleaning, vehicle maintenance, refuse collection, grounds maintenance, and catering. Tendering was designed to make public sector employees (and their unions) reduce their wage demands because they would now need to compete in the marketplace with private service providers. Should they refuse, or not make competitive offers, authorities would contract those services out, and privatize a number of services formerly provided by local government. Also, the Thatcher government required local authorities to relinquish management of council housing stock, either by selling it off to individuals or by placing management in the hands of nonprofit housing associations or tenant committees (see Wolman and Goldsmith 1992:192–93). Finally, the Education Reform Act transferred control of polytechnics to central government, and allowed schools to opt out of local authority control (Peele 1995:349; Butcher et al. 1990:68).

Local authority planning and development powers also came under attack by the Conservative government. The origins of local planning powers lay in the Town and Country Planning Act of 1947, which vested local authorities with considerable authority to regulate land use, as well as giving them the power of compulsory purchase (see Ambrose 1992; Atkinson and Moon 1994). The 1947 Act required developers to obtain permission from local planning authorities for any development. Local planning authorities based decisions on General Development Orders (which grant permission to certain types of development automatically), Use Class Orders (which establish categories of land use), and Development Plans (which set out projected land use patterns for up to 20 years). This latter function was altered when Parliament passed the Town and Country Act of 1968, replacing Development Plans with structure planning (Atkinson and Moon 1994:179). The structure planning system retained regulatory powers instituted under the 1947 Act, but sought to better integrate land-use decisions with economic, transport, and social concerns, and to insure that county and district level plans were more compatible. A third Town and Country Planning Act, enacted in 1971, instilled a stronger emphasis on economic regeneration in structure planning (Atkinson and Moon 1994:180).

From 1979 to 1989, three successive Thatcher governments loosened the regulatory grip of local planning systems in an attempt to give freer rein to market forces (see Ambrose 1992; Allmendinger and Tewdwr-Jones 1997; Atkinson and Moon 1994). Thatcherite reforms restricted local discretion in planning and development decisions in a number of ways. First, the central government set up a number of mechanisms that bypassed local authority planning powers. The 1980 Local Government Planning and Land Act created urban development corporations (UDCs) with planning and development powers independent of local authorities (Parkinson and Evans 1990). The primary mission of UDCs was to facilitate property development in inner-city areas that suffered from substantial dereliction. The central government installed UDCs in Bristol (1989) and Birmingham (1992) in the later stages of the program. In 1981, the Thatcher government also announced the creation of 11 areas as enterprise zones; another 13 were added by 1983 (Rubin and Richards 1992:433). Enterprise zones (EZs) lowered tax rates and reduced local planning controls in designated inner-city districts (Butcher et al. 1990; Harding 1989; Barnekov, Boyle, and Rich 1989). Neither Birmingham nor Bristol received EZ designation.

In addition to these bypass mechanisms, the Thatcher government directly curbed local planning powers. For instance, the Local Government Act of 1985 overhauled the structure planning system, requiring local authorities to prepare Unitary Development Plans (UDPs). The act required that UDPs adhere to central government guidance notes and ultimately pass muster with the Secretary of State for the Environment. Other planning reforms were intended to deregulate land use by simplifying planning regimes. The Thatcher government put Special Development Orders (created by the 1971 Act) to new uses, for example, giving "blanket permission for particular development in particular areas" (Atkinson and Moon 1994:185). Also, the Housing and Planning Act of 1986 allowed for the use of Simplified Planning Zones (SPZs), which provided planning permission in advance for specified land uses in designated areas (Atkinson and Moon 1994; Allmendinger and Tewdwr-Jones 1997).

Another thrust of Thatcherite intervention entailed greater central control over the implementation of urban programs. In 1982, for example, Parliament launched the Urban Development Grant (UDG) program, modeled after the American Urban Development Action Grant (Martin 1990). The UDGs, administered by the Department of Environment (DoE), served to leverage private investment for industrial, commercial, and housing projects. In 1987, the Thatcher government created a second leveraging program, Urban Regeneration Grants (URGs), for large-scale redevelopment projects. Just a year later, UDGs and URGs were folded into the City Grant program, which replicated most of the targeting functions of the earlier grants but simplified procedures for grant applicants (Martin 1990:46). Also, developers and business firms were required to apply directly to the DoE to procure City Grants, with no official role for local authorities in the administration of the program. The Conservative government also shifted the emphasis of the Urban Programme to economic development, with the proportion of funding allocated to economic development projects rising from just under 30 percent in 1979–1980 to more than 50 percent of the total Urban Programme budget in 1989–1990 (Barnekov, Boyle, and Rich 1989:146).

In a final stroke of directive intervention in 1989, the increasingly embattled Thatcher government created another set of quasi-national government organizations (quangos), called Training and Enterprise Councils (TECs). The TECs were charged with two primary responsibilities. First, they were to distribute and monitor central government grants for local training initiatives (formerly the Youth Training and Employment Training programs). A second and less clear-cut responsibility was to promote business development through economic development projects and task forces (M. Stewart 1990:6–7; Haughton and Roberts 1990, 96–97). Receiving no specific revenue stream for enterprise development, TECs were instead expected to generate funding from cost savings realized in more efficient management of training programs. By 1993, the central government had established 82 TECs in England and Wales, two of which were set up in Birmingham and Avon (Bristol) in 1990, and 21 Local Enterprise Companies (the Scottish equivalent) in Scotland (Peck and Emmerich 1993).

Competitive Urban Policy Systems in the 1990s

Margaret Thatcher's resignation in November 1990 marked the end of the most extreme conflict between central and local governments in the United Kingdom. Her successor, John Major, inherited a number of problems, including the controversy over Britain's involvement in the European Union, the growing difficulties of the poll tax, and increasing political differences between a Conservative Party-led central government and Labour Party dominance in local authorities (Peele 1995:108). As a result, the Conservative Party relaxed its grip on urban policy, changing its mode of intervention from directive to competitive, while at the same time placing a higher premium on the formation of local partnerships.

The first competitive grant, the City Challenge Grant Program, was put forward by Major's Conservative government in 1991. Under this program, 21 major cities submitted proposals to win grants from a total pot of £82 million allocated for local efforts to regenerate a city's most socially and economically distressed area. The DoE reviewed the grant proposals and picked the finalists (Pithers 1991). The City Challenge Grant system changed urban funding rather dramatically. Those cities invited to bid for funding were not assured of any allocations at all. This competitive system was meant to encourage bidding localities to produce sound regeneration strategies that involved a range of public, private, and community participants, but it also produced winners and losers in the grant-giving system (Lambert et al. 1994). The funds allocated for this program were not new monies, but were taken from existing urban programs.

Of the local authorities invited to submit proposals for the first round of grant giving in May 1991, 11 were granted £7.5 million per year for a period of five years. In the next year, all 57 local authorities with designated Urban Programme areas were invited to enter; 20 received funding. Although Birmingham received a £37.5 million City Challenge grant over a five-year period in the second round of competition, Bristol's bids failed to win approval in both rounds.

As the Conservative government reworked urban regeneration policy through the mid-1990s, the mode of intervention generally moved in the direction of promoting competition among localities and emphasizing partnership arrangements within cities. For instance, in a bold stroke in 1994, John Major swept away many of the existing urban programs and replaced them with the Single Regeneration Budget (SRB). The SRB consolidated 20 spending programs into one budget, as of FY 1994–1995 (M. Stewart 1996). The integration involved most of the traditional urban spending programs (Urban Programme, Inner Areas) but also included Housing Action Trusts and other housing programs. Part of the total amount was earmarked for specific programs and agencies (English Partnerships, Housing Action Trusts, Urban Development Corporations), with the remainder to be fought over by competing bids from localities (Stewart 1996:147). Birmingham and Bristol succeeded in the first four rounds of SRB bidding, although Bristol received far less than it had requested in the first and largest SRB pot.

The SRB is meant to allow greater local flexibility in responding to specific local needs. Moreover, it also is meant to be an administrative innovation, in that a number of formerly disparate but related regeneration programs are brought under a more coordinated budget, with input from a number of cabinet ministers, in addition to the Department of the Environment Minister. Finally, the funding is to be managed by Integrated Regional Offices that combine the extant central government regional offices under the auspices of a single regional director (Stewart 1996:148). This has reinforced an emerging shift toward a regional focus in development matters in the United Kingdom.

The introduction of the SRB and the commensurate elimination or phasing out of long-standing programs such as the Urban Programme, UDCs, and City Challenge engendered a degree of uneasiness among city leaders about their abilities to attract government grants in the future. In this atmosphere of uncertainty, the central government in 1994 invited city leaders from London, Manchester, and Birmingham to develop a vision for their cities that would guide regeneration and other initiatives over the next 20 years. A partnership framework involving local authority, business sector, and voluntary sector participation was encouraged by the central government. However, no central government funding was ever attached to City Pride, despite the substantial amounts of resources and time that were expended locally in organizing and preparing the program's vision statements. Nonetheless, local officials and their partners felt that failure to produce a collaborative City Pride vision would be punished (unofficially) by the denial of grants in the emerging competitive system.

A final competitive grant system, although strictly speaking not urban policy, is supported by the National Lottery. When the National Lottery was established in 1994, it was determined that one fourth of the income would be allotted in equal shares to five good causes. These grants were restricted to capital investments, paying up to 50 percent of a project. Interestingly, these National Lottery grants have become a de facto source of urban regeneration funding. Lottery monies disbursed by the Millennium Commission (which supports local projects that celebrate the coming of the third millennium), the National Sports Council, the National Heritage Fund, and the National Arts Council have been turned to city-center renewal efforts across Britain. Like the SRB, the system for selecting proposals has provoked intercity rivalries. Locally based, public-private partnerships have competed against each other to obtain grants that would help finance cultural development projects deemed necessary to stimulate urban economic revival. Indeed, Birmingham and Bristol have been among the successful cities in the bidding wars for high profile Millennium Commission-funded projects.

Finally, and in addition to the various competitive grant schemes, the Major government created yet another regeneration quango in 1993. English Partnerships (which originated as the Urban Regeneration Agency) was established as a nondepartmental agency to develop land for a variety of uses (commercial, industrial, housing, etc.) "in concert with other strategies and plans of local authorities, property developers and local community groups to promote regeneration, economic development and industrial competitiveness" (Littlewood and Whitney 1996:41). Funding for English Partnerships was drawn from the consolidation of two existing grant programs, Derelict Land and English Estates.

The European Dimension

The existence of a European layer in the intergovernmental system adds another dimension to the process of state structuring and restructuring for British cities. European Union (formerly European Community) funding has supported social and economic redevelopment projects in European regions through two major schemes, the European Regional Development Fund (ERDF) and the European Social Fund (ESF). Begun in 1975, the ERDF supports a regional policy in which member nations make application to the European Commission. Central governments perform a screening function and play a large role in determining which applications will be forwarded to Europe (Nugent 1989:73). The ERDF generally seeks to address uneven development among different regions of the European Union.

The European Social Fund has been in operation since 1957 and provides grants to public authorities, private companies, and voluntary organizations (Bienkowski, Walker, and Allen 1988, 245). The ESF emphasizes employment and job training schemes in member nations, with a special focus on youth. In the United Kingdom, applications were made through the central government Employment Department, which reviewed and passed along applications to the European Commission.

Since 1988, reforms in the funding mechanism altered ERDF and ESF allocations, in part because the focus of regional policy funding went from a project-based emphasis to a programmatic one (Hooghe and Keating 1994). In the 1990s, the ERDF and the ESF mechanisms each have been among the largest spending categories of the European Commission. Also, in the mid-1980s, the EU established an antipoverty program, called URBAN, that could be used to complement SRB and other central government grants.

As we discuss later, Birmingham contrived an aggressive European strategy to help finance its ambitious redevelopment agenda. As a result, it has been a major recipient of European grants since the mid-1980s, using ERDFs to carry out large-scale redevelopments in its city center. In contrast, Bristol, as a relatively prosperous city, has received little support from Europe, although it finally secured an URBAN grant in 1997.

American Federalism and the Local State

Although the U.S. Constitution is silent with respect to cities, since the 1930s, direct national-local relations have occurred primarily through a grants-in-aid system generally called "fiscal federalism." This system arose in part because of the severe impact of the Great Depression on larger U.S. cities, but also from the belief held by many large city mayors that their respective state legislatures were dominated by rural-based legislators and organized interests who had little sympathy for the plight of larger cities. A number of federal public policies have addressed problems associated with cities since the New Deal of the 1930s (poverty, employment, housing), but there has been no comprehensive national urban policy in the United States. The 1960s Great Society initiative of President Lyndon Johnson advocated programs that invoked a directive approach with fairly large amounts of categorical grant money (in transportation, education, economic opportunity, model cities, and housing) allocated to urban programs. Since the

1960s, fiscal federalism worked through three modes of intervention: permissive, withdrawal, and competitive.

The Rise of the New Federalism in the 1970s

Republican Richard Nixon's election as president in 1968 marked a turning point in national urban policy. A new federal grants-in-aid system, dubbed New Federalism, ushered in a more permissive mode of intervention. The centerpiece of Nixon's domestic legislative agenda was the 1972 State and Local Fiscal Assistance Act (see Judd and Swanstrom 1998). This act created what became known as general revenue sharing, which returned a portion of the federal tax revenues back to state and local governments with virtually no strings attached. Also under Nixon's New Federalism, a number of categorical grants were consolidated into a handful of large block grants. Block grants gave recipient state and local governments more discretion over how to use funding. The Community Development Block Grant (CDBG), established by the 1974 Housing and Community Development Act, became the hallmark federal program for urban development during this period of permissive urban policy.

Democrat Jimmy Carter elevated federal interest in cities after his election in 1976, creating an Urban and Regional Policy Group (URPG) task force that was comprised of cabinet-level secretaries from Housing and Urban Development, Health, Education and Welfare, Labor, Transportation, Commerce, and Treasury (Stowe 1980:148). The Policy Group made a number of urban-oriented proposals, but few became policies. The most prominent that came to light was the Urban Development Action Grant (UDAG) program. Lasting about 10 years, this program dispersed $4 billion to almost 2,700 projects in 2,200 cities (Harrigan 1993:414). A major beneficiary of UDAG funding was the former 13th U.S. Congressional District in Detroit (comprising much of the city's downtown and industrial corridor areas).

Federal Withdrawal 1981–1992

The 1980s brought back Republican administrations for 12 years, with Ronald Reagan (1980–1988) and George Bush (1988–1992) adapting New Federalism to their own domestic agendas. President Reagan's general approach to urban areas emphasized incentives for private business, which accomplished several of his goals: a reduction in direct federal spending, a reduced role for all levels of governments (and their bureaucracies), and implementation of a supply side perspective that believed economic problems are best solved by a relatively unfettered private sector (Peterson and

Lewis 1986). For all intents and purposes, these actions constituted a federal retreat from a national urban policy agenda.

Specific plans included a reduction in urban aid spending, accomplished first through spending cuts mandated by the Omnibus Budget Reconciliation Act of 1981, President Reagan's first budget. Reagan also pursued a federal enterprise zone policy, along the lines of the program introduced in the United Kingdom. Congress never passed such legislation, although over half of the states in the United States adopted their own enterprise zone legislation. The Reagan administration reduced revenue sharing and UDAG funding, and authorizations were finally eliminated for both programs in 1986. Funding for the CDBG program was also slashed by about a third between 1981 and 1991, though Congress did not acquiesce to every cut that President Reagan requested (Ross and Levine 1996:428). George Bush generally continued Reagan's policy of federal withdrawal.

The fiscal impact of federal withdrawal was quite striking. As figure 3.1 shows, federal aid to cities rose sharply during the permissive 1970s. As a portion of city government revenues, federal aid reached a peak of 17.3

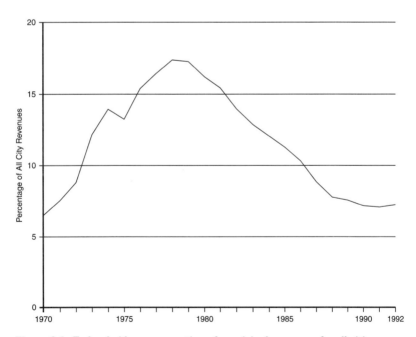

Figure 3.1. Federal aid as a proportion of municipal revenues for all cities, 1970–1992. *Source:* U.S. Bureau of the Census, *Statistical Abstract of the United States* (1970–1995); U.S. Bureau of the Census, *City Government Finances* (1978–1992).

percent in 1978 under Carter's New Partnership program. The downward pressure on intergovernmental aid began in the last year of Carter's administration and continued through the Reagan and Bush administrations. Politically, these reductions in intergovernmental aid were justified as necessary to manage the nation's growing budget deficit. The Reagan administration also claimed that scaling back federal aid would wean local governments off a fiscal addiction to federal assistance (Ross and Levine 1996: 426). By the early 1990s, the Bush administration had reduced federal aid to cities to levels comparable to the early 1970s before Nixon's New Federalism had been introduced.

The picture is less clear for individual cities. Detroit, for instance, saw federal aid (as a portion of city revenues) jump in the early 1980s and then fall steeply in the mid-1980s. By the late 1980s and early 1990s, federal aid to Detroit paralleled national trends. Boston's reliance on federal aid was never as great as Detroit's. Federal aid as a percentage of Boston's revenue base always lagged behind the national averages, and thus did not strictly conform to the Reagan administration's description of a dependent city.

Competing for Empowerment in the 1990s

Democratic president Bill Clinton took office after the 1992 election, and in some respects has taken a more traditional Democratic approach toward cities. President Clinton advocated empowerment zone legislation enacted in 1994. This new program combined some elements of the old Model Cities program and enterprise zones. Empowerment zone funding was earmarked for urban and rural areas separately, and grants were awarded to the communities that offered the best proposals and demonstrated substantial promise of public-private cooperation. The federal government would not mandate specific projects to the localities, and local coordinating councils administered the funding. The program provided for tax breaks for businesses investing within the zone's boundaries, but also direct federal assistance ($100 million) to each of the six communities winning the competition (Ross and Levine 1996:441). Detroit was among the six communities that received full empowerment zone designation. The federal empowerment zone program was expanded to include smaller amounts of funding to other cities, designated as supplemental zone cities, such as Los Angeles and Cleveland, or enhanced enterprise communities, including Boston, Houston, and Kansas City (Ross and Levine 1996:442).

Federal interest in urban problems waned when Republicans captured majorities in both the House of Representatives and the Senate in 1994. Deficit reduction emerged as the top priority for the federal government, and the urban agenda fell victim to the nation's more conservative political climate, as the federal government once again withdrew from urban policy.

State Interventions 1970–1997

Historically there have been more direct relations between states and their local governments than between localities and the federal government. Since the 1970s, state government modes of intervention have ranged from directive in regard to local fiscal policy to more permissive in economic development policy.

Since the late 1970s, American city governments have felt the bite of a growing fiscal conservatism. Referenda under the auspices of taxpayer revolts and legislation enacted by state governments in the late 1970s and early 1980s imposed limits on local property taxes in many states (see Herson and Bolland 1990). For example, the passage in 1980 of referendum Proposition 2 1/2 in Massachusetts limits to 2.5 percent the amount that Commonwealth cities can raise their property tax rates. This measure has greatly constrained Boston's revenue base, which is heavily dependent on property taxes. As a result, property taxes as a share of municipal general revenues in Boston dropped from 57.5 percent in 1981 to 34.1 percent in 1984, and remained at about that level through the rest of the 1980s (Boston Municipal Research Bureau 1990, 1995). In Detroit's case, the 1978 Headlee Amendment in Michigan imposed limits on local property taxes to specified levels unless local voters overrode the limits (Browne and Verburg 1995:63). But Headlee also required that state government pay for the cost of any new state-mandated programs, taking the funding burden off local governments. During the 1980s, many local voters authorized a waiver of the limits, and by 1994, Michigan had lowered school district property taxes, but increased the state sales tax from 4 to 6 percent. For FY 1997–1998, Detroit estimated that about 14 percent of its revenue would come from revenue sharing (where state sales taxes are shared) and about 8 percent from the local property tax (City of Detroit 1997a:ix). What is more, reductions in intergovernmental aid (see figure 3.2) compounded legal limits on local property tax levies. For Boston and Detroit, the blows of federal reductions in aid and property tax limits were cushioned by increases in state aid in the 1980s. As figure 3.2 reveals, state aid to Boston and Detroit grew substantially from the late 1970s to the early 1990s. As a result, state intervention in city fiscal policy in Massachusetts and Michigan, on balance, remained permissive.

In response to the fiscal stress caused by property tax limitations and diminishing federal aid, many city governments adopted more con-

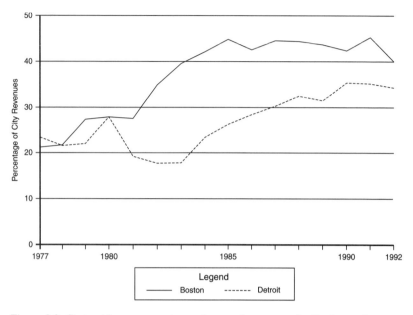

Figure 3.2. State aid as a percentage of general revenues for Boston and Detroit, 1977–1992. *Source:* U.S. Bureau of the Census, *City Government Finances* (1977–1996).

servative fiscal strategies to cut expenditures. These included contracting out services, creating off-budget public authorities, or privatizing certain services (see Sharp 1989; Herson and Bolland 1990). For example, to shift the fiscal burden off the city budget, Boston and Detroit sold off city-owned hospitals that served the poor. These off-loading strategies, however, have not appreciably altered the role of city governments as multipurpose service providers (police, fire, refuse collection, water). Simply put, the consequences of municipal fiscal restraints in the United States have been far less profound than local-state restructuring in the United Kingdom.

Moreover, state interventions in urban development policy for Massachusetts and Michigan have provided largely permissive environments for their municipalities. In Massachusetts, property tax abatements were made available in 1960 by Chapter 121A of Massachusetts Law, which gave Boston the authority to negotiate tax rates for corporations for periods up to 15 years (Boston Redevelopment Authority 1982:3). While the enabling statute was enacted in part to stabilize property tax rates (which could fluctuate normally), it also allowed the city to grant tax concessions for the purpose of facilitating redevelopment projects (Kennedy 1992:172; Barrett interview 1992). In addition, property owned by economic development corporations (EDCs) that was used to expand or retain jobs was eligible for local property tax exemption for seven years. The Prudential Building complex in Boston was among the first developments in Massachusetts to receive a property tax abatement under this legislation.

Also in 1960, the city's planning authority was vested in the Boston Redevelopment Authority (BRA) by another state statute (Chapter 652, Acts of 1960 of the Massachusetts General Laws). The Massachusetts Commonwealth later chartered the Boston Economic and Industrial Development Corporation (EDIC), which possesses the power to issue industrial revenue bonds and receive and use federal grants to leverage private investment (Brown 1987). The mayor appoints the majority of governing board members, and at least in practice, the directors of the BRA and EDIC. All this has concentrated planning and development powers in the hands of Boston mayors.

The state also created a grant-assisted program called the Commercial Area Revitalization District (CARD). Under the CARD program (administered by the Boston Redevelopment Authority), economic development incentives for the purpose of encouraging commercial development in designated areas can be offered to eligible businesses. The incentives include tax-exempt industrial revenue bonds that can fund up to 100 percent of a development project, mortgage insurance for a part of a project's financing (obtained through a conventional or industrial bond), and a "net income deduction and tax credit to be applied to state corporate excise taxes owed by a commercial enterprise" (Boston Redevelopment Authority 1982:5).

Michigan's economy was among the most severely affected by the worldwide energy crisis that began in 1973, as discussed in chapter 2. To cope with its economic problems, shortly after 1973 the state legislature enacted a number of statutes that were originally designed to provide larger, declining cities such as Detroit with policy tools that would increase the city's attractiveness to potential investors. One of the first statutes, the Plant Rehabilitation and Industrial Development Districts Act (Public Act 198, 1974), targeted industrial firms investing in a new facility or expanding an existing one within designated districts. Another (PA 175, 1975) allowed Michigan municipalities with declining areas to establish downtown development districts, to create Downtown Development Authorities (DDAs) to administer the act, and to establish tax increment financing (TIF) within the development district. Later legislation (PA 336, 1974 with Amendments 1978) enabled local governments to offer incentives such as tax abatements for industrial investment or expansion and for commercial investments, as well as giving them expanded powers to create TIF districts in areas other than downtown. The Commercial Redevelopment Districts Act (PA 255) offered tax abatements for commercial projects in 1978; the act had a sunset provision, and it expired in the early 1980s. Taking advantage of this enabling legislation, the city of Detroit created three quasi-public agencies in the 1970s — the Economic Development Corporation (EDC) in 1974, the Downtown Development Authority (DDA) in 1975, and the Detroit Economic Growth Corporation (DEGC) in 1977.

The Michigan legislature also enacted Public Act 87 (1980), known as the "quick take law," which allowed municipalities to acquire title on properties before settling with individual sellers on a purchase price. This was meant to expedite the land acquisition process dictated by a short timetable demanded by General Motors in the Poletown facility construction (see Jones and Bachelor 1993:82–83).

But in the 1990s, urban policy in Michigan took a turn toward a more directive mode of intervention. The reduction in residential property taxes (but higher sales tax) in 1993 made TIF less important, and a newly created program, the Michigan Economic Growth Authority (MEGA), gave site selection powers to the state, rather than local government. Moreover, in late 1996, the Michigan legislature passed a renaissance zones proposal (Michigan PA 376), which provided for state designation of redevelopment zones in selected cities that would offer tax and regulatory relief to businesses and residents who were located within the zone boundaries. Detroit's application was one of eight approved.

State Restructuring and Modes of Governance

State structuring and restructuring in the United Kingdom and United States have altered local governing systems in significant ways since 1970. In conjunction with urban structuring and restructuring, modes of intervention provide the context in which cities develop modes of governance. Chapter 4 specifies the relationships between urban and state restructuring and governing alignments in our four case studies. Before we turn to this more detailed comparison, however, it may be helpful to summarize how state restructuring in the United Kingdom and United States redefined local state boundaries and functions, which, in turn, created new parameters for the development of modes of governance. Table 3.2 identifies the modes of intervention used by national and state governments since 1970.

In the 1970s, national government programs in the United Kingdom, such as the Urban Programme, were quite permissive, allowing local author-

Table 3.2
National, European, and State Government Modes of Intervention, 1970–1997

	1970s	1980s	1990s
United Kingdom			
National government	Permissive	Directive	Competitive
European Union	Permissive	Permissive	Permissive
United States			
Federal government	Permissive	Withdrawal	Competitive
Massachusetts	Permissive	Permissive	Permissive
Michigan	Permissive	Permissive	Directive

ities wide latitude in their implementation. Governing alignments were local authority-centered and community development, rather than economic development, tended to dominate urban governing agendas. Conservative governments from 1979 to 1997 imposed fiscal restraints, established quangos, weakened local authority planning powers, and fundamentally altered the public sector role in providing mainline services. As in other British cities, these measures attenuated considerably the functional scope of city councils in Birmingham and Bristol. These local authorities responded to the more restrictive mode of intervention in markedly different ways, with Birmingham seeking to adjust to the new intergovernmental environment while Bristol resisted central government interventions doggedly until the early 1990s.

State restructuring in the United Kingdom also has brought about changes in local power structures. A series of reorganizations occurred, beginning with the creation of two-tier structures in 1974, followed by the demolition of metropolitan county councils in 1986, and then the restoration of unitary status to a number of district councils in 1996. During the directive period, central government quangos, such the UDCs and TECs, formed new centers of power within local governing arenas. The overall effect of these reorganizations was to fracture formal authority within local governing systems, creating multicentered governing organization. As will become clear, this did not necessarily mean turf wars would occur, although this was the case in Bristol in the late 1980s and early 1990s. It did mean, however, that neither Birmingham nor Bristol's city councils could dominate development politics in the way that they had in the 1970s. The TECs and UDCs possessed power bases of their own, and they became forces to be reckoned with in local politics.

Finally, the competitive mode of intervention affected local modes of governance in two important ways. First, the emphasis on economic development in urban regeneration through modifications in the Urban Programme and the creation of City Challenge, and later through SRBs and National Lottery funding, forced a shift in local governing agendas toward a more progrowth approach. Bristol adopted an openly progrowth agenda only after the onset of the competitive system of grants was introduced. Although the directive mode of intervention proved the most constraining for local governing systems, the competitive system of grants has placed real limits on local discretion. Government guidance and selection processes in the bidding wars have established a new set of rules of the game that permit only a modicum of leeway in developing local programs and projects. In particular, the requirement that local authorities enter into partnership with private sector interests has led to the proliferation of what Cochrane and Peck (1996) refer to as local "grant coalitions." As we discuss in chapter 4, these changes convinced a long doubting Labour majority in the Bristol City Council to enter into a network of partnership arrangements to win grants for high profile renewal projects. European grants also assumed a more competitive mode of intervention in the 1990s, which reinforced the intercity rivalry occasioned by the U.K. grant regime's emphasis on bidding for regeneration funding.

In the United States, the modes of intervention for the federal government followed a somewhat different path. The 1970s saw the introduction of general revenue sharing and block grants, and the increase in federal aid to localities established a more permissive environment for city governments to pursue local development strategies. In the 1980s, the Reagan administration ushered in a period of federal withdrawal from national urban policy; this extended into the early 1990s under President Bush. Programs like Urban Development Action Grants were eliminated and aid to cities was cut. According to Clarke and Gaile (1992), this "postfederal" era fostered a "new centrality of locality" in which city governments shouldered a much greater part of the burden of financing local development initiatives. Greater self-reliance, in turn, triggered a reordering of local economic strategies, which have moved from conventional risk-averse policies to more risk-taking entrepreneurial ones.

Federal withdrawal did not necessarily lead to entrepreneurial strategies. Detroit's progrowth agenda persisted through the 1980s even in the face of federal reductions in aid for economic development purposes, which fell from more than $50 million in fiscal year 1980–1981 to $33 million in 1991–1992 (City of Detroit 1980, 1990). In contrast, Boston saw the rise of a dual social reform–growth management governing agenda, which means that the city's governing coalition did not adopt a more entrepreneurial approach as suggested by Clarke and Gaile (1992).

Under the Clinton administration, greater attention has been paid to a national urban agenda, as demonstrated by the empowerment zone program. This marked the beginning of a more competitive mode of intervention. Despite a renewed interest in urban problems in the first Clinton administration, one of the lasting legacies of the 1980s has been a reduced federal role in urban development and in the life of cities in general.

American city governments have also experienced some narrowing in the scope of their activities. Although such contractions have been less pronounced than in the United Kingdom, fiscal constraints resulting from cutbacks in intergovernmental aid and limits placed on property taxes by state legislation or referenda have led local governments to curtail some of their traditional functions. Both Massachusetts and Michigan instituted property tax controls in the early 1980s, which depressed property taxes as a source of revenue for Boston and Detroit. Nonetheless, the functional scope of municipal governments in Boston and Detroit have been only marginally affected by these fiscal constraints. Moreover, state enabling legislation in Massachusetts and Michigan have actually enlarged the development capacity of city governments in Boston and Detroit since 1970.

State enabling legislation permitted Boston and Detroit to create quasi-public authorities that actually broadened local institutional capacity for carrying out development functions. Although in Michigan initiatives in the area of urban development became more directive, such as the MEGA program, this had little effect on local governing alignments. Unlike British state restructuring, none of the changes in national or state modes of intervention disrupted or reshaped local governing alignments in Boston or Detroit. Simply put, preservation of local autonomy (home rule) and the enabling legislation that strengthened the development capacity of local governing coalitions meant that agendas or modes of local governance in Boston or Detroit would be less susceptible to state restructuring.

4

Urban Governing Alignments and Realignments

Critical realignments, as Walter Dean Burnham (1982:10) defines them, are

> extraordinary upheavals in the flow of American electoral and policy history that occur under conditions of abnormal and general crisis. Realignment episodes involve a major increase in ideological polarization among parties and political elites, more or less abrupt but thereafter durable shifts in the nature and social location of party coalitions in the electorate, and major changes in the shape and direction of public policy.

We think that the notions of *governing alignments and realignments* are aptly suited to the study of urban politics. Urban governing alignments, as defined here, are the arrangements of urban governance, which include governing coalitions, power structures, and governing agendas. Governing coalitions are the constellations of leaders that come together around particular sets of issues or problems. Power structures, in turn, constitute the informal relations through which governing elites allocate political resources to set and carry out governing agendas. Finally, governing agendas are composed of the strategies (policies, programs, etc.) that ruling coalitions use to tackle the problems at hand. Moreover, urban polities, like national political systems, periodically undergo profound and abrupt changes in the structure and substance of governance. These critical governing realignments, wrought by social, economic, and political upheaval, reconfigure coalitional arrangements and governing agendas of cities.

This chapter chronicles the governing alignments and realignments of development politics in Birmingham, Boston, Bristol, and Detroit since 1970. Our primary objective is an understanding of the relationship between urban and state structuring and restructuring and the formation and development of governing alignments and agendas.

Birmingham: The City of Business

Brummies have traditionally taken pride in the motto that Birmingham is a "City of Business." Relations between the city's local authority and its business community generally have not been antagonistic, irrespective of which party was in power. This was certainly true from 1970 to 1997. Nonetheless, the extent and character of city council–business community cooperation in development politics changed over the period, moving from ad hoc arrangements in the 1970s to a coalitional alignment centered on a progrowth governing agenda in the early 1980s, and most recently to a progrowth regime after 1984.

The Politics of Adhocracy 1970–1979

Immediately after World War II, the Birmingham City Council undertook the task of reconstructing the city's residential and commercial areas after years of war-related privation and destruction (Birmingham City Council Development Department 1989). The regime that governed postwar Birmingham can best be described as a *technocracy*. Throughout the 1945 to 1972 period, both Conservative and Labour administrations largely deferred to the technical expertise of the city's Public Works Department on matters of redevelopment (Webman 1982).

In the early 1970s, Birmingham's governing alignment underwent a dramatic reconfiguration. The sources of this realignment lay in the seismic shifts that reshaped the city's political-economic landscape. First, the 1970s saw economic upheaval for Birmingham and the West Midlands. The international oil crisis, rising inflation, declining exports, and years of a national policy that favored other regions all worked to erode the heavy industrial base in the West Midlands and Birmingham (Spencer et al. 1986:133). Mergers among the larger manufacturing firms and the introduction of more capital-intensive processes and production facilities resulted in the closure of some older plants and labor shedding in the surviving facilities. Consolidation and rationalization in the manufacturing sector translated into dramatic reductions in the manufacturing labor force in Birmingham, which diminished from 298,900 jobs in 1971 to 241,100 in 1978 (Birmingham City Council Development Department 1989:109). Furthermore, the city's overall employment base shrank from 620,000 to 566,000 between 1971 and 1978.

Second, the central government's regional policy exacerbated problems of economic restructuring. The West Midland's industrial sector had flourished during the 1950s and 1960s. As a result, central government often refused to grant Industrial Development Certificates (IDC) to firms that wished to locate new plants or expand existing ones in the West Midlands. A report issued by the Birmingham Chamber of Industry and Commerce contended that because businesses had encountered difficulty in obtaining IDCs in the West Midlands, high-technology industrial development had been stunted. This, in turn, produced even greater reliance on the automotive industry in the region (Birmingham City Council Development Department 1989:109).

A third source of Birmingham's governing realignment was the reorganization of local government into a two-tier system. In 1974, the central government created the West Midlands County Council, and the City of Birmingham was reduced to a district authority, along with six other cities in the county, with statutory responsibilities limited to planning, housing, environmental health, and social services. Economic development, a nonstatutory responsibility, was undertaken with considerable zeal by both the Birmingham City Council and the West Midlands County Council (Spencer et al. 1986:133).

A final reason for political redirection in Birmingham was the ascendance of a new leadership in the city council. A new generation of Conservative and Labour councillors deposed the old-guard leadership that had left development policies in the hands of the public works technocracy. The Labour group in particular was more community-oriented, and when Labour gained control of the city council in 1974 it reorganized the city's development apparatus and set the city council on a very different course of development policy making (Webman 1982).

In the wake of local government reorganization, the new Labour administration recast its internal departmental and committee structure (Birmingham City Council Development Department 1989:120). An effort was made to move from a departmental management system toward a more corporate administration of the local authority. A chief executive position was created to replace the old town clerk, and a Policy and Resources Committee was established for setting the overall political direction of city council (Birmingham City Council Development Department 1989:120). The Public Works Committee, which had been a key player in the city's physical development since 1852, was disbanded and replaced by two committees, Planning and Environmental Services.

The new Labour administration also abandoned the city's long-standing Comprehensive Redevelopment Program and fashioned its first official economic development strategy in the early 1970s. This Birmingham-centered strategy, which replaced a more regional approach adopted by the technocracy, sought to retain and attract industrial development "within the city boundary" through promotional and infrastructure programs (Spencer et al. 1986:137). But a lack of consensus balkanized the process of policy making in the area of economic development, with the result that "[i]n terms of economic development, policy initiatives evolved in an *ad hoc* manner reflecting the roles of individual departments" (Spencer et al. 1986:138; emphasis added). This *adhocracy*, put simply, lacked cohesion and direction. Individual initiatives moved forward, but economic development policies and programs were not integrated into a strategic framework for regenerating the city's economy. In an attempt to instill some coherence in the city council's economic development policy making, the Planning Department's industrial development group drafted a broad policy statement called *Industry and Employment: The Birmingham Approach.* The policy statement was rejected by Conservative and Labour councillors alike. There was one exception to the rule of adhocracy. In the early 1970s the city council and the Birmingham Chamber of Commerce formed a partnership around the development of the National Exhibition Centre (see chapter 5). As it turned out, this collaboration became the embryo of a progrowth alliance that matured into a regime in the 1980s.

Forging a Progrowth Agenda: 1979–1984

In the early 1980s, Birmingham faced its worst economic crisis since the 1930s. Recession and deindustrialization ravaged the local economy. The city's unemployment rate, which stood at 7.2 percent in 1979, climbed to 19.4 percent by 1984 (Birmingham City Council 1981:4, 1984:5). Contraction of the manufacturing sector reverberated throughout the local economy, adversely affecting service employment tied to the city's industrial firms (Birmingham City Council 1986b). The service sector, which grew slightly in the 1970s, lost 17,000 jobs between 1981 and 1984 (Birmingham City Council 1984:5).

In the midst of this economic crisis, the adhocracy was abandoned and a consensus was forged among city leaders that new and drastic measures were needed to rebuild the city's economic base. It was agreed that the city should pursue an aggressive progrowth agenda to counteract the destructive forces of structural decline and cyclical downturn. During the 1979 to 1984 period, control of the city council bounced back and forth between the Labour and Conservative parties, but councillors of both parties concurred on the need for a major effort to cope with the city's dual economic crisis. When Labour gained political control of the city council in May 1980, its councillors immediately moved economic development policy to a priority position on the city's governing agenda. In 1982, when the Conservatives reclaimed control, they expanded the scope of the redevelopment program even further, setting city center revitalization as a priority on the city's policy agenda. In other words, a general consensus had formed in both parties that, in the midst of the city's dual economic crisis, economic regeneration was a critical task to be undertaken by the city council.

The city council's economic development agenda encompassed a dual strategy of regional capital and industrial development. The magnum opus of the regional capital strategy became the construction of an international convention center, first proposed by the Conservative Party in 1983 (see chapter 5). During this period, the city council also entered into a public-private partnership with Lloyds Bank and Aston University to develop a science park on the edge of the university campus (see chapter 6).

Emergence of a Progrowth Regime: 1984–1988

In May 1984, the Labour Party returned to power on the city council, and it held that power into the next decade. At the same time, a new leadership took the helm of the Labour group. This leadership was under the direction of Council Leader Sir Richard Knowles. Knowles was first elected to the council in 1972 as part of the new generation of Labour councillors that ousted the technocracy. He worked his way up through the ranks of the Labour group, including serving as chair of the planning committee. A wily and pragmatic politician, Knowles took steps to concentrate power within the Labour group among a handful of councillors and chief officers. The Knowles leadership group fashioned a regime that preempted opposition from within the city council and reinforced the alliance with business leaders around the city's progrowth agenda.

There are several reasons for the consolidation of Birmingham's progrowth alignment into a regime during the 1984 to 1988 period. The first was economic in nature. The city's economy worsened in 1984 and 1985, and further contraction of the manufacturing sector adversely affected service employment tied to the city's industrial firms (Birmingham City Council 1986b). Consequently, unemployment rose to a peak of 21.0 percent in 1985.

Second, although fiscal constraints imposed by the Thatcher government acted as financial obstacles to city council plans, they did not directly prevent the implementation of its progrowth agenda (see Birmingham City

Council 1985, 1986a, 1987, 1988, 1989). That is, the Birmingham City Council honed a sophisticated entrepreneurial strategy for attracting resources from the European Community in the 1980s, and thus was able to escape in part the tightening screws of central government fiscal constraint (see chapter 6). To some extent, the alternative revenue source enabled Birmingham's progrowth alliance to pursue a large-scale development program. Birmingham received more financial assistance from the European Community (in the form of Social and Regional Development Grant Funds) than any other local authority in Britain. In addition, unlike other major industrial cities, Birmingham was able to persuade central government to withhold direct intervention in the local authority's affairs. This owed largely to the success of the local governing coalition in convincing the Secretary of State for the Environment to forego the declaration of a UDC for Birmingham, which the Thatcher administration had seriously considered.

Finally, when the Thatcher government abolished the metropolitan county councils in 1986, including the West Midlands County Council and the Greater London Council, Birmingham became the largest unitary authority in the United Kingdom, with jurisdiction over strategic planning, transportation, and all other functions of local government. This new stature enhanced the city council's capacity to implement ambitious regional capital and industrial development strategies.

The progrowth regime that emerged out of these shifts in the city's political economy embraced a "prestige projects" strategy for city center revitalization that had been the brainchild of the previous Conservative-led council. The centerpiece of this regional capital strategy was the International Convention Centre (ICC) (see chapter 5). Other large-scale projects also were initiated to complement the ICC, including the development of a National Indoor Sports Arena, expansion of the National Exhibition Centre, and the development of a festival marketplace known as Brindley Place. Importantly, the dramatic expansion in and shift to the service base of the city's economy in the middle to late 1980s gave credence to the city council's city center prestige project plans.

The Labour-controlled city council also crafted an industrial development strategy that targeted areas beyond the city center, establishing partnerships with the business sector to regenerate areas that suffered greatly from industrial decline and dereliction. While other large city authorities, such as Sheffield and Liverpool, had taken the path of New Left municipal socialism, Birmingham's Labour leadership pioneered the use of public investment to facilitate business development in Britain. For example, in place of a UDC, the city council, the Birmingham Chamber of Industry and

Commerce, and five major developers formed Birmingham Heartlands, Limited (BHL), a nonstatutory urban development agency set up to regenerate a large swath of derelict and underutilized industrial land in East Birmingham (see chapter 5).

Although the Knowles ruling faction had deftly secured control over the city council's strategic decision making, problems arose from other quarters. In September 1985, a riot erupted in the impoverished inner-city area of Handsworth in which many buildings were burned to the ground along a main thoroughfare (Birmingham City Council Development Department 1989:139). Compounding these political troubles, a New Left faction of about 20 councillors in the Labour group voted against the leadership in protest over the lack of emphasis on social services and community development in the city council's budget (Knowles interview 1991). The Knowles ruling clique squelched the rebellion by expelling the members of the New Left faction temporarily from the Labour group. Despite the political flap over the neglect of inner-city neighborhoods and challenges from the Labour group's New Left faction, the city council did not depart from its course of pursuing development of large-scale projects in the city center. From that point on, the progrowth alliance faced little opposition, either from within or outside the city council, and appeared to have gained preemptive power over the governing agenda.

Regime Politics in the 1990s

In the 1990s, the city's business leaders emerged as dynamic players in economic development politics. The ascendance of the business community can be traced to several changes in the local political economy. These included economic restructuring, which strengthened the city's financial and professional service sector, the creation of the Birmingham Training and Enterprise Council by the central government, and government-imposed constraints on the city council's ability to finance local economic development projects without business involvement.

Restructuring of the local economy in the 1980s had greatly enlarged the city's financial and professional service sector, which comprised 11.9 percent of Birmingham's total employment by 1991. Although branch offices of national and international firms, Birmingham's financial and professional services firms had developed close ties to the regional market, servicing primarily manufacturing and commercial clients located in the West Midlands (Bore interview 1991; Willis interview 1994). As a consequence, the directors of these regional offices adopted a distinctly local orientation. This trend culminated in the creation of Birmingham City

2000 in 1990. Birmingham City 2000 rapidly matured into a powerful lobbying group for the financial and professional services firms in the city.

Another center of power emerged in Birmingham's business community when the Conservative government established the Birmingham Training and Enterprise Council (TEC) in 1990. The TEC, like City 2000, adopted a partnership style that meshed quite easily with the city's progrowth regime and also played an integral part in Birmingham's development politics.

Cooperation within the progrowth alliance intensified in the early 1990s, which spawned a whole host of new partnership bodies and joint ventures and created a dense network of working relationships among city officials and business leaders. These partnership arrangements solidified and institutionalized Birmingham's progrowth governing alliance and enabled it to carry out its regional capital and industrial development strategies more effectively. In part, Birmingham City Council's long experience in cultivating public-private partnership eased the transition from a city council–dominated governing alignment to one in which business leaders assumed a more prominent position in the governing coalition. Also, both city officials and business leaders generally agreed that a partnership model was the best vehicle for accomplishing the tasks on the city's progrowth agenda.

Mid-decade changes in the terrains of local power forced adjustments in Birmingham's governing alignments. In particular, the city council's Labour group, which remained in the majority, underwent a substantial realignment. Social restructuring was a fundamental cause. First, by 1990, ethnic minorities comprised about 20 percent of Birmingham's population. Politically, the expansion of the ethnic minority population translated into a demographic recomposition of the local Labour group. By the early 1990s, ethnic minority councillors constituted just over 30 percent of the city council Labour group. Also by the mid-1990s, women made up an even larger proportion of Labour group councillors (about one-third). Finally, the proportion of white-collar, better-educated Labour councillors had grown over the years.

Realignment of the city council began in the spring of 1993, when personal squabbles between two factions within Knowles' ruling group opened up fissures with the Labour leadership, narrowing its power base. Then a major fight within the Labour group erupted over the city council's prestige project strategy. New Left and ethnic minority councillors banded together when they discovered that although the city council had raised substantial funding for prestige projects such as the ICC, National Indoor Arena, and NEC, Birmingham's spending on basic services, particularly education, had lagged behind other local authorities. This caused a major rift within the Labour group over city council policy and the highly centralized nature of decision making.

The changing demographic profile of the city's Labour party, which in recent years saw its fastest growing constituencies among inner-city ethnic minority communities, seriously eroded the base of support for the Knowles leadership faction, which had rested on traditional white male councillors. Ethnic minority Labour councillors had in the past generally thrown in their lot with the Knowles ruling group, hoping that this support would be reciprocated in the form of greater patronage for their constituencies. But ethnic minority councillors increasingly thought that their constituents had not greatly benefited from the city's prestige development projects. Excluded from the inner sanctum of power, ethnic minority councillors became disenchanted with the policies of the Knowles leadership clique.

Initially, the Knowles faction managed to maintain control over the Labour group, but certain events seriously attenuated their influence over decision making. For instance, the May 1993 local elections reduced the Labour group's majority to a margin of five, which meant that the old guard no longer had the majority of Labour councillors in their coalition. In order to maintain their leadership position, the Knowles ruling clique offered committee chairs to New Left and other Labour councillors who had previously been denied positions of power. This broadened the political base of the Knowles faction, but it also diluted its power over Labour group decision making. To complicate things further, Teresa Stewart, a New Left Labour councillor and long-time critic of the old guard's policies, earned a surprise victory as deputy leader in 1993, and Knowles, who had been showing signs of his advanced age, promised to stand down as council leader in September 1993. In short, the internal politics of the Birmingham City Council had become much more fluid and the progrowth regime slowly began to dissolve.

Knowles' announcement of impending retirement touched off a six-month campaign for the leader's job. The central issue in this power struggle within the Labour group was the question of prestige projects versus basic service provision. In this contest for leadership positions, the old guard lost most of its support, thus allowing the New Left and ethnic minority contenders to capture most of the key group leadership positions. A more pluralistic leadership emerged victorious. This leadership was quite different from the one that had reigned since 1984. The old Labour leadership was composed solely of white men, was wholly committed to the city's progrowth agenda, and operated as an insider's clique. The new Labour group leadership mirrored to a much greater extent the demographic profile of the Labour group, with a mixture of men and women, ethnic minorities and whites. Also, in an ironic turn of fate, Teresa Stewart, who had been expelled by the Knowles clique in the 1980s, handily won the race for council Leader. The top five leadership positions now included one white female, two white males, and an Afro-Caribbean and Asian male; the new Group Executive included four whites, four Afro-Caribbeans, and four Asians. Committee chairs also were reshuffled to shake up what had become entrenched political fiefdoms for some committees.

The new, more pluralistic Labour leadership was set firmly in place after the May 1994 elections, and began to chart a new course for the city council. First, the new Labour leaders renounced the prestige project strategy, which was punctuated by the refusal of the city council leader to back a Birmingham bid for the Commonwealth games. Instead, restoration and expansion of basic service provisions, with an emphasis on education, social services, and housing, surfaced as the council's top policy priority. Efforts also were made to open up the decision-making process, allowing for greater debate over major issues such as the budget.

Despite their intentions, the new Labour leadership's efforts to disengage from the city's progrowth alliance proved more difficult than anticipated. The dense network of informal linkages among officers and business-led organizations, the city council's previous commitments to such partnerships as the Marketing Partnership and the Economic Development Partnership, and the emphasis of the central government and European grant systems on urban regeneration all limited the new Labour leadership's ability to abandon the progrowth agenda. In fact, a new generation of regional capital prestige projects was born out of the competitive grant systems (see chapters 5 and 6) so city center redevelopment and industrial regeneration remained key elements of the Birmingham City Council's governing agenda.

Boston: The Populist City?

Boston politics had long been punctuated by disputes between Irish politicians and Brahmin business elites. These traditional battle lines dissolved in the 1950s and 1960s when city officials and business leaders formed a progrowth alliance that survived into the early 1980s, at which time neighborhood populism and community activism ushered in an era of progressive politics. As a result, throughout the remainder of the 1980s, a dual coalition governed under the banners of social reform and growth management. By the 1990s, a new progrowth coalition was assembled, which shared the political limelight with community activists and city officials who remained committed to a social reform agenda.

The Politics of Downtown Development: 1976–1983

In the postwar era, Boston's market position in the U.S. array of cities deteriorated. The city experienced heavy population losses, a serious erosion in its manufacturing base, and stagnation in its central business district economy. Reacting to this decline, Boston's political leaders, professional planning officials, and downtown business elites coalesced into a powerful governing alliance in the 1950s known as the New Boston Movement (Mollenkopf 1983; Brown 1987; Dreier 1989). This progrowth coalition pursued an aggressive urban renewal program in the late 1950s and 1960s that transformed Boston's core areas. The coalition was kept intact during the early years of Kevin White's mayoral administration (1967–1983), although White had styled himself as a progressive, almost Kennedy-esque, politician in the late 1960s. White changed his political stripes in the mid-1970s, resurrecting the progrowth alliance as the dominant force in city governance during his last two terms as mayor.

Two factors help to explain White's return to a progrowth alignment in the latter half of the 1970s. First, Boston's economy fell into recession in the mid-1970s, and downtown office development slowed and unemployment rose (Dreier 1989). Second, city government faced mounting fiscal pressures in the late 1970s that resulted from the effects of a narrow property tax base, with nearly half of the city's land area occupied by tax-exempt institutions, such as state government buildings, hospitals, and universities. This was compounded by the large-scale exodus of manufacturing firms and white middle-class families from the city to suburbs (see chapter 2).

A third factor in the decision to launch an aggressive progrowth agenda was electoral politics. White's long tenure notwithstanding, his electoral coalition was never very stable. He never captured more than 55 percent of the vote, and often recast his position to win elections. For example, after narrowly escaping defeat in the 1976 mayoral election, White constructed a personal political machine through which he could shore up his electoral base and solicit campaign contributions from business allies and developers (see Ferman 1985).

In addition, the White administration revamped its development strategy after 1976. Chastened by near defeat in the 1976 election and faced with mounting fiscal problems, White largely abandoned his earlier neighborhood-oriented policies and programs and embarked on a downtown-centered revitalization approach (Kennedy 1992:202; Ganz 1992) that Ferman (1985:177) has termed a "master builder strategy." To carry out this strategy, Mayor White engineered a governing coalition in which land developers, financial interests, and downtown business elites played a central role. In the context of economic stagnation and fiscal stress, the progrowth governing coalition sought to convert Boston into a "World Class City" by attracting business and tourism (see Kennedy 1992:203–6). This regional capital strategy featured tax abatements, easily obtainable zoning variances for developers, and direct development subsidies in the form of grants and loans to promote downtown development (Ferman 1985; Mollenkopf 1983; Kennedy 1992).

Community leaders, in contrast, were largely excluded from the mayor-centered progrowth governing coalition. While the White administration had wooed the neighborhoods in its first two terms in office, it became clear that community organizers and other neighborhood interests were frozen out of the city's ruling circles in the late 1970s and early 1980s. The White administration often found itself pitted against neighborhood organizations and preservationist groups that banded together to thwart large-scale development projects that threatened extant low-income housing or historic buildings (Holtz Kay 1979; Menzies 1983; Mollenkopf 1983:chapter 5). In sum, although the progrowth coalition had pushed through a successful progrowth agenda, it was often challenged by neighborhood and community leaders and forced to make concessions. Coalitional politics characterized the city's new progrowth alignment.

Regime Politics? 1984–1989

By 1983 the consensus around the master builder strategy had collapsed under the weight of its own successes. That is, in response to the gleaming office towers and large hotels that redefined Boston's skyline almost overnight, the city's major newspapers and community leaders decried the neglect of the neighborhoods. Moreover, the spread of patronage practices in city hall led to a number of scandals, which severely tarnished the image of the White administration. As a consequence, White bowed out of the 1983 mayoral race. The succeeding mayoral administration of Raymond Flynn, in alliance with community activists, built a new governing alignment on the ruins of the old one. The new governing alliance abandoned the progrowth agenda of the White era, establishing in its place a dual agenda of social reform and growth management.

Three changes in Boston's political economy triggered the city's critical governing realignment in the mid-1980s. First, the massive development boom of the late 1970s and early 1980s had produced negative externalities, such as traffic congestion, skyrocketing housing costs, and threats to the city's historic architecture and green space. Under these circumstances, the progrowth governing agenda lost its political appeal.

Second, social restructuring of Boston's polity produced a wave of progressive politics in the 1980s. The proportion of the city's population composed of minorities (Blacks and Hispanics) grew from 17 percent in 1970 to 29 percent in 1980 (U.S. Bureau of Census 1973a, 1983). At the same time, Boston retained a fairly large, well-educated middle class (see chapter 2). What formed in the early 1980s was an interracial and interethnic liberal political coalition that came to dominate electoral politics. The 1983 mayoral election was the turning point. This election pitted Raymond Flynn, a city councillor and neighborhood populist, against Mel King, a self-styled socialist and African-American community organizer. Both candidates cultivated interethnic and interracial political bases, but Flynn garnered wider appeal, winning the contest in a landslide with two-thirds of the vote. Moreover, Flynn's urban populism proved an unqualified success in sustaining his electoral coalition through two more election cycles, gaining 67 percent of the vote in 1987 and 75 percent in 1991. He did this in part by appointing numerous minority officials to his administration (Travis 1990).

Third, the community movement in Boston has been much better organized and, consequently, has wielded more political clout than in most American cities (Preer 1987:69). At times, the myriad of community groups and activists, galvanized by issues that were perceived as threats to the city's neighborhoods, banded together into wider coalitions in order to do battle with the city's progrowth governing coalition.

The mayoral election of 1983 furnished the means for Boston's community activists to play a major role in electoral politics, serving as precinct captains and organizing grassroots get-out-the-vote efforts for Flynn. When elected, Mayor Flynn appointed community organizers as key policy makers and established close working relationships with community leaders in forging a social reform governing agenda. As a result, social reform emerged as a central component of the city's governing agenda (DiGaetano 1989; Dreier 1989).

Affordable housing dominated the new social reform agenda. To facilitate the production of affordable housing, the social reform alliance greatly expanded the role of the Boston Housing Partnership (BHP) in the construction of low and moderate income housing (see chapter 7). Community groups and the Flynn administration also won an expansion of the city's linkage policy, which channeled additional funds into the BHP's housing programs (Powers 1985a, 1985b). Finally, the social reform coalition sought to protect extant low- and moderate-income housing through enactment of condominium conversion limitations (Malone 1987; Hernandez 1987).

The Flynn administration and the city's historic preservationists and environmental activists comprised the city's growth management alliance. Protecting and improving the city's built environment and green space were the core concerns of this coalition. For example, myriad environmental groups were involved in efforts to improve the city's parks and open spaces (Primack 1989:5–6). Working closely with this alliance of environmental groups, known as the GreenSpace Alliance, the Flynn administration mapped out and implemented a five-year improvement program that covered almost all of the city's parks (Arnold 1987; Primack 1989). The Flynn administration also embarked on a mission to rezone the city's downtown and neighborhood districts through what became known as Interim Planning Overlay Districts (IPODs) (see chapter 8). The IPODs imposed much stiffer limits on development in the city (see DiGaetano 1989).

In sum, the politics of development in Boston from 1984 to 1989 were dominated by a dual social reform–growth management governing alliance. Developers and real estate interests generally acceded to a more restrictive planning process, although they bitterly opposed the city's linkage policy and limits on condominium conversions. The city administration and its community movement allies, however, had won these fights in the first two years of Flynn's first term in office. Little in the way of major opposition arose for the remainder of the decade, with Flynn winning larger and larger majorities in subsequent mayoral elections. In this sense, the dual governing coalition seemed to be wielding preemptive power, and therefore resembled a powerful regime mode of governance.

Reemergence of the Progrowth Alliance in 1990s

Boston felt the impact of economic shock waves in the early 1990s. The financial sector, the engine of economic growth in the 1980s, lost steam as more than 5,000 jobs disappeared between 1990 to 1992 and Class A office space vacancy rates jumped from 12.0 percent in 1988 to 17.1 percent in 1991 (Boston Redevelopment Authority 1993a; Amatruda 1994). Manufacturing employment also declined by 4,200 jobs over the same period. Only health services weathered the recession, actually adding more than 5,300 jobs from 1990 to 1992. Consequently, the city's economy slid into a severe depression starting in late 1989. Boston's workforce contracted from 537,661 in 1990 to 496,130 in 1992, a loss of nearly 8 percent of its job base in just two years (City of Boston 1993, 1994a). Also, unemployment rose precipitously. In 1988, Boston's unemployment rate stood at 3.3 percent, 2.2 percent below the national rate; this figure rose to a recession-level 8.4 percent in 1991, which exceeded the nation's 6.7 percent rate (Perkins 1994:14).

Added to Boston's economic woes was the city government's worsening fiscal situation. Under the Republican administration of Governor William Weld, the proportion of the city's revenue derived from state aid dropped substantially. With the state share falling from 34 percent of municipal general revenues in 1989 to 27 percent in 1993, the city's reliance on property taxes increased from 35 percent to 45 percent of its total revenues (Boston Municipal Research Bureau 1993:3). Coincidentally, the amount of tax-exempt property reached 50.8 percent of all city property in 1995, up from 46.3 percent in 1990 (Boston Municipal Research Bureau 1990:55, 1995:55), due largely to further acquisition of tax-exempt property by the state government (Boston Redevelopment Authority 1993). The dual problem of declining state financial assistance and a shrinking property tax base put the city in an ever-tightening fiscal noose, which in the early 1990s was greatly compounded by the recession-triggered collapse of the city's real estate market.

These problems occasioned a partial realignment in the city's governing structure. The mayoral administration of Raymond Flynn, which ended in July 1993, and that of his successor, Thomas Menino, agreed that aggressive promotion of development was essential to cope with the city's fiscal double bind of greater reliance on property taxes and a shrinking property tax base. Only new development would enable the city to shore up its revenue base. In response, city officials advocated regional center and industrial development strategies that targeted Boston's strongest economic sectors—financial, tourism, health, and high technology.

Business leaders were also more openly courted to participate in setting the city's new progrowth agenda. Years of corporate and banking mergers and takeovers had decimated the ranks of locally based corporate business leaders, and had the effect of weakening Boston's business leadership, which had been considered a powerful force in the 1960s and 1970s (see chapter 5). This "power failure" in the business community meant that the governing coalition that formed around the city's progrowth agenda could not graduate into a formidable regime (see Pantridge 1991). Rather, coalitional politics prevailed, with business leaders and mayoral administrations working cooperatively on particular policies and projects, but failing to exercise preemptive power over development politics.

In December 1991, the Flynn administration produced a comprehensive economic development strategy that identified six general goals: (Boston Redevelopment Authority 1991). A key area of concern was the need to target specific industries in Boston's New Economy to exploit the region's natural competitive advantages. The Flynn administration singled out five emerging industries for primary attention, principally in the high-technology sector.

The next goal was to direct a human capital governing alliance in revamping training, employment, and education programs in ways that were intended to prepare Boston's youth and adult workers for the skill requirements demanded by the New Economy. Overall Boston's new progrowth coalition pursued a "Techs Mix" reindustrialization agenda by blending elements of targeted high-tech industrial and human capital development strategies.

The biggest deal made by the Flynn administration in pursuit of its Techs Mix strategy involved a locally based biotechnology firm, Genzyme. In 1991, the *Boston Globe* reported that the "Genzyme Corp., one of the fastest-growing companies in Massachusetts, is considering North Carolina and several other areas over Massachusetts to build a $75 million manufacturing plant, citing the Bay State's economic uncertainties and infrastructure problems" (Rosenberg 1991). At the outset of the campaign, the state government opened discussions with Genzyme's CEO and president, Henri Teemer, to persuade him that Massachusetts offered the company the best environment for its new biotech pharmaceutical factory (Lavoie interview 1992; Genzyme 1991). Once the decision to locate in Massachusetts was made, site selection turned into a heated race among Boston, Cambridge, and Worcester. The Boston Redevelopment Authority (BRA) director, Stephen Coyle, presented Genzyme with a site proposal plan laden with development subsidies. At the same time, the BRA engineered a media blitz that publicized the proposed plan and the importance of attracting the biotech production facility to Boston (Lavoie interview 1992; Rosenberg 1991). Within three weeks of the initial proposal, the Boston site was selected over its two rivals (Rosenberg and Ackerman 1991).

Human capital development was another major concern of the Techs Mix strategy. The Flynn administration placed much greater emphasis on job training beginning in the early 1990s; however, Boston's business leaders controlled strategic resources that were essential for the development of effective human capital programs. The Boston Private Industry Council

(PIC), which had been seen as a model of human capital development for the rest of the country in the early 1980s, was a business-dominated group through which federal Job Training Partnership Act funding and some state training grants were channeled to Boston-based programs. Recognizing the PIC's central position in training policy, the Flynn administration curried a close and strategic working relationship with the PIC around specialized school-to-work and other vocational education programs (Moriarity 1992; Sullivan 1994).

In the autumn of 1993 a special election was called to replace Mayor Flynn, who had accepted an appointment as ambassador to the Vatican. Thomas Menino led a field of eight candidates in the September primary with 26.5 percent of the vote, and won a landslide victory in the two-candidate run-off election in November 1993 with 64.4 percent of the vote (*Boston Globe* 1993a, 1993b; Black and McGregory 1993). When Menino entered the mayor's office, he became the first Italian American to hold that office, ending a lineage of Irish mayors that extended back to the 1920s. Nonetheless, Menino's support was broad-based, crossing racial, ethnic, and class lines (*Boston Globe* 1993b).

The transition from the Flynn to the Menino administration only briefly interrupted progress on the city's progrowth agenda. No dramatic departures were made, although the Menino administration tinkered with several components of the city's economic development agenda. In particular, the Menino administration adopted a more nuts-and-bolts approach to economic revitalization, which prompted the local media to dub Menino the "Urban Mechanic" and "Mayor Fix-It."

This seamless transition from Flynn to Menino is illustrated by the consolidation of the city's development agencies. To adjust to the city's new economic reality, administrative reorganization plans began to percolate in 1992 when Flynn appointed a commission to review the city's development process (Walker 1992). In March 1993, the mayoral panel, known as the Walsh Commission, recommended that the BRA and the Economic Development and Industrial Corporation (EDIC) be merged into a single citywide development agency to eliminate the interagency duplication and rivalry (Ackerman 1993). The Walsh Commission also proposed a Mayor's Office of Economic Development to oversee economic development policy and promote business development in the city (Ackerman 1993). Before the BRA-EDIC marriage could be consummated, Flynn resigned, and the Walsh Commission's recommendations were accepted by the Menino administration. In the summer of 1993, Menino shepherded a home-rule petition through the city council and state legislature to finalize the merger of the BRA and EDIC into a single institutional entity. What is more, Menino created a new cabinet form of government in which all of the city's development agencies were put under the jurisdiction of an "economic development czar." Under the new cabinet structure, the directors of the EDIC, Public Facilities Department, and Boston Housing Authority all answered to Marisa Lago, who had been appointed to the posts of economic development czar and BRA director.

A key component of the Menino administration's economic development agenda has been to improve relations between city hall and the business community. At the Boston Tomorrow conference, held on April 5, 1994, Menino outlined his economic development plan to Boston's corporate elite (Pham 1994). The plan was based on the traditional "logic of growth" argument (see Judd and Swanstrom 1998) that government must actively encourage business investment. This would be done by developing partnerships between city hall and the business community "to provide jobs that allow people to have economic independence" (Pham 1994). Menino also formally introduced the economic development czar, Lago. Finally, Menino promised to "end the confusion and lack of coordination that now surrounds the planning and development process in Boston" (quoted in Black 1994a) by streamlining the permit process for business approvals.

Having set his agenda, Boston's "Urban Mechanic" began adjusting the machinery of economic development. In 1996, addressing a meeting of 250 business leaders organized by the Municipal Research Bureau, Menino proposed a number of business development and retention programs that underscored job creation as the city's primary economic development goal (Cassidy 1996). Menino offered four measures to generate new jobs outside the central business district. First, the city would sell off the Marine Industrial Park, which has been owned and managed by the EDIC for more than two decades, and use the proceeds from the sale to set up a business development trust fund. The trust fund would provide equity, loans, or guarantees to businesses that entered into agreements with the city to create additional employment. Greater job creation would be rewarded by more favorable terms on equity contributions, loans, and guarantees (Cassidy 1996). Second, Menino would seek to establish a sale–lease back program for retention purposes. This program would enable the BRA or the EDIC to purchase the property that businesses use for their operations, and then lease it back to the businesses on 5- or 10-year bases. Rent payments would take the place of property taxes, and could be structured to make staying in Boston more attractive. Businesses outside the downtown and Longwood medical areas would receive preferential treatment, and eligibility would be decided on a case-by-case basis (Cassidy 1996). Third, local property tax relief for businesses would be linked to job creation, with 50 new jobs set as a minimum for receipt of Chapter 121A tax abatements. Finally, Menino announced that up to 1 percent of the city's pension fund, about $30 million, would be dedicated to economic development projects.

The Menino administration also embraced a regional capital strategy, which attempted to bolster the city's convention and tourism industry. In light of the business leadership's power failure, however, the city's new progrowth coalition employed bargaining power, forming consensus on a project-by-project basis. For example, despite the general agreement that Boston needed a new and much larger convention center, disagreements among the major players over financing and location often mired the so-called Megaplex project in stalemate politics from 1993 to 1997, when it was finally approved (see chapter 5).

The partial realignment toward a progrowth politics, however, did not supplant the city's social reform coalition. Both the Flynn and Menino administrations remained committed to a social reform agenda. Working closely with community activists, both mayoral administrations continued to push for such social reform measures as affordable housing, antipoverty initiatives (including a successful bid for a federal empowerment zone grant), human investment programs for youth and disadvantaged adults, and school reform (see chapter 7). To carry out this ambitious policy agenda, the social reform coalition adeptly won a variety of federal and state grants for its innovative programs in an increasingly competitive intergovernmental system. Regime politics, however, had been replaced by coalitional politics, based on bargaining between the Menino administration and the city's community movement.

The city's preservationists and environmentalists, in contrast, had become something of a political liability for the Flynn administration, and, as a result, the growth management governing alliance foundered. Although the Menino administration has appeared more sympathetic to the concerns of the city's environmental movement, in part because the local economy had recovered by the mid-1990s, aggressive growth control or environmental strategies have yet to resurface as elements of the city's governing agenda.

Bristol: Shipshape and Bristol Fashion

Local lore in Bristol is steeped in the city's past as a seafaring center. "Shipshape and Bristol fashion," a phrase commonly used throughout the British

Isles to denote worthiness and dependability, refers to the sturdy and well-maintained ships that sailed to and from the Bristol harbor. In a wry twist, however, some Bristolians employed "shipshape and Bristol fashion" to describe the fractious and contentious local politics of the 1970s and 1980s, when growth management and progrowth factions competed with each other to control the city's development agenda. By the mid-1990s, however, conflict subsided and was replaced by progrowth coalitional politics.

Governing Realignment and Development Politics: 1970–1978

The post-War period from 1945 to 1969 in Bristol witnessed a "Long Boom" in the city's economy (Boddy, Lovering, and Bassett 1986). Though Bristol's traditional maritime industry lost its centrality in the city's economy, growth and diversification of the city's economic base produced substantial prosperity. During this period, a prodevelopment governing alliance ruled the County Borough of Bristol, which sought to maintain and enhance the city's position as a regional commercial and industrial center (Boddy, Lovering, and Bassett 1986:167). The Labour Party controlled the city council for most of these years, interrupted only by two stretches of Conservative rule (1960 to 1963 and 1967 to 1972). Regardless of which party held the reins of power, however, the city council pursued an aggressive development agenda of public infrastructure and liberal planning policies (Bristol City Council Planning Department 1988:2–3).

The 1970s saw a dramatic restructuring of Bristol's political economy. The Long Boom governing alliance had encouraged private development by establishing a permissive planning system that allowed large-scale development in the city center. The result was a downtown office boom that added 3,105,400 square feet of office space to central Bristol and 3,768,400 to the city overall from 1971 to 1976 (Bristol City Council 1993). The towering office blocks that sprang up in the city center furnished "concrete" evidence that Bristol was undergoing an economic metamorphosis, in which service industries would dominate. Bristol's service sector grew by 13 percent between 1971 and 1981. Financial services and insurance industries led the expansion of the service sector, posting a 73 percent increase in employment over the same period.

In contrast, the traditional industrial bases that had figured so prominently in the city's prosperity during the Long Boom encountered serious problems of decline and retrenchment. Between 1971 and 1981, the city's manufacturing sector lost nearly 23,000 jobs, a 21.5 percent decline. The heaviest losses were in the traditional blue-collar industries of tobacco, paper products, printing, and packaging. Even the high technology aerospace industry suffered a loss of 9.0 percent of its local work force (Boddy, Lovering, and Bassett 1986:55).

State restructuring also profoundly affected Bristol's position as a regional center. The central government, under the auspices of the Local Government Act of 1972, stripped Bristol of its status as a county borough in 1974 and demoted it to a district council in the newly created County of Avon. This meant that Bristol City Council no longer administered a full range of local governmental services, losing control over education and highway planning. The two-tier structure produced a good deal of tension between Bristol City Council and Avon County Council, with the Bristol City Council deeply resenting its subordination to Avon County. This was compounded by a partisan rivalry between the two local authorities, with Labour in control of the city council and the Conservatives holding a majority on the county council (Punter 1990:116–17). As a consequence, little coordination of strategic planning occurred between the two authorities in the 1970s.

Political-economic restructuring propelled a critical governing realignment in the early 1970s. The city council had been ruled by a "duarchy" of Conservative Leader Gervas Walker and Labour Leader Wally Jenkins for many years (Punter 1990:115–16). Decision making under this duarchy had been closed to a select few and dominated by a prodevelopment agenda. The 1971 local election, however, brought in a large number of new councillors, who took a dim view of the Long Boom regime's voracious appetite for road building and its liberal planning practices. Disputes over large-scale development rent the Labour group in particular, provoking a strong challenge to the Labour leadership in 1972. What is more, after six years of Conservative administration, the election of 1973 returned Labour to power on the city council, which ushered in a new era of governance for Bristol.

A crucial outcome of the 1973 election was a realignment in the ranks of the Labour group. According to Boddy, Lovering, and Bassett (1986:169), the waning of blue-collar manufacturing jobs and the waxing white-collar service employment "weakened the basis for traditional, class-oriented trade unionism and traditional Labour Party politics." With the old leadership's power base undermined by political realignment, the new Labour majority dismantled the centralized decision-making structures that had characterized the duarchy, and fashioned a more collective approach (Boddy, Lovering, and Bassett 1986:169). This decentering of Labour Party leadership, in turn, fractured the structure of power within the city council. Competing centers of power emerged as a result. Two major arenas of development politics developed, one that focused attention on the problem of deindustrialization, the other on externalities of overdevelopment in the city's expanding office sector. This power structure of rival progrowth and growth management alliances often frustrated attempts at constructing and coordinating a citywide development strategy.

The progrowth faction formed around the promotion of economic development and emphasized industrial regeneration and inward investment. This progrowth alliance was composed of traditional Labour councillors, including the Leader of the Bristol City Council, the city's trade unions, the city valuers (who manage the city's property and commercial enterprises) and the economic development officer of the city council. The progrowth alliance was much looser than the growth management coalition. Traditional Labour leaders and trade unions sought to rebuild Bristol's maritime and manufacturing base. The economic development officer concentrated on attracting inward investment, particularly high tech and business facilities on the outskirts of the city. The city valuers welcomed any development of commercial or other moneymaking enterprises on city-owned land (see DiGaetano and Klemanski 1993).

This progrowth alliance differed from American-style growth machines in significant ways. Business interests, for instance, were not major partners. Also, no single vision of economic development existed, so pairs of Labour committee chairs and their officers often operated independently of each other or, in the worst cases, worked at cross purposes.

The origins of Bristol's growth management alliance lay in a controversy surrounding overdevelopment of city center office space in the 1970s. Building on key victories against large-scale commercial projects, a middle class–based conservation (historical preservation) movement emerged as an influential force in Bristol's development politics. The city's amenity groups established close links with city planning officers and chairs of the City Council Planning Committee. Bristol's growth management alliance proved more effective than the antigrowth coalitions in a number of American cities (see DeLeon 1992), going far beyond simply blocking unwanted development. For example, Bristol's growth management alliance mounted an impressive conservation program (historic preservation), the fourth largest in Britain, after skillfully persuading a reluctant Labour group leadership on the city council and English Heritage, a national government agency, to supply the funding (see chapter 8).

Planning and economic development surfaced as major issues in Bristol politics during the early 1970s. The Labour administration that assumed power in 1973, for example, followed through on the decision made in 1971 to finance construction of a deep-water port on the Severn, despite central government's refusal to provide financial assistance for the project. Opened in 1977, the Royal Portbury Dock, as it became known, actually represented the final installment of the large-scale infrastructure program initiated by the Long Boom duarchy. The reasoning behind the new deep-water facility had been to modernize the city-owned port in order to accommodate the much larger ships of the postwar era, and thus restore Bristol's maritime industry to a more competitive position in the world shipping trade. The project was a major financial undertaking by the city council, with the final cost of the deepwater port reaching £37 million (Boddy, Lovering, and Bassett 1986).

In addition, a common enemy, rapid downtown office development, sometimes united the rival progrowth and growth management fragments of leadership. For example, traditional Labour leaders and their trade union constituents worried principally about the loss of blue-collar manufacturing jobs in working-class areas of South Bristol and the pressures placed on the city's housing market by office development in the city center (Boddy, Lovering, and Bassett 1986:175–76). The issue came to a head in 1973 when the Labour leadership of the city council came under pressure from key constituencies. First, the Bristol Trades Union Council dispatched a delegation to the City Council Resource and Coordination Committee to raise concerns about the sharp declines in industrial jobs and concomitant growth in downtown service employment. Second, a protest by housing action groups, in which an office building was occupied for a week, created political flak for the Labour bosses (Boddy, Lovering, and Bassett 1986:176). The immediate response to this "crisis" was issued by the new Labour leader, C. E. Merrett, who announced that office development had "gone too far" (Punter 1990:116; quoted originally in the *Bristol Evening Post,* June 20, 1973). More substantively, the planning committee declared a moratorium on all office development applications for a two-year period, with exemptions for those that demonstrated a clear planning gain for the city (Boddy, Lovering, and Bassett 1986:176; Punter 1990:116).

The Politics of Conflict 1979–1992

Tensions and conflict between rival progrowth and growth management factions in development politics intensified after 1978 for three principal reasons: there were higher levels of structural unemployment; central government initiatives limited local power to respond to problems; and Bristol's relative prosperity meant that the city was often overlooked for urban funding. First, structural decline in the city's manufacturing sector accelerated as the national economic recession deepened in the early 1980s. Economic problems spread from manufacturing to the city's service sector as unemployment in the city rose from 5.4 percent in 1980 to 10.8 percent in 1983 (Bristol City Council 1981:2, 1983:2). Despite the recession, Bristol saw another surge in office development between 1981 and 1984 (Bristol City Council 1993). This put enormous political pressure on both the prodevelopment and growth management coalitions to address the problems of economic restructuring.

Second, the Thatcher revolution of the early 1980s altered the intergovernmental context dramatically by limiting Bristol's options for responding to its mounting social and economic problems. One major effect of the Conservative government's more restrictive policies was to put the city's fisc under severe strain. The Thatcher government's directive mode of intervention imposed restrictions on local authority capital expenditures, which restrained the city council's industrial regeneration and conservation programs during this period. Bristol was perceived by the Thatcher government as a relatively prosperous city, and therefore was often passed over in the dispersal of funds from urban aid programs. This treatment incited the Labour-dominated Bristol City Council to open and active anticentral government belligerence throughout the 1980s.

The confluence of economic recession and fiscal restraint carved a new and perilous political landscape for Bristol's competing coalitions. First, the locally dominant Labour party was racked by serious internal dissension. In March 1980, Labour secured a majority of 53 out of 84 seats on the city council, but this large majority belied simmering tensions within the Labour group. A sizable minority of Labour councillors, first elected in 1979, broke ranks with the Labour group on a number of crucial issues (Egginton 1980). The dissident faction of left-wing councillors belonged to a younger generation of Labour politicians, who tended to be better educated and less tied to Labourist traditions (Barker 1981:18–19). Tensions erupted into an all-out donnybrook when eight dissidents split publicly with the Labour group over a dispute on the 1980–1981 budget (Harrison 1979; Shorney 1980b; Webber 1980d). The continuing debt incurred in financing city dock improvements in the 1970s had caused a severe drain on the city council's resources. The rebellious faction claimed that the proposed budget substantially reduced basic service expenditures and they voted against it in the general council (Webber 1980a). The Labour leadership promptly expelled the rebels from the group (Barker 1981:3; Webber 1980e). Backed by the local district party organization, the outcasts appealed the expulsion to the National Executive Committee of the Labour party, which restored them to the Bristol Labour Group "with 'reasonable' committee places"(Barker 1981:3; see also Shorney 1980a; Webber 1980b, 1980c). Some bitterness persisted, with a similar clash occurring over proposed rent increases for council housing in March 1981 (Barker 1981:4; Webber 1981).

In 1984, after a year of a hung council, the Labour Party again captured a sizable majority on the Bristol City Council, which it has maintained ever since. The character of the Labour group on the city council, nonetheless, had undergone a political transformation. Traditional Labour councillors, whose allegiances were to the city's trade unions and blue-collar constituents, found that the ranks of the New Left wing of the Labour group had grown. A split between soft and hard factions within the New Left wing further cleaved the Labour group (Boddy, Lovington, and Bassett 1986:181; Dalby 1989). Traditional Labour politicians remained in the majority of the Labour group, however, and they therefore retained control of most of the leadership positions, including council leader. Nevertheless, the New Left contingent secured a sizable minority of the Labour seats, and, as a consequence, gained a number of key committee chairs. The strength of the New Left faction became apparent when the city council adopted a "socialist strategy" in 1986. This flirtation with New Left governance quickly faded, as central government restrictions on council spending made impractical the costly program of municipal socialism.

Bristol's development politics in the 1980s reflected the generally raucous nature of city governance. Development policy making embroiled rival growth management and progrowth coalitions in disputes over planning and regeneration in which each side attempted to exercise dominating power over the other to achieve their goals (see DiGaetano and Klemanski 1993; Stewart 1995). For example, an imbroglio over the issue of restrictive planning controls on city center development, known as the "planning difficulties," set city planners and amenity groups, on the one hand, against an alliance of architects, real estate interests, and the Bristol Chamber of Commerce, on the other (see chapter 8). Squabbles also broke out within the city council between city valuers and economic development officers, on the one hand, and city planners, on the other, in dealing with companies that sought to build on city-owned land (Whyatt 1993).

Finally, a war raged between the city council and the Thatcher government (especially with the Department of the Environment) over who should control the development process in Bristol (see Punter 1990). The Thatcher government imposed an urban development corporation (UDC) on a 900-acre industrial area just east of the city center in 1989. The Bristol

City Council fought a protracted legal campaign to prevent the establishment of the Bristol UDC, as it would possess extensive and independent
(from the city council) planning and development powers over the designated area. The city council took the litigation all the way to the House of
Lords, the final arbiter of such disputes, but lost the fight to stop the UDC.
Moreover, throughout the tenure of the Bristol UDC, which came to the
end of its designated seven-year life in 1995, the relationship between the
UDC and the city council was one of open and often vitriolic warfare (Di-
Gaetano 1997).

Emergence of a Progrowth Agenda in the 1990s

The causes of governing realignment in the mid-1990s in Bristol were man-
ifold. In the early 1990s, the local economy suffered from a recession so
severe that local notables claimed that it was the worst to affect the city
since the Great Depression. Overall unemployment multiplied from a low
of 5 percent in 1990 to almost 14 percent in 1992 (Cairns 1993; Jackson and
Elliot 1992). Even Bristol's financial services sector retrenched, and the for-
est of power cranes that silhouetted Bristol's skyline during the boom years
of the 1980s virtually disappeared. All sectors of the local economy contracted as the national recession deepened. Moreover, industrial restructuring of the Greater Bristol economy accompanied the recession of the
early 1990s. Whitehall, in recognition of the end of the cold war, began
to pare back the nation's military-industrial complex. The South West,
which had benefited in the 1970s and 1980s from defense industry expansion, now faced a military build-down. National defense downsizing
forced Rolls Royce and British Aerospace, the two defense industry giants
in the region, to slash their work forces. Defense-dependent subcontrac-
tors and supplier companies in the Bristol area also felt the domino effect
of cutbacks among the area's major defense producers (West interview
1993).

As Bristol entered into this new era of economic uncertainty, intergovernmental restructuring further reduced the ability of the city council
to cope with problems of economic regeneration. In the 1980s and early
1990s, city council Labour leaders had resisted government intervention-
ism and remained cool to business participation in development politics.
Additional central government constraints on revenue and capital expenditures forced the city to curb its economic development activities. The
city council also lost its monopoly over local regeneration and planning
functions. The creation of the Bristol Development Corporation and the

Avon TEC further hemmed in the city council's planning and economic development role, at the same time providing business elites bases of power from which to remake the city's governing alignment.

In addition, in the 1970s, many urban-related central government and European Union grants were increasingly distributed through highly competitive bidding processes (see Stewart 1994). These pushed the city council into an alliance with the private sector and with central government quangos such as Avon TEC, something proud Bristolian Labour politicians had traditionally been loathe to do (DiGaetano 1997).

This reordering of the local governing system meant that business leaders, largely excluded from the city's governing coalitions in the 1980s, began to play an influential role in local politics in the 1990s. The shock of the city and region's recession and restructuring had jolted the Bristol business leaders into action. The city's corporate leaders formed the Bristol Initiative in the early 1990s to work on some of Bristol's most pressing social and economic issues. Many of these business leaders belonged to the legendary Merchant Adventurers, an exclusive organization that had figured prominently in Bristol's social, economic, and political life since the eighteenth century. The Bristol Initiative eventually merged with the Bristol Chamber of Commerce, with the new organization renamed the Bristol Chamber of Commerce and Initiative, and became a potent force in local affairs.

By 1993, the local Labour leadership recognized that, unless they cooperated with the city's business leaders, intergovernmental funding for urban redevelopment projects could never be obtained. Added to this, Bristol's business elite had become much better organized and much more astute about local politics. On this new political landscape a progrowth alliance formed around a regional capital strategy in the mid-1990s. An interlocking directorate of leaders from the city council, the Bristol Chamber of Commerce and Initiative, the local media, cultural institutions, the tourism industry, and the city's large employers began to unite around an effort to protect and enhance Bristol's position as the nerve center of the region's commercial, financial, and cultural industries.

The idea of creating a regional development partnership germinated from the concerns of Bristol's new corporate elite about defense industry downsizing and the erosion of Avon County's position in national and global markets. These business leaders included the regional managing directors and chief executives of British Aerospace, Rolls Royce, British Gas Southwest, and Bristol and West Building Society. Their chief worry was that the local economy was in serious trouble, and that local government possessed neither the capacity nor the will to address the region's deepening economic malaise (Geohegan 1993; Hider 1994).

Early in 1992, the new corporate elite, brought together as directors of the boards of the Avon TEC and the Bristol Initiative, met informally and resolved to forge a regional body to wrestle with the twin problems of recession and defense industry decline (Geoghegan 1993). Using their positions as directors of the Bristol Initiative and the Avon TEC, this small band of corporate executives, whose companies all had direct and place-based interests in the local economy, engineered the building of a county-wide development partnership.

The Avon TEC underwrote much of the initial expense for organizing meetings, conducting surveys, and commissioning reports necessary to unite the disparate public and private interests into a regional growth alliance (Hider 1993; Geoghegan 1993). The major stumbling block was convincing the local authorities to cooperate; each was suspicious of the others and worried about protecting its own political turf. To establish the common ground, a Task Force was formed. It commissioned a series of reports that identified the weaknesses in the region's economy and recommended a number of strategic proposals for joint action in the areas of inward investment, European funding, and smaller regeneration projects (Avon Economic Development Conference 1993; Jackson and Elliot 1992). On this basis, the corporate leaders organized the Avon Economic Development Forum, again largely funded by the Avon TEC. To the forum they invited local business leaders, politicians from Avon County Council and the six district authorities (including Bristol), and representatives from the three Avon-based universities and the Trade Union Council. As hoped, the task force and Avon Economic Development Forum worked to allay the suspicions and fears of the participating politicians. At a March 1993 conference all parties agreed to the formation of the Western Development Partnership (WDP). Since then, the WDP has served as the chief coordinator for inward investment initiatives for the area once covered by Avon County (now defunct).

Bristol's emergent progrowth coalition also organized a network of partnerships to carry out its regional capital strategy (see chapter 5). First, in 1993, the Bristol City Council, the South West Arts Council, and the Bristol Chamber of Commerce and Initiative formed the Bristol Cultural Development Partnership to enhance Bristol's cultural infrastructure as a means for encouraging economic development. The Bristol City Council also entered into the Harbourside Partnership with other landowners (Lloyd's

Bank, British Gas, British Rail, and the JT Group) to regenerate Cannon's Marsh and Wapping Wharf. Later, the Avon TEC and the Bristol Chamber of Commerce and Initiative won government funding to set up a Business Link, which they jointly operate. Finally, in 1995, business leaders and the city council created Bristol 2000 to oversee the development of several high profile development projects on the city's historic Floating Harbour. These included a new performing arts center and a triad of natural science–related discovery centers, both of which received Millennium Commission grants to help finance both projects (Bristol City Council 1995, 1996).

The success of the city's progrowth alliance in the mid-1990s suggests that the adage "shipshape and Bristol fashion" might regain its old meaning. Proliferation of public-private partnerships around the economic regeneration issues in the mid-1990s may indeed signal that Bristol's progrowth coalition may be solidifying into a regime. Whether bargaining power has graduated to preemptive power is not clear, however, although the city's regional capital strategy appears to dominate Bristol's governing agenda.

Detroit: The Motor City Seeks a Renaissance

Beginning in the 1970s, Detroit politics revealed a split personality of sorts. Although a fair amount of consensus existed between political and business leaders on economic development issues, the city's political leadership was becoming predominantly black, while the business establishment remained largely white. The issue of race and power has remained a source of tension in Detroit for many years, at times hindering the willingness of political and business leaders to sustain a consensus around development strategies or specific projects.

Regime Formation in Detroit in the 1970s

The initial impetus for governing realignment in Detroit came from economic and social restructuring. First, the flight of business firms from the city after the 1967 race riot was dramatic. While employment in the city of Detroit rose 4.9 percent (4.2 percent in manufacturing alone) from 1962 to 1967, employment from 1967 to 1972 declined by 14 percent, with a 13.7 percent decrease in manufacturing (Darden 1987:23). In short, by the early 1970s, deindustrialization and business departures and failures were undermining Detroit's once vibrant economy. Meanwhile, social restructuring was changing the composition of the Motor City's population. Due primarily to white flight to the suburbs, Detroit's African-American community emerged as a majority in the city's population by the early 1970s. Economic contraction and racial recomposition of Detroit's population set the stage for a governing realignment that brought together the city's white corporate establishment and its first African-American mayor, Coleman A. Young, into a progrowth regime.

Progrowth realignment was initiated by Detroit's white business establishment. This corporate elite put into place some development plans and organizations such as Detroit Renaissance, Inc., and the New Detroit Committee (later New Detroit, Inc.). These organizations were designed to rebuild the city, not only in terms of bricks and mortar, but also as a way to heal the area's post-riot social and racial wounds after 1967. Seeking a complete recovery and rebirth, Detroit began to market itself as the "Renaissance City," also applying the label to the Renaissance Center, a major office, hotel, and shopping complex built on the riverfront in the 1970s.

The election of Young in 1973 completed the realignment to a progrowth regime. Young, a former state senator and union organizer, ran against John Nichols in the general election. Nichols, a white former Detroit police chief, had won the primary on an anticrime platform, and promoted himself as intending to take an "administrative approach" to the problems of Detroit, as opposed to Young's "legislative approach" (Rich 1989:103). The 1973 election also was the first mayoral election after the 1970 Census reported a majority black electorate in Detroit (228,000 registered black voters to 220,000 registered white voters). Young's success in the 1973 election rested largely on his ability to turn Nichols' self-described strength into a liability in the minds of the voters. Young claimed that Nichols was merely a one-issue candidate (anticrime), while Young embraced a number of issues and emphasized substantial plans to rebuild the city's economy. During this first campaign, Young promoted his vision of Detroit's economic redevelopment, which included a plan to rebuild the city's riverfront properties "from bridge to bridge" (i.e., from the Belle Isle Bridge roughly at the city's eastern border to the Ambassador Bridge located near the city's western border). Much of this riverfront property at that time had fallen into disuse, and contained warehouses or old rail yards (Weathers interview 1992).

The 1973 election also brought about some changes in the city's governmental structure. A new charter was adopted that provided for a few changes that made for a much stronger mayor and relatively weaker city council. One provision allowed the mayor more appointment power over department heads, an authority not granted by the previous charter passed in 1917.

Mayor Young had a loyal following throughout his five terms, especially among older black voters who felt a shared experience with him, that of growing up in the South and moving to an industrializing northern city that promised high wage jobs and a life freer of the racial prejudices of pre–World War II days (Kiley 1992). A pragmatist on economic development issues, Young expended considerable energy on issues related to race and power, pushing early for an affirmative action hiring plan for the police department and enforcement of the city's residency requirement for city employees. The percentage of black police officers increased from 5 percent in 1967 to 25 percent in 1976 (Darden et al. 1987: 75) then to 65 percent in 1987 (Edmonds 1987).

Shortly after Mayor Young's first election, a consensus among business and political leaders emerged around a progrowth agenda, with an emphasis on riverfront-downtown commercial and office developments. During those early years, the mayor found support from homegrown business leaders such as Henry Ford II, financier Max Fisher, and real estate developer Al Taubman. Young also cultivated ties with such organizations like Detroit Renaissance, Inc., a nonprofit organization that began in 1970 and is made up exclusively of CEOs from Detroit-area businesses. It was meant to be the organizational vehicle for implementing the redevelopment strategies of the local business leadership.

At about this time, the Young administration created two separate executive development units — a Planning Department and a Community and Economic Development Department (C&EDD). This enlarged bureaucracy worked closely with public-private partnerships, such as the Detroit Economic Growth Corporation (DEGC), the Downtown Development Authority (DDA), and the Economic Development Corporation (EDC), all created in the 1970s to help facilitate, finance, and administer development projects. Detroit's progrowth regime helped to build marquee projects. The Renaissance Center (completed during Mayor Young's first term in office) was the earliest and most obvious product of their efforts, but the organization became involved in a number of other revitalization efforts, such as the Joe Louis Arena, Hart Plaza, and Trolley Plaza. Preemptive power existed in Detroit through the 1970s, with a shared orientation toward a regional capital strategy that emphasized downtown and riverfront commercial developments.

Trouble in Motown: 1981–1987

In the early 1980s, Detroit's economy took another tumble during the automobile recession, in which the Big Three automakers lost approximately

$3.5 billion in 1980. Conflict arose over the progrowth agenda during this time from some city council members and from increasingly organized and vocal neighborhood organizations opposed to specific projects. Also, a series of federal investigations (but no indictments) of Mayor Young focused on government contracting improprieties in his administration. Withdrawing to an ever tighter circle of friends and supporters, he maintained his mass following, his electoral strength peaking in the 1981 election when he received over 65 percent of the vote.

At the same time, the city's intergovernmental environment was changing, mostly for the worse. Ronald Reagan's election as president in 1980 changed the federal government's mode of intervention from permissive to withdrawal. Detroit in particular was hurt by federal withdrawal because of the special relationship that had developed between Jimmy Carter and Coleman Young during the previous four years. James Blanchard, a Democrat and former U.S. Congressman, was elected Michigan's governor in 1982. This meant that Detroit still had a somewhat sympathetic ear in Lansing. However, Governor Blanchard and Mayor Young never established the strong personal friendship that Young had developed with Blanchard's predecessor, Republican William Milliken. As a consequence, federal and state aid to Detroit for economic development declined during the 1980s.

Detroit's ruling partners supported a dual regional capital-industrial development strategy in the 1980s. Despite the federal withdrawal, Detroit scored a huge (but highly controversial) success with the construction of a high-technology automobile production facility, a General Motors Buick–Oldsmobile–Cadillac assembly plant, called the "Poletown" plant (see chapter 6). Mayor Young continued to cultivate private investors during the 1980s, but his relations with businesspeople tended to become less public, in part a reaction to the highly publicized protests and legal actions taken by residents opposing the Poletown project. Young came to rely on a 13-member, all male, all black inner-circle advisory group that the local press dubbed Young's "kitchen cabinet." This group met monthly, and included his political lieutenants, and local church, educational, civic, and legal leaders, but no business leaders (Edmonds 1987).

A small group of developers and business leaders were personal friends and thus became trusted and favored investors in the city, especially for commercial development projects. Although some of the investors were relatively new to the Detroit development scene by the 1980s (such as Greektown investors Ted Gatzaros and Jim Papas), a number of veteran business leaders remained, including Taubman (primarily a suburban shopping mall developer) and Fisher (who made his fortune in the gas and oil business, then later in real estate). Taubman and Fisher led the effort to build an upscale residential complex and marina on the river called River-front West Apartments. Peter Stroh, chair of the Stroh Brewery Company, also had developed a strong business relationship with the mayor begin-ning in the late 1970s that continued through development of Brewery Park and the Stroh River Place complex.

Over time, Young had made judgments about the loyalty and com-mitment business leaders had to the city and to him, personally. Conse-quently, this inner circle had the best access, received the fastest approval, and generally had the easiest time in putting together the necessary pub-lic and private resources to complete a project in the city. They also were among the first the mayor called when the city needed assistance. Conrad Mallett Jr. (interview 1989), who had worked in Mayor Young's organization during the early 1980s (and later became Michigan Supreme Court Chief Justice), put the mayor's perspective in this light: "Coleman Young likes to talk about 'pedigree' — where you came from; who you are. This use of pedi-gree was important in many of the mayor's choices — people in his organi-zation, even including the selection of political consultants. Could others vouch for your capability and loyalty? That was what was important."

This increasing personalization of decision making and its concomi-tant secrecy made the mayor even more central in deciding which pro-jects and developers would be favored with the necessary local government support on land siting, building permits, gap financing, and tax incen-tives. About the same time, a number of locally based corporations brought in new CEOs who were not born and reared in Detroit. Only a few of the early investors from the 1970s remained, including Fisher, Taubman, and Stroh. As Young later recounted, "I was comfortable with the old leadership. I knew them and they knew me. The new guys didn't know me. What's the saying? 'A clean broom sweeps?' One of the things they swept out was con-cern for the city of Detroit" (quoted in Pepper 1996a). As a result, the De-troit progrowth regime fell apart during the early 1980s, leaving a loose coali-tion of interests that generally remained committed to the city's regional capital and industrial renewal strategies. But the coalition members began to spar over the means to achieve the progrowth agenda, in part due to a lack of mutual trust. Those projects that were built were largely reactions to opportunities that presented themselves to the city, rather than the im-plementation of a shared vision among regime partners. Development deals were struck, but they tended to be made on a project-by-project basis.

Scarcer local resources in the late 1980s helped create a shifting of interests and priorities among coalition partners in Detroit. Local governments were not the only organizations that faced a revenue squeeze during this period. Private businesses continued to reorganize themselves in an effort to remain competitive. In many cases, this meant that private funding or even simple investments for economic development projects were not as available as they had been in the past. Furthermore, increased tensions around issues of race and power in the city exacerbated the problems caused by external economic and political forces. Relations between the private sector and local government were quite cool by the beginning of the mayor's fourth term in 1985.

Much of the dissension between Mayor Young and the local business establishment was provoked by fundamental disagreements over the Detroit Strategic Plan. Initiated in 1987 by Detroit Renaissance, Inc., and not by the mayor, the Detroit Strategic Plan attempted to address the city's myriad problems by first creating five task forces to investigate and report on the status of those problems (jobs and economic development, education, crime, city image, and race relations). The Project's joint chairs were Walter J. McCarthy Jr., Chair and CEO of Detroit Edison, and Alan E. Schwartz, senior partner of a prominent Detroit law firm. The planning project process began its task force hearings in January 1987.

Several problems quickly arose. A power struggle locked Mayor Young and the business community in open conflict, primarily over who properly should lead the city into the future. Part of this struggle was expressed through specific disputes about the direction the task forces would take and even the topics they would investigate. For example, the original process did not include a task force on race relations, which the mayor demanded. Such disputes set an adversarial tone for the entire planning process. The simple fact that Detroit Renaissance unilaterally took initiative for strategic planning implied a lack of leadership by the mayor, exacerbating tensions among the groups involved, and the mayor did not enthusiastically participate in the planning process.

The 122-page strategic planning report was released in November 1987, with recommendations from each of the five task forces (*The Report of the Detroit Strategic Planning Project,* 1987). A decade later, the report's impact remained minimal. Much of the planned funding was not released by Detroit Renaissance, and the mayor had already gone on record as saying that he would implement only those recommendations that he preferred. But even council member Mel Ravitz, the mayor's frequent adversary, saw little value in the plan, for many of the reasons that seemed to echo the mayor's view. As Ravitz explained in a January 27, 1992 interview with the authors, "There was nothing new in that Plan, nothing new. The issues they addressed were almost cliché-ish in what they proposed.... Why it took them a year and $750,000 to formulate them, I don't know. If they had merely looked back in the archives, they would have found proposals of the same sort...but never implemented." The fallout from the Strategic Plan heightened the tensions within the development coalition, so that political and business leaders focused on their differences rather than their commonalities and shared goals.

The city's uneasy coalition continued through the late 1980s, using bargaining power to put together a few development projects, but also failing on several proposals (casinos, the Comerica Tower–demolition of Ford Auditorium, and the first Tiger Stadium proposal). Although Young's double-digit margin of victory would be regarded with great pride by many candidates, the mayor's re-election margin was 10 points smaller than his 1981 triumph. There were a few projects completed during his last term, however. A new Chrysler Jefferson Avenue North plant was built, although with as much controversy as the Poletown plant (see chapter 6). The expansion of the Cobo Convention Center was completed in 1989, as were several commercial developments (see chapter 5).

A Re-Emerging Progrowth Regime? 1994–1997

Mayor Young's run for re-election in 1989 proved to be his last hurrah. This time, he defeated Thomas Barrow 56 percent to 44 percent (Willing 1992). During Mayor Young's last term, more and more business leaders called for his retirement—first privately, then publicly. The mayor's secrecy and personalized approach to local decision making hurt his relations with the media, and with those outside his close circle of advisers and confidants. In June 1993, just prior to the filing deadline for the November election, Mayor Young announced that he would not seek re-election. A field of seven primary election candidates was whittled down to former State Supreme Court Justice Dennis Archer, who took 53 percent of the primary vote, to attorney and former police commissioner Sharon McPhail's 26 percent. The other five candidates combined for the remaining 21 percent (Toy and Trent 1993). Archer's self-conscious style in the campaign was conciliatory and healing, and he made a number of gestures toward the business community and the suburbs, both of whom had felt slighted or annoyed by Mayor Young in his last two terms. In the general election, Archer won with 57 percent of the vote (Vlasic, Toy, and Kiska 1993), and in the minds of many, his election heralded a new era in Detroit politics, one that held great promise for fostering cooperation in city-suburban and public-private sector relations.

Archer's first term of office brought considerable optimism to the city, especially from those who previously objected to Young's combativeness. The local media especially praised Mayor Archer's conciliatory and open style, and Detroit's receipt of one of six federal empowerment zone grants was considered a major coup for his new administration. This was especially true in terms of consensual politics in the city, because empowerment zone grants required and favored those applications that could demonstrate broad-based cooperation and support from a variety of local sources (business, government, labor, neighborhoods, and so on). Mayor Archer also forged an agreement with the Detroit Lions professional football team and the Detroit Tigers baseball team to build two new sports stadiums side by side in the Foxtown area of the city. In regard to both the empowerment zones and new stadiums, the local media highlighted the cooperation and coalition-building skills of Mayor Archer.

Since Archer's election in 1993, Detroit's business leadership has taken a renewed interest in the city's renaissance. Part of that effort has included the creation of the Greater Downtown Partnership, Inc., an organization of business, civic, and philanthropic leaders that sought to renew Detroit's declining downtown retail area. The group has tried to avoid the publicity often associated with downtown projects (and the resulting high costs for land acquisition as a result), but has indicated a desire to redevelop the site of the old Hudson's department store building, which has been vacant since 1983 (Pepper 1996b).

As Mayor Archer's first term ended in 1997, the consensus among observers was that, despite some inefficiencies and turnover in economic development leadership positions, Archer skillfully courted the business community, the local media, and surrounding suburbs. Thus, there is a strong possibility that a reformation of a progrowth regime may occur in Detroit, with a focus on a regional capital strategy (that now includes gambling casinos, sports stadiums, and entertainment-cultural attractions).

Explaining Governing Alignments and Realignments

The stories of development politics in Birmingham, Boston, Bristol, and Detroit reveal that governing realignments occurred during periods of social, economic, and political turbulence. If the seismic dislocations were severe enough and major departures from existing governing arrangements and agendas ensued, then critical realignments took place. These alignments were constructed by the new constellation of city leaders that appeared in the midst of realignment-induced political turmoil.

Each of the four cities underwent critical governing realignments during the 1970 to 1997 period (see table 4.1). Birmingham experienced two critical realignments, one in the early 1970s and one in the early 1980s. The first was brought on by the combined effects of economic contraction, restructuring of the local authority into a two-tier system, and the emergence of a new generation of local political leadership. Under these circumstances,

---

Table 4.1

Governing Alignments and Realignments in Birmingham, Boston, Bristol, and Detroit 1970–1997

Birmingham
Critical realignment, 1973–1974
Adhocracy, 1974–1975
Critical realignment, 1979–1980
Progrowth coalition, 1980–1983
Progrowth regime, 1984–1993
Partial realignment, 1993–1994
Progrowth coalition, 1994–1997

Boston
Progrowth coalition, 1975–1983
Critical realignment, 1983–1984
Dual social reform and growth management regimes, 1984–1989
Partial realignment, 1990
Dual progrowth and social reform coalitions, 1990–1997

Bristol
Critical realignment, 1973–1974
Rival progrowth and growth management factions, 1974–1992
Critical realignment, 1993–1994
Progrowth coalition, 1994–1997

Detroit
Critical realignment, 1973–1974
Progrowth regime, 1974–1979
Progrowth coalition, 1980–1994
Emerging progrowth regime, 1994–1997

---

an adhocracy ousted the long-standing technocracy in development politics. Under the adhocracy, development decision making became decentralized and fragmented, with little consensus achieved around economic development strategy. Again in the early 1980s, critical realignment struck as the twin economic crises of deindustrialization and deep recession galvanized both Conservative and Labour parties into action around a progrowth agenda. By the mid-1980s progrowth politics dominated the city's governing agenda, and a regime was built around dual regional capital and industrial development strategies.

Only one critical realignment unfolded in Boston during the 1970–1997 period. In 1983, rapid economic growth and its attendant negative externalities, social restructuring in the form of racial, ethnic, and class recomposition of the population, and the mobilization of a well-developed community movement culminated in the election of Raymond Flynn as mayor. This governing realignment dislodged the progrowth agenda that had dominated the city's development politics for decades. The new governing alignment featured a dual regime, in which the Flynn administration formed alliances with community activists around affordable housing and environmental improvement and historic preservation strategies, respectively.

Bristol, like Birmingham, experienced two critical realignments in the postindustrial era. Burgeoning city center development, downgrading the Bristol City Council to district authority, and the rise of a new generation of Labour leaders converged to topple the Long Boom duarchy in the early 1970s. The governing alignment that replaced the duarchy featured rival progrowth and growth management factions in Bristol's development politics. This alignment persisted into the early 1990s, when a second critical realignment occurred. Educed by a dual economic crisis of defense industry downsizing and deep recession and the introduction of a competitive mode of intervention, a progrowth governing alignment replaced the rival faction mode of governance that had characterized development politics for so long.

Detroit, like Boston, has undergone one critical governing realignment since 1970. The turbulence caused by rapid deindustrialization and economic contraction, white middle-class flight, and the resultant emergence of an African American majority led to the demise of the law-and-order governing alignment that had emerged after the 1967 riot. The mobilization of Detroit's white corporate elite around a Renaissance agenda and the election of Coleman Young as mayor in 1973 jelled into a regional capital regime that ruled Detroit until the late 1970s. Beginning in the early

1980s, however, internal tensions and the external pressures of federal withdrawal and deepening economic decline and recession reduced the progrowth governing alignment to a loose coalitional structure. The new alignment revolved around a dual regional capital and industrial development strategies.

Three of the cities also underwent partial governing realignments. The realignment in Birmingham in the mid-1990s, brought on by social restructuring (which resulted in growing numbers of ethnic minorities, women, and white-collar Labour councillors) and the subsequent crisis in the Knowles leadership, produced a balanced back-to-basics and progrowth governing agenda. In the early 1990s, recession and declining intergovernmental aid combined in Boston to disrupt the growth management regime. In its place, the Flynn and Menino administrations forged alliances with the city's business leaders around regional capital and Techs Mix reindustrialization strategies. The social reform alliance held together, although a coalitional structure replaced regime politics. Finally, due in large part to social restructuring (an increase in the number of better educated, white-collar residents), the rise of the New Left contingent in Bristol's local Labour party further fragmented the existing factional power structure.

Part II
Progrowth Politics

The Politics of Regional Primacy

The notion that the engines of postindustrial urban economies have been driven by downtown functions such as *command centers* for corporate headquarters (Sassen 1991) or financial and business service centers (Fainstein 1994) has become widely accepted (see also Judd and Swanstrom 1998:chapter 13). Accordingly, efforts to revitalize downtown economies by offering public subsidies to office and commercial development in the 1970s and 1980s have been referred to as *corporate center strategies* (Hill 1983; see also Judd and Swanstrom 1998). It is our contention that these conceptions of downtown economies and the strategies to redevelop them in the 1980s and 1990s gauge too narrowly the nature and structure of central city downtowns. Postindustrial city centers of Great Britain and the United States (as well as other industrial nations) are not simply corporate command or financial centers, but integrate business, commercial, and cultural functions. What is more, downtown renewal strategies over the last 15 years have reflected this complex mix of economic functions.

In the postindustrial urban hierarchy, Birmingham, Boston, Bristol, and Detroit, in varying degrees, constitute *regional capitals* in the global economy. Further, the four cities have pursued regional capital strategies that promote development of city center business and financial service industries, specialized shopping districts, and cultural and tourism facilities. Boston and Bristol have been undisputed regional capitals, with little competition from other regional contenders for the title. Birmingham and Detroit performed the principal function of manufacturing centers, and have only recently aspired to regional capital status. In doing so, these former industrial giants have struggled to shake off their images as gritty factory towns through large-scale downtown renewal programs.

Birmingham: The City of Business

Birmingham has long prided it itself as the *City of Business,* based on manufacturing and trades. Manufacturing, although declining as a source of employment, remained a core industry for the West Midlands, particularly automobile manufacturing. But if the nation's financial and professional services remain concentrated in London, Birmingham has carved out a niche as a regional business center, specializing in financial and professional services for the West Midlands manufacturing sector. The impending consolidation of the European Union set for 1992 promised to spur this on. According to the former chair of the Economic Development Committee, Albert Bore (July 19, 1991 interview):

> You can see a development in that within Europe, because if there is a federalization with Europe, it's quite clear that we're going to get a number of regional centers. Each regional center is going to become a center for business and professional services. Birmingham can position itself alongside the likes of Lyon, France, and Frankfurt, Germany. But you can see a European edge to that change is quite interesting to follow through.

In short, Birmingham sought to position itself as a regional capital in the new global economy.

Birmingham's Prestige Project Strategy

The genesis of Birmingham's regional capital strategy lies in the development of the National Exhibition Center in the 1970s. The Birmingham Chamber of Industry and Commerce conceived the idea that the West Midlands should be considered as an alternative location to London for a national exhibition center. The chamber submitted evidence to the House of Commons Committee on Export Promotion in 1968 that the nation lacked sufficient facilities to promote trade and industry (Birmingham City Council 1989:115). Working together, the leader of the city council, Alderman Sir Francis Griffin, and the director of the Birmingham Chamber, Robert Boone, with the backing of many local interests, assiduously lobbied Whitehall to name Greater Birmingham as the locale for the proposed national exhibition center. In January 1970, despite a very strong counter-lobbying effort by London, the government gave Birmingham the nod, and what became an enduring partnership between the Birmingham City Council and the Birmingham Chamber was born.

From its inception, the National Exhibition Centre (NEC) was a joint venture between the City Council and the Chamber. The City Council purchased the Warren Farm at Bickenhill, located a few miles outside the Birmingham city limits for the NEC development. The site offered access to the Birmingham Airport, the recently electrified rail line to London, and an interchange of several motorways and dual carriageways. The city council supplied the funding necessary to build the NEC, and N.E.C., Ltd., a company limited by guarantee, was formed to construct and manage the facilities. The Birmingham Chamber of Commerce was responsible for the day-to-day operation and marketing of the NEC, while the city council had majority representation on the board of directors (Birmingham City Council 1989:115). The NEC proved enormously successful, attracting hordes of exhibitions and producing substantial revenues for the city. These revenues and the borrowing power of the N.E.C., Ltd., were later applied to the construction of other flagship developments, as well as to its own expansion.

In the midst of wrenching economic restructuring and a deep recession in the early 1980s, the Birmingham City Council embarked on a massive physical redevelopment program to transform Birmingham into a world-class "City of Business." The jewel in the crown of the city's prestige project strategy was the International Convention Centre (ICC). The plan to construct a convention center was hatched in 1983 during the interregnum of Conservative rule on the city council. It was thought that Birmingham's strategic location at the center of Britain's transportation network and the established reputation of the city-owned National Exhibition Centre would enable Birmingham to capture a large share of the nation's business conference trade. A bipartisan consensus around the initiative carried the project, so that when Labour regained control of the city council in 1984, Birmingham's City Council broadened the development agenda to an array of interrelated *prestige projects.* These included the International Convention Centre, the National Indoor Arena (sports), expansion of the city's National Exhibition Centre, and large-scale pedestrianization of the central area.

The success of Birmingham's prestige project strategy program lay in the use of preemptive power by the city's progrowth coalition. An inner circle of senior politicians and officers, led by the council leader, Sir Richard Knowles, tightly controlled the prestige project agenda. It was decided that prestige projects would be controlled at the center through the Council's Finance and Policy Committee. To minimize opposition to the prestige project strategy, the Knowles' ruling faction concealed details about financing of the projects until they were presented to the Labour Group as a fait accompli (Brooks interview, 1993; Stewart interview, 1994). Councillor Martin Brooks, who became chair of the Economic Development Committee in 1993, depicted the city council power structure under Knowles' leadership as follows:

> A lot of these initiatives have been dealt with in a very cen-
> tralized way. I think it's the fact that the Finance and Manage-
> ment Committee is the *supreme policy making committee* of the
> council. A lot of these initiatives were being dealt with through
> the mechanisms of the Finance and Management Committee,
> and a lot of other committees that have a direct involvement, or
> should have a direct involvement, don't necessarily know very
> much about the overall strategy in some of these areas.

The decentralized committee system enabled the Knowles leadership to obscure the degree to which it had concentrated power at the center.

The city council funded its prestige project program by cobbling together financial packages from a variety of sources (Birmingham City Council 1987:8, 1992:8). First, the prestige projects were implemented through the management structure of the National Exhibition Centre Limited, the holding company for the NEC that is jointly controlled by the city council and the Birmingham Chamber of Industry and Commerce, to circumvent increasingly restrictive central government rules on borrowing and expenditures. The city council also received substantial funding from the European Community, including £50 million for the ICC, £32 million for the expansion of the NEC, £2 million for the development of Centenary Square, £1 million for the refurbishment of the Birmingham Repertory Theater, and £3 million for pedestrianization of the central area (Birmingham City Council 1992:8) (figure 5.1).

  Shielded by the Byzantine nature of city council structures, the Knowles ruling clique shepherded the prestige projects through to completion in the early 1990s, at a cost to the city of more than £330 million (Loftman and Nevin 1992:21). In the meantime, a high-profile promotional campaign to boost the ICC and other megaprojects was marshaled, with enthusiastic cooperation from the local media and business community to win public approbation.

  By the early 1990s, the city's prestige project strategy had completely changed the face of Birmingham's city center. The £180 million ICC had been built and was in full operation along with the adjoining £31 million five-star Hyatt Hotel (with one-third city council ownership). The £57 million NIA had opened its doors to sporting events of every variety (figure 5.2), and the NEC had completed its expansion program by adding four new

Figure 5.1. Centenary Square, with (left to right): Hyatt Hotel, the ICC, and Repertory Theatre. Photo by Alan DiGaetano.

exhibition halls. Finally, Centenary Square and Victoria Square pedestrian malls had turned the city's civic center into a showpiece for convention business and tourism. Also, Brindley Place, a 26-acre private development area, situated directly across the canal from the ICC and planned in the mid-1980s, came to life with construction of an aquarium, office towers, restaurants, shops, and market rate housing. Finally, the Gas Street Basin, which had been the central interchange of the Falzey-Birmingham Canal, had been converted into an entertainment district with pedestrian gaslight canal walks, historic pubs, and other amenities (Birmingham City Council 1989).

The city council augmented its physical redevelopment strategy in 1990 by luring the Sadler Wells Royal Ballet (renamed the Birmingham Royal Ballet) and the D'Oyly Carte Opera Company from London. This equipped Birmingham with a full complement of high quality performing arts groups, such as the Birmingham Repertory Company and the Birmingham Symphony Orchestra. The symphony took up residence in the ICC's new concert hall when it was completed.

The Highbury Initiative and the Emergence of City 2000

In the late 1980s, a more explicit regional capital strategy was fashioned out of what became known as the Highbury Initiative. The Highbury Initiative marked a turning point in the relationship between the Birmingham

Figure 5.2. The Falzey-Birmingham Canal, Sea-Life Aquarium, and the National Indoor Arena. Photo by Alan DiGaetano.

City Council and the city's business leaders. Highbury (named for the setting) actually consisted of two symposia, the first in 1988 and the second in 1989, that probed the question of city center revitalization and its importance for long-range economic development of the city (Christie et al. 1991:97).

For the 1988 gathering, the city council and the government-run City Action Team (CAT) organized an international symposium that was attended by public officials (local and central government), business elites, architects, chartered surveyors, developers, landowners, artists, and a number of experts from overseas (Loftman and Nevin 1992:40). This first meeting of the Highbury Initiative produced a plan for renewing the city center in three ways: (1) downgrading the Inner Ring Road to give pedestrians greater access to and priority in the CBD; (2) projecting an upscale image of the CBD; and (3) identifying and promoting the development of different districts of the city center, like the Jewellery Quarter, the Financial Quarter, the Gun Quarter, and the Media Quarter (Loftman and Nevin 1992:41).

The city council and CAT sponsored a second symposium in 1989, inviting 33 business leaders. This gathering built on the foundation laid by the first, turning to the problem of how to expedite implementation of the regional capital strategy through such projects as the ICC (Loftman and Nevin 1992:41).

The Highbury Initiative spawned a number of consultations and joint working operations around city center issues between the city council and the city's financial and professional firms (Maxwell 1995). Out of these interactions came the idea for Birmingham City 2000. It was the senior partner of KMPG Peat Marwick in Birmingham, Roger Dickens, who called a meeting of city center business executives to discuss the creation of an organization that would advance the interests of the city's financial services and professional industry. After several informal discussions, a handful of business leaders, led by Dickens, founded Birmingham City 2000 in 1990.

City 2000 quickly became a major player in economic development politics, contributing expertise and a wide network of business and political contacts to the city's progrowth regime. Moreover, City 2000 openly and actively embraced Birmingham's regional capital strategy. For example, City 2000 has lobbied the city council on local issues, such as pedestrianization of the city center and the formulation of a marketing strategy for promoting Birmingham as a regional capital (Maxwell interview 1995).

After the Highbury Initiative, a new rhetorical focus crept into the lexicon of economic development discourse in Birmingham. According to city and business leaders alike, the central purpose of economic development activity was to position Birmingham as a regional capital, so that the city could better compete in the global economy (Bore interview 1991; Moore interview 1993). The down payment of the city's regional capital strategy was the development of the city council's prestige projects. These projects were seen as essential public infrastructure for transforming Birmingham into a national and international business center. The second phase of Birmingham's regional capital strategy consisted of promotional efforts to encourage business investment in the city center and attract conference trade and business tourism.

The Politics of Place Marketing

In the 1980s, the city council sponsored several promotional schemes to burnish Birmingham's image as England's City of Business. Each of these formed integral parts of the prestige project strategy. In 1992, the Knowles ruling clique and Chief Executive Roger Taylor became troubled about Birmingham's ability to market itself as a business center to the outside world. Blame fell on the city council's public affairs director, who departed the scene as a result. To find a new method to market the city, well known BBC

2 television talk show host Vincent Hanna was hired to interview all the leading players in the city, and subsequently recommend changes in the city's promotional strategies (Green 1993).

Using Hanna's report as a basis for discussion, city leaders conceived the idea of forming a marketing partnership. Chief Executive Taylor, Economic Development Committee Chair Albert Bore, and the chair of the Birmingham City 2000, Bob Gilbert, were particularly instrumental in driving this effort forward (Green interview 1993). Gilbert drew upon the professional and technical expertise of City 2000 members to produce the business plan and provide seed money to set up the Birmingham Marketing Partnership (BMP) (Moore interview 1993; Birmingham City 2000 1993). The city council committed £1.6 million annually for three years to finance the BMP operations. Many of the heavyweights in Birmingham's progrowth regime were appointed to the board of directors, which hired Michael Thorley, who came from the private sector, as the BMP chief executive in the spring of 1993.

The specific task undertaken by the BMP was to recast Birmingham's grimy industrial persona into one of a glittering regional capital for business and conference tourism (Thorley interviews, 1993, 1994). The city's recently completed prestige projects—the ICC and adjoining Hyatt Hotel, the expansion of the NEC, the NIA, and Centenary and Victoria Squares—furnished the necessary physical imagery for place marketing Birmingham as a regional capital. The BMP subsequently developed a repertoire of marketing tools to promote Birmingham as the "Gateway to the Midlands" and "Europe's Meeting Place." The BMP also plays a significant role in the city's inward investment activities.

The Fall and Rise of the Regional Capital Strategy

In 1993 support for the city's regional capital strategy ebbed considerably in the city council, as New Left, ethnic minority, and other factions of the Labour group began to question the rationale of public expenditure to underwrite private enterprise. The city council incurred an enormous debt in building the ICC, which would probably never be recouped because the convention center always ran in the red. In light of these issues, the various discontented factions merged into a loose antiprestige-project coalition that challenged the Knowles ruling bloc (Stewart interview 1994). As noted in chapter 4, this challenge resulted in a political realignment that produced a much more pluralistic Labour group leadership, with Teresa Stewart elected as Council Leader.

The new Labour leadership set about revamping the council's political agenda to emphasize education, social services, and housing. First, the new Labour leaders renounced the prestige project agenda of the previous leadership, which was punctuated by the refusal of the Leader, Stewart, to endorse a Birmingham bid for the Commonwealth games. Second, in fiscal years 1994–1995 and 1995–1996, under severe constraints imposed by central government, all city council service areas incurred deep cuts in expenditures except education, social services, and housing. Education in particular escaped cuts from the budgetary ax.

Prestige Projects Revisited

The realignment of the city council and the ascendance of the back-to-basics leadership in 1993 appeared to sound the death knell for Birmingham's prestige project strategy. In 1995, however, the central government announced plans to fund major projects through the use of National Lottery funds, which revived the quest for building prestige projects. As a consequence, the new Labour leaders grudgingly resigned themselves to another round of prestige projects.

Gearing up the city's progrowth machinery to compete for Lottery funding, city council officers, the chief executives of Birmingham City 2000, the Birmingham Chamber of Industry and Commerce, the Birmingham Marketing Partnership, and others met to develop an overall strategy for a second round of prestige projects. Each of the chief officers and business executives was given responsibility to sponsor particular projects and to ascertain their feasibility and promise. A number of major projects were considered, including a 100,000-seat national super stadium, to be built near the ICC and NIA, and hosting the National Millennium Festival at the NEC, which would finance its expansion (Dignam 1994:3). Once all the proposals were worked up and thoroughly vetted, the local authority and private sector leaders threw their collective weight behind the project proposals to be submitted to the various commissions and councils responsible for lottery funds allocation. None of these prestige projects came to fruition, however, either because they were abandoned as impractical or, in the cases of the national super stadium and the National Millennium Festival, they failed to win Lottery funding.

The Politics of Millennium Point

Despite the progrowth coalition's string of failures, Birmingham's bid to the Millennium Commission, which dispenses lottery funds for major projects that celebrate the coming of the third millennium, resuscitated the city's regional capital strategy (Percival 1995). The city council took the lead on Birmingham's Millennium Fund bid. As had been true of the prestige projects strategy of the progrowth regime in the 1980s, Millennium Point, as the project was named, was controlled at the center of the city council.

To foster ideas, Chief Executive Michael Lyons arranged a competition among the Departments of Economic Development, Planning, and Transport to design projects for the city's Millennium bid. The Planning Department's plan received the nod from the city council leadership, with a combined entertainment, educational, and high-technology industrial development format that garnered broad support within the Labour group. The chief executive's office then took charge of Millennium Point, creating a team of key department directors and various tiers of working groups of officers within the City Council. A subcommittee of the Finance and Management Committee with senior councillors was set up, with the Deputy Leader Bryan Bird assuming a crucial role in winning support for the project. To demonstrate partnership, a steering group was formed, composed of chief officers of the city council and representatives from the University of Central England, KPMG, City 2000 and other businesspeople. Sir Bernard Zissman, the former leader of Conservative Party on the city council and a prominent local businessman, expressed strong interest in the project and was given the remit to raise financial support from the private sector.

Millennium Point features a Discovery Centre for science and technology, a Technology Centre to facilitate technology transfer, research, and development, and a University of the First Age to instruct school children in the areas of science, technology, and design (Birmingham City Council, Public Relations Division n.d.). The Millennium Campus is to be located on a site in Digbeth,[1] an inner city area on the eastern edge of the city center. The area, renamed the Digbeth Millennium Quarter, will be linked to the city center by removing heavily trafficked Masshouse Circus and turning six-lane Moor Street Queensway dual carriageway into a tree-lined boulevard (Birmingham City Council 1996; Austin 1995). The cost of Millennium Point is projected to be £110 million, £50 million of which would be covered by the Millennium Fund grant.

The city's latest flagship project has not always sailed calm waters. Birmingham's Green lobby assailed Millennium Point on the grounds that it glorified science without pointing out the darker side of technological development. Also, the staff of the city's Science and Industry Museum, which would be absorbed into the Discovery Centre, reacted with hostility, bringing their union into the fray. Nearby local authorities also expressed concerns that Birmingham would seek to top slice European funds for the West Midlands to help finance the megaproject. In addition, Planning Committee Chair Stewart Stacey, who was part of the New Left wing of the Labour party, took some political flack from within the Group for teaming up with the Conservative Zissman. Further, the universities that were not to participate in the Millennium Campus activities, Birmingham and Aston, objected to their exclusion.

A final nettlesome issue was funding. Council Leader Stewart stood resolute that the city council would not allocate any of its capital spending to Millennium Point. The city would contribute the land, which the city council owns, and the remainder would be raised from other sources. To make up the difference, the city council entered negotiations with the European Union for a £22 million grant and English Partnerships for a £12.5 million grant. The private sector was expected to finance the remainder through £6 million in sponsorships and an £8 million bank loan (Teasdale 1996b).

By the autumn of 1996 most of the problems had been solved in a fashion typical of Brummie pragmatism. In October 1996 the Millennium Commission approved the £50 million grant for Millennium Point. With the financing in place, a Millennium Point Trust Company was set up and trustees were appointed from Birmingham's power elite. These included the chairman and managing director of Special Computer Holdings, Peter Rigby, as chair, the deputy leader of the city council, Brian Bird, the vice-chancellor of the University of Central England, Dr. Peter Knight, and Roger Dickens of KPMG. The chief executive of Birmingham Heartland Development Corporation, Jim Beeston, was appointed as Millennium Point's chief executive in June 1997, at which time implementation of Birmingham's latest prestige project commenced.

Planning the City of Business for the New Millennium

Birmingham's status as a regional capital is no longer in doubt. The progrowth regime's prestige project strategy of the 1980s and early 1990s laid the groundwork for the city center development boom of the mid-1990s. No longer did Birmingham's governing coalition face the dire prospects of a derelict city center. The new dilemma, in contrast, was how to manage a growing and changing city center economy. This sparked new frictions within Birmingham's governing coalition. Left-leaning councillors, planners, and environmentalists, on one side, endeavored to use strengthened planning powers to create a managed urban space and more pedestrian-oriented city center. Progrowth councillors, economic development officers and business leaders, on the other, remained committed to the regional capital strategy. These conflicts have played out in the arena of city center planning.

In the autumn of 1996, the local media chided the city council for fragmented and ill-conceived city center planning. Reacting to these criticisms, the chief executive of the city council, Lyons, called for a City Centre Symposium to take stock of the progress made since the Highbury symposia, but also to air issues related to city center planning. The city council sponsored the symposium, with some financial contribution from City 2000. Business interests, particularly from the financial and professional services sector, formed a ubiquitous presence among the 200 symposium attendees. Referred to informally as Highbury III, the symposium focused on three primary issues: (1) how to coordinate the Eastside expansion of the city center (toward Digbeth), (2) how to improve transportation in and around and access to the city center, and (3) how to encourage more housing in the city center (Sparks 1997).

The need for coherent city center planning was made poignantly clear in the week of the symposium, when proposals for two massive commercial developments were unveiled. Hampton Trust (property developers) and Carlton Communication announced their intention to develop a £200 million mixed use entertainment and office complex on the site of the Central Television studios on Broad Street near the ICC and Brindley Place (Mowbray 1997). The proposal received mixed reviews. Progrowth city councillors and business leaders lauded the project as an exciting addition to the city center. City planners, who had been in behind-closed-door talks with the developers, viewed the project design, which featured an enclosed shopping and entertainment complex and what would be Birmingham's tallest office tower, as poorly conceived.

The next day, Land Securities (a developer) proposed a £400-million upscale retail complex to replace the existing Martineau Square markets on the east side of the city center (Sparks interview, June 3, 1997). This development, named Martineau Galleries, posed a conundrum for city planners. Shortly before this announcement, the developer (Hammerson) had submitted an application for planning permission to replace the Bull Ring, a dreary 1960s-style shopping center that had been the subject of a string of failed redevelopment proposals over the years. City planners felt that this latest £300-million retail complex would probably materialize, but feared that the city center retail market would not be able to support both retail complexes. Business leaders and the Economic Development Department, on the other hand, welcomed both schemes. Further, the issues of access and available parking became highlighted at the symposium, as the city center was poised to absorb more than £900 million of commercial and residential investment.

Birmingham's policy makers now wrestled with the problem of overdevelopment wrought by the successes of the city's prestige project strategy. In fact, the issue that ignited the most heated debate at the symposium was *access* to the city center. Representatives from the city council tended to favor limiting car access to the city center, enlarging pedestrian areas, and establishing better mass transportation links (Grimley 1997). City center business leaders countered that any transport strategy for the city center should not be perceived as anticar because it would have the effect of driving businesses away from the central business district. The debate itself exposed a major failing of the city council: no transport strategy had ever been written. The outcome of the symposium was that business leaders and city council officials agreed to work through the problems of access in subsequent meetings through the development of a comprehensive transport strategy (Maxwell 1996).

Boston: The Hub of New England

In the 1980s, there was little need to promote Boston's downtown development, as the downtown economy seemed to grow profusely with little encouragement from the government (figure 5.3). But by the 1990s, with the city's downtown economy in shambles, concerns arose about Boston's role as New England's regional economic hub. In response, the Flynn administration convened a series of meetings with government, business, and community leaders to formulate a recipe for revitalizing the local economy (Sege 1991). The new political consensus that emerged from these meetings ranked job creation as the city's highest economic development priority (Gillis interview 1992; Sullivan interview 1992).

In the transition from the Flynn to the Menino administration, commitment to a progrowth agenda strengthened. A key component of the Menino administration's economic development agenda has been to improve relations between city hall and the business community (Pham 1994). On January 17, 1994, Menino, in a speech to a chamber of commerce gathering of 450 business leaders, drew a sharp distinction between his administration and Flynn's: "For years, city government has acted as an opponent of business rather than an ally.... City government has acted as a gatekeeper to slow business down, rather than a responsible partner to

Figure 5.3. Boston skyline. Photo by John S. Klemanski.

find ways to help business grow. That will exist no more" (quoted in Black 1994a). Menino has indeed developed a closer working relationship with the city's business establishment than his predecessor (Sullivan interview 1994; Coughlin interview 1994). But doubts lingered about whether business leaders were equipped to handle a prominent role in development politics.

Power Outage in Boston's Business Leadership

Like many other regional centers in the United States, Boston has witnessed a significant change in the ownership of corporate and financial firms located downtown. Prior to the 1980s, most prominent banks, insurance companies, and corporations were locally based, and these companies supplied the core leadership group of CEOs. During the 1980s and 1990s, due to a rash of mergers and failures, ownership of many of these corporate and financial companies was transferred to holding companies outside the Boston region. According to some, Boston became a "town of branch managers" (Pantridge 1991). And because these firms were no longer locally based, CEO commitment to civic improvement in Boston waned (Coughlin interview 1994; Pantridge 1991; Dreier interview 1992; Ackerman 1996b; Snyder 1988). Consequently, Boston's downtown business leadership experienced what some called a "power failure," as corporate leaders no longer stepped into the breach at critical moments to settle controversial political issues (Pantridge 1991). In the 1990s, a new generation of CEOs began to take up the seats of power vacated by the old guard (Edgerly 1992; Snyder 1988; Ackerman 1996b). To staunch the power drain caused by corporate and financial sector restructuring, these Young Turks turned their attention to shoring up the city's leading business organizations.

The Greater Boston Chamber of Commerce (GBCC) was perceived as disengaged from public affairs in the 1980s, concentrating instead on member services and conferences. In the 1990s, Boston's new corporate leadership reasserted the chamber as a force in city and state politics. In 1992, the former Parks Commissioner under Mayor Flynn and director of the Artery Business Community for three years, William Coughlin, assumed the position of President of the GBCC. In addition, the CEO of Boston Edison, Paul O'Brien, took over as chair of the chamber.

Coughlin, O'Brien, and O'Brien's successor, Fletcher Wiley, a senior partner in a Boston law firm, undertook to hone the chamber into an effective tool for achieving the goal of "international competitiveness" (Coughlin 1992, interview 1994; Klocke interview 1992). To this end, in January 1996, the chamber announced an aggressive agenda to promote economic growth in the region (Muller 1996), but weaknesses in the chamber persisted. For example, after a six-month search for a new president to replace Coughlin, the chamber board vote ended in deadlock (Ackerman 1996b). At this impasse the chamber suspended the search, with Coughlin agreeing to stay on as long as needed. After a protracted internal struggle, a compromise candidate, Paul Guzzi, was finally appointed chamber president in March 1996 (Blanton 1996). In short, the chamber's recently adopted aggressive style belied deep divisions within its leadership.

A second organization slated for renewal was the once awe-inspiring Coordinating Committee, composed of Boston's most influential CEOs and known colloquially as the "Vault" (because it had originally met in the safe of a leading local bank). In the 1980s, the Vault had fallen into disrepair and many of the city's leading corporate managers no longer bothered to attend its monthly meetings (Edgerly interview, August 8, 1992). Heartened by the energetic leadership of O'Brien, however, prominent business executives returned to the Vault after years of absence (O'Brien interview, July 30, 1992). This enthusiasm quickly waned with the departure of O'Brien as chair in 1993, himself a victim of a corporate merger. At this point, Vault members debated whether to disband the group entirely. Urged to continue by other business organizations, such as the Chamber and the Boston Private Industry Council, the new chair of the Vault, Stephen Brown of John Hancock insurance, attempted to rehabilitate the group's organization and agenda (Coughlin interview 1994; Sullivan interview 1994). These renewal efforts ultimately failed, and the legendary Vault closed its door for good in 1997.

Simply put, Boston's downtown business establishment in the 1990s could no longer generate high voltage leadership. In fact, persistent fragmentation within the business community became the subject of a lively debate in a three-hour forum held at the Bank of Boston early in December 1995 (Kindleberger 1995b). Attended by more than 250 business leaders, the panelists and attendees could not even reach a consensus on whether Boston's business leadership had been a failure. The keynote speaker, Harvard Business School professor Rosabeth Moss Kanter, observed that the Boston business community lacked a "grand vision" because of the "rise of growth companies with different priorities" (quoted in Kindleberger 1995b). In other words, if not a power failure, at the very least Boston's business leadership was experiencing a brownout.

Boston's Regional Capital Strategy

Recession and corporate restructuring in the late 1980s and early 1990s threatened to undermine Boston's dominant position as New England's regional capital. In reaction to the twin threats of recession and corporate restructuring, a new governing coalition emerged that developed an aggressive progrowth governing agenda, in which a regional capital strategy formed a key element.

Given the weakness of Boston's business community, regional capital politics of the 1990s produced a coalitional mode of governance. That is, the city's progrowth governing coalition employed bargaining power, forming consensus on a project-by-project basis. An example of this coalitional form of politics was the development of a new Boston Gardens (a sports arena for the Boston Celtics and Bruins), renamed Fleetcenter (Howe 1993b). Begun in 1988, complex negotiations among the developer, state and city officials, and a consortium of banks who proposed to underwrite the $160 million Fleetcenter sports arena broke down at a number of junctures. This stalled the final agreement until early 1993 (Howe 1993a, 1993b; Howe and Lehigh 1993).

Under the Menino administration a more explicit regional capital strategy materialized, as the development of a new convention center was made the showpiece of its economic development agenda. Convention center politics, however, became entangled in a protracted struggle over financing and site location that delayed the project for more than four years.

Megaplex or Megamess?

In January 1993, Governor William Weld proposed building a new state-operated convention center to grab a larger slice of the national and international convention and conference trade. The existing Hynes Convention Center had been judged too small a venue to host many of the larger conventions and conference events. The primary revenue source of funding for the estimated $700-million convention center would be state revenue bonds that would be included in the state's capital budget. The politics of funding the convention center turned rancorous when Governor Weld urged that a stadium be attached to the convention center project as a way to avert the departure of the New England Patriots football club from Massachusetts, a possibility hinted at by the team's management (Howe 1993c). The local press dubbed the combined convention center and sports stadium project the "Megaplex."

Paying for the sports stadium proved to be a major stumbling block, because it brought the total bill for the project to near $1 billion. Governor Weld opposed any kind of tax increase, and looked to private contributions to help finance the Megaplex (Vaillancourt and Canellos 1995). To make the project more politically viable, Mayor Menino proposed a stand-alone convention center paid for by a combination of state and city financing from taxes or fees assessed on the tourism industry (Kindleberger 1994b). The state legislative leadership cast a dubious eye on public funding for the sports stadium portion of the Megaplex, fearing that it would unduly burden the state fisc.

Little agreement on financing the Megaplex existed within the business community, either. First, because they vigorously endorsed the Megaplex, the city's downtown business elite formed an organization, the Massachusetts Alliance for Jobs Growth, to identify private sources of funding for the project (Bailey 1994). This ended in failure, with almost no one else actively supporting the organization's recommendations (Kindleberger 1994a). The tourist industry, in turn, balked at Menino's proposal for assessing substantial levies on tourism businesses, such as hotels and taxis (Kindleberger 1995c). Robert Kraft, owner of the Patriots football club, offered to pick up much of the tab for building a new sports stadium, but not all of it. Moreover, the Patriots preferred to finance stadium construction through a state bond issue, to be repaid over 25 years.

Site selection also posed a major obstacle. Four major sites were under consideration, with different constellations of interests supporting each. The Menino administration backed a South Boston site, located on the edge of the central business district near the waterfront. The South Boston site would allow convention center users ready access to downtown attractions (Vaillancourt 1994; Kindleberger 1995b). Also, much of the land for the proposed South Boston site was already in public hands, which would minimize problems of real estate speculation and relocation. A second site, in Roxbury, was advocated by black community and business leaders, and eventually by the Weld administration. The Roxbury site, located in a largely industrial area known as CrossTown, was promoted by its backers as a means to regenerate one of the city's most depressed inner-city neighborhoods. A group of local developers sought to build the Megaplex on a third site in the Copley-Kenmore area. This group proposed to expand the existing Hynes Convention Center and develop a retail-hotel complex that would be linked to the city's baseball stadium, Fenway Park. A fourth site was targeted by yet another group of developers; it lay near the Boston Harbor in an area adjacent to a major artery (Southeast Expressway) south of the city's downtown (Vaillancourt 1994; Kindleberger 1995c, 1995d).

Both the South Boston and the Copley-Kenmore sites provoked substantial neighborhood opposition. Community leaders from each neighborhood voiced concerns about added congestion, business and residential displacement, rising property values, and threats to historic buildings (Isa and Nelson 1994; Kindleberger 1995d).

In early 1995, to keep the Megaplex alive, the major players held a "summit" meeting and agreed to form a commission with representatives from state and local governments, as well as the business community (Kindleberger 1995a). The purpose of this commission was to work out a compromise among the competing financing and site selection proposals. The commission selected the South Boston site and fashioned a complex package of public and private financing mechanisms. When the commission published its recommendations in April 1995, rather than forging consensus, the financing and site selection proposals reignited the disputes that had been smoldering during the commission's deliberations. Because the compromise plan failed to dampen the tensions within the progrowth coalition, Megaplex financing went down to its third defeat in the state legislature in the autumn of 1995 (Vaillancourt and Kindleberger 1995).

In early 1996, to break the legislative impasse, Menino offered to increase the city's financial contribution. His offer received a warm reception from state legislative leaders (Halbfinger 1996; Zernike 1996), but the absence of a sports stadium caused some consternation among downtown business leaders. Also, tourist industry interests railed against additional levies to be imposed on hotels, taxis, and car rentals.

By December 1996, the original Megaplex proposal had all but expired, as the convention center and sports stadium were now being considered for separate sites. Also, the siting of the convention center had largely been resolved, with the major players agreeing on the South Boston location. Financing continued to defy all efforts at compromise. Governor Weld persisted in his opposition to new taxes, unless they were approved by voters through a local referendum (Vaillancourt 1997b). The new House speaker and fiscal conservative, Thomas Finneran, insisted that at least half of the cost be generated through hotel and restaurant taxes and other tourism related fees. The new Senate president, Thomas Birmingham, like Weld, preferred paying for the convention center through state-issued general obligation bonds, but was willing to meet Finneran halfway on new taxes (Vaillancourt 1996). Hoteliers conceded to a 1 percent increase in hotel room taxes, but dug in against anything higher (Ackerman 1997). The Massachusetts Restaurant Association similarly opposed additional meal taxes.

On February 21, 1997, after nearly two years and $4 million in research and promotional costs, Kraft abandoned his campaign to build the New England Patriots stadium in Boston (Cassidy 1997a). He acknowledged that stiff opposition by South Boston residents and politicians had thwarted his plans to locate the stadium near the proposed convention center site. Mayor Menino, appearing pleased, reiterated an offer of a South Bay site, but promised no immediate assistance in finding another Boston location for the football stadium. Indeed, Menino chortled, "From here on, it's about the convention center" (Cassidy 1997b).

In March 1997, a second consultant's report was published. It predicted that the convention center would generate 61 percent more in revenues than had been forecast by an earlier study (Vaillancourt 1997a). In light of this good news, the mayor tendered an offer for the city to pay up to $125 million to purchase the 60-acre site in South Boston (Vaillancourt 1997c). The amount was capped at $125 million to safeguard the city's excellent bond ratings. To pay off the debt, the city would earmark anticipated increases in hotel tax revenues produced by growth in convention trade business. Leasing of city-owned land near the proposed convention center would provide an additional source of debt service revenues.

Cheered by Menino's offer of $125 million in city money for the project, Governor Weld filed a bill in May 1997 that detailed financing arrangements for the $700 million convention center (Vaillancourt and Chacon 1997). Business groups, including major hoteliers, heralded Weld's bill as a major breakthrough. But high hopes were dashed when, only moments after Weld's announcement, Finneran proclaimed that the city must increase its share to about $200 million. Also, although Weld's bill stipulated that any tax increases would be subject to voter approval, this provision was quickly dropped (Vaillancourt 1997a).

Once again Menino rose to the occasion by proposing to sell 260 new taxicab medallions to raise an additional $20 million for purchase of the convention center site (Anand 1997b). In response, Finneran stood by his $200 million figure, contending that the city should pay for site clearance and preparation as well as business relocation costs. This time a small group of Boston's business leaders, headed by BankBoston, came to the rescue with an offer of $20 million in private financing to close the gap between Menino's proposed $145 million and Finneran's new demand of $205 million from the city (Cassidy and Anand 1997). Finneran acknowledged the effort, but insisted that the $20 million could not be deducted from the city's contribution, which meant that a wide financing gap remained. The city then upped its ante to $150 million, to which Finneran in turn expressed a willingness to compromise at $160 million, with the proviso that the city assume half the funding burden in the event that costs exceed the projected $700 million (Vaillancourt and Anand 1997).

After a session of horse trading between the mayor and the House Speaker, Finneran removed a small, notched parcel from the site to lower the overall cost of purchasing the land (Cassidy and Vaillancourt 1997). The city's contribution was set at $157.8 million, and the convention center funding bill sailed through the House, winning a lopsided majority on July 15, 1997 (Vaillancourt 1997d). But this did not quite end the tale of the convention center, as the bill passed by the Senate Finance Committee excluded some of the critical compromises reached in the House bill (Finucane 1997). After several months of negotiations, Finneran and Birmingham ironed out differences between House and Senate bills, with the convention center funding legislation passing both chambers in early November (Flint 1997a).

Bristol: Capital of the West

At the beginning of the 1990s, the Bristol City Council defiantly resisted the Conservative government's efforts to foster entrepreneurship. Old guard Labour and many New Left leaders remained steadfastly committed to a philosophy of municipal socialism, viewing partnerships with business leaders with great suspicion. But state restructuring made such posturing increasingly anachronistic. By the mid-1990s, these very same Labour politicians openly embraced a regional capital strategy and entered into a raft of partnerships with business elites to carry it out.

Get Bristol Moving: The Politics of Partnership

Generally speaking, it was the younger, better-educated members of the city council Labour leadership who had become inured to the necessity of coalition politics. As the Planning Committee Chair, Andrew May, explained in an August 1, 1995, interview:

> I think the perception of partnership in the city has changed in the last few years quite dramatically in attitude as well as action. There has been a lot of shift towards a kind of bowing to the inevitable, perhaps from some peoples' point of view, that this is the way forward in terms of the city council forming alliances with others. I think that the recognition that this process has some merit in itself, that the city forms powerful alliances of interests, which have helped reposition the city itself to bid for funding, broker various sets of relationships in the city. And we can also bring to the process things that other partners can't, like legitimacy or leadership.

Labour politicians finally acquiesced to the reality that, in order to escape irrelevance in local politics, the city council needed to engage in a partnership politics while at the same time retaining its legitimacy as Bristol's democratically elected governing body.

Before the politics of partnership could be realized, Bristol's business leaders would need to put their own house in order. The Bristol Chamber of Industry and Commerce had been a marginal player in Bristol City politics for years. With a membership composed largely of small and medium-sized businesses, its activities were confined almost entirely to the provision of member services. The city council rarely if ever called upon the chamber to take part in strategic decisions, leading chief executives of the region's leading firms to disparage the chamber as a social club and, perhaps worse, politically effete.

Bristol's corporate elite, dissatisfied with both the city council's development plans and the chamber's lack of leadership and drive, founded The Bristol Initiative (TBI) in the late 1980s (Brien 1990). Corporate executives from 90 of the largest employers in Avon County joined the initiative. There was also representation from local government, including the city council chief executive, the Bristol Development Corporation, the Avon

County Council, the University of the West of England, and the Avon and Somerset Constabulary. Bristol University's vice chancellor and the Bishop of Bristol also served on the board.

In 1990, the TBI board appointed John Savage as chief executive. Savage worked tirelessly behind the scenes to establish TBI's credibility by moving a number of community-based projects forward. These projects ranged from a small but innovative housing scheme using modular units for the homeless, to boosting Bristol '97, a year-long series of events to celebrate the 500th anniversary of John Cabot's voyage from Bristol to America (Rylance 1994). Savage also gained the trust of many local Labour politicians by fighting alongside city planners against a large-scale retail scheme undertaken by the Bristol Development Corporation known as Quay Point, which threatened the city's traditional Broadmead shopping district. And, to unify the city's business community and fashion it into a powerful force in local development politics, the new corporate power elite negotiated a merger between the Bristol Chamber of Commerce and the Bristol Initiative in April 1993. In a July 7, 1993, interview Chris Geohegan, the managing director of British Aerospace's Aerobus division, related how the union between the Chamber and Initiative was arranged:

> The Initiative brought resources and energy to the nearly politically moribund Chamber, although the two organizations have maintained somewhat separate identities under the shell of the new organizational structure, the Bristol Chamber of Commerce and Initiative. The Initiative's energetic chief executive, John Savage, was installed as the new chief executive of the Bristol Chamber of Commerce and Initiative, and he has sought to use the new amalgamation to present a single voice for business community in city affairs.

The moves toward coalitional politics were, in part, facilitated by a booster campaign launched in 1992 by one of the city's local newspapers under the banner, "Get Bristol Moving." While business leaders and politicians were maneuvering behind the scenes to set things in motion, the *Western Daily Press* (1992) published a series of articles that began: "Starting today... the great debate on the future of a city crying out for leadership. This is a call to action. A call that should not go unheeded by anyone who cares for the proud, historic and uniquely resourceful city of Bristol." The series surveyed civic leaders on such issues as developing a single vision for the city and the need to strengthen Bristol's position as a regional capital and cultural center. The intent of the Get Bristol Moving campaign was to mobilize public opinion and to galvanize Bristol's civic leadership into concerted action on city center regeneration, cultural development, and tourism (see *Western Daily Press* 1992).

This call to arms produced an unprecedented period of cooperation in Bristol. Myriad interlocking partnerships appeared almost overnight. Many of these partnerships focused on rejuvenating Bristol's city center economy, and, as a consequence, they converged into a regional capital coalition. In particular, the Harbourside partnership and Bristol 2000 have undertaken the development of Bristol's regional capital megaprojects on the Floating Harbour. Other key partnerships in Bristol's regional capital alliance included the Broadmead Company, the Tourism Forum, and the Bristol Cultural Development Partnership.

By the 1990s, competition from suburban shopping centers threatened the viability of the city's major central area retail district, which was owned primarily by the city council and known as Broadmead. Also, as government restraints severely pinched the City Council's financial capacity, managing the Broadmead Shopping Centre became increasingly difficult. In 1995, the city council, Broadmead's major retailers, and the Bristol Chamber formed the Broadmead Company to revitalize, market, and manage the Broadmead shopping area (Savage interview 1995). The city council holds three of the ten seats on Broadmead's board of directors, with the others filled by the major landholders and the chamber. The chief executive of the chamber, John Savage, and the chair of city council Land and Buildings Committee serve as co-chairs on the board, and Marks and Spencer, which had recently opened a large store in Broadmead, seconded a senior executive to the Broadmead Company for two years to serve as the directing manager (Savage interview 1995). Marks and Spencer hoped to use a Broadmead renewal program as a blueprint for revitalizing other lagging urban retail centers (Edwards 1995b). The City Council and the Chamber jointly commissioned a £75,000 marketing study to assess the depth of Broadmead problems and to determine its catchment area (Savage interview 1995). Based on this study, the Broadmead partnership began implementing a £5.5 million strategy to upgrade pedestrian areas, open up new retail space, create a center for children, and lower the cost of parking in Broadmead (Edwards 1995a).

Bristol's tourist industries emerged as major sectors of the local economy, adding roughly £300 million per annum (Onions 1996). In the 1980s, the City Council Labour group had evinced little enthusiasm for the promotion of tourism in Bristol (Reid and Shorney 1992). But in the throes of a recession and with clear indications that the region's defense industry was in trouble, the city council warmed to the idea of promoting tourism, and joined with tourist industry representatives and the Bristol Chamber to form the Bristol Tourism Forum (BTF) in August 1993. The BTF formulated a tourism strategy that set out two primary objectives: increase the number of visitors from inside and outside the United Kingdom and attract a larger share of the United Kingdom's conference trade (*Western Daily Press* 1993). In addition, the city council increased its own role in promoting tourism, producing a Bristol Tourism Strategy in 1995, and launching a series of campaigns to boost tourism in 1996 (Onions 1996).

The city's fledgling progrowth coalition came to recognize that the city's cultural institutions and historic built environment furnished valuable assets for regenerating and diversifying the city's economic base. Culture as economic development constituted a crucial element of Bristol's regional capital strategy (Bassett 1993). Bristol's reputation as the West of England's center for the arts and culture, however, had tarnished in the early 1990s, as its premiere arts institutions suffered from neglect and underfinancing. To address these problems, the city council, the South West Arts Council, and the Bristol Initiative came together as a loose confederation to promote Bristol as a *City of Culture* in the United Kingdom and overseas. To pave the way for action, the three partners commissioned a £25,000 study by the consulting firm of Boyden Southwood to plumb the depths of the problems with the city's cultural and arts institutions and to formulate a cultural development strategy (*Western Daily Press* 1992). The Boyden study recommended that a cultural development strategy be devised that built on Bristol's strengths, including existing arts and tourism attractions and the large media industry presence in the city (Boyden Southwood 1992). The report also suggested that a public-private cultural development steering group be organized to coordinate arts and tourism activities and projects in Bristol, with a secretariat attached to carry out decisions made by the group.

In October 1992, the partners formally approved the cultural strategy and in April 1993 formed the Bristol Cultural Development Partnership (BCDP). The board of directors of the BCDP consists of five representatives from the city council, three from the South West Arts Action Group, three from the Bristol Chamber, and several from Bristol's arts community. Once all parties had agreed to the cultural strategy, the partnership recruited a head of cultural planning and jointly put up £65,000 annually to fund promotional activities (Kelly interview 1995). The city council has contributed £25,000 each year, and has supplied office space for the BCDP's operations, while the other two partners provided £20,000 each annually to the BCDP's core funding. To widen the partnership network, representatives from other culturally oriented organizations were added to the BCDP board, including the Avon Community Arts Network, the Compact for the Arts in Bristol and Avon, a local arts cooperative called Artspace, and the University of the West of England. The city's directors of Leisure and Planning serve as technical advisers to the BCDP (Kelly interview July 12, 1995).

Andrew Kelly was appointed Head of Cultural Planning on April 1, 1993, with the responsibilities of mediating between art funders and providers, raising money for cultural development initiatives, lobbying government and other agencies on behalf of Bristol's cultural institutions, and promoting cultural development projects (Bristol City Council 1993; Kelly interview July 12, 1995). Kelly clearly conceived of cultural development as a tool for place marketing, and has plunged the partnership into a number of initiatives to improve Bristol's edge as the cultural capital of the West. These have included submission of applications to become a Cultural City in the Eurocities Network and a joint bid with Bath for a £250,000 grant to host the City of Photography and Electronic Image celebration in 1998, sponsored by the Arts Council under its Great Britain's Arts 2000 program (Bristol City Council 1993; Rylance 1994; Savage interview, July 5, 1994). The City of Photography bid ultimately failed.

English Partnerships assumed responsibility for the defunct Bristol Development Corporation (BDC) in 1996. Relations between the city council and the BDC had been extremely contentious, with the city council opposing almost all the BDC's initiatives. When English Partnerships took charge of the unfinished projects left by the defunct BDC, however, a spirit of cooperation replaced the old animosity. Although not a partnership per se, English Partnerships became a willing and active supporter of Bristol's regional capital strategy.

The Politics of Waterside Redevelopment

The various elements of the city's regional capital strategy—cultural, commercial, and residential development—converged in Bristol's Harbourside development initiative. The focal point of waterside redevelopment was Cannon's Marsh, astride Bristol's Floating Harbour and an important part of Bristol's proud maritime history since the eighteenth century (see figure 5.4). In the postwar period, however, the Floating Harbour's economic functions became obsolete, and Cannon's Marsh slipped into dereliction. Redevelopment planning for Cannon's Marsh has stirred up a hornet's nest of political controversy and animosity since the 1960s.

Figure 5.4. Bristol's Floating Harbour. Photo by Alan DiGaetano.

By the mid-1990s, the political climate in Bristol had calmed considerably, and planning around Cannon's Marsh clearly reflected this change. In 1993, the landowners involved in Cannon's Marsh, including the Bristol City Council, Lloyds Bank, British Gas, British Rail, and the JT Group, formed a partnership to regenerate the area. The creation of the Harbourside Partnership, as it became known, was a response to the previous difficulties of reaching agreement among the landholders. The partners also invited the Bristol Chamber of Commerce and Initiative to join the Harbourside Strategy Group, which was responsible for planning and developing Cannon's Marsh. Ironing out differences among the members of the Harbourside Partnership consumed more than a year of delicate negotiations. In June 1993, the partnership hired a firm of chartered surveyors, Drivers Jonas, to craft a development framework for the 66-acre Harbourside site. The partners rejected Drivers Jonas' initial proposal, which had to be reworked significantly (May interview 1994), but the revised development framework, which envisioned a mixed use development with an aquarium, an office complex, and market rate housing, was finally approved in early 1995 (Kershaw interview 1994; May interview 1994).

The partnership unveiled its £500 million blueprint for regenerating the Cannon's Marsh and Wapping Wharf in April 1995 (Edwards 1995b). Under the Harbourside Planning Brief, approved in May 1995, Cannon's Marsh was slated for an aquarium, 950 housing units and 613,000 square feet of office space, a 600-space underground parking facility, and two public squares and walkways (Bristol 2000 n.d.; Bristol City Council 1995; Edwards 1995b). To attract office and other commercial development to Harbourside, as noted, city planners agreed to lighten onerous development burdens on private developers. City planners prepared the groundwork for development with pre-established planning permissions, decisions on listed structures, and remediation of polluted land (Kershaw interview 1995). This new, prepackaged planning approach streamlined the development process for large-scale projects to make Bristol more competitive with its chief rivals, including London and Plymouth (May interview 1995). This plan was again revised to accommodate several new flagship initiatives. Savage of the chamber and Kelly of the BCDP urged the Harbourside Partnership to transform part of Cannon's Marsh into a cultural quarter, which led to the abandonment of Drivers Jonas' aquarium idea, which mimicked the one in Baltimore's Inner Harbor. In its stead, Kelly proposed a science-oriented theme and prepared a feasibility study to make his case.

Once consensus was reached on the overall framework for Harbourside, the city council and BCDP asked the chairman of the newly privatized Wessex Water company, Nicholas Hood, to coordinate a Millennium fund bid for the proposed science projects. Hood formed a working group of chartered surveyors, accountants, and other professionals to draw up plans and secure financing to move the science center project forward (Kelly interview 1996). Out of these informal arrangements was born Bristol 2000. A public-private partnership, Bristol 2000 united the Bristol City Council, Wessex Water, Investment South West Arts, and Bristol Chamber of Commerce and Initiative (Hood interview 1995).

In April 1995, Bristol 2000 submitted its £41 million bid (half the projected cost) to the Millennium Commission to develop a triad of science-related discovery centers (Bristol City Council 1995). The Wildlife Discovery Center is billed as an "electronic zoo," using audiovisual technology, such as virtual reality, to inform visitors about animals in their natural habitat (Bristol City Council 1994:3). Attached to the Wildlife Discovery Center would be a large-format cinema that would show wildlife films. Finally, Bristol Exploratory, a hands-on science museum currently located adjacent to the Temple Meads railway station, would be renamed Science World and relocated to a Harbourside site to complete the triad. These science discovery center projects have been designed to draw on Bristol's large media industry presence and the existence of local expertise in wildlife film production (de Groot interview 1995; Hood interview 1995).

On another front, Kelly implored the Harbourside Partnership to build a replacement for the city's poorly designed concert hall, Colston Hall at the Cannon's Marsh site (Kelly interviews 1995, and 1996; Savage interview 1995). The city council initially sought to retain control over the Center for Performing Arts (CPA) project, but Kelly and others again convinced them that a partnership arrangement would prove more efficacious. In 1996, a Performance World Trust was set up under the umbrella of Bristol 2000 to prepare the Arts Council bid and muster support for the CPA in the city's business community. Louis Sherwood, the chairman of the HTV Group (a regional television company) and a member of the fabled Merchant Venturers, was appointed as chair of the Performance World Trust board of directors. The proposed CPA is to include a concert hall with seating for 2,300 that can be enlarged for major events and a second auditorium equipped "with flexible staging suitable for more intimate and experimental presentations" (Bristol 2000 n.d.).

Financial arrangements for the three science worlds and the CPA were quite complex, and failure to win the Millennium and Arts Council bids would scuttle implementation of the Harbourside plan. The total cost of the Three Worlds development project is estimated at £130 million, with Millennium Fund and Art Council grants to cover about half. The remainder of the financing was to come from the Bristol City Council, English Partnerships, the landholders in the Harbourside Partnership, the Single Regeneration Budget, a Derelict Land Grant, and, interestingly, the Smithsonian Institute. English Partnerships agreed to provide £16 million in long-term loans for front-end funding of the development costs (Welfare interview 1996).

In the midst of all this cooperation, some opposition to Harbourside percolated up from the city's growth management movement. At a public hearing in April 1995, the Bristol Civil Society and other amenity groups assailed the Harbourside plan as allowing too much space for office development (Bristol City Council 1995; Edwards 1995b). Andrew May, the Planning Committee Chair, rebuffed the attack by countering that it was time to "get real" and recognize that the office development was essential to pay for the leisure and infrastructure portions of the Harbourside plan (Bristol City Council 1995; Edwards 1995b). May, who had been a ready ally of amenity groups in the past, assumed a more pragmatic view on center city regeneration.

By 1997, many of the pieces of the £400 million Harbourside regeneration program had fallen into place. Bristol's Millennium bid won final approval in the summer of 1996 for the £41 million in matching funds to finance Wild Screen and Discovery Worlds. Bristol 2000 appointed a director, Gillian Thomas, to oversee the £82 million development project. A Bristol 2000 bureaucracy of 75 staff members was pulled together; implementation of the two science worlds was under way; and the Performance World Trust selected a futuristic glass and steel design for the £98.5 million CPA, on which the local press immediately conferred the dubious title, "Exploding Greenhouse" (Harrison 1996). The project also successfully bid for millennium funds from the National Lottery (Bristol City Council 1999). In the meantime, English Partnerships agreed to provide £21 million for developing the public squares and walkways for the areas in and around the CPA and the two science worlds in Harbourside (Bristol Harbourside 1997).

Detroit: The Renaissance City

Detroit has been known as America's automobile capital for most of this century. As the city's fortunes declined, Detroit's civic and political leaders turned increasingly to a regional capital strategy, beginning in the 1970s, that emphasized redevelopment of the city's riverfront and the Woodward Avenue corridor.

Renaissance Politics and Regime Formation in the 1970s

In contrast to Birmingham and Boston, Detroit's corporate elite, rather than its political leadership, launched the city's regional capital strategy in the early 1970s. The premier private sector redevelopment organization in Detroit since its inception in 1970 has been Detroit Renaissance, Inc., a nonprofit organization comprised of the CEOs of Detroit-area businesses. This group was meant to be the organizational vehicle that would implement the redevelopment strategy of the local business leadership (Detroit Renaissance, Inc. 1990). The group's members have been involved in a number of revitalization efforts: physical and economic planning, land banking through a special fund, beautification projects, and technical assistance to neighborhood organizations. Detroit Renaissance was also the incubator for the defining project of this era of Detroit's redevelopment—the Renaissance Center.

The Renaissance Center (RenCen) originally was a 33-acre complex that included the 73-story Westin Hotel, four 39-story office towers, plus retail stores and restaurants, located on the Detroit River near Woodward and Jefferson Avenues—the symbolic heart of downtown Detroit (figure 5.5). A later development (Phase II) added two office towers to the complex. The project resulted mostly from the efforts of Detroit Renaissance,

Figure 5.5. Detroit riverfront and skyline. Photo by John S. Klemanski.

and specifically Henry Ford II, who put together most of the private financing for the project. Ford leveraged contributions from other business interests, committed over $81 million of Ford Motor Company money, and convinced a consortium of banks to lend the group another $200 million for construction purposes (Jones 1983:182–184). The RenCen and Detroit as the Renaissance City, became symbols of the city's redevelopment, tourism, and convention trade marketing strategy.

When Coleman A. Young was first elected mayor in 1973, he brought a strong congruence of interests between local political and business leaders regarding Detroit's regional capital strategy. Young's first campaign advocated a riverfront development strategy that already had been articulated by the private sector's Detroit Renaissance a few years earlier. Young proved an able coalition builder, forging a formidable progrowth alliance with the city's downtown business leadership that preempted most opposition and kept most other issues off the local agenda. Although his labor union organizing days had left him wary of business and he remained concerned about a white-dominated business elite in an increasingly black city, he worked with a small group of trusted investors, as well as business organizations such as Detroit Renaissance. He also reorganized the local bureaucracy to create a support system that could implement the emerging regime's strategy.

Young's alliances extended high up into the intergovernmental system to then-President Jimmy Carter and Michigan Governor William Milliken. Young recounted his relationship with Milliken during the mayor's first term of office:

> Hard times have a way of encouraging a mayor's trust in bipartisan coalitions. Although it startled many, I had to deal immediately with Republicans or watch my city fade from the map, block by forsaken block. I also had to deal with the state of Michigan, because it was obvious that Lansing would have to participate somehow in the recovery of Detroit. Fortunately, the governor of Michigan at the time was the finest and fairest the state has had, despite his party affiliation. Bill Milliken was not your typical Republican. . . . Milliken's social policy more closely resembled a Democrat's. . . . It included . . . an active urban agenda." (Young and Wheeler 1994:218)

Tensions in Regional Capital Politics: 1981–1993

The economic, intergovernmental, and political context of Detroit in the 1980s was far worse than in the 1970s, precipitating a fiscal crisis that was avoided only by lobbying the state legislature for a local income tax, campaigning for passage of a local referendum, and restructuring city labor union contracts (Mallett 1989). Because of the difficulties facing the auto manufacturers during the early 1980s, they tended to play a smaller role in the city's redevelopment during this time, and their leaders took relatively secondary roles in the various redevelopment organizations. Peter Stroh, chair of the Stroh Brewery Company and a native Detroiter, felt that much of Detroit's problems were due to diminishing corporate and mayoral involvement. As Stroh explained in a March 4, 1993, interview:

> My understanding is that the mayor in the past ten years has withdrawn. At the same time, an awful lot of business leadership in this city, particularly the auto companies, has withdrawn. Well, the other forces at work that we ought to talk about is the fact that Detroit's companies are no longer led by Detroiters, they're led by professionals who may come from anywhere. They don't have the longstanding ties to Detroit that somebody like Henry Ford II might have.

These problems also reached deep down into city hall. For many years, the mayor had been able to construct a rolling majority of support on the city council, but opposition to some projects and to his secretive style began to create more open conflict. Near the end of Mayor Young's final term, Mel Ravitz (interview 1992) explained the mayoral-council dynamic:

> We have a nonharmonious relationship between the mayor and at least some of us on the city council. If things were different we could more easily talk about policy-making in Detroit. With the mayor's executive power to make and implement policy, the council can try to make contrary policy, but we don't have the ability to implement it. Sometimes we try to advise, recommend, urge, beg, and plead with the mayor to adopt a different policy than what he proposed, without much success. One of the things that now seems to be the norm, is that we go to court to resolve our differences.

The progrowth alliance suffered for other reasons as well. Mayor Young came under a series of FBI investigations for alleged kickbacks on city contracts involving the Vista waste hauling company and Magnum Oil supply company. Although no indictments were ever returned, the mayor grew more hostile to the media, the federal government, and perhaps most importantly, a number of private sector leaders who did not come to his defense as he thought they should. As he later explained, "I don't think there's any doubt that from that time on [in 1980] I sort of had a fortress mentality. I was shocked to the extent that these [expletive] would go. I viewed [the investigations] as an attack on me" (Pepper 1996a:1C).

Local economic development decision making, then, was becoming stultified as a consequence of these events. The increasing personalization and secrecy made the mayor even more central to deciding which developers would be favored with the necessary local government cooperation on land siting, building permits, gap financing, and tax incentives. What little opposition to this increasingly secret style was marginalized and handled by the mayor and his staff. Most of the vocal opposition centered on aspects of specific projects, not the city's overall development strategy. The progrowth alliance maintained its focus on downtown-riverfront developments — the major differences were that the group was smaller than it had been in the 1970s and regional capital politics had drifted into a coalition mode of governance.

Riverfront Developments: 1981–1993

Detroit's regional capital strategy continued into the 1980s, but it lacked the purchase of a defining project like the RenCen to generate optimism and enthusiasm. Nonetheless, a number of developments moved through the pipeline to help Detroit compete for the tourist and convention trade.

These included construction of the Joe Louis Arena and expansion of Cobo Hall (now the Cobo Exhibition-Convention Center). Other developments occurred in the 1980s, including Stroh River Place and Harbortown, both located east of the RenCen on the river as mixed-use developments anchored by a hotel or upscale residential development.

Stroh River Place became the new site for the Stroh Brewery Company headquarters, whose former brewery and offices had been located on Gratiot Avenue. This development in turn spurred some projects in the area between it and the RenCen called the Warehouse District. Stroh River Place was meant to be a "town within a town," as it included an entire range of facilities and an upscale restaurant, along with the residential and hotel development phase. The $159 million complex even included a Detroit police ministation onsite. Located about a mile east of the RenCen, the complex was opened in 1985, with additional phases completed after that. Peter Stroh showed his willingness to invest in the city through this development, as well as a later office project called Brewery Park, built on the site of the old Stroh brewery.

The 50-acre, $250 million Harbortown development was financed by the real estate arms of the local gas utility company, ANR (American Natural Resources) Development Corporation and MichCon (Michigan Consolidated Gas Company) Development Corporation. Harbortown, located about a half mile east of the RenCen, was also meant to be a self-contained project, with residential developments (a high-rise apartment building, plus two-story condominiums), along with a shopping center and a boat marina.

The Rebirth of Renaissance Politics: 1993–1997

With Dennis Archer's election as mayor in 1993, and with new faces in city government and in the executive suites of local businesses, a re-formation of Detroit's progrowth coalition appeared to occur. The Detroit Economic Growth Corporation, led since 1995 by C. Beth DunCombe, a longtime civic activist, prominent local attorney, and Archer's sister-in-law, maintained its importance in the mayor's administration. DunCombe's influence in development policy casts a wide net, as she serves as co-chair of the Detroit–Wayne County Stadium Authority and co-chair of the mayor's advisory committee on casino gambling, in addition to her presidency of the DEGC.

Change, or at least the appearance of change, came quickly after Archer's election. The local media adored Archer's more accessible, open style, contrasting it favorably to Mayor Young's secretiveness and hostility

(Costello 1994:1A). Under Mayor Archer, the city also reviewed its marketing strategy. Early on, Archer began offering his vision of Detroit as a "world-class city," focusing on the economic development investments made during his term of office. By the end of his first term, Detroit as a world-class city was very much a part of Archer's public speeches and of the city's publications (City of Detroit Communication and Creative Services Department 1997). The city boasted that between January 1994 (when Archer took office) and April 1997, about $5.5 billion had been invested or committed to the city. The range of investments illustrates more of a regional capital approach by the city than ever before: 20 commercial projects valued at over $630,000,000, 15 industrial projects valued at over $73,000,000, 18 institutional projects valued at over $280,000,000, 15 office projects valued at over $480,000,000, 20 residential projects valued at about $113,000,000, and 48 projects associated with the empowerment zone, with a value of over $3.9 billion (City of Detroit June 1997). In addition, the city launched a $25-million advertising campaign (targeting magazines and newspapers) promoting the city with the slogan "It's a great time in Detroit." Some local businesses adopted the slogan in their own advertising as well (Wilson 1997).

Rebirth also seemed to be occurring in Detroit's business circles. A number of new board members joined Detroit Renaissance during the 1990s, including Michael Ilitch, CEO of Little Caesar's pizza company and owner of the Detroit Tigers (baseball) and Detroit Red Wings (hockey). Ilitch had endeared himself to city boosters with his involvement in the two teams that remained in Detroit (the Piston basketball and Lions football teams moved to Pontiac in the 1970s), and because he moved his corporate headquarters back to Detroit and renovated a 5,000-seat former entertainment jewel, the Fox Theater. Associated projects (restaurants, theaters) near the Fox came to be called Foxtown. Another new board member was Dave Bing, the owner of Bing Steel and a former star of the Pistons basketball team. In addition, longtime Detroit Renaissance President Robert McCabe was replaced, first by Robert Keller, then by Michael Glusac (in 1995), and then by former Michigan House Speaker Paul Hillegonds (in 1997).

With those changes in the Detroit Renaissance Board of Directors, a new mission statement was created, and Detroit Renaissance decided to stop sponsoring events (such as the Grand Prix), and focus their CEO energies more directly on Detroit's redevelopment. Some of the newer members had begun to question the emphasis on sponsoring events that the organization had taken for the most part in its recent history. As Glusac explained in an October 2, 1995, interview,

> The impetus to review the organization's mission and goals came mostly from the younger CEOs on the Board. They felt the vision ought to be altered, or they should simply turn the work product over to their vice-presidents. If we had stayed in the "events" business, there would have been no need for the CEOs of major corporations to continue to spend time with these matters. This wasn't a proper use of the talent we had on the board.

Consequently, Detroit Renaissance created a number of spin-off organizations and activities, including the Detroit Investment Fund and the Greater Downtown Partnership.

In October 1994, the organization announced its commitment to create the Detroit Investment Fund, which would provide approximately $52 million in venture capital for investments in Detroit. Approximately $20 million of the total was pledged by the big three automakers (Pepper 1994:1A). The private, for-profit fund, established to help in job creation and economic development, called on investments made by the 42 member companies of Detroit Renaissance, Inc. (Gargaro 1995:18). The fund is similar to Cleveland's Development Partnership Fund, raised by Cleveland Tomorrow, the organization that is that city's counterpart to Detroit Renaissance. The Detroit Investment Fund is managed by Detroit Ventures, Inc., and by July 31, 1995, all of the targeted $52 million committed to the fund had been received from members (Glusac 1995).

Three aspects of the fund make it unique among other efforts to rebuild Detroit. First, it involves only private money, rather than contributions from such traditional sources as public employee pension funds. Second, it is a for-profit enterprise, and would thus become a partner in the ventures in which it invested. Third, the fund's range of activities will extend beyond previous efforts to include investments in real estate developments, high-tech or industrial parks, community development banks, and many other ventures.

A clear signal that the city's regional capital regime was reemerging was the creation of the Greater Downtown Partnership (GDP). In cooperation with Mayor Archer, the business community and Detroit Renaissance formed the GDP in 1996. The group's members included representatives from the big three automakers, foundations, banks, corporations, and the city government (Oguntoyinbo 1996:1B). The group was to focus on retail developments within the Central Business District, and to acquire property, provide loans, address the problem of the long-vacant Hudson's Building, and generally improve the Woodward Avenue corridor. Members provided the initial $4 million in seed money, and Lawrence Marantette, a vice president of community and environmental affairs for ANR Pipeline Co. and President of ANR Real Estate Co. (associated with the local gas utility company), was appointed full-time president and CEO of the organization.

The resurrection of Detroit's regional capital regime was accompanied by a lineup of megaprojects that would reclaim the limelight that had been lost in the 1980s. These included three gambling casinos, side-by-side sports stadiums for the professional baseball and football teams, along with ancillary restaurant and entertainment developments. Expansion of the Detroit Medical Center and development of Orchestra Place, a site next to the historic and renovated Orchestra Hall and across from the Medical Center, also proceeded in the mid-to-late 1990s.

Playing Hardball: The Politics of Sports Stadiums

Among the projects in the works were new side-by-side stadiums that would bring the baseball Tigers (from the team's old location just west of downtown) and the football Lions (from the city of Pontiac) together in the Foxtown area of the city. The initial costs were projected at $240 million for a 42,000-seat baseball stadium and $225 million for a 65,000- to 75,000-seat football stadium. With parking, offices, and practice facilities added to that, the total projections were $505 million, with various public contributions expected to pay about half (48 percent) of the costs (Lam and Fricker 1996:1A). The state of Michigan promised $50 million in support for infrastructure improvements and land acquisition through its Michigan Strategic Fund (now called Michigan Renaissance Fund). Many other details need to be worked out, including the actual purchase and relocation of businesses on the proposed site of the stadiums, various contributions by the state, county, and local agencies (such as the Downtown Development Authority), and voter passage of tourist taxes that would help pay for stadium construction (through increases in hotel and motel room taxes, rental car taxes, and taxi fares).

The side-by-side stadium concept designed to bring the Detroit Lions football team back to Detroit from northern Oakland County's Pontiac Silverdome was considered a major victory for Detroit and Archer, and a bit of a surprise. The Lions were the first Detroit professional sports team to leave the city (in the mid-1970s), and it had received substantial local and state funding to construct the 80,000-seat Pontiac Silverdome. Much of the credit in securing the commitment of the Lions to move back downtown went to Archer and to Lions Vice Chairman William Clay Ford Jr., part of the younger generation of the Ford family that owns the Lions football team (Pepper 1996b:1D). Indeed, a *Detroit Free Press* headline heralded Archer's leadership in swinging the new sports stadium deal, announced on August 21, 1996, as a "Team effort."

Ground was officially broken for construction of Tiger Stadium in September 1997. The Lions deal will take longer to develop, and the team still needs to work with the city of Pontiac and the Silverdome, as they have a lease and commitment to play there until the year 2004. Regardless of those possible impediments, Archer's stock went up tremendously after the sports stadiums deal was announced. In addition, a number of ancillary investments near the site of the stadiums were announced shortly after that.

Gambling on Detroit

In November 1996, Michigan voters approved Proposal E, which allowed the construction of three gambling casinos in Detroit. Given the ballot language and a subsequent ordinance passed unanimously by the city council in June 1997, preferences would be given to two operators with local connections, Atwater Casino Group and Greektown LLC (DeHaven 1997:1A). Mayor Archer selected Atwater and Greektown, along with MGM Grand, as the three finalists.

Casino gambling as an economic development strategy has a long and controversial history in Detroit (see Rich 1990). While local voters consistently opposed casinos through the 1970s and 1980s, Mayor Young's efforts to use casino gambling as an economic development strategy suggests an element of a regional capital strategy in Detroit as early as the 1970s. To a degree, the failure of the business community and some local leaders and organizations to support Mayor Young's gambling initiatives contributed to the further decline of Detroit's progrowth coalition during the 1970s and 1980s.

By the early 1990s, a successful casino in Canada, Casino Windsor, spurred another ballot proposal that was approved. The three casinos approved for Detroit will invest between $500 and $700 million each, and all have proposed multifaceted entertainment venues that include hotels, restaurants, theaters, and family-oriented musical–variety shows (Wilson, DeHaven, and Hackney 1997:3A). Each casino would create between 3,000 and 4,000 jobs, and promised "extras" to entice the city to approve their proposal. The extras include contributions to a community fund, money to demolish abandoned houses, funding for office renovation, and so on (Ankeny 1997). While actual construction of casinos has not yet occurred as of this writing, Detroit's foray into gaming as an economic development approach illustrates a renewed regional capital strategy in the 1990s.

Conclusion

Regional capital strategies in Birmingham, Boston, Bristol, and Detroit have converged in several respects. First, all four cities have anchored their regional capital strategies in the development of megaprojects that have been seen as the principal means to achieve regional primacy by restructuring downtown areas into cultural and entertainment districts.

Despite these palpable similarities, however, regional capital megaproject politics have not always engendered consensus and comity within local governing coalitions. Regional capital politics in Birmingham moved from a regime to a coalitional power structure. In Boston, a fragile progrowth alliance was formed, which slowed progress on its regional capital strategy considerably. Bristol, in turn, saw the rise of a powerful regional capital coalition in the mid-1990s, although it is not yet clear whether a regime can be constructed out of the phalanx of partnerships that emerged. Finally, in Detroit, a progrowth regime that had formed during the 1970s moved to an uneasy coalition during much of the 1980s, then shifted to competing factions during Coleman Young's last two terms of office. With Dennis Archer's election in 1993 and re-election in 1997, a re-emerging coalition seems to have blossomed again, in large part because of Archer's more conciliatory style. Although Detroit will seemingly be tied always to the automobile industry, much of the energy of this renewed coalition has centered on a regional capital strategy that now includes megaprojects such as professional sports stadiums, gambling casinos, and cultural-entertainment projects.

6

Coping with Industrial Decline

Birmingham and Detroit emerged as respective national centers for car production in Great Britain and the United States in the first part of the twentieth century. Once powerful engines of national growth, these industrial behemoths have seen their economic importance ebb considerably over the last half century. National and international competition has led industrial firms to locate new factories or mills in suburban or exurban settings, often overseas, either to be closer to target markets or to take advantage of cheaper sources of labor. As a consequence, large-scale production facilities in Birmingham and Detroit became rarer sights. Moreover, the two Motor Cities have been particularly vulnerable to postindustrial economic restructuring. Lacking the diversified manufacturing sector of some cities or the requisite skill base to adapt easily to a high-technology service economy, single industry cities such as Birmingham and Detroit have taken the brunt of postindustrial urban deindustrialization.

Although many big cities simply abandoned industrial development in the face of postindustrial economic restructuring, in what initially may have appeared to be a fool's errand, Birmingham and Detroit embarked on aggressive industrial development strategies. In Birmingham, the progrowth regime adopted a two-pronged strategy of industrial retention and diversification. Detroit's progrowth alliance concentrated on industrial retention.

Birmingham: Industrial Retention and Diversification

The dual economic crises of recession and structural decline shocked the Birmingham City Council into creating a broad-based economic redevelopment program that began in the early 1980s. Bipartisan consensus emerged around the city's economic development agenda, which meant that proj-

Figure 6.1. Aston Science Park, Birmingham. Photo by Alan DiGaetano.

ects or programs initiated by one party were carried through when another party gained control of the council. This began with the creation of an Economic Development Committee in 1980 under a Labour majority. In 1982, to modernize and diversify the city's economic base, the Birmingham City Council, then under Conservative rule, joined Lloyds Bank and Aston University in developing Aston Science Park (figure 6.1), which serves as an incubator facility for high-technology industry. When Labour took power in 1984, it embraced the science park wholeheartedly, expanding it well into the 1990s.

Regime Politics and Industrial Development

The transformation of Birmingham's economic development politics into a progrowth regime was engineered largely by the ruling faction headed by Sir Richard Knowles after Labour returned to power in 1984. Birmingham's economic development strategy ran on a separate track from the city's prestige project strategy. The chair of the Economic Development Committee, Councillor Albert Bore, became the chief architect of the city's economic development strategy from 1984 to 1993. Bore earned a Ph.D. in physics and became a faculty member of Aston University in Birmingham. He gradually worked his way up through the local Labour party ranks, first as a party organizer, then winning a city council seat in 1980. Bore, seen as both an able politician and the city council's expert on economic development matters, eventually became Knowles' right-hand man in council politics.

Under Bore's leadership, the city council devised its first comprehensive economic strategy in 1985. Four basic elements comprised this strategy: (1) retention and modernization of the existing industrial base, (2) diversification of the local economy through expansion of the service sector and development of new industries, (3) support for supplier firms dependent on the city's basic industries, and (4) human capital development through training and community programs (Birmingham City Council 1986a).

To carry out this strategy, the council strengthened its capacity to promote economic development in a variety of ways. To finance the council's ever expanding economic development activities, expenditures grew steadily from £12.5 million in fiscal year 1980–1981 to £53.8 million in 1990–1991 (Birmingham City Council 1981, 1991). To supplement the city council's own resources, Bore began prospecting for European funding. In a July 19, 1991, interview Bore related that in 1985, "We then started to try and prise open the door to European monies, and we found that, in terms of European Structural Funds, we had become very clearly eligible because the unemployment situation in Birmingham and the West Midlands had soared to levels which were well beyond the average unemployment in Europe." But the European Commission (EC) was reluctant to award large structural fund grants to Birmingham because the British government had not designated the city or the West Midlands as areas needing economic development assistance. According to Bore (interview 1996):

> Development area status therefore became a goal, not just in its own right, but as a means to access European monies. We actually battled hard with government on the economic indicators, loss of employment, the downsizing of the manufacturing sector, unemployment levels across the city. At that time, using government figures, unemployment levels in the city were in excess of 20 percent, and there were areas of the city in which it was in excess of 50 percent. And so in 1985, development area status was awarded.

With Intermediate Development status secured, the city council developed an elaborate system of lobbying to mine this new lode of European grants. This entailed setting up a permanent office in Brussels as a base camp from which to lobby the EC for development and other grants. The amount of funding acquired from European grants testifies to the progrowth regime's prowess in working the European grant system. Over the 12-year period from 1985 to 1996, the city council received more than £254 million from Europe for economic development purposes, which enabled the city to bypass, to some extent, the increasingly restrictive fiscal limits imposed by the central government (Birmingham City Council 1996b).

Birmingham City Council also honed its bureaucratic capacity and expertise to formulate and implement economic development policy. When Bore first became chair of the Economic Development Committee, he convinced the council to establish an economic development unit within the Planning Department. Later, in 1986, when the Thatcher government abolished all the Metropolitan County Councils, the city council folded a portion of the defunct West Midlands County Council economic development unit into a Development Department in the city's new unitary local authority. The city council also transferred economic development staff from Planning and Valuation and Estates to the Development Department (Birmingham City Council 1989:130). In 1989, a separate Economic Development Department was created, which became Britain's largest by far with a staff that ballooned to more than 400 by the early 1990s.

The city council's growing economic development capacity produced a broad range of property development, business services, and training and employment programs over the 1980s and 1990s. For example, to implement the city's industrial retention strategy, the city council constructed two business parks (Woodgate Valley, 60 acres, and Small Heath, 24 acres) to provide facilities for small and medium-sized supplier and service firms that were linked to Birmingham's traditional manufacturing sector (Birmingham City Council 1985, 1986a). Furthermore, in the late 1980s, the city council developed support services designed to improve manufacturing skills and processes, such as customized training centers for the plastics and other industries (Birmingham City Council 1989:24).

Functional partnerships also played an important part in Birmingham's industrial development strategy. In 1986, the city council and Birmingham University established a second science park, the Birmingham Research Park, located on the university's campus in Edgbaston (Birmingham City Council 1986a:28). Of the public-private partnerships formed around economic development functions in the 1980s, however, the most ambitious was Birmingham Heartlands Limited.

Creation of Birmingham Heartlands Limited

East Birmingham had long been a target for renewal by the City Council (Docklands Consultative Committee Support Unit 1993:3). As early as 1985, the city council had considered the idea of forming a renewal agency with a jurisdiction over two traditional manufacturing areas, Newtown and Nechells, that had suffered from substantial dereliction of industrial property (Birmingham City Council 1986a). Despite this important economic reason, politics was decisive in the birth of the Birmingham Heartlands Limited (BHL). The Thatcher government was seriously considering Birmingham as a candidate for one of its second-generation urban development corporations (UDCs). By proposing the establishment of a nonstatutory, locally controlled urban development agency (UDA), Birmingham City Council hoped to retain planning powers over the area. The city council moved to form the UDA in 1986, beginning a year-long battle to prevent the imposition of a UDC (Docklands Consultative Committee Support Unit 1993:4).

The city council was not alone in its opposition to a UDC. In a private meeting with Council Leader Knowles, John Douglas, then chair of the Birmingham Chamber of Industry and Commerce, broached the idea of setting up a public-private partnership to regenerate East Birmingham. In the taxi ride back to the Council House after the meeting, Knowles enjoined the head of the Economic Development Unit, Richard Green, to "get on with some ideas" about the formation of what became Birmingham Heartlands (Green interview July 29, 1993).

The Knowles ruling bloc orchestrated a well-planned campaign to convince Secretary of State for the Environment Nicholas Ridley that a UDC was not needed in Birmingham. First, the city council hired the consulting firm of Roger Tym Partners to conduct a study of the East Birmingham area's social and economic problems. Based upon the findings of this study, the city council drafted a regeneration strategy for East Birmingham, which called for the creation of a private sector-led UDA that would maintain an arm's length relationship to the local authority. Second, to bring Ridley around to the idea that such a UDA would operate just as effectively as a UDC, the city council enlisted the aid of its chief business ally, the Birmingham Chamber of Industry and Commerce, to lobby Whitehall. A final political ploy was to empower the Birmingham Chamber to nominate the chair of UDA. The strategy worked, and the Conservative minister accepted the proposed UDA (Docklands Consultative Committee Support Group 1993:5).

The BHL was formally established in March 1988, with Sir Reginald Eyre as its chair. Sir Reginald, who served as Conservative MP for Birmingham from 1965 to 1987 and held several junior posts in Conservative governments, had been instrumental in the formation of the BHL. He also had strong links to the local business community, both as a senior partner in a firm of solicitors and through his service on the chamber's governing board. The BHL was structured as a consortium, composed of five private developers (65 percent share of ownership), the city council (35 percent share of ownership), and the chamber (one share). The board of directors seated three representatives from the city council, including Economic Development Chair Bore, the five founding private developers,[1] and one chamber representative. The five developers nominated the BHL chief executive, and the city council named the finance director (Birmingham Heartlands 1989). A small staff, seconded from both city council and the private sector, carried out the day-to-day operations (Bishop interview 1991).

The objective of Heartlands UDA was to facilitate economic regeneration of the East Birmingham area. This included coordination of infrastructure improvements, industrial and office park development, and a small amount of housing construction and rehabilitation. Because the Birmingham Heartlands was locally controlled, however, it possessed none of the powers wielded by statutory UDCs. Also, unlike government-sponsored UDCs, Birmingham Heartlands could not count on a dedicated cash flow from Parliament, and thus was forced to piece together government grants and developer commitments on a project-by-project basis (Beeston interview 1993). Nevertheless, the BHL chalked up two major accomplishments in the 1988 to 1992 period: the development of a campus-style office park called Water Links and an "urban village," known as Bordesley Village, located on the southwestern edge of the Heartland's development area near the city center. The BHL had its failures as well. For example, Star Site, a flagship office and commercial development envisioned in the development strategy, never materialized. Also, the BHL made little progress in industrial retention, partly because of the depressed property market of the early 1990s.

Regime Adjustment: 1990–1993

In the 1990s, Birmingham's progrowth regime found it necessary to adjust to a new political landscape. The Birmingham City Council had reigned as undisputed master of the city's economic development agenda in the 1980s. Partnerships such as Birmingham Heartlands and Aston Science Park provided coalitional vehicles to implement economic development strategies and projects, but the city council clearly dominated these alliances. This changed in the early 1990s, as central government restrictions on local authority expenditures tightened and the availability of government grants became contingent upon a strong showing of private sector involvement.

First, the Birmingham Chamber of Industry and Commerce, which had a long tradition of engagement in Birmingham's economic development politics, emerged as a central player in the progrowth alliance in the early 1990s. For example, Birmingham Chamber President John Douglas led the charge to convince Parliament that the West Midlands ought to be declared a Development Area, which would qualify the region for additional funds for economic development purposes (Duckers and Morris 1993). Private conversations between Douglas and Trade and Industry Minister Tim Sainsbury proved crucial in upgrading Birmingham to full development area status (Morris 1993).

The creation of the Birmingham Training and Enterprise Council (TEC) in 1990 further altered the distribution of power in economic development politics. Initially, the decision to create a Birmingham TEC incited protests from both the chamber and the city council, which had developed their own programs for training and enterprise development. When the TEC was imposed over these objections, the chamber strongly urged the Secretary of State for Trade and Industry to accept its nominee as chair of the TEC board. However, the chamber candidate was found wanting and after a rather long search, Bass Taverns chairman Charles Darby was appointed chair of the TEC.

Despite this somewhat rocky beginning, the TEC managed to smooth relations with both the chamber and the city council. Once convened, the board defined the central task of the TEC as strategic, with its modus operandi the development of a wide array of networks and partnerships to achieve its objectives for training and business development (Darby interview 1993; Cragg interview 1993). Importantly, the TEC's partnership strategy blended seamlessly into the city's existing governing alliance. As a consequence, the TEC became an integral part of Birmingham's progrowth regime (Cragg interview August 8, 1993; Darby interview August 9, 1993; Birmingham Training and Enterprise Council n.d.).

The Economic Development Department, the TEC, and the chamber formed an economic development triumvirate that wove a dense web of partnerships and joint operations that solidified Birmingham's progrowth regime. For example, in 1991, after extensive and sometimes contentious talks, the chief executives and board chairs of the Birmingham Chamber and the TEC, along with Bore and Green from the city, negotiated an agreement to form the Birmingham Economic Development Partnership (BEDP) (Darby interview August 9, 1993). The purpose of the BEDP was to integrate the business development strategies and programs that the TEC, the

Economic Development Department, and the Birmingham Chamber had previously undertaken separately. In 1992, BEDP received its first real opportunity to move its integrated business development plan forward when it won a bid for Business Link funding from the Department of Trade and Industry (DTI) — £1.74 million over three years (Birmingham Training and Enterprise Council 1993). Birmingham's Business Link, which operates under the umbrella of the BEDP, acts as a nerve center for receiving and disseminating information about business development and advice services available in Birmingham. In 1994, the BEDP incorporated a second line of business services into the system, named Start-Up Link, to serve firms with fewer than 10 employees. Finally, the city council, the chamber, and the TEC joined forces on Birmingham's bid in the second round of City Challenge, which brought in £37 million over five years to regenerate Newtown-South Aston, one of the city's most deprived inner city areas.

Creation of the Heartlands Development Corporation

A second point of regime adjustment in the early 1990s could be found in the politics of Birmingham Heartlands. The successes of Waterlinks and Bordesley Village notwithstanding, it was felt that the nonstatutory BHL had achieved only modest results by 1992. Unable to rely on a guaranteed stream of government funding and stymied by the collapse of the city's property market in the early 1990s, the Heartlands UDA was seen as lacking the wherewithal to leverage private investment in its East Birmingham area of operation (Beeston interview 1993; Bore interview 1993).

The Knowles ruling clique concluded that some other mechanism was needed to regenerate the area. To remedy the problem of unstable revenue streams, the city council submitted a bid for City Challenge funding in the 1991–1992 cycle that would cover a substantial swath of the Heartlands redevelopment area, but it lost in the first round of the competition. Undaunted by this setback, in October 1991, the Labour leadership in the city council, Chief Executive Roger Taylor, and the Heartland's board tendered a proposal to the central government to declare Heartlands a UDC. Reminiscent of the city's prestige projects, this decision and subsequent negotiations with the central government were closely guarded secrets, even from the Labour group and the Economic Development Committee. The inner circle of Labour leaders and officers wished to limit the amount of debate and thus forestall any potential controversy over the proposed UDC, for it might be construed as a reversal of their principled stand against the imposition of a UDC in 1987.

The Finance and Management Committee, the city council's central policy body (chaired by Knowles), sent a report to Secretary of State for the Environment Michael Heseltine, recommending that Birmingham Heartlands be declared a UDC. Heseltine, who had been a staunch advocate of UDCs since their inception, expressed a willingness to consider the proposal. The city council requested that a Heartlands UDC be allocated a total of £103 million over a five-year period. The city council would hold half the seats on the board, with the remainder filled by the central government (Beeston interview August 6, 1993; Taylor interview August 9, 1993). According to the Finance and Management Committee proposal (submitted October 21, 1991), this would "ensure the effective combination of the powers and resources of the UDC with those of the City Council" (Docklands Consultative Committee Support Unit 1993:8). The strategy and activities of the proposed UDC would vary little from the BHL, but the means for carrying them out would differ markedly. Heseltine approved the Birmingham Heartlands Development Corporation (BHDC), although the funding level was set at £50 million, less than half the amount requested by the city council—about £7.5 million per annum.

The BHDC was clearly an anomaly among UDCs, as no other in the country allowed a local authority to control half the seats on a UDC governing board. Sir Reginald Eyre, former chair of BHL, was selected to chair the new BHDC, an appointment that was fully supported by the city council (Beeston interview 1993; Docklands Consultative Committee Support Unit 1993:8). As with the old Heartlands, consensus and comity prevailed at board meetings of the BHDC. This is not surprising, given that all of the councillors appointed by the Secretary of State for the Environment belonged to the progrowth faction of the city council.[2] Despite the fact that a tenant's group from Nechells lobbied for local representation on the BHDC board, no community leaders were appointed (Docklands Consultative Committee Support Unit 1993:8).

The conversion to a UDC brought a larger and much more reliable revenue stream from the central government. This paid some dividends almost immediately. For example, the BHDC managed a deal with Leyland DAF (which produces vans) that enabled the company to stay afloat. The BHDC purchased a piece of property from DAF for £4 million, which supplied sufficient capital to the company's management to buy out of its bankrupt parent company and thus continue operation of its Heartlands factory (interviews with Bishop July 20, 1994, and August 8, 1996). Having UDC status also vested Birmingham Heartlands with formal planning and development authority. The change in administrative structure and powers, however, did not alter the Birmingham Heartlands mission. The newly constituted board adopted without revision the old BHL development framework as their own strategic plan. In addition, BHDC Chief Executive Jim Beeston, originally seconded to the old BHL from the city council, maintained a close and cooperative relationship with the local authority. For example, the UDC carefully abided by the city's Unitary Development Plan, although as an independent planning authority it was not obliged to do so (Beeston interview August 6, 1993). In other words, the creation of a UDC did not disturb the close association between Birmingham Heartlands and the city council.

A Shift to Coalitional Politics, 1993–1997

Beginning in 1993, the Labour group embraced a "Back-to-Basics" agenda of improvements in education, social services, and housing under direction of the new Council Leader, Teresa Stewart. Not surprisingly, economic development lost ground as a council priority, with department expenditures dropping from £53.8 million in fiscal year 1991–1992 to £32.0 million in 1995–1996. But the Back-to-Basics Labour councillors failed to dismantle Birmingham's economic development agenda. The Labour leadership itself was divided on the issue, with Deputy Leader Bryan Bird, who also served on the BHDC board, quite keen to promote large-scale development projects. Furthermore, Bore's successor as Economic Development Committee chair, Martin Brooks, himself a progrowth politician, served on the Labour group Executive Committee. Similarly, the new Chief Executive Michael Lyons espoused a strong commitment to economic development. Given the plurality of views on economic development, an accommodation was eventually worked out in which the progrowth agenda would not be abandoned, but transmuted to a more diversified approach. In part, this meant a heavier reliance on attracting private investment rather than large-scale infrastructure projects financed by the city council. Through this compromise, economic development politics shifted to a coalitional mode of governance.

Maintaining a Foothold in the Auto Industry Base

In the mid-1990s, growth in manufactured exports, greatly facilitated by a devaluation in sterling and a cut in interest rates from 10 to 6 percent, galvanized the West Midlands economy into recovery (Birmingham Economic Information Center n.d.:9; Cheeseright 1993). The expansion of manufacturing output (Wachman 1993), in turn, spurred greater demand for industrial property in Birmingham and the West Midlands (Causer 1993; *Birmingham Post* 1994; E. O'Brien 1993). According to a report published by the Birmingham Economic Information Center (n.d.:10), the "revival in the fortunes of the City's manufacturing sector may have fueled a significant increase in fixed investment by Birmingham companies in equipment, land, and buildings." Finally, the assignment of Birmingham to full Development Area status in 1993 complemented these market advantages by making firms within the city limits eligible for a larger pool of capital investment grants (Duckers 1993:1).

What worried Birmingham's economic development triumvirate was that investment in plant and training by Birmingham's small and medium-sized manufacturing companies, particularly those involved in the production of automotive component parts, lagged behind the region and the nation (Birmingham Economic Information Center n.d.:14). With increased demand for auto parts by the large car companies located in the region, which had modernized their production processes and set up just-in-time supply systems to operate more efficiently in an increasingly competitive market, Birmingham's antiquated component parts factories found it difficult to compete. The failure to modernize plant and equipment and improve planning and organization of work processes meant that in terms of productivity and output, Birmingham's manufacturing sector performed comparatively poorly during the recovery of the mid-1990s (Birmingham Economic Information Center n.d.:7–8; Cragg interview July 19, 1994).

In response to the changing economic landscape, Birmingham's economic development triumvirate began developing an integrated set of strategies and policies to enhance flexibility in production. They developed programs to encourage outsourcing of supplies and services as the means to slim company operations and focus on core competencies, and tried to restructure supply chains to meet the growing demands of large manufacturing concerns (Birmingham City Council 1996a). For example, in 1994, the TEC, the city council, and Central England University combined forces to enlarge the capacity of the city's Advanced Manufacturing Centre, which was renamed the Birmingham Centre for Manufacturing (BCM). The jointly operated BCM furnished customized training and recruitment for Birmingham-based companies (Green interview, July 28, 1994). Also in 1997, the TEC, in consultation with the City Council and others, developed a regional program to reduce the cost of operations, upgrade the production process, and improve the delivery system in the West Midlands automotive supplier base. Accelerate, as the program is called, received £11.5 million from Europe, £3 million from local agencies, and £13.5 million from West Midlands companies over three years (Accelerate n.d.). Finally, the economic development triumvirate also put together another partnership — Locate in Birmingham — that established a "one-stop shop" for inward investment advice and assistance services (Locate in Birmingham n.d.).

The Politics of Auto Factory Location: Snaring a Jaguar

In the midst of the flurry of activity aimed at modernizing the city's manufacturing sector, a major injection of auto industry investment appeared from an expected quarter, Ford Motor Company. In 1989, Ford Motor Company purchased one of Britain's classic car manufacturers, Jaguar. After the acquisition, the Birmingham Economic Development Department and BHDC made a number of overtures to the managers of the Jaguar autobody plant in Castle Bromwich, assisting them in small ways with their operations (Beeston interview, August 10, 1995; Green interview 1995). It was through these contacts that Birmingham officials caught wind of Ford's decision to produce a new line of small sports cars, the Jaguar X200. Ford was considering locations in Britain, Germany, Japan, Mexico, Portugal, and the United States (Jacobs 1995). After several months the search boiled down to the Ford plant in Wixom, Michigan, and Birmingham's Castle Bromwich autobody facility.

Snaring the Jaguar X200 operation required heavy public subsidies as bait. The incentive package used to capture the Jaguar assembly plant was extremely complex, featuring multiple tiers and arenas of bargaining. Moreover, officials kept a tightly sealed lid on the negotiations until a bargain could be struck. Ford opened negotiations with the DTI in late 1994, with Ford Motor Company chairman Alex Trotman and Secretary of State for Trade Michael Heseltine meeting in December to bring the deal to closure (Lorenz 1995). The sticking point was that Heseltine had offered £60 million in assistance for the £400 million project, and Ford was angling for more. By the end of February, Heseltine raised the ante to £80 million in direct aid, which satisfied Ford, but still required approval from the European Commission (EC). When the EC balked at the size of the direct aid in the government assistance package, the DTI reduced the amount of direct aid and added indirect assistance, such as training and recruitment services, to maintain the level of assistance at £80 million.

While these stratospheric bargaining sessions were going on between Trotman and Heseltine in London, a number of political and technical problems had to be resolved at ground-level in Birmingham. First, competition for the X200 plant initially triggered rivalry between Birmingham and nearby Coventry, which is home to a large Jaguar assembly plant and the company's British headquarters. When it became clear that Ford preferred the Birmingham site, a deal was struck between Birmingham and Coventry to develop a joint training and recruitment program as part of the overall incentive package for Ford, which allayed some of the ill feelings between the two auto cities. The joint program brought together a cumbersome alliance of local agencies, which included the city councils and TECs of both cities and Heartlands UDC, to provide customized technical training and recruitment for the plant. In addition, the Castle Vale Housing Action Trust, charged with the responsibility to regenerate the large council estate located on the front doorstep of the Jaguar plant, negotiated a separate jobs linkage pact for Castle Vale residents.

A second problem surfaced when Ford insisted on additional land for expanding the existing Jaguar facility for production and warehousing purposes. To satisfy this demand, English Partnerships, the central government regeneration agency, acquired two parcels of land, which included the old and empty Fort Dunlop factory and a smaller 280,000-square-foot factory, both situated on the southwestern boundary of the original Jaguar property. English Partnerships purchased the historic Dunlop building (it had been a Spitfire factory in World War II) from Tarmac Richardsons Developments. Richardsons had already received planning permission for a mixed-use retail and leisure facility for Fort Dunlop, and to persuade the developers to sell, the city council agreed to transfer its planning agreement to another site in Birmingham owned by Tarmac Richardsons (Green interview August 7, 1995). English Partnerships also entered into a joint venture with Tarmac Richardsons to develop a 13-acre industrial park on an adjacent parcel to accommodate just-in-time component part suppliers (Cheeseright 1995a).

The £80 million size of the public subsidy suggests just how important the Jaguar investment of £400 million was to both central government and the local authorities and agencies involved. The subsidy package broke down as follows: (1) the DTI provided £48 million in regional selective assistance; (2) English Partnerships invested £15 million to purchase the Dunlop property, which will be turned over to Ford for expansion of the existing Jaguar plant; (3) local authorities and agencies contributed £17 million for recruitment, training, and environmental improvements (Cheeseright 1995a). Estimates for the number of new jobs that will be generated by the Jaguar project have ranged from 5,000 to 7,000 new jobs, with 1,000 to 1,500 new hires at the Jaguar assembly plant and the rest among component parts firms (Lorenz 1995; *Birmingham Voice* 1995). Moreover, the property market in Birmingham reacted almost instantaneously to Ford's decision to locate the X200 facility in Birmingham, with industrial parks in the vicinity filling up quite rapidly with automotive component suppliers (Turpin 1995).

Birmingham's success in snaring the Jaguar plant owed as much to environmental factors as to the inducement package offered to Ford. First, the resurgence in Britain's automobile industry, which is concentrated in the West Midlands, meant that Birmingham would offer a good location, with easy access to component supplies and a financial services sector that has substantial expertise in serving the car industry (Cheeseright 1995b). Second, the Birmingham site afforded excellent transport links, with close proximity to the M6 and M42 Motorways and abutment to a Spine Road being built by the city council that traverses the Heartlands development area from east to west.

Piercing the Greenbelt for High-Tech Development
While greenfield sites in other parts of the Midlands were being gobbled up by Toyota and Peugot, the absence of large parcels of land for modern manufacturing operations greatly impaired Birmingham's ability to attract sizable high technology or other industrial investment. In 1995, Dutch-owned Philips Electronics began searching for a location in Great Britain to build a new microelectronics manufacturing plant. Regional planning guidance from the Department of Environment suggested the West Midlands as a favored location. Acting on this suggestion, Philips contacted the West Midlands Development Agency (WMDA) about the availability of a site in the West Midlands. Although WMDA had received similar inquiries in the past, Birmingham always had lost out because it lacked a suitable site (Richards interview 1996). In this case two sites were identified, one in Wolverhampton and another in Birmingham's greenbelt in the Sutton Coldfield district. Philips preferred the Birmingham site, but its location in the greenbelt complicated matters considerably. Philips also insisted that its interest in the site, known as Peddimore, remain a secret or it would look elsewhere.

The next step was to win city council approval. To comply with Philips' insistence on secrecy, WMDA acted as a front for the company and submitted an application for planning permission to build an electronics plant at Peddimore, which WMDA obviously had no real intention of doing (Richards 1996). Planners and the economic development staff, who were often at loggerheads on development issues, formed a remarkably united front on this project. Indeed, they assisted WMDA in preparing the planning application and recommended its approval by the city council. Nonetheless, some "Green" voices in the Labour group protested the incursion into the greenbelt, arguing that once done, it might open a floodgate for further greenbelt development. These environmental Socialists contended that brownfield sites ought to be recycled and pieced together for the large industrial park. Prodevelopment forces in the city council countered that even if brownfield parcels were reclaimed, it would be impossible to find a sufficient number of contiguous parcels to assemble the 137 acres necessary for the microelectronics plant.

As the debate in council chambers raged, a second front in opposition emerged among the city's conservationists and residents of Sutton Coldfield. Championed by Conservative MP Sir Norman Fowler, this antidevelopment coalition warned that the proposed industrial park would generate unacceptable levels of noise and air pollution, snarl the area in perpetual traffic congestion, destroy valuable pasture land, endanger wildlife, and threaten a Bronze Age settlement (Langford 1996; Percival 1996; Teasdale 1996a). The antidevelopment forces mobilized the full panoply of oppositional politics, as they organized meetings, filed petitions, made their case in the local media, and launched a letter-writing campaign to persuade the city council to deny planning permission to the microelectronics factory.

Prodevelopment forces repelled the antidevelopment attack by trotting out tried and true arguments about how the microelectronic plant would produce 3,800 jobs (1,135 at the plant, the remainder from supplier firms). They also dismissed the claims about negative externalities as wildly exaggerated. City planners assured all parties that both noise and air pollution could easily be abated to levels below the legal limits (Percival 1996).[3]

In the end, the words of the opposition fell on deaf ears, and the City Council Planning Committee granted planning permission in July 1996 (Green interview 1996). But this was not the end of the story. Although the city council owned most of the land for the proposed electronics facility, any such development required approval of Secretary of State of the Environment John Gummer, because it was located in the greenbelt. Gummer had two options, to refer the matter back to the local authority, or to hold a public inquiry into the matter. Gummer chose the latter. Some local observers noted that this decision may have been politically motivated, as the opposition to the project surfaced in the Conservative stronghold of Sutton Coldfield and it was the Conservative MP, Sir Norman Fowler, who had demanded the public inquiry (Langford 1996). The public hearing was scheduled for December 1996. The upcoming national election and subsequent victory by the Labour party postponed further the decision on Peddimore, which was still pending in July 1997.

The public inquiry inspector appointed by Gummer wrote a report that indicated that the factory development should not be given planning permission to locate on the greenbelt site, which elated the Peddimore Action group, as the opposition alliance called itself. However, the new Labour Deputy Prime Minister, John Prescott, overturned the inspector's ruling in September 1997, thereby clearing the way for the development of an electronics plant in Peddimore (Flurry 1997).

New Frictions in the Economic Development Triumvirate

Coalitional politics exposed cracks in the armor of Birmingham's economic development triumvirate. As Chief Executive of the City Council Michael Lyons explained in a June 10, 1997, interview,

> There are still tensions. . . . The TEC, which is cash-rich, is a small organization, is not encumbered by the democratic process unduly, and is able to move incredibly quickly. . . . So people get very irritated when there are some joint discussions and a week later the TEC has done something, badged it, and all our thinking appears as a TEC initiative. There is a degree of frustration. But there are still those who take the long term view and say the TEC gets things done and that is the price you have to pay for using their money. So it is a managed friction really. The TEC is in a rather fragile position, with a change of government nobody really knows what is going to happen to the TECs.

Drafting a citywide economic development strategy in 1997 exemplified the politics of managed friction in Birmingham. The Economic Development Department had for years published economic development strategies for Birmingham. The other partners in the progrowth alliance, however, while signing off on the documents, had always perceived them as belonging to the city council. In early 1997, the Economic Development Department, the TEC, and the chamber agreed to write an economic development strategy under the auspices of the BEDP. The process turned out to be a painful one.

Early on, it became clear that the three partners held different perspectives on the future course of economic development in Birmingham (Cragg interview June 2, 1997). The chief executive of the TEC, David Cragg, thought that the Economic Development Department was overly concerned with local politics, which translated into a microscopic view of economic development. Chamber Chief Executive Bob Moore (interview, June 4, 1997) saw the city council as acting overly proprietary, and seeking to "highjack" the strategy. Moore perceived this inclination to dominate the strategic process as stemming from the city council's worries about accountability in the spending of public money. Director Economic Development Department Richard Green (interview, June 5, 1997), in turn, noted that the TEC fiercely opposed any language that hinted that some communities might receive more regeneration funding than others. Nonetheless, the bruising process did produce a broad-based Economic Development Strategy (Economic Development Strategy for Birmingham 1997). After final consultation by partnership members, an economic strategy document for the years 1998–2000 was published. In sum, the very fact that the economic development triumvirate was able to manage the friction generated by the process of writing the Economic Development Strategy bore witness to the tensile strength of the city's progrowth coalition.

Detroit: "The Reason We Exist"

During Mayor Coleman Young's first years in office, the city's progrowth approach took on a dual strategy, emphasizing riverfront commercial and office developments along with an industrial retention strategy focusing on the automobile industry. Detroit's historical reliance on the big three automobile manufacturers made the city and many of its residents relatively wealthy in the earlier part of the century. But as a single industry city, Detroit also suffered when the automobile industry faced stiff international competition and the energy crisis in the 1970s.

As the second prong of Detroit's dual strategy, industrial retention focused primarily on large automobile manufacturing plants, as well as on suppliers to the auto industry. For Coleman Young, a former autoworker and labor union organizer himself, the auto industry was more than simply "important" to the city of Detroit. Young was fond of quoting the historian Arthur Pound (1940), who had written, "Fundamentally, modern Detroit exists to build and sell motor cars, and once it quits doing that it will lose its chief reason for existence" (quoted in Young and Wheeler 1994:233). Young felt that, in many respects, making cars was indeed "the reason we exist." Much political effort was expended by the mayor and city government in providing the resources and incentives to retain the large automobile manufacturing facilities, which had become increasingly footloose. Although some opposition existed over the specific application of the progrowth strategy, that opposition (which occasionally included one or two city council members) was largely marginalized throughout Mayor Young's time in office. The combination of automobile executives, along with federal, state, and city government support, created a powerful industrial retention coalition that intended to keep automobile production in the city.

The Politics of Industrial Retention

Although an industrial development strategy might appear obvious for a city such as Detroit, it was not always so. Before 1974, the city's redevelopment emphasis was not on industrial redevelopment (Thomas 1989:151). However, by the time Coleman Young took office, the city's economic development organizational resources had been fortified by a revised city charter, as well as the 1974 federal Housing and Community Development Act, which opened up funding for spending in areas of economic development that had not existed previously. By 1975, the state of Michigan also passed a series of statutes that allowed local governments to offer tax abatements for new industrial investments, provided for the public taking of land for development projects, and allowed local governments to create a number of quasi-public development agencies designed to facilitate redevelopment. These resources combined to help finance, clear the sites, and construct two state-of-the-art auto assembly facilities — the General Motors Poletown plant and the Chrysler Jefferson Avenue North expansion.

The Central Industrial Park Project: "Poletown"

The Poletown plant was one of the largest U.S. industrial development projects implemented up to that time, and as such, garnered much interest among national and local media, legal observers (Alderman and Kennedy 1991), political activists such as Ralph Nader and associates (Wylie 1989), and urban scholars (Fasenfest 1986; Jones and Bachelor 1993). The term "Poletown" came from the large Polish-American population that had lived in that area (part of the site included property in Hamtramck, an enclave city that had one of the largest Polish populations of *any* city in the world during the early 1900s).

Officially called the Central Industrial Park Project, the 465-acre Poletown project came about as a result of an offer in the late 1970s by General Motors Chairman Thomas Murphy to Mayor Young to find a several-hundred-acre site (the original estimate was between 500 and 600 acres) for a modern automobile manufacturing plant, to clear it, provide financial inducements, and bring the required infrastructure up to specification. All of this was to be accomplished within one year. This kind of development policy-making was typical of Detroit under Mayor Young. The mayor dominated the economic development agenda, and took an active and personal interest in his two favorite growth goals, the riverfront and the auto industry. Economic development policy-making in Detroit tended to be especially private and secretive during that time.

Implementing the deal proved more complicated. There were 1,200 residential, commercial, and industrial structures already on the site, including such powerfully symbolic buildings as a hospital, public schools, and 16 churches, including a historic Polish Catholic Church. The controversy led to high-profile demonstrations involving organizers working for Ralph Nader, and a legal battle that ended up before the Michigan Supreme Court. In *Poletown Neighborhood Council v. City of Detroit* (410 MICH 616) the court majority ruled that the city could take land under eminent domain provisions (and a separate "quick take" statute passed by the Michigan legislature in anticipation of this project), even for essentially "private" purposes (that is, for the General Motors Corporation).

Some questions and criticisms remain about the wisdom of this redevelopment project. The projected 6,000 jobs the facility was to employ never fully materialized during the 1980s, although approximately 5,400 workers operated on two shifts briefly in 1985 (Braunstein and Prater 1989). About $300 million in public funding was spent on the Poletown plant, including land acquisition costs of over $130 million, more than twice the projected total. Even into the 1990s, the city still was using a substantial amount of its Community Development Block Grant (CDBG) annual funding to pay off the Poletown debt. As the automobile industry continues to face its usual cycle of highs and lows, layoffs at the plant (both temporary and permanent) have made the project seem less beneficial for the city and its residents. Despite these concerns, Coleman Young pointed to the Poletown project as one of the highlights of his administration. In describing the controversy over the project, the mayor said,

> it actually put three thousand people back to work, half as many as I had optimistically hoped for but more than enough to make the effort worthwhile. In the times when GM runs two shifts at Poletown, which it began to do permanently in June of 1993, the facility employs four thousand. That's strictly a bonus for me. . . . Regardless of the numbers, the important thing was to keep making cars in Detroit — to preserve the Motor City's "chief reason for existence," as Arthur Pound put it. I was a proud mayor the day that first Cadillac rolled off the line. To me, it made up for nearly every goddamn person, plant, and corporate headquarters that had hightailed it to the suburbs over the previous twenty years. (Young and Wheeler 1994:249)

Regardless of the controversy about how General Motors built its plant and whether even the conventional wisdom over its benefits to the city exceeded its costs, the Poletown facility was remarkable for the speed and efficiency with which it went from a handshake agreement to completion.

Chrysler's Jefferson Avenue North Project

By the early 1980s, Detroit's progrowth coalition was shaken—less from disagreements around the dual strategy as from land-taking controversies over the Poletown project along with Mayor Young's increasing distrust of local business leaders. Despite these and other difficulties, Mayor Young pursued an arrangement with Chrysler Chairman Lee Iacocca that was similar to the city's deal with Thomas Murphy of General Motors. Over time, Chrysler Corporation has been the auto manufacturer with the greatest presence in Detroit proper. Part of Young's negotiating tactic was to remind Iacocca of the support the city had given Chrysler during the federal bailout of the company in the late 1970s (Young and Wheeler 1994:250). It proved an effective negotiating technique.

But Chrysler had negotiating power as well. By the mid-1980s, Chrysler had come to Detroit looking for site clearance, tax incentives, and other public supports (along with a renegotiation of its labor agreement with UAW Local 7) to build a modern high-tech production and assembly facility, much in the same way that General Motors had done with its Poletown plant project. Chrysler had intended to shut down the Jefferson Avenue plant in 1987, after a planned phaseout of the old K-car model line (*Detroit News* 1986). For Mayor Young, keeping Chrysler in Detroit was both essential to the local economy and an important symbol underscoring Detroit's continued standing as a world leader in automobile production. As Young later recounted:

> The Jefferson Avenue Assembly Plant was . . . a coup for the city of Detroit. Not only did it take up where the Central Industrial Park left off in terms of reindustrializing the city, it also firmly reestablished Detroit's previously precarious position as the heart and leader of the world's automotive community. There is not another city in America . . . with one state-of-the-art automobile plant, much less two. . . . There can be no dispute that the parlaying of Poletown and Chrysler Jefferson has grandly preserved Detroit's tradition as the Motor City. (Young and Wheeler 1994:252)

Public costs for this project originally were estimated to be about $200 million. Unexpected environmental clean up costs added considerably to that original estimate, and by 1989, the Community and Economic Development Department revealed that public financing costs had reached $264 million (Prater 1989). Similar to the Poletown project of a few years earlier, public resources that include a number of city, state, and federal financial incentives were combined to provide the funding needed to complete the incentive package. These incentives included locally available bonds, land write-downs and tax abatements, state of Michigan job training funds (the only new program available since Poletown), and funding for infrastructure improvements. In addition, federal loans, loan guarantees and Urban Development Action Grants were made available (Kushma 1986).

Officially dedicated on March 31, 1992, the new Chrysler Jefferson Avenue North facility (figure 6.2) was a $1-billion, 637-acre, 1.75-million-square-foot state-of-the-art production plant that was to make the company's popular Jeep Grand Cherokee vehicles (*New York Times* 1992:8L). Although the new facility replaced the "Old Jeff," the land requirements for modern automobile production also mandated a similar neighborhood residential and business relocation and site preparation as had occurred with the General Motors Poletown plant a few years earlier.

To prepare the site, the city again purchased the remaining property in private hands, razed 854 houses, and relocated about 2,000 residents

Figure 6.2. Chrysler Jefferson Avenue North plant, Detroit. Photo by John S. Klemanski.

still living in the surrounding neighborhood. Over 100 businesses also were moved to make the site ready for new construction. In the Chrysler case, much of the land in question already was vacant, although this did not prevent another controversy over land acquisition. Similar criticisms arose about the wisdom of using scarce public resources to benefit a profit-making corporation, as well as the relocation of businesses and neighborhood residents that had occurred during the Poletown project (McGraw 1988). Further, the Chrysler project included a land appraisal controversy that created a near-scandal for the city government.

The land acquisition controversy is amply detailed elsewhere (see Jones and Bachelor 1993), but the problem arose largely because the city was operating under a strict timetable dictated by Chrysler. Land acquisition and appraisal of the property was done so quickly that the value of the property was overestimated.

Appraisers set the cost of the inventory ($40 million) and buildings ($2 million) at a value over what the city had set aside for *all* of the project's land acquisition costs (McGraw 1988). Chrysler later altered its plans for the paint plant, which made the purchase and the tight deadline unnecessary, but the city had already committed to buy the buildings and inventory.

The huge cost overruns on land acquisition, and especially the process whereby the city needlessly overpaid millions of dollars for property it then resold to the original owners, became the subject of an FBI investigation. Although no formal charges ultimately were brought against any city official, the controversy surrounding this project led to the 1988 resignation of Emmet Moten as Director of the Community and Economic Development Department, and brought into further question the city's progrowth strategy.

Industrial Retention and Expansion in the 1990s

With Dennis Archer's election as mayor in 1993, the business community saw a more positive, conciliatory leader. Though Archer has not necessarily focused his efforts at industrial retention to the same degree that Coleman Young did, he oversaw a number of industrial and manufacturing investments during his first term in office. Easily the largest commitment of money came from Chrysler Corporation, which promised a $1.5 billion investment over a period between 1997 and 2002. About $750 million was earmarked for expansion of the Jefferson Avenue North plant, $300 million was targeted for new products and parts at the company's Detroit Axle facility, and $150 million was to increase production at the Chrysler

Mack engine plant. The company already had begun a $750 million conversion of the former Dodge Viper assembly plant to an engine plant for its future truck and Jeep models that would take Chrysler's total commitment to over $2 billion (Phillips 1997b). Moreover, the automaker already had expanded the Jefferson Avenue North operations in 1994 with a $120 million investment designed to increase production of its Jeep Cherokee sports utility vehicles, by adding a third shift and hiring 800 more workers. Chrysler's Chairman Robert Eaton (who in 1997 also was serving as chair of Detroit Renaissance, Inc.) remarked that the investments will "create opportunity for Chrysler and the city that will last well into the next century" (Phillips 1997a).

In addition, General Motors expanded its Poletown plant in 1996 at a cost of $250 million. A General Motors spokesperson said that the company enlarged the facility "because it made good business sense" (Solomon 1997). Still other investment and commitments in manufacturing occurred during Mayor Archer's first term, including a $350 million rehabilitation and remodeling of facility and equipment by American Axle and Manufacturing Inc., located a short distance from the Poletown facility, and smaller investments of $15 to $25 million by Strong Steel Products LLC and Thyssen Steel Group for expansion and construction of steel processing facilities (Solomon 1997).

Detroit Earns Empowerment Zone Approval

The 1994 federal Empowerment Zones program targeted federal social services funding and tax breaks to areas designated by cities making application for funding. Much like the other competitive grants, empowerment zone designation criteria included a city's ability to demonstrate broad-based cooperation among businesses, labor unions, neighborhood organizations, government, and educational institutions located in the city making application.

Certainly one of Mayor Archer's early triumphs in forging cooperation among different parties was Detroit's award as one of only six cities to receive full empowerment zone funding. Full empowerment zone status meant that the federal government would provide $100 million in social services grants over a two-year period to be spent by the city over a ten-year period. The empowerment zone competition required a lengthy proposal emphasizing cooperation and wide participation within a city. In Detroit, an Empowerment Zone Coordinating Council (selected by the mayor), comprising neighborhood activists, business representatives, and local government staff members, put together the city's application to the federal government. Leading the entire group was Gloria Robinson, director of the city's newly reorganized Planning and Development Department (essentially a merger of the former Planning Department and the Community & Economic Development Department). Robinson, a former Wayne County planning official, was given particular credit for leading the application process through on a day-to-day basis, and bringing together representatives of many of the groups needed to demonstrate full participation (Costello 1994).

The governing body was to be a 50-member Empowerment Zone Development Corporation, whose members were nominated by the Zone's Coordinating Council, the mayor, and other officials such as Michigan's governor, John Engler, and Wayne County Executive Edward McNamara. The Planning and Development Department was to disburse the funding (Stevens 1994). An 18.35-square-mile area covering parts of southwest Detroit, the central Woodward Avenue corridor, and parts of the east side, were included within Detroit's empowerment zone boundaries. While some of those areas could attract commercial or office investments, many of the areas within the zone would most likely see industrial developments.

The impact of Detroit's empowerment zone award on the city was immense, both in monetary and symbolic terms. Not only was federal funding forthcoming, but major private sector commitments of investment were made. As Mayor Archer put it (1998),

> In addition to federal funding, we had a commitment of $1.974 billion and $1.1 billion in commitments . . . to loan money to businesses that would locate in the zone. That wasn't considered exciting news, at least as it was treated by the media. . . . Then, in March 1995, Bob Eaton [Chairman of Chrysler Corporation] called up from Argentina. He said, "Chrysler Corporation would like to invest $750 million in the city of Detroit. Are you interested?" I said, "Of course, I'd be very interested."

Only one year into his first term as mayor, Archer had pulled together a widely based coalition of businesses, neighborhood organizations, and government officials in a city that had been more familiar with conflict, especially in Coleman Young's last term of office. As the *Detroit Free Press* summarized:

> A new mayor, a spirit of teamwork that included community groups and business and a realization that time was running out for the city triggered a chain reaction that clinched a $100 million federal empowerment zone for Detroit. Federal officials said . . .

that Detroit won the prize because its plan was community-
driven, linked a wide variety of social service programs, and
showed a high level of commitment from corporations and civic
groups. (Costello 1994)

By late 1997, banks had loaned nearly $900 million within the zone,
most of that to automobile suppliers. Approximately 2,750 new jobs were
created, with almost $4 billion projected to be invested eventually (Ankeny
and Gargaro 1997). Of that total, Chrysler Corporation has committed over
$1 billion for expansion of its Mack Avenue engine plant, which will add
about 1,000 jobs to the facility. About 85 percent of the industrial development within the empowerment zone has come from auto suppliers. Such
a shift in local development politics during Mayor Archer's first term suggests the possibility that a progrowth regime might re-form in Detroit during the 1990s.

The Politics of Renaissance Zones

In December 1996, the Michigan legislature passed a pet project of Republican Governor John Engler, called Renaissance Zones. Under the original renaissance zone proposal, cities would designate certain areas (with
a maximum size of 5,000 acres) that would be free of all state and local
taxes (except sales tax and bond millages) for a 12-year period beginning
January 1, 1997 (Pluta 1995). The intent of the plan was to revitalize distressed areas by encouraging residential, commercial, and industrial growth.
This supply-side approach to revitalization (i.e., lowering taxes and business costs) found favor with the Republican-majority state legislature, but
Dennis Archer was a strong and public supporter of the proposal as well.
Because some city governments and the Michigan Municipal League were
opposed to the original proposal in 1995, Republican Governor Engler
used Democratic Mayor Archer's support as an aid to passing this legislation (Lane 1995).

Detroit's application was approved, and the city's renaissance zone
actually comprised six parcels situated in different parts of the city, mostly
intended for industrial development purposes. For example, of the six
parcels identified for renaissance zone designation (totaling 1,345 acres),
all were either meant to encourage industrial developments (specifically
industrial parks) or industrial with a small commercial or retail development (Dixon and Christoff 1996). Though anyone (business, resident) lo-
cating inside the zone boundaries would have their taxes waived, virtually
all of the areas identified by Detroit were meant to support industrial developments.

Conclusion

Birmingham and Detroit have clearly attempted to preserve their positions as manufacturing centers, devising industrial strategies tailored to retention of automobile production. However, despite this similarity, the politics of industrial development in Birmingham and Detroit have differed.

In Birmingham, governing alignments shifted from an adhocracy in the 1970s to a regime in the mid-1980s. Birmingham's progrowth alliance actively pursued an aggressive dual industrial diversification-retention strategy. The rise and development of Birmingham's progrowth regime is reflected in city council's allocation of resources to economic development. As figure 6.3 shows, economic development expenditures as a percentage of total city council spending rose steadily from the early 1980s to 1992. Regime politics was reinforced by the formation of public-private partnerships in the 1980s, notably Aston Science Park and Birmingham Heartlands. Even the appearance of the Birmingham TEC did not disrupt the progrowth alliance's regime power structure, as it joined the city council and the Birmingham Chamber of Commerce in forming an economic devel-

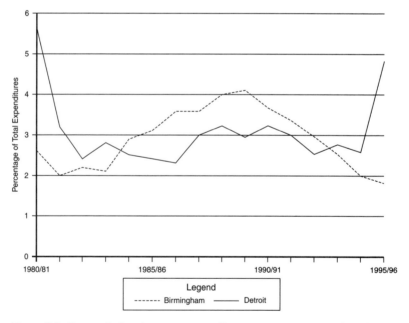

Figure 6.3. Economic development expenditures as a percentage of total expenditures for Birmingham City Council and the City of Detroit, 1980–1981 to 1995–1996. *Source:* Birmingham City Council, *Annual Report and Accounts* (1991–1996); City of Detroit, *Budget* (1981–1996).

opment triumvirate in the early 1990s. The Economic Development Partnership, which focuses on business development services, exemplifies the close cooperation among the city council, TEC, and the chamber around economic development issues. Similarly, the city council adapted to the more competitive mode of intervention by negotiating a UDC with central government for the Heartlands area on which the city controlled half the seats on the board.

Birmingham's political-economic landscape changed in the mid-1990s. Demographic changes in the city's electorate narrowed the Knowles-Bore ruling clique's political base in the Labour group. A new, more pluralistic Labour leadership downgraded the status of economic development on the city council's governing agenda. The economic development triumvirate survived this political reshuffling, although the power structure shifted from a regime to coalitional arrangements. The level of economic development expenditures mirrored this shift, dropping substantially after 1992 (see figure 6.3). At the same time, Britain's manufacturing sector rebounded, which provided Birmingham with a number of opportunities to pursue its industrial diversification and retention strategy.

Coalitional politics complicated the industrial development process. The intricacies of the Jaguar project are a case in point, which involved a complex set of intergovernmental and public-private bargaining tiers and arenas. The politics surrounding a proposed microelectronics industrial park to be located in the greenbelt illustrates further that Birmingham's preemptive regime had undoubtedly given way to a far less consensual mode of governance. Tensions even arose within the economic development triumvirate around the task of writing a joint economic development strategy.

Detroit's approach to industrial retention has taken two different paths over the past 25 years. During the progrowth regime years of the 1970s, industrial development received little attention. In the early 1980s, however, industrial retention became a cause célèbre when Coleman Young negotiated a deal to locate an automobile assembly plant in Poletown. This was partially attached to Young's view of auto factory work as a real option for African Americans who had not attended college and saw these jobs as an opportunity for high wages and decent benefits. Young always saw Detroit as the Motor City automobile production center of the world, and intended to hold onto the title.

The controversy stirred up by Poletown, however, also showed that regime politics would characterize industrial development politics in Detroit. The development of Chrysler's Jefferson Avenue assembly plant ignited similar, although not as intense, conflict. Simply, a coalitional structure, with the Young administration reacting to opportunities afforded by GM and Chrysler, had replaced the progrowth regime in economic development politics. Moreover, the city's industrial development strategy hinged on marriages of convenience between the Young administration and the auto companies. As figure 6.3 shows, Detroit's economic development expenditures spiked during development of the Poletown plant in the early 1980s and the Jefferson Avenue factory in the middle to late 1980s.

Dennis Archer has taken an approach that has appeared to spread his interests across many different kinds of investments. Nonetheless, the improved political climate and image of Detroit that has come with Mayor Archer's administrations has engendered an interest by investors in Detroit. Part of that interest has been a major commitment of private investment that is more or less associated with the empowerment zone, but another major commitment came specifically from Chrysler Corporation to expand and renovate its current facilities. Interestingly, despite the many controversies over the Poletown and Jefferson Avenue factories, both facilities have expanded their operations in the past five years. In sum, even with a greater emphasis on a regional capital strategy after 1993, the city of Detroit has remained bound to the automobile industry.

Part III
The Dilemmas of
Progressive Urban Politics

7

The Politics of Social Reform

In American cities, social reform traditionally has been overshadowed by the specter of progrowth politics (see Logan and Molotch 1987). But in the 1980s, social reform coalitions gained prominence in a number of cities, including San Francisco, Santa Monica, Minneapolis, and even Chicago (see Bennett 1989; DeLeon 1992; Clavel 1986; Nickel 1995; Ferman 1996). These challenges to the dominance of progrowth politics met with considerable success, fostering policies and programs that centered on community rather than downtown development.

Social reform has a more continuous history in British urban politics, given the socialist predilections of the Labour party. Labourist traditions of local socialism were rooted in the nation's trade union movement and focused on equity in consumption policy, such as housing and social services. The 1980s saw the rise of a "New Urban Left" in a number of cities that challenged the Labourist tradition, and advocated a governing agenda featuring improvements in public transport, job creation, and equal opportunities in the labor market (Stoker 1988). New Left coalitions in Sheffield, Leeds, and London, however, were not mobilized as challenges to local growth coalitions, as none existed (Boddy and Fudge 1984; Lawless 1990). The New Urban Left instead pushed local social reform agendas, in part as a reaction to the Thatcher government's attempts to promote market-based local development policy, but also to advocate a more community-based politics that departed from the Labourist tradition in local governance. By the end of the 1980s, Conservative government constraints on local authority spending and administration effectively suffocated the New Left's experiments in municipal socialism (Stoker 1988).

Palpable differences appear in the political-economic context of urban social reform politics that arose in the United States and the United Kingdom during the 1980s. A common thread, however, does wend its way through urban social reform in both countries. In the United States, urban social reform politics in the 1980s grew out of the community movements that organized around issues of inequality and neighborhood development. As Clavel and Kleniewski (1990:223) relate:

> Another important condition fostering progressive policy has been the development of strong community-based organizations of various types. These were crucial in places like Boston and Chicago, forming a major part of the electoral mobilization that elected Flynn and [Harold] Washington. Community groups' organizational capacities had grown slowly through the 1970s, often fueled by local social and economic problems: housing, jobs, women's and gay rights, and so on. . . . Mature community-based organizations have also, in some cases, proved to have unexpected administrative benefits for elected officials attempting to put new policy initiatives into place, since their research and advocacy experience may provide them with better issue resources than available to newly elected local government.

Similarly, Britain's New Urban Left forged close ties to community-based movements. Gerry Stoker (1988:194) explains:

> The fact that the Urban Left's response emerged at the level of local government, in part, reflects that since 1979 Labour's only effective power base has been at the local level. It also corresponds with the close relationship between the Urban Left and a range of community-based and campaigning organizations. The rise from the 1960s of women's movement, black groups, ecological and environmental organizations, peace campaigners, the shop stewards' movement in industry and inner city community action contributed to a changed climate of ideas. . . . It is no accident that many of the officers and councillors of the Urban Left have been, and in many cases remain, involved in the community-based and campaigning political movements.

To understand this common thread in urban social reform politics, our comparative study integrates elements of urban social movement and modes of governance theories (see Fainstein and Hirst 1995) by focusing on the relationship between community movement mobilization and governing coalition formation. Following from this, we argue that a crucial condition for the construction and maintenance of a social reform governing agenda is the development of a strong community movement. This means that a city's community movement attains a position of *strategic* importance in urban politics when community activists have developed institutional bases of power that local politicians find useful in the process of governance. Our comparison of Boston and Bristol explores three dimensions of social reform politics: (1) the form and strength of community movement mobilization, (2) the nature of the alliances that form around social reform issues, and (3) the ability of social reform coalitions to implement governing agendas.

Urban Social Reform in the 1970s and 1980s

Bristol and Boston provide an interesting comparative study of urban social reform politics. The two cities experienced similar social and economic changes from 1970 to 1989. Both witnessed explosive economic growth as each assumed new economic functions as regional financial centers and prospered from the growth of regionally based high-technology and defense industries. Moreover, both cities retained a strong middle-class presence, which spawned growth management coalitions in the 1970s and 1980s to cope with the difficulties of overheated downtown development booms (see DiGaetano 1989; Punter 1990). Despite these similarities, social reform became a dominant element of Boston's governing agenda, while Bristol's New Left failed to gain ascendance over the city council's traditional Labourist leadership.

Community Mobilization in Boston and Bristol

A necessary precondition for the rise of a social reform governing coalition is the development of a well-organized and politically powerful community movement. Boston and Bristol, although similar in many ways, saw quite different patterns of community movement mobilization in the 1970s and 1980s. Boston's community movement emerged as a powerful force in local politics, while in Bristol community activists failed to establish an independent power base.

The Rise of Community-Based Politics in Boston

Boston's community movement mobilized as an oppositional force in city politics during the 1970s, but by the 1980s, it had begun to develop political skills and resources useful for coalition building around social reform issues. The leaders of Boston's community movement employed pressure tactics, insider politics, and effective use of the local media to force social reform measures onto the city's governing agenda. In part, this was a consequence of forming alliances within and across sectors of the community movement, such as the Boston Affordable Housing Coalition and the Boston Jobs Coalition, before mounting issue-based campaigns. This also has meant that much of the social reform agenda actually originated in the city's community movement rather than city hall.

Another key institutional resource developed by Boston's community leaders has been electoral mobilization. In 1983, Boston voters approved the replacement of at-large elections with a mixed at-large–district system. This charter revision altered the form of representation on the city council and school committee, enlarging the sphere of political influence for community leaders. The switch to district representation for nine of thirteen city council members and all of the school committee members fostered close working relations between district representatives and community leaders (Preer 1987:69). As one close observer put it, "district representatives maintain close contacts with groups, and groups hold their representatives accountable" (Preer 1987:69). What is more, community activists played a major role in mayoral election campaigns, organizing grassroots get-out-the-vote efforts for local candidates.

In sum, boasting more than 300 neighborhood and other associations, the community movement in Boston has been much better organized and, consequently, has wielded greater political clout than in most American cities. By adopting electoral and coalitional strategies, community leaders legitimized their actions in the eyes of government officials, and were thus perceived more as constructive, rather than disruptive, agents in the body politic. This allowed community organizers to form alliances with certain city officials and thus gain a foothold in city hall.

Community Movement Growth and Dependency in Bristol

Community movement mobilization in Bristol during the 1980s stood in stark relief to Boston's powerful community movement. Although a variety of coalitions, fora, and networks formed within the community movement, no single organization or set of overarching coalitions effectively could claim to represent the voluntary sector in strategic decision making at the citywide level or even in particular policy areas. This lack of cohesion within the community sector was reinforced by differences in function, scope, and geography among the groups. In this context, the community sector's two generalist organizations, the Bristol Voluntary Services Council (BVSC) and the Bristol Community Groups Network, never managed to build citywide constituencies among the community groups that operated in Bristol.

Nonetheless, the community sector in Bristol grew in the 1980s, as the Bristol City Council allocated a comparatively large portion of its Urban Programme funding to support community group activities. According to the director of the BVSC, George Garlick (interview July 13, 1994), the "Bristol [City Council] was a very generous funder of community organizations in the 1980s through the Urban Programme. Whereas nationally, . . . about 50 percent of Urban Programme money went to voluntary organizations, in Bristol . . . 85 percent went to voluntary organizations. So they influenced the way that central government grant was spent in favor of voluntary organizations."

Much of the money dispensed to community groups by the city council came in the form of core funding, which enabled these groups to survive and in some cases hire staff to run the day-to-day operations. The willingness of the Bristol City Council to supply core funding rather than simply project-based grants accounts, in part, for the growth spurt in community organizations during the 1980s in Bristol. The downside of this relationship, however, was that the very existence of community groups hinged on city council support. Moreover, individual city councillors formed political ties to groups that operated within their bailiwick, ensuring that they received a share of the urban aid being distributed by the city council (Garlick interview 1994; Erskine interview 1997). The system for allocating financial assistance to community groups was based on political patronage and fostered a relationship of fiscal dependency for the community movement. The nature of these funding arrangements therefore produced bilateral relations between particular politicians and community groups, with community groups viewing each other as competitors for the same pots of money. Consequently, Bristol's community movement remained fragmented and fiscally dependent on Bristol City Council and other government bodies (e.g., Avon County Council) and foundations (Bishop interview 1993; Garlick interview 1994).

Building Social Reform Alliances

In the 1980s, coalition building around social reform issues in Boston and Bristol diverged. Boston's well-organized and politically powerful community movement, which had engaged in oppositional politics in the 1960s and 1970s (see Mollenkopf 1983), entered into a governing coalition with the mayoral administration of Raymond Flynn in the 1980s that forged a preemptive social reform agenda. The weakness and fragmentation in Bristol's community movement, compounded by divisions within the ruling Labour party on the city council, meant that social reform failed to gain prominence on Bristol's governing agenda.

The Rise of a Social Reform Regime in Boston

In the late 1970s and early 1980s, social reform politics was more limited, and played out through oppositional politics and some bargaining between Kevin White's mayoral administration and community activists. By the mid-1980s, under the banner of "economic justice," the Flynn administration, community activists, and a handful of progressive business leaders coalesced into a regime-like power structure around a social reform governing agenda. Boston's social reform regime centered on efforts to produce affordable housing and attain greater equal opportunity in the job market. The underlying strategy deployed was to redistribute some of the benefits of a booming downtown economy—money, jobs, housing—to the city's poor and working-class neighborhoods. In the 1980s, affordable housing became the central element of the city's social reform agenda.

In February 1983, the Boston City Council deliberated on an affordable housing linkage policy modeled after San Francisco's (Vennochi 1983). When the ordinance came to his desk in June 1983, Mayor White vetoed the measure because he felt it was too stringent. Within a month, however, White impaneled an advisory committee to draft an alternative linkage policy. The policy failed to generate much heat in the upcoming 1983 mayoral election, as White had already announced his decision to bow out of the race and all the candidates advocated some kind of linkage program.

Despite unanimity among the mayoral candidates, dissension arose within the ranks of the advisory committee. Business and real estate representatives opposed any form of linkage program, while housing activists on the panel sought an expansive linkage policy. In October, after a compromise had been ironed out among the contending forces, the advisory committee recommended a linkage formula that would require developers of commercial projects to pay a $5 fee for each square foot of space built over the 100,000 square feet limit (Vennochi 1983). The money generated from the linkage fees, which could be paid over a twelve-year period, would be used to construct affordable housing. White endorsed the advisory committee's proposal, and established Boston's linkage policy through an executive order in the twilight days of his administration.

Boston Fair Share and the Boston Affordable Housing Coalition assailed White's linkage policy as grossly inadequate. The mayoral candidate, Flynn, who had fought for housing reform during his years on the city council, lent his voice to the chorus of criticism. This embryonic social reform coalition argued that the linkage fees were too low, that housing as well as commercial development should have been subject to linkage fees, and that the twelve-year payment period was too long. These criticisms notwithstanding, revisions in the linkage formula awaited Flynn's succession to the mayor's office.

By the early 1980s, Boston's economy entered a period of sustained expansion. In this environment, affordable housing for Boston's poorer and minority residents surfaced as the catalytic issue in Boston's social reform politics. Rapid economic development in Boston produced the spillover effects of escalating housing costs and the creation of a severe housing shortage (Muzzio and Bailey 1986). For example, the city's average housing rent increased from $540 in 1985 to $788 in 1987, and the median price for a single-family house more than doubled from $80,000 to $180,000 between 1982 and 1987 (Malone 1988). Second, the number of condominiums in Boston rose from 14,556 in 1983 to 31,556 in 1986, comprising 12.2 percent of Boston's housing stock (Howe 1987; Malone 1988). In reaction to these threats to the city's affordable housing stock, community activists laid siege to the White administration's downtown-centered, progrowth agenda, but exacted few concessions in the form of protection and construction of affordable housing. After 1983, community activists and the Flynn administration coalesced around a governing agenda of "economic justice," and affordable housing became the central focus of this social reform alliance.

Flynn imparted a lively populist appeal to his constituents, cultivating the persona of "Everyman" by immersing himself in the everyday life of Boston neighborhoods. On any given day, he could be found jogging through Boston's diverse neighborhoods, playing basketball with teenagers on neighborhood courts (Flynn had played for Providence College), or frequenting neighborhood taverns to socialize with working-class patrons. Electorally, Flynn's urban populism was an unqualified success. Flynn constructed a broad-based electoral coalition that bridged the class and racial divisions that had riven the city's politics at least since the early 1970s, when federal court-ordered school busing had caused these rifts to deepen. Opinion polls consistently attested to Flynn's extraordinary popularity, with approval ratings of 77 percent in 1985, 83 percent in 1987, and 75 percent in 1989 (Mooney 1989). Flynn overwhelmed his opponents during the 1987 mayoral election, garnering 67 percent of the total vote.

Flynn's self-styled neighborhood populism facilitated the transition made by Boston's community movement from outsider to insider politics. Wielding their newfound electoral power, community leaders pressed for changes in the city's governing agenda that would address neighborhood concerns and problems more directly. Flynn, in turn, appointed community organizers as key policy makers, dubbed the "Sandinistas" by the local press. Because many of them had earned their political spurs in community organizing and therefore had long-standing ties to the community movement, Flynn's left-wing Sandinistas were predisposed to working with community organizations in constructing a social reform governing agenda (Dreier interview 1992; McGuigan interview 1992).

The Flynn administration coalesced with community activists around a broad affordable housing legislative agenda. For example, Massachusetts Fair Share, the Massachusetts Tenants Organization, the Association of Community Organizations for Reform Now (ACORN), and other community groups banded together with the Flynn administration to enact a revision in the city's linkage policy. The proposed revision would increase linkage fees on large-scale commercial development and reduce the number of years, from twelve to seven, over which linkage installments could be paid (Powers 1985b). The real estate industry immediately went on the defensive. The Greater Boston Real Estate Board (GBREB) labored strenuously to derail the linkage revision, first in the city council and then in the courts (Powers 1985a; Dreier 1989:47). After several setbacks, the affordable housing alliance finally triumphed over the GBREB, when the Boston Zoning Commission approved the change to the city's housing code in 1986 (Dreier 1989:47; Boston Redevelopment Authority 1988).

The affordable housing coalition's legislative agenda also included measures to protect existing low- and moderate-income housing. First, the Flynn administration, tenants groups, and sympathetic members of the city council attempted to strengthen Boston's rent control system. The White administration's actions in the 1970s had lifted rent control from more than 50,000 units. The affordable housing coalition secured amendments that widened the coverage and put more teeth into the enforcement of rent control by extending the authority of the Boston Rent Equity Board.

Second, this same coalition, alarmed by the extent to which gentrification had eroded the stock of affordable housing, proposed ordinances that would impose limits on condominium conversions. These proposals encountered truculent opposition from an alliance of developers, real estate interests, and progrowth members of the city council. This opposition stymied passage of two condominium limitation proposals and diluted the power of a third. Nevertheless, the affordable housing coalition eventually succeeded in pushing through the city council a much more restrictive condominium conversion limitation in June 1987 (Malone 1987; Hernandez 1987).

In many ways, these legislative victories cemented the bonds of the emerging social reform regime and set the stage for implementing its affordable housing agenda. In 1986, Flynn pledged that 3,400 new housing units would be built in Boston over the next year. To fulfill this promise, the Flynn administration devised a complex of interlocking policies and programs designed to produce or preserve affordable housing.[1] First, the Neighborhood Housing Trust Fund (NHTF) became the cash cow for affordable housing construction.[2] By 1988, the housing linkage program subsidized 35 housing developments with 2,092 units, of which 84 percent were classified as affordable housing. In addition to the NHTF, the Flynn administration established the Neighborhood Stabilization Fund, which generated funds by the sale of "quick start" parcels that the city owned, which were used to assist low- and moderate-income residents in holding onto their homes (Boston Redevelopment Authority 1987:2).

The Flynn administration introduced or enlarged programs for the development of affordable owner-occupied housing, which included the use of abandoned property, city-owned property, tax abatements, and an infill-housing program for affordable housing projects (City of Boston 1987). Moreover, in collaboration with the Boston state house delegation, Flynn ushered a bill through Beacon Hill's legislative labyrinth that would reduce the time available for tax delinquent landowners to reclaim abandoned housing. The city also gained the authority to offer tax abatements for the development of tax delinquent abandoned buildings with one to six units, which would permit nonprofit developers and low- and moderate-income residents to refurbish vacated housing without having to pay back taxes on the property (City of Boston 1987:44–45).

To complement the funding and property disposition programs that subsidized low- and moderate-income housing production, the Flynn administration also instituted two additional linkage programs. Inclusionary zoning, which was initiated in 1986, obligated developers who received zoning relief for private housing projects of at least 10 units in the downtown area and at least 25 units in the neighborhoods to set aside for low- and moderate-income residents. The amount of affordable housing included would be equal to or greater than 10 percent of the total number of units (City of Boston 1987:26–27). Parcel-to-parcel linkage, in turn, made it a condition of development approval that for-profit developers of city-owned downtown parcels also participate in the redevelopment of specified neighborhood parcels (DiGaetano 1989:269).

The Flynn administration utilized community development corporations (CDCs) as the city's primary vehicle for expanding the affordable housing stock in the city's poorer neighborhoods (City of Boston 1987; McGuigan interview 1992). Policy Sandinistas, such as Peter Dreier, the Boston Redevelopment Authority Housing Director, and Lisa Chapnick, the director of the Public Facilities Department (the city's housing development agency), cultivated close ties to leaders of the CDCs and together devised new mechanisms for financing, building, and refurbishing affordable housing (Dreier interview 1992; McGuigan interview 1992). As Chapnick explained, "CDCs are Boston's secret weapon. When I do business with a CDC, I know that what they want is what the [Flynn] administration wants — preservation of affordable housing for the long term. . . . When the city declares war on abandoned buildings, CDCs are the primary weapon" (quoted in Radin 1987b:30). Boston's CDCs became the workhorses of the city's affordable housing production.

The CDCs in Boston originated in the community protest groups that sprang up in the 1960s (Fisher 1984; Robb 1985:49). When first formed, CDCs in Boston were able to construct or refurbish only a few homeowner units a year. From the mid- to late-1980s, CDCs, particularly through involvement in the Boston Housing Partnership (discussed later), concentrated on building and rehabilitating larger-scale, multifamily housing (Hagopian interview 1994). Furthermore, the role of CDCs in policy-making was heightened by their willingness to pool their resources in order to increase their political clout. In 1980, CDC leaders in Boston and across the state formed the Massachusetts Association of Community Development Corporations (MACDC). Because 22 of the 49 MACDC members were based in Boston proper, one of the permanent committees, the Boston Committee, focused on Boston neighborhood development problems (Libby interview 1992).

Another partner in Boston's program to implement the affordable housing program was the Boston Housing Partnership (BHP). In 1982, Paul Grogan, the director of the White administration's Neighborhood Development Agency, approached William Edgerly (interview August 8, 1992), CEO and chair of the State Street Bank, about creating a public-private partnership around the problem of affordable housing. Edgerly convinced the heads of a number of other banks to come on board, and by 1983 BHP was born. From that point on the BHP served as an umbrella agency for cooperative efforts among city and state officials, CDCs, and business leaders to tackle the problem of a dwindling stock of affordable housing in Boston. The BHP's small central staff, funded largely out of state and city grants, performed the functions of coordinating funding among the various projects and providing technical assistance to CDCs. The CDCs, in

turn, undertook the job of selecting and purchasing buildings for rehabilitation, hiring the architects and contractors to carry out the renovations,
monitoring the work in progress, choosing the tenants, and eventually managing the apartments when they were completed and filled (City of Boston
1987:46).

To finance affordable housing projects, the BHP pooled $38 million
from city, state, and private sources for the first phase (1985–1987) of its
program. The BHP housing program, like the city's, produced much of its
affordable housing through CDCs. Seven hundred units of affordable housing were refurbished by 10 CDCs in 69 buildings during the first phase.
The BHP also operated a Small Building Program, which provided rent
subsidies and rehabilitation funds to 160 units of small owner-occupied
housing (City of Boston 1987:48)

Bristol: Social Reform Politics in the 1980s

Bristol has been considered one of Britain's more prosperous big cities,
endowed with a strong financial services sector and situated in a region
that has attracted substantial high tech and other investment over the last
three decades. Although the city possessed pockets of poverty, it also had
a sizable middle class and served as the cultural center of the region. This
relative prosperity meant that the amount of urban aid that Bristol received from the central government was quite small compared to Britain's
other major cities. In addition, at least in the 1980s, the relationship between the Labour-dominated Bristol City Council and the Thatcher government was marred by suspicion and conflict. In this political and economic environment, despite the presence of a large community movement
and an emerging New Left contingent within the city council's Labour group,
a social reform governing agenda failed to materialize.

In 1980, a riot ripped through St. Paul's, an inner-city district popu-
lated by a relatively large percentage of Afro-Caribbeans. The event caused
a considerable political stir in Bristol and the nation, as it was the first in a
spate of disturbances that rocked Britain's larger cities in the 1980s. When
the central government refused to hold a public inquiry on the matter, local leaders formed a Tripartite Committee to investigate the underlying
reasons for the social disorder. The Tripartite Committee, which was composed of representatives from the Bristol City Council, Avon County Council, and the Bristol Committee for Racial Equality, concentrated on the
problem of inner-city deprivation. To address the problem, the Tripartite
Committee was subdivided into three working groups — community facilities, employment, and education — to devise policy proposals. The pro-

posals were submitted to the Home Office in July 1981, but no firm commitment from the central government for additional funding ensued. Without government financial support, Bristol's strategic antipoverty alliance crumbled. Moreover, leadership in the Bristol community movement, as noted, proved too poorly organized to sustain a long-term peak coalition with the county and city councils.

Consequently, the city council resumed full responsibility for strategic decision making on inner-city regeneration. For example, on the basis of a research report on poverty in Bristol, in which the Planning Department compiled Department of Environment data that showed Bristol ranked twelfth among urban authorities on inner-city deprivation in 1981, the city council requested Urban Programme status. As with an earlier attempt, the request was denied. Nonetheless, the information generated by this effort was employed in acquiring European Social Funding in 1984 (Boddy, Lovering, and Bassett 1986:188–89), which supplied additional resources to the city's own Inner Area Program. As a result, the city council became a generous financial supporter of community groups in the later half of the 1980s. The city council's poverty program was given a boost in 1987 when the Conservative government finally granted Bristol Urban Programme status. Nevertheless, the failure to form a social reform governing alliance around the city's antipoverty effort meant that the city council managed a dispersed network of relationships with individual community groups that delivered publicly funded community development programs.

Bristol's Labour party, which held a majority on the Bristol City Council for all but two years in the 1980s, was racked by factionalism. Traditional Labour councillors, who maintained strong ties to the city's trade unions and blue-collar constituents, sought to minimize or even marginalize the growing number of New Left politicians appearing in the ranks of the local Labour party. A split between soft and hard factions of the New Left wing exacerbated further the factionalism within the Labour group (Dalby 1989; Robertson interview August 8, 1991).

Traditional Labour politicians comprised the majority of Labour group, and therefore retained control of most of the leadership positions. Hence, when New Left councillors broke ranks with the Labour leadership over the city council's budget in 1980, they were temporarily removed from the group. Bitterness over this issue festered even after the rebels were restored to the Labour group by the national Labour party. When Labour returned to power in 1984 after two years of hung councils, the New Left contingent secured a sizable minority of the Labour seats, gaining a number of key committee chairs. The strength of the New Left faction became apparent when the city council adopted a "socialist strategy" in 1986. The spirited enthusiasm around Bristol's Socialist Strategy quickly withered, however, when it became apparent that central government restrictions on city council spending made impossible the costly programs envisaged by the New Left's plans for municipal socialism.

Recasting Social Reform Politics in the 1990s

The 1990s brought realignments in social reform politics to both Boston and Bristol. In Boston, the social reform coalition lost its clear dominance in the 1990s. The onset of economic hard times and cutbacks in federal and state aid for housing and other programs meant that tradeoffs were made between progrowth and social reform forces. Social reform maintained a prominent position on the city's governing agenda, but shifted to broader-based coalitional politics among city hall officials, business leaders, and community activists. Bristol, which had not fostered a strong community movement in the 1980s, witnessed the emergence of an embryonic social reform governing coalition in the mid-1990s. The central government set requirements for community participation in Single Regeneration Budget bids and projects that enabled community activists to gain a foothold in strategic decision making around regeneration issues.

Coalitional Politics in Boston

The Flynn administration altered its governing strategy dramatically in the early 1990s. With the bottoming out of the housing market and the loss of revenue from the linkage program and other sources, the city's affordable housing strategy diminished in importance. The new governing agenda consisted of four strategic foci: (1) a community-based anticrime program, (2) a broad-based educational reform effort, (3) improvement in community health care facilities and programs, and (4) an aggressive and targeted economic development strategy (Sullivan interview 1992, 1994). Each of the first three initiatives undertaken by the Flynn administration clearly fit within the broader strategic aim of social reform, and were designed to address problems faced by the city's most disadvantaged neighborhoods. The anticrime effort, which was a reaction to the rise in drug and gang crime, incorporated community policing methods and youth initiatives, such as the Safe Neighborhoods program. To reform the city's school system, the Flynn administration convinced the state legislature to abolish the elected school board and replace it with a new one appointed by the mayor. The centerpiece of the Healthy Boston initiative was the building of a new Boston City Hospital. The Flynn administration, despite reducing the priority of affordable housing, remained steadfastly committed to the city's neighborhoods and disadvantaged residents.

Having learned the lesson that community mobilization can be an effective governing tool, the Flynn administration also began devising ways in which CDCs could be used as vehicles for stimulating economic growth in the neighborhoods. In 1991, for example, the Flynn administration, MACDC, and three locally based banks developed a micro-loan program for financing small business start-ups and expansion in Boston neighborhoods (Libby interview 1992; Gillis interview 1992).

The director of Economic Development and Industrial Corporation, Don Gillis, supplied the rationale for using CDCs to promote neighborhood economic development in a 1992 interview:

> Community development corporations, with their locally based
> elections of boards of directors, have a strong community base.
> They are very effective advocates in the community, and some of
> them have gotten more into economic development. Some of
> them are seeking to expand their role, like in business you have
> to move into new markets because some of the old markets are
> drying up. Housing development resources are drying up. So the
> availability of new opportunities, a notion of survival, but also
> identifying community priorities make CDCs effective agents for
> economic development.

In the spring of 1992, Gillis engineered a new form of collaborative framework, christened the Boston Economic Growth Partnership (BEGP). The BEGP brought together city officials from the EDIC and Public Facilities Department (PFD), the heads of five CDCs, MACDC, two foundations (Boston Foundation and Hyams Foundation), and utility (Boston Edison) and banking officials (Bank of Boston and Fleet Bank) around the issue of neighborhood economic development (Gillis interview June 23, 1992; Economic Development and Industrial Development Corporation n.d.:3). The purpose of the BEGP was to replicate the successes of the Boston Housing Partnership by using CDCs as the principal vehicles for neighborhood economic development (Economic Development and Industrial Corporation n.d.). Thus, the social reform governing coalition switched its emphasis from affordable housing to job creation (Gillis interview June 23, 1992; Economic Development and Industrial Corporation n.d.). Before the BEGP could become fully operational, Flynn accepted a post as ambassador to the Vatican, leaving the new partnership in limbo.

The Menino administration never revived the BEGP, and instead developed ways to invigorate neighborhood business districts that forged direct links with neighborhood business owners, rather than working through CDCs (Lago interview 1994; Griggsby interview 1994). The Menino administration, for instance, launched a $2.5-million, city-funded neighborhood business renewal program based on the Mainstreets model.

In sharp relief to Flynn's energetic and confrontational populism, Menino adopted a low-key and consensus-building leadership style. Despite the contrasting styles of leadership, however, the substance of governance maintained a remarkable continuity (Kranish 1993; Black 1993; McGrory 1993; Lehigh 1994). Although Menino had campaigned as a candidate for "change," some social reform measures proposed or initiated under Flynn were brought to fruition by the Menino administration, such as school reform (Hagopian interview 1994; Lago interview 1994; Sullivan interview 1994). The resilience of social reform politics also was revealed in the alliance between the Menino administration and community leaders around the passage of a "living wage" ordinance. This ordinance requires companies that receive financial assistance from, or have contracts with, the city to pay a minimum of $7.49 per hour to their Boston employees (Flint 1997b). Business leaders objected strongly to the measure, but the Menino administration dismissed their concerns and signed the ordinance into law in August 1997. In addition to these initiatives, two other issues highlight the durability of Boston's social reform coalition: eliminating biases in bank lending and the effort to secure an empowerment zone grant.

The Politics of Bank Lending Practices

In 1992, the Boston Federal Reserve Bank published a report that exposed a yawning disparity between whites and minorities in the lending practices of Boston banks (Walker 1995a). In response to the revelation that banks had disproportionately denied mortgages to residents in Boston's poorer and minority neighborhoods, an alliance among the Flynn administration and community groups, including ACORN (Association of Community Organizations for Reform Now), the Massachusetts Alliance for Affordable Housing, and a host of neighborhood-based groups, launched a campaign to end unfair bank lending practices (Canellos 1992; Walker 1995a). Rather than resisting, most Boston banks tacitly agreed that biases existed in their lending practices and entered into negotiations with the Flynn administration and community groups about how to resolve the problem (Walker 1995a). For example, Fleet Bank negotiated a deal with the Flynn administration and the Massachusetts Alliance for Affordable Housing to establish an $8-million lending program to enable low- and moderate-income Boston residents to become first-time home buyers (Benning 1992).

It should be noted that the alliance between community leaders and the Flynn administration, although generally amicable, became unsettled over the lending bias issue. For some community activists felt betrayed when the Flynn administration struck a behind-the-scenes deal with one of the larger banks without consulting the community groups that had mobilized around the issue. The bitterness engendered by this action led some community leaders to accuse Flynn of political grandstanding (interviews with Vargas July 28, 1992, and Hagopian August 12, 1992).

Change in mayoral administrations did not disrupt the bank lending effort. Mayor Flynn issued an executive order that established a linked deposit policy, which required banks to comply with federal guidelines on minority lending, as established by the Community Reinvestment Act of 1977. Failure to improve rates of lending to Boston's poorer and minority neighborhoods could be punished by a withdrawal of city funds held in deposit at those banks (Walker 1995b). In 1995, the Menino administration pushed the Linked Deposit policy through the city council, giving it a legal status that would, unlike an executive order, carry over from administration to administration (Walker 1993, 1995b). The new Linked Deposit policy also required an annual review of lending practices of those banks holding city deposits. In addition, the Flynn and Menino administrations and community groups, such as Massachusetts Affordable Housing Alliance, used negative publicity to keep the heat on banks.

A three-year study of mortgage lending in Boston published in August 1995 reported a substantial rise in inner-city lending by local banks. Between 1990 and 1993, bank loans to minorities in Boston doubled, which diverged from national patterns in which lending rates to minority applicants dropped (Blanton 1995). The city's annual surveys of eleven banks also indicated that bank lending performance overall in minority communities, which included affordable housing and mortgage lending, economic development, services, and banking employment, improved appreciably (Walker 1995b).

Empowerment Zone Politics

Antipoverty efforts in Boston throughout the 1980s had been fragmented and addressed more indirectly through the city's affordable housing and jobs programs. This trend continued through the early 1990s until the federal government afforded an opportunity for a more concerted attack on poverty—the Empowerment Zone program. Boston entered the race for empowerment zone designation in a field of 78 cities (Hohler 1994b).

The Menino administration initiated the bid for an empowerment zone, but preparation of the city's proposal was an exercise in inclusive decision making and consensus building. In January 1994, Menino appointed a steering committee to write the plan. The 121-member committee was composed of city and state government officials, community activists, and business leaders (City of Boston 1994b; Hohler 1994a; Walker 1994d). Under the gun of the nearly impossible deadline of six months, formulation of the plan entailed a massive undertaking of grassroots organizing and public consultation through the medium of community-based meetings (City of Boston 1994b; Coughlin 1994; Hagopian interview September 6, 1994; Lago interview September 6, 1994). Although haggling among community activists over the precise boundaries of the proposed empowerment zone had to be resolved through a gerrymandering process, the strategic decision-making process was generally deemed to be open and well-coordinated (Hagopian interview September 6, 1994).

Menino personally filed the city's empowerment zone proposal, entitled *Boston Works*, with HUD on June 30, 1994. Boston's bid was considered to be a long shot, given the city's relatively prosperous image and Washington politics that favored larger cities, such as New York and Chicago (Hohler 1994a; Walker 1994b). Nonetheless, once submitted, Boston's social reform alliance launched a sophisticated and multipronged campaign of insider lobbying to win empowerment zone designation. First, Menino and a local contingent of business leaders, community activists, and other civic leaders made the formal presentation to HUD (Coughlin 1994). Second, the Menino administration organized meetings with officials in the Clinton administration who had direct ties to Massachusetts to solicit their aid in the battle for empowerment zone funding (Hohler 1994b). Finally, Boston's congressional delegation, which included the state's seasoned and powerful Senators, John Kerry and Edward Kennedy, as well as Boston's Representatives, Joseph Moakley and Joseph Kennedy, II, maneuvered behind the scenes on behalf of Boston's bid (Hohler 1994b).

In the midst of this full-scale assault, Representative Kennedy learned from Clinton administration officials that, although the selection panel was impressed by the city's proposal, Boston was unlikely to receive the full $100 million grant (Black 1994b). The Clinton administration then decided to create a second tier of $25 million grants that excluded the social service component of the empowerment zone grant (Hohler 1994c). Seeing the possibility of salvaging the *Boston Works* initiative, the Menino administration quickly regrouped and applied for the second-tier grant (Walker 1994b).

To improve the chances of this second proposal, a coalition of Boston banks (Bank of Boston, BayBank, Citizens Bank, Shawmut Bank, State Street Bank, US Trust, the Boston Companies, and Boston Bank of Commerce) pledged $35 million in loans and other assistance as part of the *Boston Works* renewal program (Walker 1994a). The strategy worked, as Boston, along with four other cities, received an Enterprise Community Zone (ECZ) grant.

The deftness displayed by the empowerment zone coalition in winning the ECZ grant did not carry over into implementation of the program (see Anand 1997a). It took the Menino administration 10 months to select the 37-member advisory board that would make recommendations on loans to ECZ businesses. As a result, two and a half years into the program, only one loan had been approved. This loan was used to build a textile factory in Roxbury. Only $2.9 million in commitments had been secured and 59 jobs created (all associated with the textile factory) by the end of May 1997. Another problem with the program emerged when Menino appointed the former director of a CDC, Reginald Nunnally, as executive director of the ECZ. Nunnally's appointment drew fire because he was thought to be too inexperienced to run the $44 million program. Nunnally himself admitted his lack of knowledge about marketing and finances (Anand 1997a). Because of such bureaucratic problems, the $35 million in loans to ECZ businesses pledged by the eight banks was slow to appear.

Affordable Housing Revisited

When Boston's economy began to recover in the mid-1990s, Menino decided to overhaul the city's affordable housing policy. To stabilize inner-city neighborhoods, the Menino administration created programs to facilitate home ownership for moderate-income families. To promote neighborhood commercial development, the Menino administration began a city-funded Main Street program (interviews with Griggsby September 7, 1994, and Lago September 6, 1994). Despite these efforts, affordable housing resurfaced as a volatile issue when a state-wide referendum in November 1994 outlawed, beginning on January 1, 1995, the use of rent control regulations by all communities in Massachusetts. Only Boston, Brookline, and Cambridge actually operated rent control programs under the nullified state legislation. The Menino administration immediately called for passage of a home rule petition that would allow Boston to reinstate rent control (Walker 1994c). The home-rule petition issue pitted the Greater Boston Real Estate Board against an alliance of tenants groups and the Menino administration. The city council approved the petition, and the state legislature, after intensive lobbying campaigns by both sides, enacted exemptions for the three cities. Governor William Weld, a staunch opponent of rent control, vetoed the legislation. Backpedaling a bit, Weld eventually signed legislation that permitted a two-year phaseout of rent control, rather than bringing it to an abrupt halt (Oser 1996).

Although Boston procured a two-year reprieve for parts of its rent control program, a serious problem still loomed—displacement of poor tenants by rapid rent increases as the extension expired at the end of 1996 (Chacon 1996b). In the meantime, the Boston Tenants Coalition pressed the Menino administration to adopt measures that would cushion the impact of the final phaseout on January 1, 1997 (Anand 1995b). In a deal negotiated among the Menino administration, the Rental Housing Association (an industry group of landlords), and the Boston Tenants Coalition, city officials agreed to conduct a telephone survey of the 22,000 tenants affected by decontrol to determine what sort of measures would be needed (Anand 1995a). Little in the way of action followed.

In the final months of the rent control extension period, housing activists stepped up pressure on Menino to provide rent subsidies for those tenants subject to escalating rents after the first of January (Anand 1996). Initially, Menino refused to allocate city funding for tenants adversely affected by rent decontrol. But Menino eventually succumbed to political browbeating by the housing alliance and, in October 1996, unveiled a "safety net" proposal that would commit $2 million in rental subsidies and $6 million in extant funding to affordable housing construction for low-income elderly residents (Chacon 1996a).

In early 1997, the Menino administration, the Massachusetts Housing Partnership Fund (MHPF), and BankBoston announced a collaborative effort to encourage small-property landlords and investors to renovate existing or build new rental housing (Anand 1997). The Hidden Assets program, as it is called, will be funded by the MHPF and the city. The MHPF will contribute $5 million in low-interest loans, and the city will furnish $1 million in long-term loans that can be converted to grants.[3] Nonprofit developers, such as CDCs, are also eligible for the program. Landlords who receive the loans and grants must agree to set aside at least 51 percent of the units for "people with household incomes at or below 80 percent of the area median income" (Anand 1997c). In short, although commitment to affordable housing was revived with the issue of eliminating rent control, it was clear that social reform politics in Boston had changed. The alliance between the Menino administration and housing activists was no longer based on preemptive power, thus marking the end of regime politics.

Urban Regeneration Politics in Bristol in the 1990s

Bristol's track record on antipoverty initiatives has been less than noteworthy. Even under the old Urban Programme, antipoverty efforts were not coordinated on the basis of any strategic plan or agenda. In terms of urban regeneration, the handful of neighborhood-based initiatives undertaken in the city's poorest areas, like Hartcliff–Withywood and Easton, featured cooperation between the city council and individual community organizations (J. Bishop interview 1993). However, nothing approaching Boston's social reform alliance emerged.

In part, this resulted from the fragmentation in Bristol's community movement. In raw numbers, Bristol's community movement had become quite large, with an estimated 1,200 community-based organizations by 1994, yet the relationship of dependency on the local authority for financial support remained in place. Moreover, the city council altered the basis of financial assistance to community groups in the 1990s. In the 1980s, the Bristol City Council had been willing to supply community groups with core funding, which enabled them to sustain operational support, such as paid staff and office premises. Foundations and other private sources generally limited grant giving to specific activities and projects. In the 1990s, under restraint of central government dicta to reduce direct service delivery, the Bristol City Council transformed its relationship with community groups into a contractual one where funding was given for the provision of specific services (Garlick interview 1994; J. Bishop interview 1993). As a result, funding for core activities dwindled, making it more difficult for community groups to maintain administrative functions.

The introduction of a more competitive intergovernmental grant system, however, altered relations between the Bristol City Council and Bristol's community movement. Single Regeneration Budget and some European grants require the participation of community leaders. This transformed relations between the city council and the community movement, putting it on a more mutually dependent footing in the arena of regeneration policy-making. Comparing Bristol's City Challenge bid and subsequent Single Regeneration bids illustrates this realignment in social reform politics.

The Politics of Urban Regeneration

The central government invited Bristol to submit a proposal for the first round of City Challenge in 1991. Bristol City Council leaders were ambivalent about the competitive program, paying only lip service to the local campaign to win the City Challenge grant. The job was shouldered almost entirely by city council officers, led by the Housing Department (Lambert et al. 1994). The initiative received little support or guidance from city councillors, with the exception of those representing the wards involved (Hartcliffe and Withywood). Moreover, with little experience in such cooperative efforts, council coordination with Avon County Council, the business sector, and community leaders proved awkward and sometimes contentious. The bid ultimately failed. When Environment Secretary Michael Heseltine invited Bristol to compete in the second round of City Challenge, participants mounted a much better organized effort. According to Lambert et al. (1994:12), "The key differences from the first round bid were the establishment of a full-time team comprising officers from the city and county, and nominated partners from the private sector, the university and the community, led by a senior officer from the Planning Department." City Council Labour leaders remained unenthusiastic. According to Malpass (n.d.:15), in a steering group meeting after Bristol's failure to win in the second round was announced, "a Labour councillor was reported to have said that it was now 'back to normal, no fancy delivery mechanisms, no central government involvement, back to the local authority taking charge.'" Bristol politicians it seems had not yet mastered the art of partnership.

The Conservative government opened the bidding process for Single Regeneration Budget (SRB) funding in 1994. Bristol's first SRB bid kindled ill feelings between the city council and community leaders. The roots of the controversy over the SRB bid were buried deep in the history of city council–community relations. As with City Challenge, there was little involvement by members of the Labour group in the first SRB round (Holland interview July 7, 1996). Instead, city council and Western Training and Enterprise Council (WESTEC) officers and staff patched together a number of their pet projects to comprise the SRB bid. To satisfy SRB's clear requirement for collaboration, the Bristol City Council and WESTEC formed a dummy Bristol Regeneration Partnership (BRP) to coordinate the bidding process (Bee interview June 17, 1997). The chamber of commerce was added later to BRP. The SRB bid was then presented to business and community leaders for their stamp of approval (interviews with Garlick July 13, 1994; de Groot, July 5, 1995; Kershaw July 7, 1995; Sandbrook July 19, 1995; Savage July 18, 1995).

The bid, under the heading of *Bristol 2020*, focused on the regeneration of what was known locally as the "Crescent of Deprivation and Opportunity." This crescent touched wards from Lawrence Weston in the city's northwest corner, through Southmead, Lockleaze, the inner-city areas of St. Paul's and Lawrence Hill, and Knowle West to the southwesternmost neighborhoods of Hartcliffe and Withywood (Bristol Regeneration Partnership 1995).

The fait accompli SRB proposal, which needed to be rushed along to meet the deadline set by the Regional Government Office (RGO), incensed some community leaders (Garlick interview 1994; de Groot interview 1995; Kershaw interview 1995). Moreover, tensions worsened as the community leaders accused city council officers of seeking to dominate the planning and consultation process (Garlick interview July 13, 1994). City council officers recognized the problem, but blamed the lack of consultation on the short time frame imposed by the central government (de Groot interview July 5, 1995).

At this juncture, two leading community activists, who saw the SRB agenda being pulled too far into the orbit of city council influence, went to the RGO and reported that Bristol's SRB bid would not be supported by the community sector leadership (Erskine interview 1996; Fowler interview 1996). In its stead, a number of community organizations under the umbrella of the Bristol Community Groups Network submitted a separate SRB bid for a large-scale, community capacity-building project. After a process of negotiation between city council officers and community leaders, this bid was appended to the city's bid. The capacity-building project was scaled back from £20 million to £280 thousand. To placate the rebellious community activists, city council officers acquiesced to certain concessions in the final SRB proposal. This marked a shift in the dynamics of SRB politics, with community leaders assuming a more strategic role in the process.

Community leaders from the Bristol Council on Equality, the Black Voluntary Sector, the Greater Bristol Trust, and the BVSC formed a steering group to discuss the feasibility of a peak organization that would develop community-based regeneration strategies. An open meeting was held in which a structure and management committee was created for what became the Voluntary Organization Standing Conference on Urban Regeneration (VOSCUR) (Erskine interview 1996). The stated purpose of VOSCUR was to ensure that Bristol's community organizations were directly involved from the early preparatory stages of bids through to implementation of programs funded by grants from the central government and European Union (Garlick 1995b). The VOSCUR group received the £280,000 in SRB funding for community capacity building over five years, which enabled the fledgling community organization to hire its own staff (Erskine 1996).

Under director Jean Erskine, VOSCUR has steered a course that has not tied it closely to the BRP. Rather than devoting most or all of its resources (it has a staff of only 1.5) to jockeying for position within the BRP, VOSCUR has found it more efficacious to engage in individual partnerships, particularly with the city council, around single projects. For example, VOSCUR teamed up with the city council and community groups in Hengrove Park to regenerate a 220-acre brownfield site in South Bristol (Erskine interview June 8, 1997).

VOSCUR has not been without its critics. Some local notables felt that a process for decision making around regeneration issues should have been put in place first, before setting up the governing structure (Sandbrook interview July 19, 1995). Moreover, reflecting persistent divisions within Bristol's community movement, some peak community organizations, such as the BCVS, Agenda 21 (environmental), and Choices for Bristol, evinced some suspicions that VOSCUR may try to encroach on their territory (Erskine interview July 10, 1996). In other words, in an environment of city council cutbacks on community development funding, some community leaders viewed VOSCUR as another competitor in a universe of rapidly diminishing resources. By 1997, the local culture had changed somewhat, with greater cross sector discourse and coordination emerging. Interestingly, this has occurred since the BVSC was put out of commission, when the city council withdrew funding in March 1997 on the grounds that BCVS had become ineffectual.

Most parties agreed that Bristol's first bid for SRB funding was a rush job that lacked coordination. Under pressure of time, the SRB bid had been roughly hewn without much consideration of strategic priorities or creating an integrated system of urban regeneration. Furthermore, when Bristol learned that it had received less than half the funding proposed in its bid, adjustments had to be made in the city's SRB spending priorities. Bristol had requested £17 million over four years, but the Major government granted only £800,000 for Bristol's antipoverty initiatives for 1995, and a total of £7.85 million over six years (Garlick 1995a). At this point, the BRP revisited the question of strategy and mission (interviews with Sandbrook July 19, 1995, and Kershaw July 7, 1995). Formed in name only for the first SRB proposal, the BRP provided the forum for adjusting the city's regeneration priorities to the reduced level of funding (Kershaw interview July 7, 1995). Now that the BRP was fully operational, it coordinated and integrated the process of preparing the city's second and third round SRB bids, both of which were successful. The BRP also appointed six staff of its own (previously it had been staffed by the city council) in late 1996 to carry out its SRB responsibilities.

In June 1997, the BRP board, after a somewhat quarrelsome debate between community and business leaders, constituted the partnership as an industrial provident society (with charitable status). Business sector representatives on the board would have preferred to incorporate as a company limited by guarantee. Membership was broadened to include representatives of the Avon and Somerset Constabulary, the local health authority, the universities, two colleges of further education, the Trades Union Council, and VOSCUR. The BRP may, however, be in danger of developing into a single-purpose partnership that bids for and implements SRB funded projects. As the new chair of the City Council Planning Committee, Helen Holland, who is also the chair of the BRP, explained in a June 17, 1997, interview, "We have reappraised how people are going to input into the partnership, and there is a lot of stuff going on about what else the partnership is going to get involved because it did necessarily get weighed down with SRB project management."

A number of local leaders expressed misgivings about the BRP, questioning its ability to serve as a coordinating agent for regeneration citywide. According to Jean Erskine (1997), the director of VOSCUR, chief executives of its member organizations rarely attended BRP officer meetings, sending lower-tier officers in their place. This was seen as a warning sign that the BRP may be in danger of becoming marginalized. For instance, the city council, on its own, submitted a bid and won a £3.6 million URBAN grant for three inner-city wards from the European Commission (Shorney 1997). The city council had considered handing over implementation of the URBAN project, which entails youth, sport, and music programs in Easton, Lawrence Hill, and Ashley, to the BRP (Holland interview June 17, 1997). Holland worried that the BRP may not possess the capacity to navigate the Byzantine rules laid down to govern the URBAN program. "Although I want the partnership (BRP) to have that kind of role, I don't want to set them up to fail, really. I think that there will be dangers of asking the BRP to oversee that process" (Holland interview June 17, 1997).

A final sign that social reform politics was on the rise could be seen in the city council's new community development agenda. A realignment in the city council that started in 1996 with the establishment of Bristol as a unitary authority resulted in the election of more community development-oriented Labour councillors to leadership positions in 1997. The old guard Council Leader, Graham Robertson, stepped down and was replaced by a more left-leaning Council Leader, George Micklewright. Micklewright, who had been chair of the Housing Committee and a powerful figure behind the scenes for years, placed greater emphasis on community development. Also, Councillor Helen Holland, who replaced Andrew May as Planning Committee chair in May 1997, had been more closely aligned with community regeneration politics through her involvement with the failed City Challenge bids and as chair of the BRP. Social reform, as a result, has risen as a priority on the city council agenda. Four key initiatives demonstrate the expansion of the city council's social reform agenda: On Site, which is a resident jobs and training program; Business Match, which encourages businesses to purchase goods and services from Bristol-based companies; a Third Sector strategy to support community-based economic development; and a Regeneration Bids strategy to maximize the city's ability to attract grants and other external funding for job creation and antipoverty projects (Bristol City Council n.d.). Whether this will translate into the development of a stable social reform governing coalition is not yet clear.

Conclusion

Differences in state structure notwithstanding, it has been argued here that the development of a well-organized community with institutional electoral and policy resources that are independent of local government are crucial building blocks for the construction of sustainable social reform governing alliances. For example, the differences in the scale and relative importance of social reform agendas in Boston and Bristol in the 1980s and 1990s can be explained in large part by differences in political clout and coherence of the community movements in the two cities. Boston's community movement coalesced with the Flynn administration in the 1980s to form a powerful social reform regime. Although circumstances of a depressed property market undermined the regime power structure, the city's social reform governing coalition remained intact well into the Menino administration. Bristol has been less hospitable to social reform politics. The city's weak and fragmented community movement could not overcome its dependence on the city council through the 1980s and early 1990s. Changes in central government and European grant systems, however, may have given Bristol's community activists the leverage necessary to form a social reform governing coalition through such organizations as the BRP and VOSCUR. In addition, the city council's new leadership is more concerned with issues of community development. Whether this incipient social reform coalition will graduate into a stable governing alliance remains to be seen.

8

The Dilemmas of Growth Management Politics

Leavened by the forces that degraded urban life — sprawl, pollution, traffic congestion, and the destruction of green space and historic architecture — the politics of growth management in American cities arose in reaction to the externalities of rapid growth. In some cases, growth management movements found strong allies among state and local government officials. For example, in Portland, Oregon, and Seattle, Washington, growth management governing coalitions installed elaborate systems to regulate land use locally and regionally (see Caves 1992; Egan 1996). In other cases, growth management movements encountered resistance or apathy from government officials. Particularly (but not exclusively) in the western United States, these growth management activists resorted to what Caves (1992) called "ballot box planning," which imposed growth controls on urban and other areas through state and local referenda and initiatives. Growth management in Britain, in turn, is a much older and more respected tradition. An island nation with comparatively limited space, Britain's greenbelt policies and strong planning systems have long enabled local authorities to contain urban sprawl. Restrictive land use powers and policies were, to some extent, rolled back by the Thatcher government in the 1980s in deference to market forces. The Major government, believing that the Thatcher government had gone too far, restored some measure of local planning and development power in the early 1990s as a buffer against what were seen as the worst effects of an unbridled market economy.

Boston and Bristol were both caught up in the politics of growth management. Growth management alliances in our "prosperous" cities formed around issues of modulating the pace and kind of development, with particular concerns for historic preservation and protection of green space.

The Rise of Growth Management Politics in Boston and Bristol

In the 1960s and early 1970s, mobilization of Boston's growth management movement developed unevenly, with isolated episodes of resistance to large-scale development. For example, grassroots opposition to a federal highway scheme in south Boston delayed the project for more than a decade (Kennedy 1992:198–200). Some consolidation occurred in the 1970s when some 20 groups including Boston Harbor Associates, Boston Society of Architects, Boston Society of Landscape Architects, and the Citizen Housing and Planning Association united as the Boston Preservation Alliance (BPA) to safeguard the city's built environment (Kay 1979; Menzies 1983; Frisby 1984; Yudis 1984). As the political arm of the preservation movement, the BPA won its first major contest when the White administration agreed to establish the Boston Landmarks Commission to review and recommend buildings for designation as historic landmarks (Collins, Waters, and Dotson 1991:48). In contrast, environmental groups were much slower to consolidate their power. It was not until 1985, for instance, that environmental groups cohered around a common agenda by forming the Boston GreenSpace Alliance.

In Bristol, two citywide groups emerged as the self-appointed guardians of the city's built environment. One was the Bristol Civic Society, which was founded in 1905 and was composed primarily of professionals (architects, barristers and solicitors, academics, engineers, and planners). The society maintained only a small staff and relied on expertise and free services from its membership to carry out its historic preservation agenda (*Bristol Evening Post* 1987). The Bristol Visual and Environmental Group, largely a one-woman show since its inception in 1971, became an outspoken lobbying group on any development matters involving historic buildings or aesthetic considerations in physical development (Punter 1990). Bristol's growth management movement coalesced in the midst of a controversy surrounding the construction of city center office blocs in the early 1970s. Building on key victories against large-scale commercial projects, this middle-class conservation movement exerted considerable influence in Bristol's development politics by the mid-1970s.

Three factors seem common to the rise of growth management movements in Boston and Bristol. First, both were primarily middle-class movements, with professionals dominating leadership positions. Second, both cities possessed large stocks of historic buildings and a substantial number of parks, squares, and other areas of green space; that is, a built environment worth preserving. Finally, and not surprisingly, political mobi-

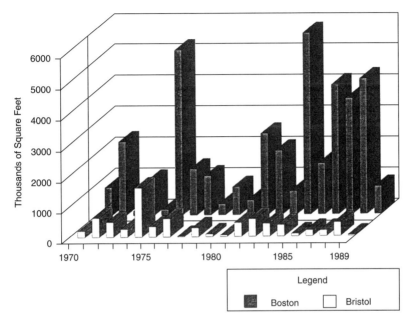

Figure 8.1. Office development in Boston and Bristol, 1970–1989. *Source:* Boston Redevelopment Authority, Policy Development and Research Department (April 1989); Bristol City Council, Planning and Development Services (April 1995).

lization occurred in periods of rapid development. Figure 8.1 shows office construction in Boston from 1975 to 1989 and office completions in Bristol from 1974 to 1990. Political mobilization in Boston around growth management issues reached its peak in the mid-1980s, which, according to figure 8.1, coincided with the acme of the city's downtown office construction boom. Similarly, in Bristol, the rise to prominence of the conservation movement occurred in the mid-1970s, which corresponded to the city's biggest office boom in recent history. Despite these similarities, modes of governance around growth management agendas diverged.

Boston: Managing the Urban Environment

Boston's growth management movement never achieved the strength or durability of its social reform counterpart (see chapter 5). In fact, it was largely through its connection to social reform issues that the growth management movement was able to enter into a governing alliance with the Flynn administration in the mid-1980s. Nonetheless, and in contrast to the years of the White administration, planning in Boston from 1984 to 1989 was dominated by the city's growth management governing alliance. Developers and real estate interests generally acceded to the increasingly restrictive planning process, so that little in the way of major opposition arose for the remainder of the decade. In this sense, it appeared that Boston's growth management governing alliance wielded preemptive power, and therefore resembled a powerful regime mode of governance.

The chief architect of the Flynn administration's development strategy was Boston Redevelopment Authority (BRA) director Stephen Coyle. On Coyle's watch, the BRA reassumed its role as the citywide planning agency and took the lead in formulating and carrying out the Flynn administration's growth management strategy (Rezendes and Aucoin 1991). In doing so, Coyle became the gatekeeper in the development process, proving a tough negotiator with developers on issues of building design and size, while at the same time exacting developer contributions for affordable housing and jobs programs (King 1990:7–8). This was greatly aided by Boston's hot real estate market, which gave Coyle an edge over developers eager to construct giant corporate towers in downtown Boston. Overall, Coyle is credited with rezoning the entire city, installing a process that institutionalized citizen participation in neighborhood planning, and expanding the city's housing and jobs linkage programs (Frisby 1987; Rezendes and Aucoin 1991; King 1990:7–9).

Managing Growth in the Boom Eighties

Boston experienced a massive office development boom in the 1980s (see figure 8.1). To cope with the city's rapid pace of growth, in June 1985 the Flynn administration announced a comprehensive plan that attempted to balance concerns of regulating development and "economic justice." The master plan proposed nine new initiatives: (1) tougher downtown development restrictions, (2) the creation of targeted development areas, (3) rezoning the entire city; (4) expansion of the city's linkage program, (4) incentives for housing production, (5) expansion of job training and employment programs, (6) measures to protect and improve open space, (7) preservation of about 255 buildings, (8) improvement of the city's transportation facilities, including pedestrian and bicycle traffic, and (9) expansion of citizen participation in the planning and development process (Powers 1985c). To carry out this ambitious plan, the Flynn administration restored citywide planning authority to the BRA, which had been curtailed under Mayor White (Boston Redevelopment Authority 1986; Kennedy 1992). Flynn also greatly enlarged the BRA staff, from about 165 in 1984 to 315 in 1987, to perform the agency's expanded functions (Boston Redevelopment Authority 1986, 1992).

Shortly after the inauguration of Boston's growth management plan, the BRA embarked on the lengthy and painstaking process of revising the city's zoning codes. As a stop-gap measure, the BRA created interim planning overlay districts (IPODs) to serve as zoning tools until the rezoning process was completed. The IPODs established guidelines and strategies for development design, historic preservation, housing affordability, traffic management, and public improvements (Brown et al. 1987). By 1989, eight IPODs had been put in place and five permanent zoning districts had been established (Boston Redevelopment Authority 1989:4).

To control the rate and kind of development that took place within the downtown IPOD, the BRA identified five categories of subdistricts—priority preservation, restricted growth, medium growth, economic development, and special planned development areas in the financial district—and established height and size limits for each (Prince and the Boston Redevelopment Authority 1991:83; Brown et al. 1987). Instruments for managing development in Boston's neighborhoods, in turn, included limits on building heights, transportation and parking controls, urban design requirements, and open space planning (Prince and the Boston Redevelopment Authority 1991:90). Furthermore, a community-based master plan was formulated for Chinatown, and IPODs were adopted for a number of neighborhoods (Boston Redevelopment Authority 1987:3). To protect open space, which accounted for 11.2 percent (3,600 acres) of Boston's total land area, the Flynn administration fashioned an open space zoning district with nine subdistrict categories (Prince and the Boston Redevelopment Authority 1991:99). The BRA also developed a master plan for the city's waterfront that was designed to guarantee public access to the waterfront through the creation of a Harborpark by stringing together small and large open spaces abutting the Boston Harbor with a pedestrian walkway named Harborwalk (Boston Redevelopment Authority 1987:9). The BRA completed the downtown zoning code revision by the end of 1991 and the remainder of the city by 1993 (Ackerman 1991, 1992; Barrett interview July 7, 1992).

The Flynn administration also overhauled the city's development review structures and processes in an effort to protect the city's neighborhoods from the negative impacts of development and raise standards of environmental quality and urban design. Amendments to the city's Development Review Requirements toughened the requirements for development approvals and provided for a public review of development projects to judge whether developers adhered to development standards (Brown et al. 1987; Prince and the Boston Redevelopment Authority 1991:89). Development proposals were subjected to review by the city's Historic Landmark Commission, the Civic Design Commission, and Community Advisory Committees, as well as the Zoning Commission. All told, the phalanx of regulatory and review agencies meant that developers underwent close scrutiny when proposing development projects.

Urban Populist Planning

Urban populism infused development politics in the middle to late 1980s with a strong element of participatory planning. Community leaders rallied around the cause of greater neighborhood participation in the planning process under the banner of the Coalition for Community Control of Development (CCCD)(Lupo 1987a). Acquiescing to CCCD's demands, the Flynn administration established Community Advisory Committees (CACs), which considered the design and environmental impacts of proposed developments and, when deemed necessary, recommended zoning and other restrictions (Lupo 1987b; Radin 1987b).

The democratizing effects of CACs should not be overstated, however, for the neighborhood councils functioned in an advisory capacity, and most members of these councils were initially handpicked by the Flynn administration (Lupo 1987b). Nonetheless, CACs usually exercised de facto veto power over development in their neighborhoods, as the Flynn administration was very reluctant to proceed with a project unless it had passed muster with these neighborhood planning bodies (Barrett interview July 7, 1992; Lupo 1987b). Finally, the Flynn administration's commitment to a participatory planning process was repeatedly demonstrated by the enormous efforts to win neighborhood approval for specific projects. For instance, in 1987, BRA staff conducted approximately 45 neighborhood meetings a month, with BRA Director "Coyle personally attending up to nine neighborhood meetings a month" (Frisby 1987). In later years, board members of CACs were elected by the neighborhoods, rather than being appointed by the mayor.

Returning Luster to Boston's Emerald Necklace

In the early part of the century, Frederick Law Olmsted designed Boston's park system, known locally as the Emerald Necklace. From the late-1970s to the early 1980s, the management of the city's park and recreation system slackened and, as a consequence, Boston's Emerald Necklace lost much of its luster (Primack 1989:3–4). During this period, myriad environmental groups sought to refurbish the city's parks and open spaces, but these efforts were fragmented, often focusing on a single park or area.

In 1984, old Yankee conservationists, leftist community gardening activists, minority neighborhood leaders, traditional environmental and beautification activists, and some business owners, whose property was situated in close proximity to a park, began to coalesce around the issue of restoring the city's park system (Primack 1989:5–6). In August 1985, leaders from 20 groups and several public agencies founded the Boston Green-Space Alliance (BGA) to act as a citywide advocate in preserving and improving the city's natural environs (Primack 1989:6). This proved no mean feat, given the cacophony of ideological viewpoints espoused by the diverse groups involved (Primack interview July 6, 1992). BGA leaders worked out a semblance of consensus and in 1985 deployed a lobbying campaign that combined *Boston Globe* exposé articles on the deteriorating conditions of city parks and face-to-face meetings with city officials (Primack 1989:7, interview July 6, 1992). By the spring of 1986, however, it became clear that the BGA's strategy to persuade Mayor Flynn that "parks fit in well with his own neighborhood and youth-oriented agenda" had failed to hit home (Primack 1989:7, interview July 6, 1992).

The green space campaign was given a boost in the summer of that year when the Boston Foundation, a local philanthropic organization, sponsored a seminar that focused on Boston's parks and open spaces. More than 100 city and state officials, environmentalists and preservationists, business leaders, and community organizers attended the seminar series (Arnold 1987). The goal of this 18-month-long forum, known as the Carol B. Goldberg Seminar, was to exchange and develop ideas that linked improvement of the city's park system to a strategy to combat problems of poverty in Boston (Boston Foundation 1987). Seminar participants issued a report in October 1987, which concluded that a comprehensive park and green space improvement program could be a powerful instrument in any effort to enrich the quality of life for all Boston residents, as well as serve as a vehicle for alleviating problems associated with poverty (Boston Foundation 1987:21). The report listed 10 general recommendations and offered guidelines for launching a citywide program to rehabilitate Boston's park system. The formula agreed upon by seminar participants envisioned public-private cooperation as the modus operandi to accomplish this task.

The BGA played a key role in the forum, and was subsequently selected to monitor the progress made in carrying out the proposed agenda. This became the basis of an ongoing working relationship between the

Flynn administration and the BGA. In its capacity as monitor, the BGA served as both consultant, working with the BRA, PFD, and the Parks Department on designing and implementing various programs related to open space preservation and use, and watchdog, reviewing city zoning and other land use plans (Primack interview July 6, 1992). The immediate consequence of this alliance was that the Flynn administration undertook the job of rehabilitating the city's entire park system through its capital spending program (Arnold 1987; Primack 1989). First, Flynn appointed William Coughlin as the city parks commissioner to clean house in a department that had gained a reputation as a haven for patronage and mismanagement. Second, the Parks Department, working closely with the GreenSpace Alliance and the PFD, mapped out and implemented a five-year improvement program that covered almost all of the city's parks (Primack 1990, interview July 6, 1992). The restoration of Boston's Emerald Necklace was completed by 1992.

Bristol: Growth Management and the Politics of Conflict

During the Long Boom (1945–1970), a progrowth governing coalition orchestrated a massive reconstruction of war-torn Bristol using a program of large-scale public infrastructure development (Boddy, Lovering, and Basset 1986:171). Under this Long Boom regime, planning decisions were subordinated to economic and engineering concerns and decision making took place behind closed doors, allowing little or no consultation with the public (Punter 1990:114). When the development boom reached its pinnacle in the early 1970s (see figure 8.1), however, the Bristol Civic Society and the Bristol Visual and Environment Group, in conjunction with a host of neighborhood amenity and resident groups, mounted a number of energetic and well-publicized campaigns against big development projects. Their actions won the incipient growth management movement a good deal of public approbation (Punter 1990:119–20). What is more, public anger incited by the city council's prodevelopment policies spilled over into the 1973 local election, which returned the Labour Party to power.

The new Labour administration implemented a number of institutional and policy changes that dismantled the Long Boom planning system, replacing it with one that enforced strict land use and design requirements. First, the city council divided the existing Planning and Land Committee into two separate committees, the Planning and Traffic Committee and the Land and General Purposes Committee. This freed planners from worries about how such decisions might affect the value or financial returns of city property holdings. Thus liberated, the Planning Committee imposed a two-year moratorium on new planning permission applications for office development (Punter 1990:116). The Planning Department also was separated from the City Engineering Department, enabling city planners to chart a course not dictated by the city engineers' preoccupation with infrastructure expansion (Punter 1990:117).

In addition, a durable conservation alliance formed in the mid-1970s, consisting of city planners, the chair of the City Council Planning Committee, prominent amenity groups such as the Bristol Civic Society, and English Heritage (the national, government-funded historic conservation agency). Bristol's conservation program, which provided subsidies for refurbishing the city's substantial stock of Georgian and Victorian buildings, was the fourth largest in Britain.

Over the years of its implementation the conservation program met with some resistance from the Labour group's leadership, especially over funding issues. The fact that English Heritage supplied the lion's share of funding for conserving Bristol's historic architecture, and some deft political maneuvering by the chief planner, Iain Patterson, enabled the conservation program to run through two very successful five-year phases from 1977 to 1987 (see Punter 1990).

Bristol's conservation program existed as a sheltered harbor in the otherwise tumultuous sea of growth management politics. Bristol's growth management alliance came under fierce attack on a number of fronts. Two issues—the erosion of city planning powers and the City Centre Draft Plan—illustrate how competing factions of progrowth and growth management interests became locked in combat during in the 1980s.

City Planning Powers under Attack

At the end of 1985, the Bristol Chamber of Commerce, the Bristol Society of Architects, and Bristol Property Agents issued a report that slammed Bristol's Planning Department (Prestage 1986). The report, entitled "Planning Difficulties in Bristol," drew on a survey of 64 development industry practices and firms that had dealings with the Planning Department, and concluded that Bristol had acquired a reputation for poor planning performance and antidevelopment attitudes (Prestage 1986). The "Planning Difficulties" report was submitted to Chief Executive Walter Miller, who sympathized with the development industry's concerns. Miller dispatched the report to the Planning Committee in March 1986, which determined that the allegations should be investigated and handed it over to the Planning Director, Patterson. Patterson responded by drafting a counter report that refuted the charges, and defended the city's restrictive development practices as a necessary buffer against overdevelopment. Moreover, amenity group leaders actively supported Patterson in the Planning Difficulties controversy (Punter 1990:275, 276).

Nonetheless, Patterson, under direction from Planning Committee Chair Andrew May, recommended a review of the city's planning practices to determine how to improve the process further (Punter 1990:275). At this point, a meeting was arranged to bring together the authors of the "Planning Difficulties" report, the planning officers, and the Planning Committee chair to iron out differences. This attempt at conciliation ended in disaster. The chamber of commerce failed to attend, and the property agents who did attend stormed out of the meeting, leaving a single architect to brave the city planners alone (Punter 1990:276).

City planners subsequently went on the offensive, using the media to rebut the "Planning Difficulties" report at every opportunity (Prestage 1986). Patterson defended the city council's restrictive planning regimen as the instrument for ensuring a high standard of development, which would, in turn, protect Bristol's high quality of life and environment (Prestage 1986). In response to the charge that the Planning Department was antidevelopment, Patterson contended that "[t]here will always be friction between planners and developers. The only way to avoid it is if we nod, smile and keep taking the free lunches" (quoted from Prestage 1986). It became clear that the planners had won this round in the fight over planning.

Nevertheless, pressures within the city council forced the Planning Department to modify its review and approval process. The chair of the Planning Committee, May, was concerned about the image and workings of the city's planning system, and moved to install a more flexible planning system, which would reduce criticism from the private sector and avoid a showdown with central government (Punter 1990:277). May convened regular meetings between the Planning Department and the Bristol Society of Architects to work out kinks in the review process. Greater cooperation between the architects and planners drove a wedge through the "Planning Difficulties" alliance, which, in turn, politically isolated property agents (Punter 1990:277).

May, through the Planning Committee and in alliance with the chief executive, also sought to reform the planning application and review processes by (1) rationalizing decision making in the Development Unit and Design Sections and reducing the discretion of the Planning Director over individual projects; (2) upgrading the Planning Department's computer system; (3) instituting annual performance reviews for the application process, the work program, and the workload of the Planning Department;

and (4) increasing public awareness and participation in the development planning process through fora for public consultation (Punter 1990:277–78). The last of these changes reflected Councillor May's New Left orientation, while the first three showed his desire to move planning to a strategic level. Amenity groups, in contrast, regarded this relaxation of the planning regimen as the first step in dismantling the growth management system that safeguarded Bristol's built environment (Punter 1990:283).

Bristol's planning system came under attack from another quarter when the Secretary of State for the Environment set out policies that weakened local authority power to regulate development. This was done by establishing an appeals process that permitted developers to overturn city council decisions on planning applications more easily (interviews with Fiddler July 9, 1993; Patterson August 8,1991; May August 1, 1991). This had a major impact on Bristol's planning process. The office development boom in Bristol had pushed planners to the limit, and to curtail office and other commercial development, city planners refused a comparatively high rate of development applications. For example, Bristol City Council denied 19 percent of all development applications in 1985, against a national rate of 14 percent (Punter 1990:282). In response to these denials, developers took their cases to the DoE, which, in turn, granted development permission in about half the cases. In 1982, only 29 percent of all planning appeals from Bristol had been granted by the DoE; by 1985, under the new appeal process, the proportion of planning decisions overturned by the DoE had skyrocketed to 48 percent, well above the national average of 41 percent (Ellis 1986).

Buried under a mountain of planning applications and sensing that decisions to deny projects could be easily overturned by appeal, city planning officials relaxed their grip on the development process. Reluctance to deny applications stemmed first from the cost of fighting appeals to the DoE, and second from the belief that denials would probably be overturned by the DoE, anyway. The consequence was that the rate of application refusal dropped precipitously after 1985, a clear signal that Bristol's development control system had been seriously eroded (Punter 1990: 282–85).

A final blow to Bristol's planning power was dealt by the Thatcher government, when the Secretary of State for the Environment announced on December 7, 1987, that an urban development corporation would be declared for a large industrial area east of the city center (Punter 1990:293). The city council had been warned of this eventuality by Conservative councillors, who had been notified by a "senior government source" in April 1987 (Punter 1990:293).

The proposal to establish a UDC in Bristol alarmed and outraged the city council for several reasons. First, a UDC would mean the loss of planning power over the area, and any development plans that were made by the UDC need not conform to the city council's own plans and policies (interviews with Robinson July 6, 1993 and May August 1, 1991). Second, New Left Labour councillors viewed UDCs as a threat to local democracy, being accountable only to the central government (Moreton 1989; May interview August 1, 1991). Finally, the area to be handed over to the UDC did not really fit the typical description of an urban regeneration area. Only a small portion of the land was derelict and even a smaller amount was vacant. The city council considered the area to be a necessary, if unpleasant, "dirty backyard" where industries could operate away from residential and commercial areas (interviews with West July 5, 1991, and May August 1, 1991).

In February 1988, the Planning Committee began to research the procedures for objecting to the UDC's approval. After reporting its findings, the city council decided on a 38 to 22 vote to file a formal objection to the DoE (Punter 1990:294). In the meantime, the DoE extended the boundaries of the proposed UDC to include the Old Market area and a portion of the inner circuit road that the city council had planned to use for an expansion of its central shopping area, known as Broadmead (Punter 1990:296). The proposed extension provoked a slew of objections and counter responses between the city's planning director and the Junior Minister for the Environment. Eventually a meeting of all the principal players was called, including the minister, the DoE regional officer, the leader of the Bristol City Council, the planning committee chair, the chief executive, the planning director, and other senior officers (Punter 1990:296). The meeting generated much heat, with the minister seeking to persuade the city council to withdraw its objection, and city officials attempting to convince the DoE to abandon the UDC boundary extension proposal (Punter 1990: 296). Nothing was resolved.

At this point, May, the Planning Committee chair, spearheaded the drive to raise a formal objection before the Select Committee of the House of Lords, in spite of strong opposition from a number of senior Labour councillors (Punter 1990:296–97). However, the Avon County Council, which had often been at odds with the Bristol City Council, voiced strong support for the formal objection, and a petition was submitted to the House of Lords on June 22, 1988 (Bristol City Planning Officer and Avon County Planning Officer 1991). At the hearing held by the Select Committee in October 1988, the regional director of the DoE argued that a UDC was necessary in Bristol because the local authority had been too slow to regenerate the designated area. He also claimed that the area required substantial highway improvement to facilitate the flow of traffic into and through that sector of the city (Punter 1990:298). In its final report, the Select Committee, although it had rejected many of the DoE's claims about the city council's neglect of the area, upheld the UDC declaration because it felt that such an agency would be better equipped to regenerate the area (Punter 1990: 298). The city council did win one concession when the Select Committee recommended that most of the area under the proposed extension be excluded from UDC jurisdiction (Bristol City Planning Officer and Avon County Planning Officer 1991:2). The Bristol Development Corporation was officially incorporated in January 1989, and began operation in the following February.

The City Centre Local Plan: An Exercise in Democracy?
Consideration of a City Centre Local Plan started as early as 1983, but did not make much progress until 1985, when Avon County put its structure plan in place (Punter 1990:320). With Planning Committee chair Andrew May at the helm, the process of drawing up a local plan was injected with a strong dose of participatory politics. Borrowing ideas from New Left models in Sheffield and Leeds, May and the planning officers attempted to democratize the process of local planning.

To accomplish this task, planning fora were set up to discuss the content of the local plan. Seventy groups were represented in these fora, drawing from interests across the spectrum: amenity, business, residential, professional, trades, and public associations (Punter 1990:320). Three fora were organized around particular topics: (1) conservation, traffic, and quality of the environment; (2) economy, trading, and professional interests; and (3) housing, community groups, recreation, and the arts (Bristol City Council 1987). A City Centre Local Plan Team, composed of three city planners (one for each forum), was created to coordinate the effort. Each forum produced topic papers that were then used in formulating the policies and planning areas for directing city center development. While the Planning Committee and planning officers generally won praise for their labors to broaden public involvement, some complained that less-organized and minority groups had been left out (J. Bishop interview July 7, 1993).

The plan that surfaced from this more participatory decision-making process rested on the principle that areas should be ranked according to their development priority and function (Bristol City Council, Planning Department n.d.). The draft plan abandoned the site-by-site, ad hoc style that had previously characterized the Planning Department's practices, and informed the city's planning system with a more strategic orientation. The City Center Plan set a clear agenda for its 10-year life: "to promote the city's role as a regional Center for business, cultural and recreational facilities" (Bristol City Council 1987).

Although most applauded the broad objectives of the draft plan, battle lines were drawn on a number of particulars. First, the strategic area approach regulated the amount and character of office development, limiting building size to a maximum of 65,000 square feet within the central business district. Property developers approved of the plan's strategic character, which would partially relieve them of the earlier procedures and practices that they considered rigid and bogged down in the minutiae that often delayed office development. Nonetheless, the city's property agents charged that implementation of the plan would choke off Bristol's thriving financial sector office market. Furthermore, the plan imposed a limit of one parking space per 5,000 square feet of office space. This severe restriction on available parking, coupled with the Labour Council's opposition to a proposed privately owned Avon Metro Area light rail system, moved one property agent to describe the plan as "absolutely ludicrous." It came as no surprise that the city's amenity groups praised the City Centre Draft Plan. Restrictions on large-scale development, an emphasis on pedestrian over vehicular traffic in the city center, with links to public transportation to outlying areas, and continued priority for conservation and protection of green space all conformed to the growth management agenda (Sutton 1990).

Growth Management in the 1990s: An Endangered Species?

The political profile of environmental and historic preservation groups receded considerably in Boston and Bristol during the 1990s. The political climate no longer favored aggressive growth management politics. The severe recession that beleaguered both cities appeared to render trivial arguments about balanced growth and restrictive planning. Also, central government funding for the conservation program dried up in Britain. As a consequence, development politics in the 1990s increasingly embraced the logic of growth, which placed a high premium on stimulating, rather than controlling, physical development. In short, growth management politics seemed to become an endangered species in Boston and Bristol.

Boston: Growth Management's Reincarnation?

As the growth management regime collapsed, historic preservationists and environmental activists alike attempted a political reincarnation that would better fit the new reality of growth politics. As development slowed to a trickle, the Flynn administration increasingly viewed historic preservationists as obstructionists. When the Boston Preservation Alliance objected to the demolition of several older buildings in the combat zone (the downtown area district once designated as the city's pornography district), BRA director Paul Barrett dismissed their concerns (Canellos 1993). In response, preservationists adjusted their political pitch to the new reality of progrowth politics. In the 1993 mayoral election, preservationists urged mayoral candidates Menino and James Brett to formulate "aggressive policies and pass ordinances to save the city's historic buildings from the wrecking ball" (Clements 1993). As chair of Boston Landmarks Commission Alan Schwartz intoned, "There has been a lot of frustration that people don't see historic preservation as a major economic generator for the city of Boston. And what we're saying is that whoever the new mayor is needs to recognize that and make it a major piece of any new economic development strategy that he comes up with.... This really has to be a top priority of city governments" (quoted from Clements 1993).

During the 1993 mayoral election, the Landmarks Commission laid out a six-point plan to use historic preservation as an economic development tool. The plan proposed delaying permits for demolition of older buildings, tax abatements for preservation of older buildings, and additional city government support for the city's seven historic districts (Clements 1993). The proposal stirred little interest during or after the election campaign.

Environmental activists also lost their attraction as governing coalition partners in the 1990s (Primack interview July 6, 1992). The city's park improvement program had been accomplished, creating an internal crisis for the Boston GreenSpace Alliance. With its guiding mission completed, member group support eroded, and the BGA leadership cast about for a new mission to reunite the fractious coalition (Primack 1990). In common with historic preservationists, however, environmental activists adopted a new agenda that echoed the Menino administration's concerns about economic development and social reform. The grassroots group, E.C.O., for instance, pushed the city to enlarge its recycling program (Chacon 1995b). Also, greater emphasis was placed on improving the environmental conditions in the city's poorer neighborhoods, as indicated by the creation of the Environmental Diversity Forum and the Massachusetts Environmental Justice Network, a coalition of lawyers (Allen 1994; Chacon 1995b).

In response to this new agenda, the Menino administration unveiled an Environmental Blueprint and Action Plan in 1995 that listed 48 specific projects, from recycling automotive materials to a feasibility study for urban fish farms (Chacon 1995b). Menino said he would also seek to "create more green space in congested neighborhoods" and would convene a conference on the issue of a "sustainable Boston" (quoted from Chacon 1995b). To burnish further his "green" credentials, Menino elevated the chief of Environmental Services to a cabinet-level post. Finally, Menino began to deliver on some of his promises by late 1995, when his administration proposed new parks for a West Roxbury landfill site and a 93-acre site along an abandoned rail bed in East Boston (Chacon 1995a). In both cases, the Menino administration worked closely with neighborhood activists and groups in designing the parks.

Nevertheless, Menino's Environmental Blueprint elicited only tepid praise from environmental leaders. Andrew McCloud, from E.C.O, said, "We're glad to see that he [Menino] has addressed some interdepartmental issues among different agencies, which has always been a problem. But I think he's not being informed well by some of his people" (quoted from Chacon 1995b). Mary Ann Nelson, a national board member of the Sierra Club, complained that "[T]o me, it looks like a packaging deal. Some things that are already going on have just been presented in a different way" (quoted from Chacon 1995b). Finally, Vivien McCloud, the executive director of the Boston Harbor Association, was more optimistic, noting that "[W]hile some say this plan isn't ambitious, it is doable. And that's a positive step" (quoted from Chacon 1995b). McCloud also noted that the city's environmental affairs department was sorely underfunded and understaffed, with a budget of less than half a million dollars and a staff of only twelve people. These remarks gave voice to feelings that environmental issues no longer occupied a central position on the city's governing agenda.

Bristol: Growth Management Falters

Due to the recession, Bristol's growth management coalition also faltered in the 1990s. City center office and commercial development came to a grinding halt, which effectively obviated restrictive planning policies. The conservation program also lost steam, as much of the central area historic building stock had been restored during the 1980s development boom. Also, a number of actions taken by the city council revealed that it was backing away from its aggressive growth management policies of the past. For instance, as part of the city's Green Policy, the Local Draft Plan had originally called for pedestrianization of the central boulevard area in the downtown district known as St. Augustine's Parade. In the midst of a recession, however, the Royal Automobile Club, the Bristol Property Agents, the

Bristol Development Corporation, and even the DoE all decried the pedestrianization plan, and argued that, if implemented, it would damage future employment prospects in the city center. More importantly, progrowth elements in the council, such as the City Valuer, urged that the pedestrianization proposal be axed because it would discourage office and commercial activity (Shorney 1992). Even Planning Committee chairman Andrew May conceded that the Local Plan "needs to be brought up to date to deal with the economic problems of the City. It does mean a much sharper focus on promoting economic development and trying to develop new sectors of employment" (quoted in Shorney 1992).

Another very important change occurred with the retirement in 1993 of Iain Patterson, the planning director of 15 years. A controversial and commanding figure in the city's planning politics, Patterson proved a formidable ally to Bristol's growth management movement. Patterson was succeeded by Diana Kershaw, Bristol City Council's first female chief officer. Kershaw's talents and inclinations lay in promoting and negotiating economic development, rather than conservation and development control. In fact, she considered conservation and restrictive planning as stumbling blocks to effective city center development, particularly in the throes of market stagnation. Kershaw proposed to disband the Design and Control units of the Planning Department, but May rejected the idea (Kershaw interview July 5, 1994). Nonetheless, even May had became more willing to compromise on design control, conservation, and green policies in cases where development would not proceed without a more flexible approach to planning (May interview July 13, 1994). This dramatic transition in city council attitudes allowed progrowth politics to emerge as the dominant force.

Despite these setbacks, the growth management coalition achieved a measure of success. For instance, conservation groups and the Planning Committee joined forces to preserve a number of historic buildings and park land in Stoke Park, located on the northern boundary of Bristol. After intense negotiations, the Health Authority agreed to sell the buildings and land to the city council for preservation purposes (Alsford 1992).

But such victories had become rare moments in the 1990s, and the growth management coalition managed to survive only by assuming a more defensive posture. For instance, amenity groups banded together against the development of a Tesco superstore in the late 1980s to protect a playing field in Golden Hill, a neighborhood area in the north central part of Bristol. The amenity groups and the council's Planning Committee fought the superstore project every step of the way. First, the Planning Committee denied planning permission, and when reversed on an appeal to the

DoE, took the case to the High Court of Britain on the ground that the playing field constituted precious open space that would be lost to unwelcome and unnecessary commercial development. Although the battle dragged on for four years, all was lost when the High Court ruled in June 1992 in favor of Tesco (Hansford 1992).

The endurance of the antisuperstore campaign demonstrates the resiliency of Bristol's growth management alliance. It also suggests that growth management forces in Bristol had fallen back to a defensive position. Unable to move conservation or green policy forward, it increasingly resorted to rearguard actions to delay or block unwanted development projects. In short, it had become something akin to what DeLeon (1992) describes as an "antiregime."

Conclusion

Growth management politics in Boston and Bristol since the 1970s bear some remarkable similarities. First, common to the character of Boston and Bristol's growth management movements was the middle-class base of support. Second, the impetus of political mobilization for their growth management movements could be found in development booms that threatened historic architecture or green space in both cities. Third, growth management coalitions in both cities strengthened planning systems and development control measures. Fourth, large-scale physical rehabilitation programs were undertaken by growth management coalitions, which in Boston refurbished the city's entire park system and in Bristol, through the conservation program, restored a very large proportion of the city's Georgian architecture and squares. Finally, growth management politics in Boston and Bristol receded in the 1990s, as economic recession and shifts in the political climate made growth management more difficult to justify.

There also were some notable differences between Boston and Bristol. During the 1980s, in Boston, the Flynn administration and the growth management movement formed a preemptive governing coalition that met with little resistance from developers or other progrowth factions. Bristol, in contrast, featured competing factions of progrowth and growth management coalitions that engulfed the planning process in a perpetual state of conflict. Also, in Bristol, the intervention of the Thatcher government weakened local planning powers, thus curbing the ability of city planners to regulate development. Thus there were wide differences in the governing capacity of growth management alliances in Boston and Bristol.

Part IV
Modes of Governance
as Explanation

9

Explaining Modes of Governance

The primary focus of this book has been to compare postindustrial urban development politics in the United Kingdom and the United States. The object of this analysis has been what we termed modes of governance, which embody the "who, how, and what" of governing large cities. Adopting a comparative case study approach, we have sought to show how governing coalitions (who), power structures (how), and governing agendas (what) have varied between and within the United Kingdom and the United States. We also have endeavored to demonstrate that commonalities in the practice of urban politics exist, principally the process of building and maintaining coalitions.

A thesis that runs throughout the book is that governing alignments and agendas form and develop as intertwined bundles of city leadership alliances and policies. Based on our detailed descriptions of development politics in Birmingham, Boston, Bristol, and Detroit, table 9.1 shows that governing coalition composition (who governs) and the content of governing agenda (what is done) are closely correlated. Progrowth agendas in all four cities have been set by some combination of city government officials and economic interests (primarily business elites). Growth management agendas in Boston and Bristol have been associated with coalitions of city government officials and environmental or historic preservation activists. Finally, the social reform agenda in Boston developed under the auspices of governing alliances between the mayoral administrations of Flynn and Menino and elements of the city's community movement.

As table 9.1 also shows, however, urban power structures varied both across time and cities, in some even when the composition of governing coalitions had not altered significantly. For example, in Birmingham gov-

Table 9.1

Comparing Urban Governing Coalitions, Power Structures, and Agendas

	Governing Coalitions	Power Structures	Governing Agendas
Birmingham			
1974–1997	City Council leaders and officers and business elites	Coalition (1974–1983) Regime (1984–1993) Coalition (1994–1997)	Progrowth
Boston			
1975–1983	K. White administration, downtown business elites and developers	Coalition	Progrowth
1984–1989	Flynn administration and community activists	Regime	Social reform
	Flynn administration and environmentalists	Regime	Growth management
1990–1997	Flynn and Menino administrations and community activists	Coalition	Social reform
	Flynn and Menino administrations and downtown business elites	Coalition	Progrowth
Bristol			
1973–1992	City Council leaders, planners and amenity groups	Rival factions	Growth management
	City Council leaders, economic development officers and city valuers, and real estate interests and developers	Rival factions	Progrowth
1993–1997	City Council leaders and officers, and business elites	Coalition	Progrowth

Table 9.1 *(continued)*

	Governing Coalitions	Power Structures	Governing Agendas
Detroit			
1974–1997	Young and Archer administrations and downtown business elites	Regime (1974–1979) Coalition (1980–1997)	Progrowth

erning realignments from 1974 to 1997 did not dramatically change the composition of the city's governing coalition or its attendant policy agenda. Nonetheless, the configuration of power shifted from coalitional in the 1970s to a regime in the middle 1980s to the early 1990s, and reverted back to coalitional politics in the middle 1990s. Similarly, the power structure of the ruling progrowth alliance in Detroit underwent a realignment. Emerging as a regime in the 1970s, tensions arose among the ruling partners in the 1980s that replaced preemptive with coalitional politics. In short, our findings fail to corroborate either community power theories (pluralist versus elite) or regime theory.

Missing from our discussion of the modes of governance thus far, however, is a causal explanation for *how and why* governing alignments and agendas arise, develop, and eventually are displaced by others over time. To aid in our etiological inquiry of urban governing alignments and realignments, we draw on three theoretical perspectives. First, urban political economy underscores the importance of the regional, national and even international political-economic environment in explaining the form and content of urban politics. Political culture and institutions form the cardinal elements of a second perspective, and occupy a middle range of theorizing. The third perspective operates at the micro-level of theory and focuses attention on the role of leadership in local political decision making. Considering the utility of each of these theories for comparative analysis of urban politics, our purpose is to develop a theoretical framework that integrates all three levels of theorizing — macro, mezo, and micro — into a single explanation of modes of governance.

The Political Economy of Urban Governance

Urban political economy is predicated on the assumption that urban politics is a product of the division of labor between state and market in city affairs (see Harloe 1977; Peterson 1981; Smith 1984; Logan and Swanstrom

1990). Comparative urban political economy, by extension, attempts to explain how this structural divide shapes the contours of urban governance within and across countries (see Gurr and King 1987; Keating 1991). Paul Kantor, Hank Savitch, and Serena Vicari Haddock (1997:349), for example, have recently developed a political economy framework for comparing urban regimes by examining the "bargaining context" of cities. Kantor, Savitch, and Haddock (1997:349–50, emphasis in original) define regimes as "governmental agents that function to *bargain out the terms of cooperation* between the public and private sector in a liberal-democratic political economy." The focus of their analysis is the relationship between local governments and business interests, contending that "government must bargain over the conditions for inducing capital investment from private-sector markets to achieve economic goals that are shared by dominant political elites."

The political economies of liberal democracies structure these "bargaining contexts" through democratic conditions, market position, and intergovernmental environment. Democratic conditions range from highly competitive popular control systems, which encourage the formation of inclusive governing alliances and thus limit business influence, to less competitive ones that foster exclusionary coalitions in which business elites play a more influential role. Market positions are "determined by location, transportation, or concentrations of specialty services (high technology, corporate finance, and headquarters)," which "make cities more or less appealing to private investors." Finally, intergovernmental systems establish the parameters of bargaining contexts through the provision of "direct aid, political access (to national government), or planning regulations," which either enhance or weaken the hands of local governments (Kantor, Savitch, and Haddock 1997:351).

According to Kantor, Savitch, and Haddock (1997:350), "Ultimately, these factors constrain the very composition of [local] governing coalitions (encouraging who does and does not participate), the mode of bringing about public-private cooperation, and dominant policy agendas (collective versus selective benefits, residential versus commercial development, downtown versus neighborhood investments)." Based on the political-economic criteria of market position (favorable, unfavorable) and intergovernmental system (integrated, dispersed), Kantor, Savitch, and Haddock distinguish four bargaining contexts and two urban regimes associated with each: dirigist (planner, distributor); dependent private (vendor, radical); dependent public (grantsman, clientelist); and mercantile (commercial, free enterprise).

Unfortunately, application of the political-economic model devised by Kantor, Savitch, and Haddock does not gain much purchase on governing alignments in our four case cities. Birmingham's "dependent private" bargaining context, according to the bargaining context criteria, should have produced a radical regime (local mobilization, programmatic parties and high participation, and "open governing coalitions that pursue symbolic politics directed at a mass audience" [Kantor, Savitch, and Haddock 1997:358]). However, Birmingham saw the rise of what they refer to as a "grantsman regime," which uses "public aid for business revival and collective social benefits" (361).

Similarly, a commercial regime, which experiences the political cross pressures to incorporate business demands as well as demands for participation by neighborhood and civic interests, should have emerged in Boston's "mercantile" bargaining context (favorable market position and dispersed intergovernmental system). Instead, what formed was something akin to a modified planner regime, which "draw[s] on formidable bargaining resources to organize open governing coalitions that are dominated by party, government, and bureaucratic interests and that hold sway over business participants" (Kantor, Savitch, and Haddock 1997:354). And Bristol's "dependent public" bargaining context, with its favorable market position and dispersed intergovernmental system, should have engendered a commercial regime. What developed instead was a hybrid of weak grantsman and planner regimes.

The only city in our study that conforms to Kantor, Savitch, and Haddock's typology is Detroit (which was included in their study as well). A bargaining context of an unfavorable market position and a dispersed intergovernmental system fostered Detroit's vendor regime, in which city officials "are inclined to sell the city's wares at bargain prices . . . hoping the city can keep its declining capital from sliding still further" (Kantor, Savitch, and Haddock 1997:358).

The point here is not to dismiss outright the comparative framework wrought by Kantor, Savitch, and Haddock, which is probably the most sophisticated of its kind. Rather, our intention is to signal the dangers of over reliance on a political economy perspective in comparing modes of governance. That is, although cross-national differences in urban political economy certainly effect differences in modes of governance, we hold that the specific modes of governance that emerge are in fact products of a far more complicated set of influences and processes. Simply put, factors such as political traditions, local circumstances, and leadership also must be taken into account.

Culture, Institutions, and Urban Governance

A second theoretical perspective posits culture and institutional development as the primary explanatory factors of urban politics (see, for example, Banfield and Wilson 1963; Elazar 1970). Sam Bass Warner (1968) crafted one of the most notable cultural theories of urban politics and development. Warner explains the development of Philadelphia from the late eighteenth to the early twentieth centuries largely in terms of the American tradition of privatism, which "[i]n its essence, lay in its concentration upon the individual and the individual's search for wealth" (Warner 1968:3). Interestingly, Barnekov, Boyle, and Rich (1989) invoke the concept of privatism to explain the evolution of urban policy in the United Kingdom and United States from the 1960s to the 1980s.

In a variation of Warner's theory of privatism, Meredith Ramsay (1996:96) also purports to reveal "how local institutions, beliefs, values, norms, and traditions shape local regimes." As Ramsay explains:

> Culture is linked to political and economic action through the
> social construction of policy issues. Such ideological
> constructions are here referred to as narrative, discourse and
> story. In complex urban politics, there are likely to be multiple
> narratives, each competing for dominance in interpreting local
> events and prescribing the direction of public affairs. The
> outcome of this competition is important because government
> action is shaped by the story that gains the ascendancy.

Like Warner, Ramsay claims that privatism ranks as the "privileged narrative" in the American cities. This means that "[d]iverse local voices are conventionally devalued and displaced by a generalized and homogenized interpretation that elevates the common currency of jobs, revenue, and trade as the measures of local success" (Ramsay 1996:96–97). Furthermore, the political culture of privatism is "socially embedded" (see Polanyi 1957) in public authority and establishes the foundation for building local political institutions, such as urban regimes.

Barbara Ferman (1996) takes this reasoning a step further by analyzing what she calls the "institutional framework" of "urban arenas." Urban arenas, which include electoral, civic, business and intergovernmental "spheres of activity" consist of "particular frameworks and underlying political cultures that lend a structure to" activities within a local political system (Ferman 1996:4–5). Ferman (8) contends that the institutional framework "contains critical elements that collectively set the tone for how particular institutions operate, thereby shaping expectations of acceptable forms of behavior. These elements include decision-making rules, patterns of re-source distribution, degree of formalization, general orientation, and gov-erning orientation." Institutions such as political parties and public-pri-vate partnerships routinize norms and expectations in the political process, which, in turn, become "important determinants of actions...empower-ing certain types of activities while constraining others" (8). For Ferman, local political culture and arenas are mutually reinforcing, and together establish the logic of urban arenas (10). As a result, political change un-folds as a "long-term, comprehensive, dynamic process that must incor-porate political education; it requires alteration in values, perceptions, ex-pectations, and ultimately behavior" (9).

For our four cities, application of Ramsay's narrative theory and Fer-man's institutional analysis is relatively simple. For example, while pri-vatism perhaps reigned as the hegemonic narrative in Detroit and Birm-ingham, in Boston, at least in the 1980s, the more communitarian narratives of social reform and growth management gained ascendance. In both cases, the institutional frameworks of various partnership arrangements were formed to consolidate the dominance of ruling narratives. In contrast, a cacophony of competing voices — privatism, municipal socialism, and growth management — became institutionalized in the highly contested politics of Bristol's development policy-making arena through the 1970s and 1980s. Beginning in the early 1990s, however, privatism seems to have prevailed, and has been reinforced by an integrated network of public-pri-vate partnerships around city center revitalization.

The utility of the cultural-institutional approach lies in its concep-tion of governing alignments as framed by values and rules. This perspec-tive falls short, however, in at least one important way. Local governing alignments in our four cities experienced a good deal of flux and instabil-ity over time. This raises a troubling question for theories of political cul-ture. If local narratives and institutions are socially embedded and there-fore resistant to change, why did they shift so abruptly in Boston and Bristol? Put another way, cultural-institutional theories fail to account adequately for abrupt changes in the modes of governance.

Leadership and Urban Governance

The study of political leadership has stimulated considerable interest in urban political science over the last two decades. A bountiful literature on the subject has covered a wide range of topics, including constraints on leadership, leadership style, and leadership skills (see P. Clark 1969; Pressman 1972; Kotter and Lawrence 1974; Lupsha 1974; Stone 1982; Ferman 1985; Svara 1990; Fuchs 1992). Our particular concern with urban leadership pertains to the use and structure of political power—or what Judd and Parkinson (1990) call leadership capacity.

Clarence Stone (1995:97), borrowing heavily from the work of James McGregor Burns (1978), puts the following construction on political leadership:

> Although Burns distinguishes between leadership and "naked power wielding," he sees leadership as a form of power. It is a way of making something happen that would otherwise not take place. Hence, Burns offers "contribution to change" as a test of leadership. Thus, from Burns, we have a conception of leadership with three essential elements: leadership is a purposeful activity, it operates interactively with a body of followers, and it is a form of power or causation. Put succinctly, leadership is "collectively purposeful causation."

Having thus defined leadership, Stone (1995) formulates a means to measure leadership capacity by comparing the performance of five American mayors (James Curley of Boston, Richard Daley and Harold Washington of Chicago, Richard Lee of New Haven, and Fiorello La Guardia of New York). He evaluates leadership ability by determining whether mayors make a "*departure* [original emphasis] from an established course, and [that] the change is purposeful" (106). Starting from what he calls a "base point" (existing conditions), Stone examines three areas of leadership performance to ascertain whether a mayor has "taken the path of least resistance" or chartered a new one (106). These three leadership tasks include scope of policy impact (minimal, redistributive), impact on followers (little, significant), and institution building (none, some, extensive) (105–8).

Stone concedes that his conception of leadership capacity, which is based on *personal* leadership, fits less comfortably when applied to British urban politics. "[D]isciplined parties, a strong merit-system tradition with top posts held by career civil servants, and a national context of parliamentary government" means that "there is no twin to the popularly elected executive in the United States" (110–11). As a consequence, Stone concludes that there is a " 'muted style' of local governmental leadership in the United Kingdom" (111).

Stone's theory of leadership poses at least one difficulty for comparative analysis. For Boston and Detroit, the performance of mayors Flynn and Young, respectively, yields easily to Stone's conception of personal leadership. In the United Kingdom, however, local leadership assumes a *collective* form, as illustrated by Birmingham's economic development triumvirate of the 1990s and Bristol's growth management and progrowth factions of the 1970s and 1980s. Despite these limitations we think that his approach offers critical insights for a comparative analysis of urban political leadership. Whether personal or collective, one can still profitably employ Stone's notion of a "base point" by which to assess leadership performance. Moreover, the means of evaluating leadership performance — scope of policy, impact on followers, and institution building — all provide useful measures of governing capacity.

Comparing Urban Governing Alignments and Agendas

Our position is relatively simple. Each of the three theories of urban politics, taken alone, furnish necessary, but insufficient, explanations of the modes of governance. Explication therefore requires use of all three theoretical domains — political economy, institutions, and leadership. What is more, a comparative analysis of modes of governance must examine the interplay between urban and state structuring and restructuring and leadership as it unfolds in the alignment and realignment of urban governing structures and agendas. To interrogate these complex interactions over time and cross-nationally, we now compare the *formation, development,* and *demise* for each of the governing alignments discussed in this book. What we hope to achieve is a comparative understanding of the politics of growth, growth management, and social reform.

Comparing Progrowth Politics

The logic of growth has been widely viewed as a compelling force in American urban politics (Peterson 1981; Mollenkopf 1983; Judd and Swanstrom 1994; Ferman 1996). John Logan and Harvey Molotch (1987) attribute the dominance of growth politics to the perseverance of what they call the urban "growth machine," which is an enduring alliance of political leaders, real estate interests, and others that have a direct or indirect stake in growth and development. Stone (1989, 1993), similarly, attributes the systemic bias in favor of progrowth politics to the "privileged position" of business leaders in urban politics. As noted, Ramsay (1996) points to the hegemonic narrative of privatism as the reason for the move toward growth politics. None of these explanations of progrowth politics suffice for comparative analysis. For growth machines, a privileged position for business elites, and privatism simply have not been constituting features of postindustrial urban politics in the United Kingdom.

This raises a central question for comparative urban analysis. What explains the differences between progrowth politics in the United Kingdom and the United States? One answer lies in the stark differences in state structure and local governing systems. The prevalence of progrowth politics in the United States can be attributed to the decentralized structure of the American state, which allows greater local autonomy from national government but also subjects American local governments to much greater dependency on the local economy for resources (see Harding 1994; Kantor, Savitch, and Haddock 1997). Intergovernmental aid, for example, comprises a smaller proportion of local government revenues in the United States, so that city governments have been far more dependent on the local marketplace as a source of revenues, primarily through property taxes. Similarly, municipal borrowing comes in the form of local bonds floated on the private bond market and managed by private credit agencies. Local government's fiscal dependence on the economy gives the business community its privileged position in urban politics and provides the institutional foundation of local growth machines. This dependence is compounded by the candidate-centered nature of local elections, in which the developers and business elites have become a primary source of campaign contributions for mayoral candidates. Local governing systems in the United States expose city governments to business influence to a far greater degree than local authorities in Britain. This environment predisposes urban politicians to seek alliances with resource rich business interests to pursue progrowth governing agendas in the struggle to maintain fiscal stability.

In sharp contrast, Great Britain's centralized state structure shelters local authorities from many of the exigencies of the market economy. For instance, local authorities receive a far greater share of their revenues from the central government and British intergovernmental grants traditionally are disbursed on the principle of fiscal equalization among localities (Harding 1994:360). Further shielding local authorities from the throes of market forces, the central government guarantees local governments against bankruptcy.

Two interrelated consequences redound from this more centralized state structure. First, local authorities are obliged to follow the lead taken by central government, so that national urban policy often becomes local policy. Second, local authorities are fiscally far less vulnerable to fluctuations in economic cycles. British local authorities depend far less on local business investment (but far more on central government aid) for generating local public revenues. Added to this, strong party organizations mean that local candidates need not solicit campaign contributions from wealthy business contributors. Consequently, British urban politicians, particularly in Labour-dominated authorities, historically have been far less inclined to seek grand alliances with local business elites around development agendas.

The logic of progrowth politics in Britain, in other words, is based on very different premises from the American calculus of growth. Rather than as a fiscal necessity, local authorities in the United Kingdom in the postwar period embarked on large-scale redevelopment programs to rebuild war-damaged areas and inner-city slums. Infrastructure development was a matter of modernizing and upgrading the city's transport system. Public works and planning officers often dominated the prodevelopment governing alignments that carried out these massive renewal efforts (see Webman 1982; Birmingham City Council 1989; Punter 1990). In postwar urban development politics, a technocratic, rather than fiscal, logic obtained.

A new species of urban progrowth politics arose during the Thatcher era, however, principally from changes in the central government's mode of intervention (see Harding 1991). Moving from a permissive mode of intervention in the 1970s to a directive one in the 1980s, the Thatcher government forced a progrowth agenda on local governing systems through the imposition of enterprise zones, simplified planning regimes, UDCs, TECs, and changes in the grant system that emphasized economic development initiatives. Moreover, UDCs and TECs gave business leaders a direct role in local development policy-making. A further change in the mode of intervention in the 1990s to a more competitive system encouraged the formation of local partnership arrangements. As noted, the partnership requirement of the competitive mode of intervention spawned grant coalitions among local authority officials, TECs, and local business leaders (see Cochrane and Peck 1996). Budding growth coalitions in places like Manchester and Sheffield have been resource-driven, coming together for the expressed purpose of winning central government and European regeneration grants (see Lawless 1990; Cochrane and Peck 1996; Stewart 1996).

These explanations of progrowth politics remind us that the differences in American and British urban governance stem from differences in the political economies and cultures of the two countries. Decentralized state structures (which allow for a privileged position for business elites and the development of growth machines) and the weakness of political parties have meant that progrowth urban politics flourishes in the United States, whereas the centralized state, a strong party tradition, and broad powers of local authorities inoculated British urban politics against the logic of growth. When the central government altered its mode of intervention to privilege business leaders in the development decision-making process, however, progrowth coalitions began to surface in British urban politics.

Broadly speaking, urban and state structuring and restructuring explain the differences in the development of progrowth politics in the United Kingdom and the United States. Left unexplained, however, are the variations among cities within each of the two countries. For this, a much more specific analysis of urban governing alignments is necessary.

Formation of Progrowth Alliances

The timing for the emergence of progrowth governing coalitions differ substantially among our four cities. The inception of Birmingham's progrowth alliance can be traced back to the early 1970s when the Labour-controlled local authority combined forces with the Birmingham Chamber to develop the National Exhibition Centre. Similarly, the progrowth alliance in Detroit found its origins in the early 1970s, when the Motor City's white business establishment orchestrated the development of the Renaissance Center. This megaproject was supported enthusiastically by the administration of Coleman Young, the city's first African-American mayor, although the city played a secondary role in its development. Boston's progrowth governing alliance appeared in the early 1990s, when Raymond Flynn's administration adopted an aggressive economic development strategy. Bristol's progrowth coalition emerged even later, around 1993, when local business leaders spearheaded the drive to create the Western Development Partnership.

Massive deindustrialization acted as the catalyst for the forging of progrowth alliances between local political and business leaders in Birmingham and Detroit. In Boston, it was the deep recession of the early 1990s that convinced the Flynn administration to realign the city's governing coalition, first by abandoning its growth management partners and then by opening negotiations with business elites around a progrowth agenda. The construction of Bristol's progrowth coalition was a response to the combined effects of economic and state restructuring. The collapse of the city center development market and severe contraction in the defense industry produced an economic crisis for Bristol, which had enjoyed a period of almost uninterrupted economic prosperity since the early 1970s. Coincidentally, partnership requirements established by the competitive mode of intervention persuaded the Labour leadership on Bristol City Council to form a progrowth alliance with the city's increasingly powerful business leadership.

Development of Progrowth Alignments

Progrowth politics followed a variegated pattern of development among the four cities. Birmingham's progrowth alliance developed into a regime in the 1980s around a progrowth agenda that featured both regional capital and industrial development strategies. The Knowles ruling clique worked quietly behind the scenes to assure that the city's prestige project strategy, which showcased the International Convention Centre, would encounter little or no political resistance. Furthermore, cooperation between the city council and the local business community marked Birmingham's industrial diversification and retention politics in the 1980s, as signified by the formation of the Aston Science Park and the Birmingham Heartlands UDA.

By the late 1980s, the rapid growth of Birmingham's financial and professional services sector altered the dynamics of the city's power structure. City center business leaders organized themselves into a powerful force in regional capital politics through the establishment of Birmingham City 2000. The creation of the Birmingham Marketing Partnership further secured the position of city center business leaders in the city's progrowth regime. The appearance of the Birmingham TEC in 1990, imposed through the directive mode of intervention of the Thatcher government, briefly disturbed the balance of power in the city's industrial development politics. Three centers of power emerged on this new political landscape: the City Council Economic Development Department, the Birmingham Chamber of Commerce, and the TEC. Working through the Economic Development Partnership, City Challenge, and informal networks, these three power centers quickly merged into an economic development triumvirate. In part, the cooperative relations among the three resulted from the shift to the competitive grant system that made partnership a requisite for all local regeneration efforts.

A second realignment occurred in Birmingham's progrowth governing alliance, when the Knowles ruling clique lost control of the Labour group. In this case, an internal power struggle ensued, which mirrored the demographic shifts (the rising numbers of women and ethnic minorities) in the local Labour party. When the more pluralistic group leadership headed by Teresa Stewart took power, a back-to-basics agenda supplanted the progrowth agenda as the city council's top priority. Nonetheless, the progrowth alliance held together, but development politics shifted into a coalitional mode of governance. Also, central government restrictions on local authority finances precluded using city council capital expenditures to finance prestige projects. As a result the new generation of prestige projects, including Millennium Point, had to be funded by lottery and other grants obtained through the competitive grant system. Coalitional politics also structured the economic development triumvirate's industrial development efforts, such as the development of the Jaguar plant in Castle Vale. Coalitional politics meant growing tensions within the triumvirate, as revealed by the exercise of writing a joint economic development strategy. Finally, Birmingham's progrowth alliance began to encounter serious opposition to major economic development projects. The proposal to develop a microelectronics plant in the greenbelt is a case in point.

Boston's progrowth alliance in the 1990s constituted a loose confederation between local politicians and the Hub's business elite. Both Flynn and Menino attempted to fashion a governing alignment in which Boston's downtown business elite would play a leading role. However, postindustrial economic restructuring, in the form of mergers and consolidation in the city's financial and corporate sectors, caused the city's downtown business establishment to experience a "power failure." Megaplex politics exposed deep divisions within the progrowth alliance, despite the general consensus around a regional capital strategy.

In Bristol, rival factions contested for dominance in the arena of development politics in the 1970s and 1980s. By the mid-1990s, however, a progrowth alliance sprang to life, when a handful of business leaders, building on their new institutional power bases in the Bristol Initiative and the Avon TEC (later named Western TEC), engineered the formation of the Western Development Partnership. Subsequently, these business leaders, primarily through the amalgamated Bristol Chamber and Initiative, joined forces with the city council in forming an interlocking network of partnerships around a regional capital strategy. Initially, it was the combined effects of an ever-tightening noose of central government fiscal constraints and the lure of government grants dispensed through a competitive system that goaded Bristol's truculent Labour leadership toward a coalitional mode of governance. Once suspicions had been allayed, partnerships proliferated, including Broadmead, Cultural Development, Harbourside, and Bristol 2000.

Detroit's progrowth alliance quickly crystallized into a powerful regime around the city's regional capital strategy in the 1970s. The hallmark of this progrowth alignment was the development of the Renaissance Center. By the 1980s, however, seized by internal strife, the progrowth coalition slipped into a loose coalitional mode of governance. Scandals, endless disputes with the suburbs over race and economic development issues (such as a light rail line), and a falling out with the city's white business establishment over strategic planning and casino gambling increasingly isolated Young's mayoral administration. Dwindling federal funds for economic development during the Reagan and Bush administrations further hindered efforts to carry out the city's dual agenda of downtown revitalization and industrial renewal. Reduced to a coalitional power structure, cooperation often could be achieved only around individual projects, such as the Poletown and Chrysler Jefferson Avenue North auto assembly plants.

Two changes in the Motor City's political economy turned the tide of progrowth politics in Detroit in the mid-1990s. First, the national recovery produced a boom in the country's manufacturing sector, which spelled robust growth in the automobile industry. Detroit's economic prospects, as a result, improved markedly. The city's new mayor, Dennis Archer, capitalized on Detroit's rising economic fortunes by repairing much of the political damage inflicted by the disputes of the 1980s and the early 1990s. With a renewed feeling of optimism, the Archer administration and downtown business elites renovated the city's governing structure by forging a new consensus around a regional capital strategy. Major projects, like the new Tiger baseball stadium, previously stalled by internecine conflict, suddenly came to life again. Similarly, the Detroit Lions, in Pontiac since the 1970s, negotiated a return to downtown Detroit in a new football stadium. Even casino gambling won approval from Detroit's voters.

In addition, two changes in the intergovernmental mode of intervention abetted Archer's efforts to rehabilitate the city's progrowth coalition. First, the Clinton administration's Empowerment Zone program offered an opportunity for tackling Detroit's deepening problems of inner city and industrial decline. The Archer administration deftly organized a coalition of business and community leaders around the Empowerment Zone bid, which won designation in 1994. Later Archer supported Governor Engler's Renaissance Zone initiative, which gained for Detroit several added incentives for industrial investment.

Explaining Progrowth Politics

For all four cities, the common denominator in the formation of progrowth governing alliances was the condition of the local economy. Dislocations caused by economic restructuring, often accompanied by wrenching recession, set the stage for the rise of progrowth alignments. This might lead some to believe that cities face an economic imperative, as suggested by Paul Peterson (1981). To hold with Peterson that city governments *must* promote economic development, however, ignores the critical role played by state structuring and restructuring. In the decentralized federal system of the United States, municipal governments like Boston and Detroit are clearly subject to market-based fiscal constraints. In Britain, however, central government policies and grant systems insulate local authorities from the fiscal imperatives of local economic growth. In short, economic restructuring and recession are perhaps necessary conditions, but can account for the rise of progrowth politics only when state structures are taken into consideration.

Birmingham's progrowth alliance first arose in the 1970s, during a period of permissive intervention that did not discourage its formation. Similarly, the rise of Boston's progrowth coalition was not hampered by federal withdrawal, particularly given the permissive mode of intervention in Massachusetts at the time. In Bristol, the competitive mode of intervention was a crucial factor in the rise of progrowth politics in the early 1990s. Finally, Detroit's progrowth regime emerged in an intergovernmental system, in which both federal and state modes of intervention were permissive.

In Boston, the Flynn and Menino administrations actively sought to cultivate good relations with the business community. Bristol's business leadership displayed exceptional political acumen in bringing an intransigent Labour leadership into the fold. Similarly, Detroit's corporate elite responded to the city's worsening social and economic circumstances by forming Detroit Renaissance, Inc., and developing the Renaissance Center.

The interplay between urban and state restructuring can also be seen in the development of progrowth politics. In Birmingham, the local authority dominated the progrowth regime in the 1980s. By the early 1990s, central government directive and later competitive interventions circumscribed the ability of the city council to finance its prestige project strategy. Furthermore, the rise of new centers of powers, including Birmingham TEC and City 2000, meant that the city council could no longer dictate the terms of alliance. In Bristol, a conflict-ridden mode of governance characterized development politics in the 1970s and 1980s. Rival progrowth and growth management factions vied for ascendance, with the local authority serving as the political battleground on which these contests were fought. By the 1990s, economic crisis and the installment of a competitive mode of intervention coaxed city council Labour leaders into a politics of partnership with the local business elite around the city's regional capital strategy.

In the context of a decentralized local governing system, economic conditions have had an even greater impact on the development of progrowth politics in Boston and Detroit. The anemic state of Boston's progrowth alliance has resulted, in part, from an economic restructuring that decimated the ranks of a once powerful downtown business establishment. Detroit's progrowth governing coalition also felt the effects of state and economic restructuring. Federal withdrawal and continued economic decline in the 1980s and early 1990s exacerbated internal tensions in the progrowth coalition, contributing to its loss of governing capacity.

Differences in governing alignments and agendas among the four cities, nonetheless, cannot wholly be explained by differences in urban political economy. Local leadership also played a key, mediating role. For example, different logics characterized political leadership in the two British cities. The political pragmatism of Birmingham's city council leaders and the more recalcitrant ideological approach taken by Bristol's Labour leadership engendered very different development politics in the 1970s and 1980s. Similarly, adept handling by Bristol's enterprising business leadership smoothed the transition from conflict-ridden development politics in the 1980s to the politics of partnership in the 1990s. In Detroit, the Young administration's steadfast commitment to retaining the city's base in the auto industry is somewhat unusual in the United States.

Growth Management Politics in Comparative Perspective

The study of local growth management politics in the United States has been quite extensive (Caves 1992; DeLeon 1992; Stein 1993). Several findings from this body of research are relevant here. First, as with the politics of social reform, growth management politics depends on the level of grassroots political mobilization. Often dubbed "antigrowth" movements, growth management political mobilization is most likely to surface in cities with more highly educated and affluent residents and during periods of rapid development (see Protash and Baldassare 1983; Logan and Zhou 1993; Clark and Goetz 1994). As Logan et al. (1997:614) explain, "it is in communities with higher levels of socioeconomic status, those experiencing a recent environmental threat, and those with stronger civic organization that serious challenges to the growth machine will arise."

The study of growth management politics, by contrast, has excited relatively little interest among urban scholars in Britain. Instead, concern has focused on the effects of centrally curtailed local planning powers in the 1980s (see Ambrose 1992; Atkinson and Moon 1994; Allmendinger and Tewdwr-Jones 1997). There are some exceptions to this rule, however (see Punter 1990). Brindley, Rydin, and Stoker (1989), for instance, compare planning politics in six English cities. They distinguish local planning styles that result from the interaction between local attitudes toward market processes (market critical and market led) and the state of the local economy (buoyant, stable, depressed) (8–10). Two of these planning styles, regulative planning and popular planning, relate directly to the politics of growth management. Regulative planning is rooted in Britain's strong planning traditions and law. Based on the technical expertise of professional planners, this approach employs comprehensive planning through the exercise of local authority development powers (14–15). Citing the case of Cambridge, Brindley, Rydin, and Stoker observe that regulative planning emerged under conditions of a buoyant local economy and the dominance of a market-critical ideology. The second growth management style, popular planning, grew out of community opposition in the 1960s to highway and urban renewal policies that threatened particular neighborhoods (17). Since then, advocates of popular planning have moved beyond the defensive politics of confrontation to introduce community-based planning processes (18). There also has been a close association between the rise of the New Left and acceptance of community-based planning (19). According to Brindley, Rydin, and Stoker (1989), the use of popular planning occurred in the 1970s and 1980s under circumstances of a stable economy and market-critical local attitudes.

Combining the criteria established by American and British studies, we can highlight four conditions that putatively encourage the formation of growth management governing coalitions in the United Kingdom and the United States. The first is that a city must possess a sizable, well-educated, and affluent middle-class community. The second is that the city must be experiencing a sustained period of rapid development that threatens to erode the quality of urban life. Third, strong civic organization serves as a crucial catalyst for community mobilization around growth management issues. Finally, how, or even whether, a growth management governing coalition arises, also depends on market-critical attitudes of local government officials.

Formation of Growth Management Alliances

Of our four cities, only Boston and Bristol witnessed the formation of growth management governing alignments. Unlike Birmingham and Detroit, Boston and Bristol experienced rapid economic development and possessed sizable middle-class communities. In Boston, the formation of a growth management governing coalition occurred when growth management mobilization converged with the election of Flynn in the mid-1980s. In Bristol, years of protest by middle-class amenity groups against unsightly concrete office towers and large-scale infrastructure projects finally bore fruit, when a new Labour party leadership took the reins of power in 1973. What emerged was a growth management governing faction composed of community-oriented councillors, city planners, and amenity groups.

Development of Growth Management Alignments

Local factors largely explain the transformation of Boston's growth management movement into a powerful governing coalition. The Flynn administration, with its close ties to the city's community movement, forged a restrictive system of development regulation through its Interim Planning Overlay Districts and Neighborhood Advisory Councils. Environmental groups and the Flynn administration coalesced around the rehabilitation of the city's park system. In short, Boston's development politics moved well beyond the defensive strategy of antigrowth mobilization into a positive program of growth management.

In Bristol, the City Council Planning Committee, planning officers, and amenity group leaders hammered out a three-pronged strategy to protect and enhance the city's historic built environment. This growth management agenda incorporated three intersecting policies: (1) a conservation program to preserve the city's historic built environment through renovation and conversion of listed buildings to commercial and housing uses; (2) planning policies to regulate office and other city center architectural design; and (3) an office policy that invoked controls on the rate and kind of office development in the city center. Growth management in Bristol never completely surmounted the politics of factional competition. The growth management faction often met stiff resistance from its progrowth rivals over planning and development policy in the 1970s and early 1980s. Moreover, directive interventions by the Thatcher government narrowed Bristol's planning authority. The imposition of the Bristol Development Corporation is a case in point. With little hope of overcoming the Conservative government's full-scale assault on local planning powers, Bristol's growth management alliance adopted a siege mentality. Summoning those planning powers still at hand, the growth management alliance deployed defensive tactics to protect historic sites and open space under the threat of large-scale development. As in the battle for Golden Hill, however, central government often overruled the city council in favor of private development.

Demise of Growth Management Alliances

Of the three types of governing alignments considered here, growth management alliances appear to be the most fragile. Growth management coalitions in Boston and Bristol ruptured during the recession of the early 1990s. With historic architecture and open spaces no longer under the threat of rapid development, the political commitment of local politicians to growth management wavered. In the case of Boston, the Flynn administration broke with its growth management allies and pursued an aggressive progrowth agenda. Mayor Menino, although more receptive to environmental activists, failed to resurrect the growth management governing alliance. Bristol's growth management alliance suffered a similar fate. As city council leaders turned their attention to the city's emerging regional capital status, amenity groups continued to snipe at large-scale developments such as Harbourside. Such guerilla actions proved ineffective as city planners and many New Left politicians had since abandoned the cause of growth management.

Explaining Growth Management Politics

The comparison of growth management politics in Boston and Bristol largely confirms the received wisdom. Indeed, what distinguished Boston and Bristol from Birmingham and Detroit were the four preconditions for growth management politics. Boston and Bristol retained substantial cohorts of well-educated, affluent residents that formed the basis of their local growth management movements. The threat of rapid development triggered growth management mobilization in the 1970s and 1980s, which took place under the auspices of established historic preservation and environmental groups that provided the leadership necessary for developing growth management strategies. Finally, growth management efforts shifted from pressure politics to participation in a governing coalition with the election of market-critical politicians to local offices.

Despite the similarity in origins, the development of growth management governing alignments in Boston and Bristol followed different courses. Boston's growth management politics moved into a regime-like mode of governance when Mayor Flynn finally reached accommodation with local growth management activists around restrictive downtown and neighborhood planning and rehabilitation of the city's park system in the mid-1980s. Governing alignments in Bristol's development politics remained fluid during the 1970s and 1980s. Unable to achieve dominance over the rival progrowth alliance, the growth management alliance never surmounted its factional character. In part, this was a consequence of the directive mode of intervention during the 1980s, in which the Thatcher government steadily curbed local authority planning powers in favor of market forces and quangos. The Bristol growth management faction persisted in trying to hurdle impediments thrown up by central government, but it was an uphill battle that eventually ended in defeat.

The demise of growth management politics in both cities can be traced to the same cause: recession. In the early 1990s, as rapid growth quickly turned into economic stagnation, growth management politics lost its raison d'être, controlling development. As a result, politicians in both cities drifted away from their allies in the growth management movement, some of whom joined emergent progrowth governing coalitions.

Comparing Social Reform Politics

The 1980s saw the emergence of urban social reform politics in the United Kingdom and the United States. At first blush, one might interpret this coincidence as local political reactions to the wave of conservative national politics ushered in by the Thatcher and Reagan administrations, respectively. The reasons behind the formation of social reform coalitions in American and British cities are, however, far more complicated.

In the United States, the ubiquity of progrowth urban politics has tended to make social reform alignments exceptions to the rule. Among the comparative handful of cities in which social reform governing coalitions seized power in the postindustrial era (e.g., Boston, Chicago, Minneapolis, San Francisco, Seattle) certain common attributes stand out (see Squires et al. 1987; Swanstrom 1989; DeLeon 1992; Nickel 1995). Synthesizing the findings of a number of studies (Clavel 1986; Smith 1989; Clavel and Kleniewski 1990), Denise Nickel (1995:375) distinguishes four antecedents to the rise of social reform politics in American cities:

> (1) an environment of rapid, but unevenly distributed, economic growth, combined with high resident service demands; (2) a community movement with sufficient electoral power to press for alternatives to mainstream progrowth development policies; (3) the waning of business elite influence in local redevelopment policy-making; and (4) diminished federal and state government intervention in local development policy.

None of these criteria for social reform is particularly applicable to British cities. On the contrary, social reform coalitions of New Left councillors, officers, and community activists were much more likely to gain control of local authorities in declining cities or counties, such as Sheffield or the West Midlands, rather than ones experiencing rapid growth as in the United States (Boddy 1984; Fudge 1984). The reasons for this are rather straightforward. In Britain, social reform agendas were generally associated with the rise of the New Left in city politics (see Boddy and Fudge 1984; Stoker 1988), which worked through the Labour Party. Labour Party gains in the 1980s occurred in large urban local authorities that were losing ground under the Thatcher revolution. New Left policies promulgated by Labour-controlled authorities, such as the Sheffield City Council, therefore constituted a political reaction to both Thatcher's market-oriented, directive mode of intervention and a groundswell of community-based organizing around nontraditional issues such as the environment and racial and gender equality.

Comparing the American and British sets of explanations delineates the different political-economic contexts in which social reform governing alignments arose in the United Kingdom and the United States. In the United Kingdom, a directive mode of intervention that placed restrictions on local authority powers combined with declining economic fortunes to set the stage for social reform coalition formation. The primary source was the New Left contingent in the Labour party. In the United States, the combination of federal withdrawal and rapid economic growth supplied the platform for building social reform governing coalitions. The differences in fiscal structures of local governing systems partly explain why such starkly different contexts would give rise to social reform politics. The common factor in both countries was community movement mobilization. The New Left grew out of community organizing around environmental, women's, inner-city poverty, and other issues. Moreover, ties between New Left Labour politicians and community-based organizations remained strong (see Boddy and Fudge 1984; Stoker 1988). In American cities, community organizers moved into the political arena, becoming the foot soldiers of electoral campaigns in a setting of weak local parties. In this respect, the origins of urban social reform governing alliances in the United Kingdom and the United States are quite similar. How urban social reform alignments developed, however, reflects the differences in party and intergovernmental systems of the two countries.

Formation of Social Reform Alliances

The genesis of social reform politics in Boston and Bristol lay in community mobilization. In Boston, the community movement shifted from a confrontational politics in the 1960s and early 1970s to a more accommodationist strategy in the late 1970s and early 1980s (see Fisher 1984). Community organizers won a number of victories in the late 1970s and early

1980s, including the city's linkage policy. The relationship between Boston's community activists and city hall did not transform into a governing coalition until Flynn took office in 1984. This transpired as a result of the crucial role that community leaders played in the election of Flynn in 1983.

Social reform politics in Bristol broke onto the local scene with the riots that took place in St. Paul's in 1981. It appeared that community and Labour leaders (particularly the New Left faction) on the city council were on the brink of forming a social reform governing coalition through the local Tripartite committee. The central government's refusal to allocate Urban Programme funding, however, quashed the incipient social reform alliance. What developed instead was a system of clientelism between individual Labour councillors and particular community organizations. It was not until the 1990s, with the institution of the competitive grant system, that the possibility of a social reform alignment resurfaced. The defining moment occurred when community leaders defied the city council by proposing an alternative to the city's Single Regeneration Budget (SRB) plan. Possessing newfound institutional leverage, the community movement could now enter into a bargaining relationship with the city council.

Development of Social Reform Alignments

Social reform politics in Boston and Bristol developed along divergent paths. Boston's community movement coalesced with the Flynn administration in the 1980s around the governing tasks of protecting and producing affordable housing. Tenant groups and the Flynn administration teamed up to push condominium limitations and other protective measures through Boston's city council. A booming local economy supplied the resources, in part through the city's expanded linkage policy, to fund affordable housing development. Community development corporations became the instruments through which these programs were implemented. In other words, social reform alignments were based on a regime mode of governance in which an alliance of city officials and community activists wielded preemptive power. Circumstances of a depressed property market in the early 1990s realigned Boston's social reform politics. Unable to finance affordable housing development by redirecting the benefits of economic growth to the city's poorer neighborhoods, the social reform alliance altered its governing agenda. The new social reform politics addressed community economic development (e.g., enhanced enterprise zones), bank lending practices, and rent control. Furthermore, when economic conditions improved in the mid-1990s, the Menino administration and community activists joined forces to enact a social wage policy for Boston. The resilience of Boston's social reform alignment seems to surpass similar alliances in other American cities, such as San Francisco and Chicago, which did not survive into the 1990s.

Development of social reform politics in Bristol traveled a far bumpier road than in Boston. The ascendance of a New Left contingent in the local Labour party coincided with the racial disturbances in St. Paul's, the predominantly Afro-Caribbean district in Bristol's inner city. The Tripartite Committee of politicians, officers, and community leaders foundered in the absence of central government financial support. What is more, restrictive fiscal policies issued by the Thatcher government rendered the council's socialist strategy, largely a product of the New Left faction of the Labour group, impracticable. Nevertheless, through the 1980s the city council increased its allocation of grants to community-based organizations. These social reform alignments developed into a system of clientelism in which individual Labour councillors who represented areas of high deprivation ensured that community groups in their districts received a slice of Urban Programme or other available funding.

Central government intervention in the 1990s forced a realignment in the clientele system that had subordinated community groups to the city council. With the introduction of the competitive mode of intervention, first with City Challenge and later with the Single Regeneration Budget (SRB), a coalitional mode of governance emerged. The creation of the Bristol Regeneration Partnership (BRP) and Voluntary Organization Standing Conference on Urban Regeneration (VOSCUR) institutionalized the alliance of community activists and the city council into a social reform governing alignment. This social reform governing coalition coexists with the enduring network of clientelistic relations between individual councillors and community groups.

Explaining Social Reform Politics

Differences in state structure notwithstanding, it has been argued here that the development of a well organized community movement, with institutional (electoral and policy) resources that are independent of local government, are the crucial building blocks for the construction of sustainable social reform governing alliances. For example, differences in the origins and development of social reform politics in Boston and Bristol in the 1980s and 1990s can be explained in large part by differences in the political clout and coherence of the community movements in the two cities. Bristol has been less hospitable to social reform politics. The city's weak and fragmented community movement could not overcome its dependency on the city council through the 1980s and early 1990s. Changes in central government and European grant systems, however, may have given Bristol's community activists the leverage necessary to form a social reform governing coalition through such organizations as the BRP and VOSCUR. Also, the city council's new leadership is more concerned with issues of community development. Whether this embryonic social reform coalition will mature into a stable governing alliance remains to be seen.

Differences in electoral and intergovernmental systems, however, do explain many of the differences in the development of social reform alignments and agendas between Boston and Bristol. For instance, the permeability of candidate-centered campaign organizations in American cities means that community activists can deploy their organizational resources in local elections to gain access to city governing coalitions. In contrast, strong parties in Britain preclude electoral mobilization by community leaders. The New Left, it should be emphasized, worked *through* the Labour party, not from an independent power base outside it. State structures also mattered. Britain's more centralized state structure enabled the Thatcherite directive mode of intervention to dampen or defuse local social reform impulses, as was the case in Bristol in the 1980s. As a result, rather than forming a social reform governing alliance, a system of political clientelism evolved around community-development policies and programs.

In the context of a weak state, the federal withdrawal under the Reagan administration actually had little direct impact on the development of Boston's social reform regime in the 1980s. This is because increased state aid and a buoyant local economy (a source of increased local revenues) compensated for the loss of federal funding for affordable housing and other development programs, at least in part.

Economic changes had a far greater impact in Boston than in Bristol. The slump in Boston's economy in the early 1990s brought the social reform regime's affordable housing development to a grinding halt. It also forced the social reform governing alignment into a coalitional brand of politics. The social reform alliance persisted, but it no longer exercised preemptive power over the city's governing agenda. Insulated to a far greater degree by central government sources of funding, Bristol City Council's urban programs were largely unaffected by the peaks and troughs of the local business cycle. Only when Conservative governments reduced urban policy funding in the early 1990s did the Bristol City Council cut grant allocations to community organizations.

Assessing the Results

To establish the links between political economy and leadership in urban development politics, we compared the formation, development, and demise of progrowth, social reform, and growth management alignments in Birmingham, Boston, Bristol, and Detroit (see table 9.2). What is striking about all three areas of urban development politics is that the impetus for the formation of urban governing alignments are all found to originate in changes in the urban political economy. In other words, urban leaders reacted to urban and state restructuring by aligning or realigning local governing arrangements. How this was done, however, depended on the nature of urban and state restructuring and the capacity and predilections of local leaders.

A second point can be made. As table 9.2 indicates, governing coalitions (progrowth, social reform, growth management) and power structures (rival factions, coalitions, and regimes) do not correlate directly with any particular urban political economy. In other words, the causal relations implicated in the formation, development, and demise of urban governing alignments are not linear in character. This is because urban governing alignments are political constructs that reflect both the urban political-economic context in which they are built and the abilities and predispositions of their architects, local political and civic leaders. In this sense, causation is an interactive process between the macro forces of urban political economy (urban and state structuring and restructuring), and between urban political economy and leadership (logic and capacity).

Urban Power Structures Revisited

Based on the preceding comparison of urban governance in the United Kingdom and the United States, we have come to the conclusion that our original conception of urban power structures warrants some refinement and evaluation. First, in an attempt to distinguish structures of power within coalitional politics, we modified our original typology to accommodate three distinct forms of coalitional governing alignments. Then, having crafted a more sensitive instrument for analyzing the configuration of power, we reached some conclusions about the relationship between the type of power structure and the capacity to govern.

A Revised Typology of Urban Power Structures

In chapter 1, we identified three types of power: dominating, bargaining, and preemptive. Each form the basis of different configurations of power: rival factions, coalitions, and regimes. Cognizant of the fact that real world

Table 9.2

Modes of Urban Governance in Birmingham, Boston, Bristol, and Detroit, 1970–1997

Agenda	Formation	Development	Demise
Progrowth			
Birmingham	Economic restructuring	Coalition (1974–1983) to regime (1984–1993) to coalition (1994–1997)	
Boston	Economic restructuring and recession	Coalition (1990–1997)	
Bristol	Economic restructuring and recession	Coalition (1993–1997)	
Detroit	Economic restructuring	Regime (1970–1979) to coalition (1980–1994) to emerging regime (1994–1997)	
Social Reform			
Boston	Community movement mobilization	Regime (1984–1989) to coalition (1990–1997)	
Bristol	Community movement mobilization and competitive mode of intervention	Coalition (1994–1997)	
Growth Management			
Boston	Rapid growth and middle-class mobilization	Regime (1984–1989)	Recession
Bristol	Rapid growth and middle-class mobilization	Rival factions (1973–1992)	Recession and competitive mode of intervention

Table 9.3

Urban Power Structures

Forms of Power	Configuration of Power
Dominating	Rival factions
Dominating and bargaining	Contingent coalition
Bargaining	Enduring coalition
Bargaining and dominating	Prevailing coalition
Preemptive	Regime

politics almost never conforms to such neatly packaged theoretical constructs, we think that the subtle shades of gray that exist within coalitional politics require clearer definition. As portrayed in table 9.3, our revised typology amends the original category of coalitional politics by subdividing it into three separate power structures.

Contingent coalitions can be rival or nonaligned factions that form an alliance around a particular issue or project. Dominating power may be the prevalent form, but bargaining occurs if common ground can be found for tradeoffs and compromises. In Boston, the White administration and community activists, who were often at odds over development policy, put aside their differences momentarily to work out a compromise linkage policy in the early 1980s. In Detroit, the deal-making relationships developed between the Young administration and General Motors and Chrysler for the development of the Poletown and Jefferson Avenue auto factories, respectively, were clearly single project, contingent alliances.

Enduring coalitions are those based almost exclusively on bargaining power, that is, within the alliance and between factions or coalitions outside the governing coalition. Boston's volatile Megaplex politics, for example, illustrates the workings of an enduring coalition. Business leaders and politicians had formed a general consensus around a regional capital strategy, but disputes often erupted over the specifics of the financing and siting of the new convention center. The coalition endured, finally reaching agreement after four years of turbulent negotiations. Similarly, Detroit's progrowth coalition made the transition from regime to enduring coalition in the 1980s. The Young administration and the Motor City's white business elite continued to maintain working relationships around a regional capital strategy, but these relations were often strained by racial tensions and political problems.

Birmingham's progrowth regime also slipped into an enduring coalition after 1993. When a new Labour leadership took office, the progrowth coalition found that bargaining had replaced preemption as the means for accomplishing its regional capital and industrial development strategies. Tensions also arose within the economic development triumvirate, which were only allayed by painful negotiation and compromise.

Prevailing coalitions are built on bargaining power (within the governing coalition), but tend to prevail in a policy arena by exercising dominating power to overcome opponents. Boston's growth management governing alliance of the 1980s is perhaps best defined as a prevailing coalition, with its stable relations within the alliance and its ability to overcome most, although not all, opponents. Boston's powerful social reform coalition of the 1980s lost its regime power base in the early 1990s. The social reform coalition remained tightly knit (internally), and formidable enough to overcome challengers on most issues. The alliance, however, no longer exercised preemptive power, sharing the Hub's governing agenda with a sometimes competing progrowth alliance.

Bristol's progrowth coalition of the 1990s also exemplifies a prevailing coalition. The panoply of partnerships has consolidated the internal relations of the progrowth alliance. The progrowth coalition's remarkable success in pushing a regional capital strategy demonstrates its dominion over the city's development agenda, repelling most of the challenges mounted by growth management and other opponents. Bristol's prevailing coalition may be transforming into a regime structure, although it is not yet clear.

Urban Power Structures and the Nature of Governing Capacity

It is our belief that urban power structure analysis provides an essential tool for comparative urban political research. By assessing the architecture and engineering of urban power structures, we can evaluate the governing capacity in cities of different countries. Adopting two of Stone's (1995) measures of leadership capacity, scope of policy-making and institution building, we can assay the effects of the power structure on the policy-making process. Table 9.4 compares power structures that have been forged in Birmingham, Boston, Bristol, and Detroit since 1970.

The data in table 9.4 suggest that some correlation between the type of power structure and the scope of the policy agenda in our four cities exists. Beginning with the narrowest, contingent coalitions attenuate policy agendas the most. For example, in Boston a contingent coalition formed around a single issue to institute a linkage policy. Similarly, Detroit's pro-

Table 9.4

Comparing Urban Power Structures

Power Configuration	Scope of Policy Agenda	Institution Building
Rival Factions		
Bristol Growth Management vs. Progrowth (1973–1992)	Conservation, environmental protection, city center, and high technology development	None
Contingent Coalitions		
Boston Social Reform (1975–1983)	Linkage policy	None
Detroit Progrowth (industrial development, 1981–1990)	Auto industry retention	None
Enduring Coalitions		
Birmingham Progrowth (1974–1983)	Economic diversification (convention and trade show industry, high technology development, planning for prestige projects)	National Exhibition Centre, Ltd., Aston Science Park
Birmingham Progrowth (regional capital after 1993)	City center renewal (multipurpose prestige projects, housing, place marketing), strategic planning, urban design, city center transportation and access	City Pride

Table 9.4 *(continued)*

Power Configuration	Scope of Policy Agenda	Institution Building
Birmingham Progrowth (industrial development after 1993)	Auto industry retention, high technology development, training and business development	None
Boston Progrowth (1990–1997)	Downtown development, high technology development, human capital development	None
Detroit Progrowth (regional capital, 1981–1993)	Downtown renewal, strategic planning, human capital development, cultural development	Detroit Compact
Prevailing Coalitions		
Boston Progrowth (1975–1983)	Downtown development and industrial retention	Economic Development and Industrial Corporation, Boston Private Industry Council (human capital development)
Boston Social Reform (after 1989)	Bank lending practices, community economic development, affordable housing development and protection	None
Boston Growth Management (1985–1989)	Restrictive zoning, historic preservation, participatory planning, open and green space protection and improvement	Neighborhood Planning Councils, Civic Design Commission

(continued on next page)

Table 9.4 (continued)

Power Configuration	Scope of Policy Agenda	Institution Building
Bristol Progrowth (after 1992)	City center renewal, cultural development, city center shopping district, economic diversification, and inward investment	Cultural Development Partnership, Bristol 2000, Broadmead Partnership, Harbourside Partnership
Detroit Progrowth (regional capital, 1994–1997)	Cultural development, human capital development, and business development	Greater Downtown Partnership, Empowerment Zone Coordinating Committee
Regimes		
Birmingham Progrowth (regional capital, 1984–1993)	City center renewal (prestige projects, infrastructural improvement, and place marketing)	Birmingham City 2000, Birmingham Marketing Partnership
Birmingham Progrowth (industrial development, 1984–1993)	Industrial diversification and retention, business development	Birmingham Economic Development Department, Birmingham Heartlands UDA and UDC, Birmingham Economic Development Partnership

Table 9.4 (continued)

Power Configuration	Scope of Policy Agenda	Institution Building
Boston Social Reform (1984–1989)	Affordable housing development and protection	None
Detroit Progrowth (regional capital, 1970–1980)	Downtown redevelopment (commercial office and infrastructure)	Detroit Renaissance, Detroit Economic Growth Corporation, Downtown Development Authority, Community and Economic Development Department

growth contingent alliance of the 1980s coalesced around single projects—automobile assembly plants.

Regimes, although not as narrow in scope as contingent coalitions, also seem to attenuate policy agendas. The regional capital regimes in Birmingham and Detroit concentrated efforts on large-scale downtown development projects. Boston's social reform regime, similarly trained its sights almost exclusively on the production and protection of affordable housing development through its linkage policies, condominium limitations, and housing development programs.

Enduring coalitions appear to promulgate a wider range of policies than either contingent or regime power structures. Birmingham's progrowth enduring coalitions (before and after the regime era of 1984–1993) engaged in a fairly wide range of economic strategies, including city center renewal, industrial retention and diversification, strategic planning, and business and human capital development. Moreover, after 1993, inner-city regeneration became a higher priority on the city's development agenda. The governing agenda of Bristol's emergent (perhaps enduring) social reform coalition also covers a fairly wide range of policies, such as inner-city and outer estate regeneration, community economic development, and social service antipoverty initiatives. The governing agenda of Detroit's enduring progrowth regional capital coalition (after 1981) also contained a wide array of strategies: downtown renewal, strategic planning, human capital development, and cultural development.

As with enduring coalitions, governing agendas for prevailing coalitions incorporated a wider range of policies than contingent alliances or regimes. Boston's growth management prevailing coalition (1985–1989) sported a fairly broad agenda of environmental protection (restrictive planning) and environmental enhancement (park rehabilitation and historic preservation). The prevailing progrowth coalition in Boston (1970–1983) adopted a dual strategy of downtown revitalization and industrial development, both retention and diversification. Boston's prevailing social reform coalition (after 1989) broadened its governing agenda considerably to include bank lending practices, community economic development, and a social wage policy, as well as affordable housing development and protection. The agenda of Bristol's post-1992 progrowth prevailing coalition comprised a broad-based regional capital strategy that included city cultural development through prestige projects and events, city center shopping district improvement, economic diversification (Harbourside mixed-use waterfront development), and inward investment. The progrowth alliance in Detroit, which seems to have graduated to a prevailing coalition after Archer became mayor, resuscitated the dual strategy of a regional capital agenda, which included cultural development (e.g., sports stadia, casino gambling), business and human capital development, and industrial development (e.g., the empowerment and renaissance zones).

The widest governing agenda was produced by the rival factions structure in Bristol from 1970 to 1992. The governing agenda encompassed the competing policies of growth management (restrictive planning and design, conservation, and environmental improvement) and progrowth (city center office and high technology development) alignments.

The pattern of institution building also seems to have been related to the type of power structure in place. Institution building tended to be most extensive during periods in which power structures endowed urban leaders with the greatest governing capacity (prevailing and regime). During the periods in which Birmingham's progrowth regimes (regional capital and industrial development) ruled, an impressive array of agencies, partnerships and organizations were created. These included the Development and later Economic Development Departments, Birmingham Heartlands UDA and UDC, Birmingham City 2000, the Birmingham Marketing Partnership, and the Economic Development Partnership. The 1970–1983 period, in which Boston's progrowth coalition prevailed, saw the creation of the Economic Development and Industrial Corporation and the Private Industry Council. Boston's social reform regime, however, was an exception to the rule. Rather than creating new institutions, the social reform regime in Boston during the 1984–1989 period worked through informal networks and enlarged the capacity of existing agencies and partnerships, such as the Public Facilities Department (housing), the Boston Redevelopment Authority, and the Boston Housing Partnership. Finally, Detroit's progrowth regime in the 1970s fits the pattern. During this period, the Motor City's governing coalition established Detroit Renaissance, the Downtown Development Authority, the Economic Development Corporation, and the Detroit Growth Corporation. The 1973 revised City Charter also gave greater powers to the mayor, and allowed newly elected Mayor Young to create a large and wide-ranging Community and Economic Development Department.

Similarly, prevailing coalitions engaged in substantial institution building. During Boston's prevailing progrowth coalitional political era in the 1970s and early 1980s, the Economic Development and Industrial Corporation (1972) and the Boston Private Industry Council (human capital development) were created. During the brief reign of Boston's growth management prevailing coalition in the 1980s, the Civic Design Commission (reviews building design) and Neighborhood Planning Councils were formed. Bristol's prevailing progrowth coalition (1993–1997) forged a complex of interlocking partnerships: Cultural Development Partnership, Bristol 2000, Broadmead Partnership, and Harbourside Partnership. The city council also created the Economic Development Team, which more than doubled the council's economic development staff.

In stark contrast, the remaining forms of power structures engendered very little institution building. Only the enduring regional capital coalitions in Birmingham (1994–1997) and Detroit (1980–1993) formed new partnerships, Birmingham City Pride and the Detroit Compact. Rival factions in Bristol (1970–1992) and contingent coalitions in Boston (social reform 1975–1983) and Detroit (industrial development 1980–1993) produced no new institutions.

Although drawing general conclusions from a comparative set of four case studies constitutes a dubious enterprise at best, the patterns that emerged from our findings suggest two hypotheses. The first is that the configuration of power structures affects the scope of governing agendas. The narrowest governing agendas are set by contingent coalitions, which only stands to reason because they form ad hoc-bargaining alliances around a single issue or project. Regimes also attenuated governing agendas, primarily because they preempt opposing or alternative solutions to governing problems. This runs counter to Stone's (1989) conception of urban regimes, which he claims can be either inclusionary or exclusionary. Our research suggests, however, that the very nature of a regime is exclusionary, closing agenda setting to a select few (reminiscent of the elite and non-decision-making theories). Enduring and prevailing coalitions fashion much broader governing agendas, principally because they involve extensive bargaining within the ruling alliances, and often with factions or other coalitions. This means that governing is a more inclusionary process in stable and prevailing coalitional structures, allowing wider latitude for deliberation and debate about policy solutions. This also generates more conflict than in either contingent coalitions or regimes. Finally, and not surprisingly, rival factions broaden a city's governing agenda the most. Conflict among competing coalitions means that many more (and often contradictory) policy solutions will be aired. The use of dominating power also means that compromise is not the method of decision making employed. Instead, only one policy solution or, in the case of defensive politics, perhaps no policy prevails.

Our second conjecture relates to institution building. The more powerful the governing alliance, the greater likelihood it will create agencies or partnerships to institutionalize its power structure. That is, regimes and prevailing coalitions are far more likely to engage in extensive institution building than other governing alliances (enduring or contingent) or rival factions. This probably reflects both the greater cohesion within regimes and prevailing coalitions, and their capacity to dominate political arenas.

A Final Word on the Modes of Governance

Integrating perspectives on urban political economy, institutional development, and leadership capacity furnishes a comprehensive framework for the analysis of comparative urban governance. The political economy perspective stresses the importance of the international and national context for urban political development. We have attempted to capture the dynamic nature of urban political economies through the use of urban and state structuring and restructuring. The cultural perspective, in turn, focuses on the mediating role of institutions in urban governance. Our analysis of governing alignments, networks, and partnership arrangements employed such institutional analysis. The role of purposeful action lies at the heart of the leadership perspective. Our analysis of strategic decision making clearly conveys the role of purposeful leadership in building power structures and setting urban policy agendas. And combining the three perspectives has enabled us to grapple with the enduring social theoretic dilemma of structure versus agency (see Giddens 1979). The context created by urban and state structuring and restructuring (structure), the governing alignments as the institutional conduit for political processes (mediation), and strategic decision making guided by the "logics" imbued in urban leaders (agency), form a comprehensive analytical framework for explaining modes of governance. In this sense, urban governing alignments both arbitrate between and are configured and reconfigured by the dynamic interaction between the context established by urban and state structuring and restructuring and the political calculus of urban leaders.

The limitations of our study are painfully apparent. A comparative case study of four cities in two countries cannot easily justify claims that the modes of governance framework used here applies to urban politics in all or even most liberal-democratic nations. We hope that the burgeoning research in comparative urban politics will, in time, bear out some of these conclusions.

Notes

1. Modes of Governance in Comparative Perspective

1. We wish to thank Tom Halper for exercising bargaining power to help us understand the dual social production–social control nature of political power, that is, for convincing us that both the "power to" and "power over" operate simultaneously and interactively in the process of governance.

3. State Structuring and Restructuring

1. In 1969, the Wilson government also introduced a smaller urban program, Community Development Projects (CDPs)(Atkinson and Moon 1994:45). Like the UP, CDPs were designed to attack urban social pathology by targeting deprived areas. Also in common with the UP, CDPs lacked central coordination (Atkinson and Moon 1994:45–47). Squabbling between autonomous CDP work action teams, charged with coordinating the program locally, and local authorities and ministries, eventually convinced the central government to terminate the program in 1978 (Atkinson and Moon 1994:50).

5. The Politics of Regional Primacy

1. Digbeth is actually ancient Birmingham, where the medieval village was first settled.

6. Coping with Industrial Decline

1. These included Chris Bryant from Bryants, John Douglas from R. M. Douglas, Peter Galliford from Gallifords, Mike Jennings from Tarmac, and Mike Dowdy from Wimpey.

2. These included Sir Richard Knowles (deputy chair), who became Lord Mayor after he stepped down as council leader; Albert Bore, who became Labour Party Secretary and chair of the General Purposes Committee; Fred Chapman, chair of the Planning Committee until 1994; Hale, former Conservative Leader and Shadow on the Economic Development Committee; Councillor R. A. M. Brew; and C.P. Finegan, an honorary alderman.

3. The West Midlands Forum, a nonstatutory council set up to coordinate services and other activities among local authorities in the West Midlands, commissioned a study that recommended opening up greenbelt land to development in Birmingham and other local authorities. The rationale given was to improve the competitiveness of the West Midlands in attracting industrial development. Although the forum possessed no authority to approve such development, the favorable report sparked a feud within the body that eventually engulfed it in the wider controversy over the microelectronics plant (Langford 1996).

7. The Politics of Social Reform

1. Flynn's definition of affordable housing was derived from federal guidelines. It combined low-income housing, which is affordable to families of four earning $17,000 or less, and moderate-income housing, which was affordable to families of four earning between $17,000 and $27,000 (Snyder 1988).

2. Under the Linkage policy, developers of commercial projects that contained more than 100,000 square feet of floor space were obligated either to construct a specified amount of affordable housing themselves or to contribute $5.00 to the city's Housing Trust Fund for every square foot that the project exceeded the 100,000 square foot benchmark (Boston Redevelopment Authority, 1988:1). By October 1989, $76 million in commitments had been accrued from downtown developers (City of Boston n.d.).

3. The city's long-term loans provide $10,000 per unit or $20,000 for each vacant apartment built or refurbished.

References

Interviews

Barrett, Paul. 1992. Economic Development Director, Boston Redevelopment Authority (July 7).

Bee, William. 1997. Bristol Regeneration Partnership (June 17).

Beeston, Jim. 1993. Chief Executive, Birmingham Heartlands Urban Development Corporation (August 6).

———. 1995 (August 10).

Bishop, Alan. 1991. Birmingham Heartlands Urban Development Corporation (July 12).

———. 1994 (July 20).

———. 1996 (August 8).

Bishop, Jeffrey. 1993. Architect, Bristol Bridge (July 7).

Bore, Albert, 1991. Economic Development Committee Chair, Birmingham City Council (July 19).

———. 1993. Labour Party Secretary and City Councillor, Birmingham City Council (August 2).

———. 1996. Labour Party Secretary and City Councillor, Birmingham City Council (July 26).

Boyd, Lisa. 1994. Metropolitan Boston Housing Partnership (November 4).

Brooks, Martin. 1993. Economic Development Committee Chair, Birmingham City Council (August 8).

Coughlin, William. 1994. President, Greater Boston Chamber of Commerce (September 7).

Cragg, David. 1993. Chief Executive, Birmingham Training and Enterprise Council (August 8).

———. 1994 (July 19).

———. 1997 (June 2).

Darby, Charles. 1993. Chairman, Bass Taverns, Plc (August 9).

de Groot, Lucy. 1995. Chief Executive, Bristol City Council (July 5).

Dreier, Peter. 1992. Director of Housing, Boston Redevelopment Authority (July 14).

Edgerly, William. 1992. Chair and Chief Executive Officer, State Street Bank (August 8).

Erskine, Jean. 1996. Director, Voluntary Organization Standing Conference on Urban Regeneration (July 10).

———. 1997 (June 8).

Fiddler, Peter. 1993. Dean, Faculty of the Built Environment, University of the West of England (July 9).

Fowler, Ted. 1996. Bristol Regeneration Partnership (June 17).

Ganz, Herbert. 1992. Retired, Director of Research and Policy Development, Boston Redevelopment Authority (July 28).

Garlick, George. 1994. Director, Bristol Voluntary Services Council (July 13).

Geohegan, Chris. 1993. Managing Director, British Aerospace (July 7).

Gillis, Don. 1992. Director, Boston Economic Development and Industrial Corporation (June 23).

Glancy III, Alfred. 1993. Chairman, MCN Corporation; Chairman, Detroit Economic Growth Corporation; and Chairman, Detroit Renaissance, Inc., 1992–1996 (January 7).

Glusac, Michael. 1995. President, Detroit Renaissance, Inc., (October 2).

Green, Richard. 1993. Director, Economic Development Department, Birmingham City Council (July 29).

———. 1994 (July 28).

———. 1995 (August 7).

———. 1997 (June 5).

Griggsby, Charles. 1994. Director, Public Facilities Department, City of Boston (September 7).

Hagopian, Mossik. 1992. Director, Urban Edge Development Corporation (August 12).

———. 1994 (September 6).

Hider, David. 1994. Director, British Gas (July 5).

Hillegonds, Paul. 1997. President, Detroit Renaissance, Inc. (April 21).

Holland, Helen. 1996. Councillor, Bristol City Council. Chair Planning and Development Committee (July 7).

———. 1997 (June 17).

Hood, Nicholas. 1995. Chairman of the Board, Wessex Water, Plc (July 2).

Kelly, Andrew. 1995. Director, Bristol Cultural Development Partnership (July 12).

———. 1996 (July 17).

Kershaw, Diana. 1994. Director, Planning and Development, Bristol City Council (July 5).

———. 1995 (July 7).

Kiley, Tom. 1992. Partner, Marttila and Kiley Political Consultants (August 3).

Klocke, Jim. 1992. Director of Business Services, Greater Boston Chamber of Commerce (July 22).

Lago, Marisa. 1994. Chief Executive, Economic Development, and Director, Boston Redevelopment Authority (September 6).

Lavoie, Donna. 1992. Public Relations, Genzyme Corporation (July 10).

Libby, Pat. 1992. Executive Director, Massachusetts Association of Community Development Corporations (July 13).

Lyons, Michael. 1997. Chief Executive, Birmingham City Council (June 10).
McGuigan, Pat. 1992. Assistant Director, Boston Public Facilities Department (July 21).
Mallet, Conrad, Jr. 1989. Assistant to Mayor Coleman Young. Telephone interview (July 19).
Maxwell, David. 1995. Chief Executive, Birmingham City 2000 (August 9).
———. 1996 (June 6).
———. 1997 (June 3).
May, Andrew. 1991. Chair, Planning and Traffic Committee, Bristol City Council (August 1).
———. 1994. Planning and Development Committee Chair, Bristol City Council (July 13).
———. 1995 (July 19).
Moore, Bob. 1993. Chief Executive, Birmingham City 2000 (August 4).
———. 1997. Chief Executive, Birmingham Chamber of Commerce and Industry (June 4).
Moriarity, George. 1992. Acting Director, Boston Private Industry Council (August 14).
O'Brien, Paul. 1992. Chair, New England Telephone (July 30).
Patterson, Iain. 1991. Director of Planning, Bristol City Council (August 8).
Primack, Mark. 1992. Executive Director, Boston GreenSpace Alliance, Inc. (July 6).
Ravitz, Mel. 1992. Member, Detroit City Council (January 27).
Richards, Paul. 1996. Chief Executive, West Midlands Development Agency (August 9).
Robertson, Graham. 1991. Council Leader, Bristol City Council (August 8).
Robinson, Michael. 1993. Chief Executive, Bristol City Council (July 6).
Sandbrook, Martin. 1995. Deputy Director, Western Training and Enterprise Council (July 19).
Savage, John. 1994. Chief Executive, Bristol Chamber of Commerce and Initiative (July 5).
———. 1995. (July 18).
Sparks, Les. 1997. Director, Planning and Architecture, Birmingham City Council (June 3).
Stewart, John. 1994. Professor, Institute of Local Government, Birmingham University (July 21).
Stroh, Peter. 1993. Chairman, Stroh Brewery Company (March 4).
Sullivan, Neil. 1992. Chief Policy Advisor to the Mayor, City of Boston (July 15).
———. 1994. Director, Boston Private Industry Council (September 8).
Taylor, Roger. 1993. Chief Executive, Birmingham City Council (August 9).
Thorley, Michael. 1993. Chief Executive, Birmingham Marketing Partnership (July 28).
———. 1994 (July 19).
Vargas, Evelyn. 1992. Executive Director, Nuestra Comunida Development Corporation (July 28).
Weathers, James. 1992. Executive Assistant to Mayor Young (February 2).
Welfare, Jonathon. 1996. Chief Executive, Bristol 2000 (July 15).

West, Mike. 1991. Director of Economic Development, Bristol City Council (July 5).
———. 1993 (July 8).
Whyatt, Robert. 1993. City Valuer, Bristol City Council (July 14).
Willis, Peter. 1994. Chief Executive, Birmingham City 2000 (July 21).

Government, Organization, and Corporation Documents

Accelerate. n.d. Supplier Development Contract Handbook, n.d.
Amatruda, Robert. 1994. *The Boston Class A Office Market Year-End Report 1993* (April). Boston Redevelopment Authority, Policy Development and Research Department, Boston.
Avon County Council. 1990. Bristol, U.K.
Avon Economic Development Conference. 1993. *Western Development Partnership in Avon: Prospectus* (May).
Birmingham City Council. 1981. *Annual Report and Accounts.* Birmingham, U.K.
———. 1982. *Annual Report and Accounts.* Birmingham, U.K.
———. 1983. *Annual Report and Accounts.* Birmingham, U.K.
———. 1984. *Annual Report and Accounts.* Birmingham, U.K.
———. 1985. *Annual Report and Accounts.* Birmingham, U.K.
———. 1986a. *Annual Report and Accounts.* Birmingham, U.K.
———. 1986b. *1986 Review of the Economic Strategy.* Birmingham, U.K.
———. 1987. *Annual Report and Accounts.* Birmingham, U.K.
———. 1988. *Annual Report and Accounts.* Birmingham, U.K.
———. 1989. *Annual Report and Accounts.* Birmingham, U.K.
———. 1990. *Annual Report and Accounts.* Birmingham, U.K.
———. 1991. *Annual Report and Accounts.* Birmingham, U.K.
———. 1992. *Annual Report and Accounts.* Birmingham, U.K.
———. 1993. *Annual Report and Accounts.* Birmingham, U.K.
———. 1994. *Annual Report and Accounts.* Birmingham, U.K.
———. 1995. *Annual Report and Accounts.* Birmingham, U.K.
———. 1996a. *Annual Report and Accounts.* Birmingham, U.K.
———. 1996b. *Report of the Director of Economic Development to the Economic Development Committee: 1996/97 Economic Review-Issues Report* (July 31).
———. 1997. *Education in Birmingham.* http://birmingham.gov.uk/html/business/omar/educt.html.
———. 1993. *The Birmingham Economy: Annual Review 1992* (June 20). Birmingham, U.K.
———. 1996. *Economic Development Programme for Birmingham 1996–1997.* Birmingham, U.K.
Birmingham City Council Planning and Architecture. 1996. Digbeth Millennium Quarter: Planning and Urban Design for the Future. Consultation Draft (November).
Birmingham City Council, Public Relations Division. n.d. Millennium Point: The Midland's Project for the Year 2000 and Beyond. Birmingham, U.K.
Birmingham City 2000. 1993. BMP Up and Running. *Communique* Issue 9 (Summer).
Birmingham Economic Information Centre. n.d. *The Birmingham Economy Review and Prospects.* Produced by Birmingham City Council and Birmingham TEC. Birmingham, U.K.

Birmingham Heartlands. 1989. *A Strategy for East Birmingham Inner City.* Birmingham, U.K.

Birmingham Training and Enterprise Council. 1993. *Birmingham One Stop Shop for Business: Executive Summary* (January). Birmingham, U.K.

———. n.d. *Introduction To Birmingham TEC.* Birmingham: Author.

Boston Foundation. 1987. The Greening of Boston: An Action Agenda. Carol R. Goldberg Seminar, October.

Boston Municipal Research Bureau. 1990; 1995. *Boston Facts & Figures: A Statistical Perspective on Boston's Government 1990; 1995 Editions.* Boston.

———. 1993. *Securing Boston's Financial Future: A Blueprint For Boston's Future* (September). Boston.

Boston Redevelopment Authority. 1982. *Boston Redevelopment Authority Fact Book.* Boston.

———. 1986. *Planning for Boston: Initiatives for Fiscal Year 1987* (October 28). Boston.

———. 1987. *Planning for Boston.* Boston.

———. 1988. Linkage: Building Bridges of Opportunity, Affordable Homes and Jobs (Winter). Boston.

———. 1989. *Fiscal Year 1989 Briefing.* Boston.

———. 1991. Building Boston's Economic Future: An Agenda For Economic Development (December). Boston.

———. 1992. Human Resources Department memorandum. Boston.

———. 1993. *Boston's Tax Exempt Property on the Rise, Insight: A Briefing Report On A Topic of Current Interest* (July 2).

Boston Redevelopment Authority, Policy Development and Research Department. 1989. *A Summary of Development in Boston 1975–1989* (April). Boston.

———. 1993a. Boston Office Market Outpaces Other Cities, *Insight: A Briefing Report On A Topic of Current Interest* (June 11). Boston.

———. 1993b. *The Economy: Excerpt from the Official Statement of the City of Boston, Massachusetts General Obligation Refunding Bonds* (February 1). Boston.

Boyden Southwood. 1992. *A Cultural Strategy for Bristol: Final Report* (April).

Bristol City Council. 1981. *Annual Report of the Bristol City Council 1980/81.* Bristol: City of Bristol Printing and Stationery Department.

———. 1983. *Annual report of the Bristol City Council 1982/83.* Bristol, U.K.: City of Bristol Printing and Stationary Department.

———. 1987. *Annual Report of the Bristol City Council 1986/87.* Bristol, U.K.: City of Bristol Printing and Stationery Department.

———. 1990. *Annual Report of the Bristol City Council 1989/90.* Bristol, U.K. City of Bristol Printing and Stationery Department.

———. 1993. Boost for Bristol's Scene, *Bristol News,* No. 14, (Summer): 7.

———. 1994. *Bristol Development: Harbourside* (August). Bristol, U.K.: City of Bristol Printing and Stationery Department.

———. 1995. *The City and County of Bristol Key Facts: One.* Bristol, U.K. (May).

———. 1995. Harbourside "Gets Real." *Harbourside Bulletin* No. 4 (May). Bristol, U.K.

———. 1996. £41 million Win for Harbourside. *Bristol News* (June): 1.

———. 1999. *www.bristol-city.gov.uk/cgi-bin/w3menu?ammooi+*bg+f.

———. *Bristol City Centre Draft Broad Sheet.*

———. n.d. Ten Top Projects: Economic Development and Regeneration Key Projects for 1997/98. Bristol, U.K.

Bristol City Council, Planning and Development Services. 1993. *Bristol Business Development: Research Statistics* (October).

———. 1995. *Bristol Business Development: Research Statistics* (April).

Bristol City Council, Planning Department. 1987. *City Centre: Local Plan Issues* (January). Bristol, U.K.

———. 1988. *Research Report: The Role of Bristol City Council and Avon County Council in Economic Development.* Bristol, U.K.

Bristol City Planning Officer and Avon County Planning Officer. 1991. *An Evolution of Bristol Development Corporation: Two Years On* (April). Bristol, U.K.

Bristol Harbourside. 1997. *Harbour Asides* (Spring) Issue 3.

Bristol Regeneration Partnership. 1995. Bristol 2020: Submission Document.

Bristol 2000. n.d. Bristol 2000: Our Millennium Vision: Three Worlds in One City.

Brown, Jeffery. 1987. The Revitalization of Downtown Boston: History, Assessment and Case Studies. Boston: Boston Redevelopment Authority Research and Policy Department (March).

Brown, Jefferey, Francoise Carre, Gregory Perkins, and Joyce Seko. 1987. San Francisco-Boston Profile: Demographics, Economy, Development, Planning Directions. Boston: Boston Redevelopment Authority (April 9).

City of Boston. 1987. *Breaking Ground: A Report on Boston Housing Policy and Performance* (April).

———. 1993. *Economic Development and Industrial Corporation.* Boston.

———. 1994a. *Boston In Brief.* Boston.

———. 1994b. *Boston Works: Partnerships For A Sustainable Community* (June).

———. 1996. *Boston's Economy 1996* (November). Boston.

———. n.d. *Building Affordable Homes: Linkages.* Boston.

City of Clinton v. Cedar Rapids and Missouri Railroad Company. 24 Iowa 455 (1868).

City of Detroit. 1980–1996. City of Detroit *Budget* (annual editions). Detroit.

———. 1997a. *Annual Overall Economic Development Program Report and Program Projection.* Detroit.

———. 1997b. 1981–1996. City of Detroit *Budget.* Detroit.

———. 1998. 1981–1996. City of Detroit *Budget.* Detroit.

City of Detroit, Communications & Creative Services Department. 1997. *Building a World Class City II.* Detroit (June).

Detroit Renaissance, Inc. 1990. *Detroit Renaissance.* Detroit.

Docklands Consultative Committee Support Unit. 1993. *Birmingham Heartlands: A Community Audit* (June). Birmingham, U.K.

Economic Development and Industrial Corporation. n.d. *Boston Economic Development Partnership—Concept Paper.* Boston.

Economic Development Strategy for Birmingham (Draft). 1997. (May 23).

Genzyme. 1991. State and Genzyme Sign Compact to Locate Genzyme's Biopharmaceutical Plant in Massachusetts [Press Release] (November 26).

Jackson, Marion, and Matthew Elliot. 1992. Avon Economic Development Strategy: A Report For Coopers & Lybrand by LEDU: Local Economic Development Unit (July). Bristol, U.K.

Locate in Birmingham. n.d. Birmingham, U.K.

Michigan Employment Security Commission, Research and Statistics Division. *Civilian Labor Force and Wage and Salary Estimates 1979–1995* (annual reports). Lansing.

Office for National Statistics, Central Statistical Office. 1986. *Regional Trends.* London: HMSO.

———. 1989. *Regional Trends.* London: HMSO.

———. 1996. *Regional Trends.* London: HMSO.

Office for National Statistics. 1994. *Social Trends.* London: HMSO.

Office of Population Censuses and Surveys. 1954. *Census 1951: England and Wales.* London: HMSO.

———. 1963. *Census 1961: England and Wales.* London: HMSO.

———. 1975. *Census 1971: England and Wales.* London: HMSO.

———. 1984. *Census 1981: England and Wales.* London: HMSO.

———. 1995. *Census 1991: England and Wales.* London: HMSO.

———. 1993a. *1991 Census County Report: Avon.* London: HMSO.

———. 1993b. *1991 Census County Report: West Midlands.* London: HMSO.

———. 1993c. *1991 Census: Report for Great Britain.* London: HMSO.

Perkins, Gregory W. 1994. Boston Redevelopment Authority, Policy Development and Research Department. *"The Economy": Excerpt from the "Official Statement of the City of Boston, Massachusetts General Obligation Refunding Bonds"* (February 9).

Rylance, Nicola. 1993. *Bristol Chamber of Commerce and Initiative: The Initiative Program Report* (June).

———. 1994. The Bristol Chamber of Commerce and Initiative: Background to Initiative Projects and Progress (June 30).

U.S. Bureau of the Census. 1973a. *1970 Census of Population and Housing.* Washington, D.C.: U.S. Government Printing Office.

———. 1973b. *1970 Census of Population: Social and Economic Characteristics.* Washington, D.C.: U.S. Government Printing Office.

———. 1977–1996. *City Government Finances.* Washington, D.C.: U.S. Government Printing Office.

———. 1983. *1980 Census of Population and Housing.* Washington, D.C.: U.S. Government Printing Office.

———. 1993a. *1990 Census of Population and Housing.* Washington, D.C.: U.S. Government Printing Office.

———. 1993b. *1990 Census of Population: Social and Economic Characteristics.* Washington, D.C.: U.S. Government Printing Office.

U.S. Bureau of the Census. 1970. *Statistical Abstract of the United States.* Washington, D.C.: U.S. Government Printing Office.

———. 1973. *Statistical Abstract of the United States.* Washington, D.C.: U.S. Government Printing Office.

———. 1975. *Statistical Abstract of the United States.* Washington, D.C.: U.S. Government Printing Office.

———. 1976. *Statistical Abstract of the United States.* Washington, D.C.: U.S. Government Printing Office.

———. 1980. *Statistical Abstract of the United States.* Washington, D.C.: U.S. Government Printing Office.

———. 1981. *Statistical Abstract of the United States.* Washington, D.C.: U.S. Government Printing Office.

———. 1986. *Statistical Abstract of the United States.* Washington, D.C.: U.S. Government Printing Office.

———. 1987. *Statistical Abstract of the United States.* Washington, D.C.: U.S. Government Printing Office.

———. 1988. *Statistical Abstract of the United States.* Washington, D.C.: U.S. Government Printing Office.

———. 1989. *Statistical Abstract of the United States.* Washington, D.C.: U.S. Government Printing Office.

———. 1990. *Statistical Abstract of the United States.* Washington, D.C.: U.S. Government Printing Office.

———. 1992. *Statistical Abstract of the United States.* Washington, D.C.: U.S. Government Printing Office.

———. 1995. *Statistical Abstract of the United States.* Washington, D.C.: U.S. Government Printing Office.

U.S. General Accounting Office. 1993. *State and Local Finances* (October). Washington, D.C.: U.S. Government Printing Office.

West Midlands County Council, County Planning Department. 1983. *Statistics '83.* Birmingham, U.K.

Published and Other Sources

Ackerman, Jerry. 1991. "A Reshaping of the Future of Boston: Zoning Code Near Revision." *Boston Globe* (June 1).

———. 1992. "Sky Isn't the Limit, BRA Says in Zoning Proposal." *Boston Globe* (June 13): 39.

———. 1993. "Development Agency Merger to Be Urged." *Boston Globe* (March 6): 8.

———. 1996a. "Company Mergers May Take Civic Toll: With Fewer Home Offices in Boston, Charities, City Leadership Could Suffer." *Boston Globe* (July 3): 11.

———. 1996b. "Six-Month Search for New President Suspended by Chamber of Commerce." *Boston Globe* (January 9): 61, 68.

———. 1997. "Hoteliers: Tax Others for Convention Center Costs." *Boston Globe* (January 10): F3.

Alderman, Ellen, and Caroline Kennedy. 1991. *In Our Defense.* New York: Avon Books.

Alford, Robert R., and Roger Friedland. 1985. *Powers of Theory: Capitalism, the State, and Democracy.* Cambridge, U.K.: Cambridge University Press.

Allen, John, and Doreen Massey, editors. 1988. *Restructuring Britain: The Economy in Question.* London: Sage Publications, in association with The Open University.

Allen, Scot. 1994. "Environment Jobs Eyed by Flynn in Plan." *Boston Globe* (September 15).

Allmendinger, Philip, and Mark Tewdwr-Jones. 1997. "Post-Thatcherite Urban Planning and Politics: A Major Change?" *International Journal of Urban and Regional Studies* 21(1): 100–116.

Alsford, Christine. 1992. "Park Glory Revival Bid Wins Praise, *Evening Post.*" (January 1).

Ambrose, Peter. 1992. "Changing Planning Relations." In *Policy and Change in Thatcher's Britain,* edited by Paul Cloke, 97–121. Oxford, U.K.: Pergamon Press.

Anand, Geeta. 1995a. "City Readies Rent Control Survey." *Boston Globe* (October 21):65, 67.

———. 1995b. "Mayor's Help Sought as Rent Control Ends." *Boston Globe* (September 14):27.

———. 1995c. "Menino's Holiday Message: Buy Local." *Boston Globe* (November 22).

———. 1996. "Menino Urged to Finance Help for Needy Tenants." *Boston Globe* (September 26):B1, B4.

———. 1997a. "Boston's Renewal Plan Falling Short." *Boston Globe* (June 2): A1, A10.

———. 1997b. "Mayor Ups City Ante for Civic Center." *Boston Globe* (May 23): A1, B11.

———. 1997c. "Menino Unveils $6M for Rental Housing." *Boston Globe* (March 25): B2.

Ankeny, Robert. 1997. "Finalists for 3 Casinos." *Crain's Detroit Business* (August 25): 30.

Ankeny, Robert, and Paul Gargaro. 1997. "Empowered but Powerful?" *Crain's Detroit Business* (November 24): 1, 36–37.

Archer, Dennis. 1998. From This Day Forward: Laying Down the Foundations to Greatness. Speech delivered at Oakland University, Rochester, Michigan (February 16).

Arnold, David. 1987. "Parks, Space Seen as Key to Boston's Well-Being." *Boston Globe* (November 30): 19, 22.

Atkinson, Rob, and Graham Moon. 1994. *Urban Policy in Britain: The City, the State, and the Market.* Basingstoke, U.K.: Macmillan.

Austin, Carol. 1995. "Future of Digbeth—Have Your Say." *Birmingham Voice* (August 2): 2.

Bachrach Peter, and Morton S. Baratz. 1962. "Two Faces of Power." *American Political Science Review* 56: 947—52.

———. 1963. "Decisions and Nondecisions: An Analytical Framework." *American Political Science Review* 57(September): 632–42.

Bailey, Steve. 1994. "Make Room for Tom May: With Megaplex Effort, Edison's Mr. Inside Steps Out in the Spotlight." *Boston Globe,* (July 12): 33, 35.

Banfield, Edward C., and James Q. Wilson. 1963. *City Politics.* Toronto: Vintage.

Barnekov, Timothy, Robin Boyle, and Daniel Rich. 1989. *Privatism and Urban Policy in Britain and the United States.* Oxford, U.K.: Oxford University Press.

Barker, Ben. 1981. *The Operation of the Bristol Labour Party: A View from the Edge.* Working Paper 27 (Master's thesis), School for Advanced Urban Studies, University of Bristol, U.K.

Barnard, Chester I. 1968. *The Functions of the Executive.* Cambridge, MA: Harvard University Press.

Bassett, Keith. 1993. "Urban Cultural Strategies and Urban Regeneration: A Case Study and Critique." *Environment and Planning A* 25: 1773–88.

Beauregard, Robert. 1989. *Economic Restructuring and Political Response.* Newbury Park, CA: Sage.

Bennett, Larry. 1989. "Postwar Redevelopment in Chicago: The Declining Politics of Party and the Rise of Neighborhood Politics." In *Unequal Partnerships: The Political Economy of Urban Development in Postwar America,* edited by Gregory D. Squires, 161–77. New Brunswick, NJ: Rutgers University Press.

Benning, Victoria. 1992. "Fleet Commits $8M for Plan to Aid First-Time Home Buyers." *Boston Globe* (June 20).

Bienkowski, Mishka, Rhona Walker, and Kevin Allen. 1988. *Government Support for British Business*, 6th edition. Glasgow: EPRC Limited, University of Strathclyde.

Birch, Anthony H. 1993. *The Concepts and Theories of Modern Democracy*. London: Routledge.

Birmingham City Council Development Department. 1989. *Developing Birmingham 1889 to 1989: 100 Years of City Planning*. Birmingham: Author.

Birmingham Post. 1993. "EC Windfall Creates Hope of Jobs Bonanza." *Birmingham Post* (September 10).

———. 1994. "Speculators Build Hopes for Future." *Birmingham Post* (July 28): 25.

Birmingham Voice. 1995. "Jaguar and Birmingham—A World Beater." *Birmingham Voice* (August 2): 8.

Black, Chris. 1993. "Menino's Role in Contrast With Flynn's." *Boston Globe* (September 28): 31.

———. 1994a. "Menino Plans Cabinet System: New Structure Set to Manage the City." *Boston Globe* (January 18): 21, 22.

———. 1994b. "Rep. Kennedy Irks Menino with Grant Pronouncement." *Boston Globe* (December 16).

Black, Chris, and Brian McGregory. 1993. "It's for Real—Mayor Menino: Big Victory Over Brett Cuts Across Ethnic, Neighborhood Lines." *Boston Globe* (November 3): 1, 24.

Blakely, Edward J. 1994. *Planning Local Economic Development: Theory and Practice*, 2nd edition. Thousand Oaks, CA: Sage.

Blanton, Kimberly. 1995. "Minority Mortgage Lending Doubles." *Boston Globe* (August 10): 37, 41.

———. 1996. "Blueprint for Boston: Promises Action as Chamber's President." *Boston Globe* (March 22): 79, 81.

Bloch, Alice. 1990. *The Community Charge in England: Local Authority Experience*. York, U.K.: The Joseph Rowntree Foundation.

Bluestone, Barry, and Bennett Harrison. 1982. *The Deindustrialization of America: Plant Closings, Community Abandonment, and the Dismantling of Basic Industry*. New York: Basic Books.

Boddy, Martin. 1984. "Local Economic and Employment Strategies." In *Local Socialism? Labour Councils and New Left Alternatives* edited by Martin Boddy and Colin Fudge, 160–91. London: Macmillan.

Boddy, Martin, and Colin Fudge, editors. 1984. *Local Socialism?* London: Macmillan.

Boddy, Martin, John Lovering, and Keith Bassett. 1986. *Sunbelt City? A Study of Change in Britain's M4 Growth Corridor*. Oxford, U.K: Clarendon Press.

Boston Globe. 1993a. "Great Day for the Women, But the Waning of the Green." *Boston Globe* (September 23): 40.

Boston Globe. 1993b. "Menino Offers Pledge: The Ambition Stops Here." *Boston Globe* (November 4): 37.

Boyle, Robin. 1990. "Regeneration in Glasgow: Stability, Collaboration, and Inequity." In *Leadership and Urban Regeneration: Cities in North America and Europe*, edited by Dennis Judd and Michael Parkinson, 109–32. Newbury Park, CA: Sage.

Braunstein, Janet, and Constance Prater. 1989. "Controversy Encircles Jefferson Ave. Plant." *Detroit Free Press* (May 31): 1A.

Brien, Jeremy. 1990. "Partners in Prosperity." *Evening Post* (June 22): 9.

Brindley, Tim, Yvonne Rydin, and Gerry Stoker 1989. *Remaking Planning: The Politics of Urban Change in the Thatcher Years*. London: Unwin Hyman.

Bristol Evening Post. 1987. "Fighting for Bristol—Ordinary Folk Who Take on the Big Guns to Save their Towns and Cities from Devastation." (November 18).

Browne, William P., and Kenneth Verburg. 1995. *Michigan Politics and Government: Facing Change in a Complex State*. Lincoln: University of Nebraska Press.

Burnham, Walter D. 1982. *The Current Crisis in American Politics*. New York: Oxford University Press.

Burns, James McGregor. 1978. *Leadership*. New York: Harper and Row.

Butcher, Hugh, Ian G. Law, Robert Leach, and Maurice Mullard. 1990. *Local Government and Thatcherism*. London: Routledge.

Cairns, Greg. 1993. "Bristol and the West's Economy." *Bristol Economic Bulletin* 14(Spring): 12.

Canellos, Peter S. 1992. "Bank to Pay $1M in Mortgage Case." *Boston Globe* (June 20).

———. 1993. "Hungry for Developers, Boston to Pave the Way." *Boston Globe* (March 11): 1, 8.

———. 1995. "Activism '90s Style: Nonprofit Groups Aim to Teach the Needy." *Boston Globe* (November 28): 14.

Cassidy, Tina. 1996. "Menino: City to Sell Industrial Park." *Boston Globe* (January 19): 41, 49.

———. 1997a. "Kraft Gives Up on South Boston Site: Patriots Owner Says It's Back to Drawing Board as He'll Seek a Site Elsewhere in Region." *Boston Globe* (February 22): A1, A6.

———. 1997b. "A Roaring 'No' from South Boston: 1,300 Send Clear Message to Bob Kraft and His Promises." *Boston Globe* (January 9): F1, F3.

———. 1997c. "Senate Panel Version of Convention Bill Hands Reins of Facility to Joyce." *Boston Globe* (July 24): C2.

Cassidy, Tina, and Geeta Anand. 1997. "Bank Offers to Cut Gap on Civic Center: BankBoston Heads $20m Proposal; City's Share Unsettled." *Boston Globe* (July 3): A1, B8.

Cassidy, Tina, and Meg Vaillancourt. 1997. "Parcel-Cutting for Convention Center Could Boost Cost." *Boston Globe* (July 16): D1, D3.

Causer, Alan. 1993. "Nasty Surprise Just Around the Corner." *The Birmingham Post* (July 22).

Caves, Roger W. 1992. *Land Use Planning: The Ballot Box Revolution*. Newbury Park, CA: Sage.

Chacon, Richard H. 1995a. "City Sees a Park on W. Roxbury Landfill Site." *Boston Globe* (November 11): 1, 17.

———. 1995b. "Environment Plan Prompts Cautious Kudos for Menino: Advocates Say 48-Point Agenda May Lack Sweep, But One Calls It 'Doable.' " *Boston Globe* (April 10): 14.

———. 1996a. "Menino's New 'Safety Net' for Tenants Has $2 Million Rent Subsidy." *Boston Globe* (October 18): 63.

———. 1996b. "End of Rent Control Looms Over Poor." *Boston Globe* (December 23): B1, B3.

Cheeseright, Paul. 1993. "Quite a Lot of Catching up to Do." *Financial Times* (July 14).

———. 1995a. "Agency Claims 'Central' Role in Arranging Deal." *Financial Times* (July 16): 6.

———. 1995b. "Midlands Weighs Up Benefits of Jaguar Decision." *Financial Times* (July 16): 6.

Christie, Ian, Michael Carley, and Michael Fogarty, with Robin Legard. 1991. *Profitable Partnerships: A Report on Business Investment into Community.* London: Policy Studies Institute.

Clark, Gordon. 1984. "A Theory of Local Autonomy," *Annals of the Association of American Geographers* 74: 195–200.

Clark, Gordon, and Michael Dear. 1984. *The State Apparatus.* Boston: Allen and Unwin.

Clark, Peter B. 1969. "Civic Leadership: The Symbols of Legitimacy." In *Democracy in Urban America,* 2nd edition, edited by Oliver P. Williams and Charles Press, 350–65. Chicago: Rand McNally.

Clark, Terry N., and E. Goetz. 1994. "The Antigrowth machine: Can City Governments Control, Limit, or Manage Growth?" In *Urban Innovations: Creative Strategies for Turbulent Times,* edited by T. N. Clark, 105–145. Thousand Oaks, CA: Sage.

Clarke, Susan, and Gary L. Gaile. 1992. "The Next Wave: Postfederal Local Economic Development Strategies." *Economic Development Quarterly* 6(2): 187–98.

Clavel, Pierre. 1986. *The Progressive City: Planning and Participation, 1969–1984.* New Brunswick, NJ: Rutgers University Press.

Clavel, Pierre, and Nancy Kleniewski. 1990. "Space for Progressive Local Policy: Examples From the United States and the United Kingdom." In *Beyond the City Limits: Urban Policy and Economic Restructuring in Comparative Perspective,* edited by John R. Logan and Todd Swanstrom, 199–234. Philadelphia: Temple University Press.

Clements, Joe. 1993. "Preserving the Old In the New Boston." *Boston Globe* (October 23): 37.

Cochrane, Allan. 1993. *Whatever Happened to Local Government?* Buckingham, U.K.: Open University Press.

Cochrane, Allan, and Jamie Peck. 1996. "Manchester Plays Games: Exploring the Local Politics of Globalization." *Urban Studies* 33: 1319–36.

Cockburn, C. 1977. *The Local State.* London: Pluto Press.

Collins, Richard C., Elizabeth B. Waters, and A. Bruce Dotson. 1991. *America's Downtowns: Growth Politics and Preservation.* Washington, D.C.: The Preservation Press.

Costello, Nancy. 1994. "Teamwork Is Key." *Detroit Free Press* (December 22): 1A.

Coughlin, William. 1992. "Chamber Takes Aggressive Steps to Prepare Region for Competing Globally." *Banker & Trade: A Special Report — Boston Municipal Snapshot* (June 3): MS29.

Cox, Kevin, and A. Mair. 1988. "Locality and Community in the Politics of Economic Development." *Annals of the Association of American Geographers* 78: 137–46.

Dahl, Robert. 1961. *Who Governs?* New Haven, CT: Yale University Press.

———. 1986. "Power As the Control of Behavior." In *Power,* edited by Steven Lukes, 37–58. New York: New York University Press.

Dalby, Stewart. 1989. "Bristol 2: Finding the Right Balance of Development." *Financial Times* (November 24): 2.

Darden, Joe T., R. C. Hill, June Thomas, and Richard Thomas. 1987. *Detroit: Race and Uneven Development*. Philadelphia: Temple University Press.

Dawson, W. H. 1916. *Municipal Life and Government in Germany*. London: Longmans, Green.

DeHaven, Judy. 1997. "Vote Gives Local Casinos Bigger Edge." *Detroit News* (June 19): 1A, 6A.

DeLeon, Richard E. 1992. *Left Coast City: Progressive Politics in San Francisco, 1975–1992*. Lawrence: University Press of Kansas.

Detroit News (Editorial). 1986. "The Fate of Jefferson Assembly." *Detroit News* (February 23): 18A.

DiGaetano, Alan. 1989. "Urban Political Regime Formation: A Study in Contrast." *Journal of Urban Affairs* 11(3): 261–81.

———. 1991. "The Origins of Urban Political Machines in the United States: A Comparative Perspective." *Urban Affairs Quarterly* 26(3): 324–53.

———. 1991. "The Democratic Party and City Politics in the Post-Industrial Era." In *Labor-Based Parties in Post-Industrial Societies*, edited by Frances Fox Piven, 212–34. Cambridge, U.K.: Polity.

———. 1997. "Urban Governing Alignments and Realignments in Comparative Perspective: Development Politics in Boston, Massachusetts, and Bristol, England, 1980–1996. *Urban Affairs Review* 32(6): 844–70.

DiGaetano, Alan, and John S. Klemanski. 1993. "Urban Regimes in Comparative Perspective: The Politics of Urban Development in Britain." *Urban Affairs Quarterly* 29(1): 54–63.

Dignam, Conor. 1994. "Villa Boss Champions Stadium Plan." *Birmingham Post* (July 21): 3.

Dillon, John F. 1911. *Commentary on the Law of Municipal Corporations*. Boston: Little, Brown.

Dixon, Jennifer, and Chris Christoff. 1996. "11 Areas Get Chance for a Renaissance." *Detroit Free Press* (December 17): 1A.

Domhoff, William G. 1978. *Who Really Rules? New Haven and Community Power Reexamined*. Santa Monica, CA: Goodyear.

Dreier, Peter. 1989. "Economic Growth and Economic Justice in Boston." In *Unequal Partnerships: The Political Economy of Urban Redevelopment in Postwar America*, edited by Gregory D. Squires, 35–58. New Brunswick, NJ: Rutgers University Press.

Duckers, John. 1993. "Midlands Is Favourite For New Jaguar: Ford Offered Massive Cash Aid." *Birmingham Post* (July 29): 1.

Duckers, John, and Nigel Morris. 1993. "Industry In Bid For Huge Cash Lifeline: Chamber Seeks Ministers' Help." *Birmingham Post* (March 5).

Duncan, Simon, and Mark Goodwin. 1988. *The Local State and Uneven Development*. Oxford, U.K.: Polity.

Edelman, Murray. 1964. *The Symbolic Use of Politics*. Urbana: University of Illinois Press.

Edmonds, Patricia. 1987. "Detroit Solitaire: The One-Man Rule of Coleman Young." *Detroit Free Press* (April 5): 1A, 12A–14A.

Edwards, Robin. 1995a. "£5M Bid to Stop the Rot." *Evening Post* (June 21): 1, 2.

———. 1995b. "New-Look City Docks Is Set for Go-Ahead." *Evening Post* (April 29): 6.

Egan, Timothy. 1996. "Drawing a Hard Line against Urban Sprawl." *New York Times* (December 30): A1–A12.

Egginton, Steve. 1980. "Secret of the Civic Reds." *Western Daily Press* (January 21).

Eisenstadt, E. S., and L. Roniger. 1984. *Patrons, Clients, and Friends: Interpersonal Relations and the Structure of Trust in Society.* Cambridge, MA: Cambridge University Press.

Elazar, Daniel J. 1970. *Cities of the Prairie: The Metropolitan Frontier and American Politics.* New York: Basic Books.

Elkin, Stephen, 1985. "Twentieth Century Urban Regimes." *Journal of Urban Affairs* 7(2): 11–28.

———. 1987. *City and Regime in the American Republic.* Chicago: University of Chicago Press.

Ellis, Louise. 1986. "Tories Rapped on Planning Pleas." *Bristol Evening Post* (August 23).

Employment Gazette. 1970–1997.

Erie, Stephen P. 1989. *Rainbow's End: Irish-Americans and the Dilemmas of Urban Machine Politics, 1840–1985.* Berkeley: University of California Press.

Fainstein, Susan. 1994. *The City Builders: Property, Politics, and Planning in London and New York.* Oxford, U.K.: Blackwell.

Fainstein, Susan, and Clifford Hirst. 1995. "Urban Social Movements." In *Theories of Urban Politics,* edited by David Judge, Gerry Stoker, and Harold Wolman, 181–204. London: Sage.

Fairlie, J. A. 1901. *Municipal Administration.* New York: Macmillan.

Fasenfest, David. 1986. "Community Politics and Urban Redevelopment: Poletown, Detroit, and General Motors." *Urban Affairs Quarterly,* 22(1): 101–23.

Ferman, Barbara. 1985. *Governing the Ungovernable City.* Philadelphia: Temple University Press.

———. 1996. *Challenging the Growth Machine: Neighborhood Politics in Chicago and Pittsburgh.* Lawrence: University Press of Kansas.

Finucane, Martin. 1997. "Convention Center Bill Ready for Legislative Passage." *Boston Globe* (November 5).

Fisher, Robert. 1984. *Let the People Decide: Neighborhood Organizing in America.* Boston: Twayne.

Flint, Anthony. 1997a. "Mayor Hails Convention Center Deal, Pledges City Effort." *Boston Globe* (November 11): A25.

———. 1997b. "Mayor Signs Wage Law over Protest: Menino Cites Working People, Later Admits Analysis Lacking." *Boston Globe* (August 13): A1, A10.

Flury, Annie. 1997. "Residents were 'Stitched Up' in Fight over Green Belt Factory." *Birmingham Post* (September 10).

Frisby, Michael K. 1984. "Alliance Says Project Review Should Progress." *Boston Globe* (July 13): 45, 17.

———. 1987. "Coyle Learns to Live with 'Neighbors.'" *Boston Globe* (July 12): 25, 27.

Fuchs, Ester R. 1992. *Mayors and Money.* Chicago: University of Chicago Press.

Fudge, Colin. 1984. "Decentralization: Socialism Goes Local?" In *Local Socialism? Labour Councils and New Left Alternatives,* edited by Martin Boddy and Colin Fudge, 192–214. London: Macmillan.

Gargaro, Paul. 1995. "Fund Set to Nourish New Biz in Detroit." *Crain's Detroit Business* (September 4): 18.

Garlick, George. 1995a. "First Round of Single Regeneration Budget Projects Starting." *Relay* (April).

———. 1995b. "Voluntary Organization Standing Conference on Urban Regeneration—Update." *Relay* (April).

Garreau, Joel. 1991. *Edge City: Life on the New Frontier.* New York: Doubleday.

Giddens, Anthony. 1979. *Central Problems in Social Theory.* London: Macmillan.

Goodwin, Mark. 1992. "The Changing Local State." In *Policy and Change in Thatcher's Britain,* edited by Paul Cloke, 77–96. Oxford, U.K.: Pergamon Press.

Gordon, Daniel N., editor. 1973. *Social Change and Urban Politics: Readings.* Englewood Cliffs, NJ: Prentice-Hall.

Gottdiener, M. 1987. *The Decline of Urban Politics: Political Theory and the Crisis of the Local State.* Newbury Park, CA: Sage.

Gottdiener, M., and Joe R. Feagin. 1988. "The Paradigm Shift in Urban Sociology." *Urban Affairs Quarterly* 24(2): 163–187.

Gray, Virginia. 1996. "The Socioeconomic and Political Context of States." In *Politics in the American States: A Comparative Analysis,* 6th edition, edited by Virginia Gray and Herbert Jacob, 1–34. Washington, D.C.: CQ Press.

Grimley, Terry. 1997. "Visions of a Brave New City." *The Birmingham Post* (March 3).

Grodzins, Morton. 1966. *The American System.* Chicago: Rand McNally.

Gurr, T. R., and D. S. King. 1987. *The State and the City.* Chicago: University of Chicago Press.

Gyford, John. 1985. *The Politics of Local Socialism.* London: Allyn & Unwin.

Gyford, John, Steve Leach, and Chris Game. 1989. *The Changing Politics of Local Government.* London: Unwin Hyman.

Halbfinger, David. 1996. "Menino Would Tax Tourism to Get Convention Center Funds." *Boston Globe* (January 19): 18.

Hansford, Alison. 1992. "Tesco Court Victory." *Bristol Evening Post* (June 24).

Harding, Alan. 1989. "Central Control in British Urban Economic Development Programmes." In *The New Centralism: Britain Out of Step?,* edited by Colin Crouch and D. Marquand, 21–38. Oxford, U.K.: Basil Blackwell.

———. 1991. "The Rise of Urban Growth Coalitions, U.K. Style?" *Government and Policy* 9(3): 297–317.

———. 1994. "Urban Regimes and Growth Machines: Towards a Cross-National Research Agenda." *Urban Affairs Quarterly* 29(3): 356–82.

Harloe, Michael. 1977. *Captive Cities: Studies in the Political Economy of Cities and Regions.* London: John Wiley & Sons.

Harrigan, John J. 1993. *Political Change in the Metropolis,* 5th edition. New York: HarperCollins.

Harrison, David. 1979. "Labour Revolt over Cuts Is Lost." *Western Daily Press* (September 12).

———. 1996. "Our Jewel on the Waterside." *Evening Post* (August 23): 28–29.

Hasluck, Chris. 1987. *Urban Unemployment: Local Labour Markets and Employment Initiatives*. London: Longman.

Haughton, G., and P. Roberts. 1990. "Government Urban Economic Policy 1979–89: Problems and Potential." In *Local Economic Policy*, edited by Mike Campbell, 85–106. London: Cassell.

Hawley, Willis D., and Frederick M. Wirt, editors. 1974. *The Search for Community Power* (2nd ed.). Englewood Cliffs, NJ: Prentice-Hall.

Hernandez, Peggy. 1987. "Flynn Condo Plan Rebuffed by Council." *Boston Globe* (October 28): 17, 20.

Herson, J. R., and John M. Bolland. 1990. *The Urban Web: Politics, Power, and Theory*. Chicago: Nelson-Hall.

Hill, Richard Child. 1983. "Crisis in the Motor City: The Politics of Economic Development in Detroit." In *Restructuring the City: The Political Economy of Urban Redevelopment*, edited by Susan S. Fainstein, Norman I. Fainstein, Richard Child Hill, Dennis Judd, and Michael Peter Smith, 80–125. New York: Longman.

———. 1983. "Urban Political Economy: Emergence, Consolidation, and Development." In *Cities in Transformation: Class, Capital, and the State*, edited by Michael P. Smith, 123–37. Beverly Hills, CA: Sage Publishers.

Hohler, Bob. 1994a. "Menino, in D.C., Files for $94M HUD Grant." *Boston Globe*, June 30: 17.

———. 1994b. "Menino Makes Pitch for $94 Million US Grant: Boston in Competition for Empowerment Zone." *Boston Globe* (September 15): 5.

———. 1994c. "$25M Federal Grant Set for Boston Revitalization." *Boston Globe* (December 21): 65.

Holli, Melvin, editor. 1976. *Detroit*. New York: New Viewpoints.

Hooge, Liesbet, and Michael Keating. 1994. "The Politics of European Union Regional Policy." *Journal of European Public Policy* 1(3): 367–93.

Horan, Cynthia. 1991. "Beyond Governing Coalitions: Analyzing Urban Regimes in the 1990s." *Journal of Urban Affairs* 13(2): 119–35.

Howe, Peter J. 1987. "Condo Conversions Hit Working Class Boston: Many Three-Deckers Affected." *Boston Globe* (September 10): 1, 24.

———. 1993a. "Deal Remade to Build New Garden: Developers Laud Passage of Altered Bill." *Boston Globe* (January 26): 1, 12.

———. 1993b. "How the Garden Bill Grew." *Boston Globe* (January 9): 1, 15.

———. 1993c. "Weld Urges Quick OK of Megaplex: Says Patriots Could Move; Owner Denies Sale Imminent." *Boston Globe* (December 30): 1, 8.

Howe, Peter J., and Scot Lehigh. 1993. "Compromise Reached after Secret Parley." *Boston Globe* (January 26): 1, 13.

Hunter, Floyd. 1953. *Community Power Structure*. Chapel Hill: University of North Carolina Press.

Isa, Margaret, and Emily Nelson. 1994. "Kenmore-Copley Megaplex Proposal Hit: Neighbors, Community Groups Voice Fears of Traffic, Devalued Property." *Boston Globe* (June 25): 1, 4.

Jacobs, Brian D. 1992. *Fractured Cities: Capitalism, Community and Empowerment in Britain and America*. London: Routledge.

Jacobs, Kurt. 1995. "Jaguar Keeps Its Birthright." *Birmingham Post* (July 14).

John, Peter and Alistair Cole. 1998. "Urban Regimes and Local Governance in Britain and France: Policy Adaption and Coordination in Leeds and Lille." *Urban Affairs Review* 33(3): 382–404.

Jones, Bryan D. 1983. *Governing Urban America: A Policy Focus*. Boston: Little, Brown.

Jones, Bryan D., and Lynn Bachelor. 1993. *The Sustaining Hand: Community Leadership and Corporate Power*, 2nd edition, revised. Lawrence: University Press of Kansas.

Judd, Dennis, and Michael Parkinson, editors. 1990. *Leadership and Urban Regeneration*. Newbury Park, CA: Sage Publications.

Judd, Dennis, and Todd Swanstrom. 1998. *City Politics: Private Power and Public Policy*, 2nd edition. New York: HarperCollins.

Judge, David. 1995. "Pluralism." In *Theories of Urban Politics*, edited by David Judge, Gerry Stoker, and Harold Wolman, 13–34. London: Sage.

Judge, David, Gerry Stoker, and Harold Wolman, editors. 1995. *Theories of Urban Politics*. London: Sage.

Kantor, Paul, Hank Savitch, and Serena Vicari Haddock. 1997. "The Political Economy of Urban Regimes: A Comparative Perspective." *Urban Affairs Review* 32(3): 348–77.

Katznelson, Ira. 1985. "Working Class Formation and the State: Nineteenth-Century England in American Perspective." In *Bringing the State Back In*, edited by P. Evans, D. Rueschmeyer, and Theda Skocpol, 257–84. Cambridge, U.K.: Cambridge University Press.

Kay, Jane Holtz. 1979. "The Cityscape Attack Is On." *Boston Globe* (October 20).

Keating, Michael. 1991. *Comparative Urban Politics: Power and the City in the United States, Canada, Britain, and France*. Aldershot, U.K.: Edward Elgar.

Kennedy, Lawrence W. 1992. *Planning the City Upon a Hill: Boston Since 1630*. Amherst: University of Massachusetts Press.

Key, V. O., Jr. 1947. *Politics, Parties, and Pressure Groups*. New York: Thomas Y. Crowell.

Kindleberger, Richard. 1994a. "House Kills Convention Center Bill." *Boston Globe* (December 21): 1, 53.

———. 1994b. "Megaplex Backers Propose 'Tourism Fees.' " *Boston Globe* (December 3): 59.

———. 1995a. "Agency Will Study Convention Center Sites." *Boston Globe* (January 1): 43, 56.

———. 1995b. "Business Leadership in Boston Is Discussion." *Boston Globe* (December 6): 52.

———. 1995c. "A Convention Hall Plan for C Street." *Boston Globe* (November 5): 43.

———. 1995d. "Remaining Megaplex Sites Face Opposition." *Boston Globe* (April 22): 69, 73.

———. 1995e. "Top Officials Will Meet Today in Bid to Settle Megaplex Fate." *Boston Globe* (January 23): 18, 20.

King, John. 1990. "How the BRA Got Some Respect." *Planning* (May).

Knight, Richard V. 1989. "City Development and Urbanization: Building the Knowledge-based City." In *Cities in a Global Society*, edited by Richard V. Knight and Gary Gappert, 223–44. Urban Affairs Annual Reviews, Vol. 35. Newbury Park, CA: Sage.

Kotter, John, and Paul Lawrence. 1974. *Mayors in Action: Five Approaches to Urban Governance.* New York: John Wiley & Sons.

Kranish, Michael. 1993. "Menino: He's No Ray Flynn." *Boston Globe* (December 10).

Kushma, David. 1986. "Workforce at Jefferson Will Shrink." *Detroit Free Press* (October 21): 3A.

Lam, Tina, and Daniel G. Fricker. 1996. "Team Effort." *Detroit Free Press* (August 21): 1A.

Lambert, Christine, Peter Malpass, Nick Oatley, and Peter Bolan. 1994. "Competitive Urban Policy: The United Kingdom City Challenge Initiative." *Proceedings of the First International Comparative Urban Research Seminar: Shaping the Urban Future* (July 11–13). Bristol, U.K.

Lane, Amy. 1995. "Renaissance Zones on Hold in Lansing till Next Year." *Crain's Detroit Business* (November 13): 3.

Langford, Mark. 1996. "Green Belt Residents Vow to Fight." *Birmingham Post* (June 25).

Lauria, Mickey, editor. 1997. *Reconstructing Urban Regime Theory: Regulating Urban Politics in a Global Economy.* Thousand Oaks, CA: Sage.

Lawless, Paul. 1990. "Regeneration in Sheffield: From Radical Intervention to Partnership." In *Leadership and Urban Regeneration: Cities in North America and Europe,* edited by Dennis Judd and Michael Parkinson, pp. 241–57. Newbury Park, CA: Sage.

Lehigh, Scot. 1994. "Menino's Low-Key Lobbying Lacks Flynn-Like Posturing." *Boston Globe* (November 30).

Lindblom, Charles. 1977. *Politics and Markets.* New York: Basic Books.

Littlewood, Stephen, and David Whitney. 1996. "Re-forming Urban Regeneration? The Practice and Potential of English Partnerships." *Local Economy* 11(1): 39–49.

Loftman, Patrick, and Brendan Nevin. 1992. *Urban Regeneration and Social Equality: A Case Study of Birmingham 1986–1992.* Research Paper (October 1992).

Logan, John R., and Harvey Molotch. 1987. *Urban Fortunes: The Political Economy of Place.* Berkeley: University of California Press.

Logan, John R., and Todd Swanstrom, editors. 1990. *Beyond the City Limits: Urban Policy and Economic Restructuring in Comparative Perspective.* Philadelphia: Temple University Press.

Logan, John R., and M. Zhou. 1993. "The Adoption of Growth Controls in Suburban Communities." *Social Science Quarterly* 71(1): 118–29.

Logan, John R., Rachel Bridges Whaley, and Kyle Crowder. 1997. "The Character and Consequences of Growth Regimes: An Assessment of 20 Years of Research." *Urban Affairs Review* 32(5): 603–30.

Lorenz, Andrew. 1995. "Jaguar's Great Leap." *The Times* (July 16): Business Focus, 3.

Lupo, Alan. 1987a. "Helping Neighborhood Groups Preserve Turf." *Boston Globe* (July 25).

———. 1987b. "Neighborhood Planning Councils?" *Boston Globe* (January 17): 11.

Lupsha, Peter A. 1974. "Constraints on Urban Leadership, or Why Cities Cannot Be Creatively Governed." In *Improving the Quality of Urban Management,* edited by David Rogers and Willis Hawley, 607–23. Beverly Hills: Sage.

McGraw, Bill. 1988. "Chrysler Project Critics See Little Gain for City." *Detroit Free Press* (September 18): 3A.

McGrory, Brian. 1993. "Menino Sees Greatest Impact in Low-Key Strategy." *Boston Globe* (June 19): 20.

Malone, M. E. 1987. "Limited Ban on Evictions for Boston's Condos OK'd." *Boston Globe* (June 4): 1, 16.

———. 1988. "Hub Condo Conversion Rate Climbed in 1987." *Boston Globe* (April 5): 1, 20.

Malpass, Peter. n.d. "Policy Making and Local Governance: How Bristol Failed to Secure City Challenge Funding Twice" (unpublished manuscript).

Martin, Stephen. 1990. "City Grants, Urban Development Grants, and Urban Regeneration Grants." In *Local Economic Policy,* edited by Mike Campbell, 44–64. London: Cassell.

Mashberg, Tom. 1993. "Residents Hope Grant Redeems Mission." *Boston Globe* (August 25): 21, 25.

Menzies, Ian. 1983. "Preservationists Give Mayor Tour of Beleaguered Buildings." *Boston Globe* (May 9).

Mollenkopf, John H. 1983. *The Contested City.* Princeton, NJ: Princeton University Press.

———. 1992. *A Phoenix in the Ashes: The Rise and Fall of the Koch Coalition in New York City Politics.* Princeton, NJ: Princeton University Press.

Mooney, Rian C. 1989. "Poll Finds More Uneasy with Boston's Direction." *Boston Globe* (April 12): 33.

Moreton, Anthony. 1989. "A Road Worth Discussion." *The Times* (November 24).

Morris, Nigel. 1993. "Midlands to Get Massive Cash Tonic: Development Area Grant Boost." *Birmingham Post* (July 16).

Mowbray, Simon. 1997. "Leisure Complex Plan for Central TV's Site." *Birmingham Post* (February 28).

Muller, Joanne. 1996. "Chamber Plans to Push 'Economic Engines.' " *Boston Globe* (January 9): 36.

Munro, W. B. 1927. *The Government of European Cities.* New York: Macmillan.

Muzzio, Doug, and Robert Bailey. 1986. "Economic Development, Housing, and Zoning: A Tale of Two Cities." *Journal of Urban Affairs* 8 (1): 1–18.

New York Times (Detroit Journal). 1992. "Jobs Oasis Is Created, But Price Was High." *New York Times* (April 25): 8L.

Nickel, Denise R., 1995. "The Progressive City? Urban Development in Minneapolis." *Urban Affairs Review* 30(3): 355–77.

Nugent, Neill. 1989. *The Government and Politics of the European Community.* London: Macmillan.

O'Brien, Eugene. 1993. "Increased Activity Spurs Demand." *Birmingham Post* (July 22): 22.

O'Connor, James R. 1973. *Fiscal Crisis of the State.* New York: St. Martin's Press.

Oguntoyinbo, Lekan. 1996. "Group Targets Detroit Blight." *Detroit Free Press* (March 12): 1B.

Olson, Mancur. 1965. *The Logic of Collective Action.* Cambridge, MA: Harvard University Press.

Onions, Ian. 1996. "Three Cheers for a Big Tourism Boost." *Evening Post* (May 10): 15.

Oser, Alan. 1996. "Ending Rent Control the Massachusetts Way." *New York Times* (April 21): 7.

Painter, Joe. 1997. "Regulation, Regime, and Practice in Urban Politics." In *Reconstructing Urban Regime Theory: Regulating Urban Politics in a Global Economy*, edited by Mickey Lauria, 122–43. Thousand Oaks, CA: Sage.

Pantridge, Margaret. 1991. "The Power Failure." *The Boston Magazine* (October): 58, 60–61, 93–94, 96, 98.

Parkinson, Michael. 1990. In *Leadership and Urban Regeneration: Cities in North America and Europe*, edited by Dennis Judd and Michael Parkinson, 241–57. Newbury Park, CA: Sage.

Parkinson, Michael, and Richard Evans. 1990. "Urban Development Corporations." In *Local Economic Policy*, edited by Mike Campbell, 65–84. London: Cassell.

Peck, Jamie, and Mike Emmerich. 1993. "Training and Enterprise Councils: Time for Change." *Local Economy* 8(1): 4–21.

Peele, Gillian. 1995. *Governing the United Kingdom*, 3rd edition. Oxford, U.K.: Blackwell.

Pepper, Jon. 1994. "Fund to Revive City Will Top $40 Million." *Detroit News* (October 28): 1A.

———. 1996a. "Contrary to Popular Belief, Business and Mayor Coleman Young Did Get Along." *Detroit News* (September 29): 1, 3C.

———. 1996b. "A 'Miraculous' Deal Gets Done." *Detroit News* (September 1): 1D.

Percival, Jenny. 1995. "Rediscovery of the Past and Vision of the Future." *Birmingham Post* (November 11).

———. 1996. "Residents Face Electronic Shock: Factory on Green Belt Site Set for Approval." *Birmingham Post* (July 10).

Peterson, George, and Carol W. Lewis, editors. 1986. *Reagan and the Cities*. Washington, D.C.: Urban Institute Press.

Peterson, Paul. 1981. *City Limits*. Chicago: University of Chicago Press.

Pham, Alex. 1994. "Menino Lays Out Economic Plan to Executives." *Boston Globe* (April 6): 43.

Phillips, Dave. 1997a. "Archer Hails Chrysler Commitment." *Detroit News* (April 10): 1B.

———. 1997b. "Chrysler to Expand Detroit Plants." *Detroit News* (April 9): 1A.

Pickvance, Chris. 1990. "Introduction: The Institutional Context of Local Economic Development: Central Controls, Spatial Policies and Local Economic Policies." In *Race, Policy and Politics: Do Localities Matter?*, edited by M. Harloe, C. Pickvance, and J. Urry, 1–41. London: Unwin Hyman.

Pierre, Jon. 1997. "Models of Urban Governance: Exploring the Institutional Dimension of Urban Politics." Paper presented at the annual meeting of the Urban Affairs Association, Toronto, Canada, April 17–19.

Pithers, M. 1991. "Councils Win Funding for Urban Renewal." *Independent* (August 4).

Piven, Frances Fox, and Richard A. Cloward. 1971. *Regulating the Poor: The Functions of Public Welfare*. New York: Vintage Books.

Pluta, Rick. 1995. "Engler Unveils Final 'Renaissance' Plan." *Oakland Press* (September 15): A-8.

Polanyi, Karl. 1957. *The Great Transformation: The Political and Economic Origins of Our Time*. Boston: Beacon Press.

Polsby, Nelson W. 1980. *Community Power and Political Theory: A Further Look at Problems of Evidence and Inference*. New Haven, CT: Yale University Press.

Pound, Arthur. 1940. *Detroit, Dynamic City.* New York: D. Appleton-Century.

Powers, John. 1985a. "Boston Developer's Lawsuit Challenges Linkage Requirement." *Boston Globe* (June 20): 24.

———. 1985b. " 'Linkage' Revision Provokes Friction." *Boston Globe* (July 28): A13–A14.

———. 1985c. "Boston's Plan: Build with Caution." *Boston Globe* (June 22): 1, 19.

Prater, Constance. 1989. "Auto Plant Costs Soar by $100 Million." *Detroit Free Press* (July 12): 1A.

Preer, Robert. 1987. "Watchdogs of the Neighborhoods: Boston's Community Groups Are Making More Noise, and Officials Are Listening." *Boston Globe* (January 2): 69.

Pressman, Jeffrey L. 1972. "Preconditions of Mayoral Leadership." *American Political Science Review* 66(2): 511–24.

Prestage, Michael. 1986. "Policy Row Will Shape the City." *Bristol Evening Post* (January 1).

Prestwich, Roger, and Peter Taylor. 1990. *Introduction to Regional and Urban Policy in the United Kingdom.* London: Longman.

Primack, Mark. 1989. "Renaissance of an Urban Park System: The Boston Story." A paper delivered to the Rene Dubos Only One Earth Forum (May).

———. 1990. "The GreenSpace Alliance at a Crossroads." Unpublished paper. Boston.

Prince, Aaron, and the Boston Redevelopment Authority. 1991. "The Planning Process of the BRA." In *Boston by Design: A City in Development 1960–1990,* edited by Shun Kanda and Masami Kobayashi, 76–126. Tokyo: Process Architecture Publishing.

Protash, W., and M. Baldassare. 1983. "Growth Policies and Community Satisfaction: A Test and Modification of Logan's Theory." *Urban Affairs Quarterly* 18: 397–412.

Punter, John V. 1990. *Design Control in Bristol: 1940–1990.* Bristol, U.K.: Redcliffe.

Radin, Charles A. 1987a. "Mayor Puts Own Stamp on Hub Development." *Boston Globe* (January 19).

———. 1987b. "Nonprofit Groups Take Lead in Building Affordable Housing." *Boston Globe* (August 16): 30.

Ramsay, Meredith. 1996. "The Local Community: Maker of Culture and Wealth." *Journal of Urban Affairs* 18(2): 95–118.

Reed, Adolph. 1988. "The Black Urban Regime: Structural Origins and Constraints." In *Power, Community and the City,* edited by Michael P. Smith, 138–89. New Brunswick, NJ: Transaction Books.

Reid, Helen, and Jonathan Shorney. 1992. "Campaign to Attract More Visitors Is Too Little Too Late." *Western Daily Press* (March 25).

Rezendes, Michael, and Don Aucoin. 1991. "BRA Chief Coyle to End 7-Year Role." *Boston Globe* (December 20): 1, 28.

Rich, Wilbur C. 1989. *Coleman Young and Detroit Politics: From Social Activist to Power Broker.* Detroit, MI: Wayne State University Press.

———. 1990. "The Politics of Casino Gambling in Detroit." *Urban Affairs Quarterly* 23(2): 274–298.

Riker, William H., and Peter C. Ordeshook. 1973. *An Introduction to Positive Political Theory.* Englewood Cliffs, NJ: Prentice Hall.

Robb, Christine. 1985. "Rehabbing the American Dream: How Community Development Groups Make Good Neighbors." *Boston Globe Magazine* (March 31).

Rosegrant, Susan and David Lampe. 1992. *Route 128: Lessons from Boston's High-Tech Community.* New York: Basic Books.

Rosenberg, Ronald. 1991. "Boston Woos Genzyme Corp." *Boston Globe* (November 14).

Rosenberg, Ronald, and Jerry Ackerman. 1991. "Genzyme Chooses Boston." *Boston Globe* (December 5): 1, 6.

Ross, Bernard H., and Myron A. Levine. 1996. *Urban Politics: Power in Metropolitan Areas,* 5th edition. Itasca, IL: F.E. Peacock Publishers.

Rubin, Barry M., and Craig M. Richards. 1992. "A Transatlantic Comparison of Enterprise Zone Impacts." *Economic Development Quarterly* 6(4): 431–43.

Sassen, Saskia. 1991. *The Global City.* Princeton, NJ: Princeton University Press.

Saunders, Peter. 1981. *Social Theory and the Urban Question.* London: Hutchinson.

Savitch, Hank. 1988. *Post-Industrial Cities.* Princeton, NJ: Princeton University Press.

Schattschneider, E. E. 1960. *The Semi-Sovereign People.* New York: Holt, Rinehart and Winston.

Sege, Irene. 1991. "Flynn Calls Meeting on Local Economy." *Boston Globe* (November 25).

Sharp, Elaine B. 1989. *Urban Politics and Administration: From Service Delivery to Economic Development.* New York: Longman.

Shorney, Jonathon. 1980a. "About Turn on the Rebels." *Western Daily Press* (March 31).

———. 1980b. "Marxist Rebels against Labour Cuts." *Western Daily Press* (February 24).

———. 1992. "U-Turn in the City of Green Dreams." *Western Daily Press* (October 29): 2.

———. 1997. "City Hits £3M Euro Jackpot." *Western Daily Press* (May 21): 2.

Smith, Michael P., editor. 1984. *Cities in Transformation: Class, Capital, and the State.* Beverly Hills: Sage.

Snyder, Sarah. 1987. "Mayor in Grip of Housing Squeeze." *Boston Globe* (January 1).

———. 1988. "Where Have All the Powers Gone?" *Boston Globe* (December 27): 33, 37.

Solomon, Deborah. 1997. "Detroit's Top 100 Economic Developments." *Detroit Free Press* (April 15): 6–8A.

Spencer, Ken, Andy Taylor, Barbara Smith, John Mawson, Norman Flynn, and Richard Bately. 1986. *Crisis in the Industrial Heartland.* Oxford, UK: Basil Blackwell.

Squires, Gregory D., editor. 1989. *Unequal Partnerships: The Political Economy of Urban Redevelopment in Postwar America.* New Brunswick, NJ: Rutgers University Press.

Squires, Gregory D., Larry Bennett, Kathleen McCourt, and Philip Nyden. 1987. *Chicago: Race, Class, and the Response to Urban Decline.* Philadelphia: Temple University Press.

Stein, Jay M. 1993. *Growth Management: The Planning Challenge of the 1990s.* Newbury Park, CA: Sage.

Stevens, Carol. 1994. "Archer's 'Relentless' Lobbying Pays Off." *Detroit News* (December 21): 10A.

Stewart, Murray. 1990. "Urban Policy in Thatcher's England." Working Paper 90. Bristol: University of Bristol, School for Advanced Urban Studies.

————. 1994. "Between Whitehall and Town Hall: The Realignment of Urban Regeneration Policy in England." *Policy and Politics* 22(2): 133–45.

————. 1995. "Too Little, Too Late. The Politics of Local Complacency." *Journal of Urban Affairs* 18(2): 119–37.

————. 1996. "Urban Regeneration." In *Enabling or Disabling Local Government: Choices for the Future,* pp. 144–57, edited by Steve Leach, Howard Davis, and Associates. Buckingham, UK: Open University Press.

Stoker, Gerry. 1988. *The Politics of Local Government.* London: Macmillan.

————. 1995. "Regime Theory and Urban Politics." In *Theories of Urban Politics,* edited by David Judge, Gerry Stoker, and Harold Wolman, 54–71. London: Sage.

Stoker, Gerry, and Karen Mossberger. 1994. "Urban Regime Theory in Comparative Perspective." *Environment and Planning C: Government and Policy* 12: 195–212.

Stone, Clarence N. 1976. *Economic Growth and Neighborhood Discontent: System Bias in the Urban Renewal Program of Atlanta.* Chapel Hill: University of North Carolina.

————. 1980. "Systemic Power in Community Decision Making." *American Political Science Review* 74(December): 978–90.

————. 1982. "Complexity and the Changing Character of Executive Leadership." *Urban Interest* 4(Fall): 29–50.

————. 1986. "Power and Social Complexity." In *Community Power: Directions for Future Research,* edited by Robert J. Waste, 77–113. Beverly Hills: Sage.

————. 1988. "Preemptive Power: Floyd Hunter's 'Community Power Structure' Reconsidered." *American Journal of Political Science* 32(1): 82–104.

————. 1989. *Regime Politics: Governing Atlanta 1946–1988.* Lawrence: University Press of Kansas.

————. 1993. "Urban Regimes and the Capacity to Govern: A Political Economy Approach." *Journal of Urban Affairs* 15(1): 1–28.

————. 1995. "Political Leadership in Urban Politics." In *Theories of Urban Politics,* edited by David Judge, Gerry Stoker, and Harold Wolman, 96–116. London: Sage.

Stone, Clarence N., and Heywood T. Sanders, editors. 1987. *The Politics of Urban Development.* Lawrence: University Press of Kansas.

Stowe, Eric L. 1980. "Defining a National Urban Policy: Bureaucratic Conflict and Shortfall." In *Urban Revitalization,* edited by Donald B. Rosenthal, 145–63. *Urban Affairs Annual Reviews* 18. Newbury Park, CA: Sage Publications.

Sutton, Tony. 1990. "Local Plan: Agents Despair over Restrictive Clauses." *Estate Times Survey: Avon & Somerset* (March 16): 25.

Svara, James. 1990. *Official Leadership in the City: Patterns of Conflict and Cooperation.* New York: Oxford University Press.

Swanstrom, Todd. 1989. "Urban Populism, Uneven Development, and the Space for Reform." *Business Elites and Urban Development: Case Studies and Critical Perspectives,* edited by Scott Cummings, 121–52. Albany: State University Press of New York.

Teasdale, Sarah. 1996a. "Fury over Factory in Green Belt Bid." *Birmingham Post* (May 23).

————. 1996b. "Year 2000 Science Park 'to Go Ahead.'" *Evening Mail* (September 14).

Thomas, June Manning. 1989. Detroit: The Centrifugal City. In *Unequal Partnerships: The Political Economy of Urban Redevelopment in Postwar*

America, edited by Gregory D. Squires, 142–60. New Brunswick, NJ: Rutgers University Press.

Tilly, Charles. 1984. *Big Structures, Large Processes, and Huge Comparisons*. New York: Russell Sage.

Toy, Vivian S., and Kim Trent. 1993. "Archer vs. McPhail." *Detroit News* (September 15): 1A.

Travis, Toni-Michelle C. 1990. "Boston: The Unfinished Agenda." In *Racial Politics in American Cities*, edited by Rufus P. Browning, Dale Rogers Marshall, and David H. Tabb, 108–22. New York: Longman.

Turner, Robyne S. 1992. "Growth Politics and Downtown Development: The Economic Imperative in Sunbelt Cities." *Urban Affairs Quarterly* 28(1): 3–21.

Turpin, Andrew. 1995. "Developers in Rush for Top Jaguar Supply Sites." *Birmingham Post* (August 10): 21.

Vaillancourt, Meg. 1994. "New Megaplex Plan Would Alter Kenmore-Copley Area: Expanded Hynes, Stadium Near Fenway Urged." *Boston Globe* (June 24): 1, 14.

———. 1995. "Disney Eyes Waterfront for Possible Complex." *Boston Globe* (August 8): 39, 40.

———. 1996. "Convention Center Gets New Push: Birmingham Says Officials, Not Voters, Should Approve Hotel Tax to Fund Project." *Boston Globe* (July 16): D1, D12.

———. 1997a. "Convention Center Boosted: Report Says Facility to Yield 61% More Cash than Thought." *Boston Globe* (March 5): C1, C5.

———. 1997b. "Convention Center Deal Seen Near: Boston's Contribution to Project in Dispute." *Boston Globe* (June 17): D1, D17.

———. 1997c. "Convention Center Gets Boost: Mayor Proposing That City Pay Up to $125 million for South Boston Location." *Boston Globe* (March 24): A1, A4.

———. 1997d. "Mass. House OK's $700m Boston Convention Center." *Boston Globe* (July 16): D3.

Vaillancourt, Meg, and Geeta Anand. 1997. "Rifts Remain on Convention Center: Finneran Voices Optimism Despite Discord on Funding, Management." *Boston Globe* (July 4): C1, C9.

Vaillancourt, Meg, and Peter S. Canellos. 1995. "Complex Scheme Easily Undone: Political Realities Stopped Megaplex." *Boston Globe* (November 6): 1, 10.

Vaillancourt, Meg, and Richard Chacon. 1997. "Finneran: New Bill Encouraging." *Boston Globe* (May 15): C1, C5.

Vaillancourt, Meg, and Richard Kindleberger. 1995. "Megaplex Has New Obstacles: House Leaders Unveil Tough Hearing Format." *Boston Globe* (September 14): 35, 36.

Vennochi, Joan. 1983. "White Backs Linkage Plan for Housing." *Boston Globe* (October 15): 21, 22.

Vlasic, Bill, Vivian S. Toy, and Tim Kiska. 1993. "Archer off to Fast Start." *Detroit News* (November 3): 1A.

Wachman, Richard. 1993. "Robots Rule in the Heartland." *Evening Standard* (September 20).

Walker, Adrian. 1992. "Flynn Unveils Plan for Urban Renewal." *Boston Globe* (November 25).

———. 1993. "Hub Banks Rate Higher at Serving Minorities." *Boston Globe* (September 30): 1, 8.

———. 1994a. "Boston Gets $25 Million for "Empowerment Zone": City Had Applied for $94 Million from HUD." *Boston Globe* (December 22).

———. 1994b. "City Sees Options if Grant Not Won: Other Monies Likely for Low Income Areas." *Boston Globe* (December 19): 21, 24.

———. 1994c. "Landlords, Tenants Pack Hearing at City Hall to Debate Rent Control." *Boston Globe* (November 18): 36.

———. 1994d. "Plan Would Revitalize Areas along Blue Hill Avenue." *Boston Globe* (May 9): 1, 14.

———. 1995a. "Minority Loans on Steady Rise, Says City Study." *Boston Globe* (August 8): 1, 30.

———. 1995b. "Realtors Happy with Menino's Grant Program: Homeowners Get Closing-Cost Aid." *Boston Globe* (January 20).

Walton, John. 1990. "Theoretical Methods in Comparative Methods." In *Beyond the City Limits: Urban Policy and Economic Restructuring in Comparative Perspective,* edited by John R. Logan and Todd Swanstrom, 243–57. Philadelphia: Temple University Press.

Warner, Sam Bass, 1968. *The Private City.* Philadelphia: University of Pennsylvania Press.

Waste, Robert J. 1986. "Community Power and Pluralist Theory." In *Community Power: Directions For Future Research,* edited by Robert J. Waste, 117–37. Beverly Hills: Sage.

Webber, Jim. 1980a. "Call for Demo to Back Eight Labour Rebels." *Evening Post* (April 8).

———. 1980b. "Labour Group Reinstates Rebel Eight." *Evening Post* (July 5).

———. 1980c. " 'On the Carpet' Labour Rebels." *Evening Post* (June 30).

———. 1980d. "£16m Problem Is Centre of Rate Storm." *Evening Post* (March 4).

———. 1980e. "We'll Appeal, Say Sacked Labour Rebels." *Evening Post* (March 19).

———. 1981. "Left Revolt Looms on Labour View of Budget." *Evening Post* (March 2).

Webman, Jerry A. 1982. *Reviving the Industrial City: The Politics of Urban Renewal in Lyon and Birmingham.* New Brunswick, NJ: Rutgers University Press.

Western Daily Press. 1992. Get Bristol Moving series. *Western Daily Press* (February 3–7).

Western Daily Press. 1993. "City Chief in Leisure Scheme Wrangle." *Western Daily Press* (July 27).

Wheaton, Bob. 1999. "Detroit School Takeover Not Needed, Dems Say." *Oakland Press* (March 20):A-6.

Willing, Richard. 1992. "Archer Hires Big-Name Help for Mayoral Run." *Detroit News* (November 15): 1A, 11A.

Wilson, James Q. 1973. *Political Organizations.* New York: Basic Books.

Wilson, Melinda. 1997. "City Launches Campaign Touting 'Great Time in Detroit.' " *Detroit News* (November 18): 1D.

Wilson, Melinda, Judy DeHaven, and Suzette Hackney. "It's Greektown, Atwater, MGM." *Detroit News* (November 21): 3A.

Wirt, Frederick M. 1974. *Power in the City: Decision Making in San Francisco.* Berkeley: University of California Press.

Wolman, Harold, and Michael Goldsmith. 1992. *Urban Politics and Policy: A Comparative Approach.* Oxford, U.K.: Blackwell.

Wylie, Jeanie. 1989. *Poletown*. Indianapolis: Indiana University Press.

Yates, Douglas. 1977. *The Ungovernable City: The Politics of Urban Problems and Policy Making*. Cambridge, MA: MIT Press.

Young, Coleman, and Lonnie Wheeler. 1994. *Hard Stuff: The Autobiography of Mayor Coleman Young*. New York: Viking.

Yudis, Anthony J. 1984. "$1.3 Billion in Projects Get Flynn Boost." *Boston Globe* (November 1): 6.

Zernike, Kate. 1996. "Speeches Highlight Menino's Big Week: Convention Center to Top City's Agenda." *Boston Globe* (January 15): 17, 21.

Index

Alan DiGaetano is associate professor of political science at Baruch College–CUNY. He has published articles in *Urban Affairs Review, Urban Affairs Quarterly, Journal of Urban Affairs,* and *Urban History.*

John S. Klemanski is professor of political science at Oakland University in Rochester, Michigan, and has served as director of Oakland's master of public administration program. He is the coauthor (with John W. Smith) of *The Urban Politics Dictionary,* and has published articles in *Urban Affairs Quarterly, Journal of Urban Affairs,* and *Economic Development Quarterly.*